World Cinema

World Cinema
Critical Approaches

Edited by

JOHN HILL and **PAMELA CHURCH GIBSON**

Consultant Editors

Richard Dyer   E. Ann Kaplan   Paul Willemen

OXFORD
UNIVERSITY PRESS

This book has been printed digitally and produced in a standard specification
in order to ensure its continuing availability

OXFORD
UNIVERSITY PRESS

Great Clarendon Street, Oxford OX2 6DP
Oxford University Press is a department of the University of Oxford.
It furthers the University's objective of excellence in research, scholarship,
and education by publishing worldwide in

Oxford New York

Auckland   Cape Town Dar es Salaam   Hong Kong   Karachi
Kuala Lumpur Madrid Melbourne Mexico City   Nairobi
New Delhi Shanghai Taipei Toronto
With offices in
Argentina Austria Brazil Chile Czech Republic France Greece
Guatemala Hungary Italy Japan South Korea Poland Portugal
Singapore Switzerland Thailand Turkey Ukraine Vietnam

Oxford is a registered trade mark of Oxford University Press
in the UK and in certain other countries

Published in the United States
by Oxford University Press Inc., New York

© 2000 John Hill and Pamela Church Gibson

The moral rights of the author have been asserted

Database right Oxford University Press (maker)

Reprinted 2009

ISBN 978-0-19-874282-1

Printed and bound in Great Britain by CPI Antony Rowe,
Chippenham and Eastbourne

Acknowledgements

We would like to thank a number of people who have helped in the preparation of this book. We are, of course, grateful to all our contributors, some of whom worked to particularly tight deadlines. We would also like to thank our consultant editors—Richard Dyer, Ann Kaplan and Paul Willemen—for their assistance and advice. Ginette Vincendeau acted as consultant on the section on European cinema and provided invaluable help; Geoffrey Nowell-Smith also provided good advice and suggestions at an early stage.

At Oxford University Press, we would particularly like to thank our editor Andrew Lockett for his constant support and enthusiasm for the book, Tania Pickering for her invaluable assistance and Mick Belson and Ruth Marshall for their help and efficiency in preparing the manuscript for publication.

We are also grateful to Roma Gibson, Celia Britton, and Stella Bruzzi for their help. John Hill is also indebted to his colleagues David Butler, Dan Fleming and Martin McLoone at the University of Ulster for their support for the project and to the Faculty of Humanities for a well-timed period of leave of absence.

Thanks also to the staff at BFI Stills and to Timothy Seaton for his translation of the essay by Armand Mattelart (Chapter Twelve).

J. H. and P. C. G.

Contents

CONTENTS

Contributors

EDITORS

John Hill is Professor of Media Studies at the University of Ulster at Coleraine. He is the author of *Sex, Class and Realism: British Cinema 1956–63* (1986) and *British Cinema in the 1980s* (1999), co-author of *Cinema and Ireland* (1987), and co-editor of *Border Crossing: Film in Ireland, Britain and Europe* (1994), and *Big Picture, Small Screen: The Relations Between Film and Television* (1996).

Pamela Church Gibson is a Senior Lecturer in Contextual and Cultural Studies at the London College of Fashion, a constituent college of the London Institute. She is the co-editor of *Dirty Looks: Women, Pornography, Power* (1993) and has written on heritage film both for *British Cinema in the Nineties* (ed. Murphy, 1999) and for the French journal *1895*. She has a chapter on the *Alien* cycle of films in *Popular Film and Cultural Studies* (forthcoming) and is currently workin with Stella Bruzzi on a collection of essays tentatively entitled *Fashion and Culture: Theories and Explorations*.

CONSULTANT EDITORS

Richard Dyer is Professor of Film Studies at the University of Warwick. He is the author of a number of books including *Stars* (1979), *Heavenly Bodies* (1986), *The Matter of Images* (1993), *Now You See It* (1990) and *White: Essays on Race and Culture* (1997).

E. Ann Kaplan teaches at the Department of English at the Humanities Institute at Stony Brook, New York. She is the author of a number of books including *Women and Film: Both Sides of the Camera* (1983), *Motherhood and Representation: The Mother in Popular Culture and Melodrama* (1992), and *Looking For The Other: Feminism, Film, and the Imperial Gaze* (1997).

Paul Willemen is Professor of Critical Studies at Napier University, Edinburgh. He has published widely on film theory and is the author of a number of books, including *Looks and Frictions: Essays in Cultural Studies and Film Theory* (1994) and co-editor of *Questions of Third Cinema* (1989) and the *Encyclopaedia of Indian Cinema* (1994).

CONTRIBUTORS

José Arroyo is Lecturer in Film Studies at the University of Warwick and has written on Spanish and Canadian cinema.

Julianne Burton-Carvajal teaches at the University of California, Santa Cruz. Her publications include *Cinema and Social Change in Latin America* (1986) and *The Social Documentary in Latin America* (1990).

Kuan-Hsing Chen teaches at the Center for Cultural Studies in the College of Humanities and Social Sciences at the National Tsing Hua University in Taiwan. He is the author of *Intellectual Moods and Geo-Colonial Sites* (Taipei, 1996) and co-editor of *Stuart Hall: Critical Dialogues in Cultural Studies* (1996).

Ian Christie is Professor of Film and Media History at Birkbeck College, University of London. He has published widely on Russian and British Cinema, on early film, and on the avant-garde, and is author of *Arrows of Desire: The Films of Michael Powell and the Emeric Pressburger* (1994).

Stephen Crofts is a Senior Lecturer in Film and Media Studies at Griffith University, Brisbane, Australia, and the author of a study on Australian film.

CONTRIBUTORS

Chris Darke is a freelance writer and part-time lecturer at the University of Warwick and has contributed to *Sight and Sound*, *Screen*, and other publications.

Wimal Dissanayake is a Senior Fellow at the East-West Center, Hawaii, and editor of *Melodrama and Asian Cinema* (1993), *Colonialism and Nationalism in Asian Cinema* (1994), and the *East West Journal*.

Jill Forbes is Professor of French at Queen Mary and Westfield College, University of London, and is author of *The Cinema in France after the New Wave* (1992), *Les Enfants du paradis* (1997), co-editor of *French Cultural Studies* (1995) and co-author of *Studies in European Cinema* (2000).

Cathy Fowler is a Lecturer in Film Studies at the Southampton Institute of Higher Education and is author of a forthcoming study on Belgian Cinema.

Freda Freiberg teaches at Monash University, Melbourne, and is author of *Women in Mizoguchi Films* (1981) and editor of *Don't Shoot Darling! Women's Independent Film-making in Australia* (1987).

Daniel J. Goulding is a Professor of Film Studies and Theatre Arts at Oberlin College, Ohio. He is author of *Liberated Cinema: The Yugoslav Experience* (1985) and *Occupation in 26 Pictures* (1998) and contributing editor of *Post New Wave Cinema in the Soviet Union and Eastern Europe* (1989) and *Five Filmmakers: Tarkovsky, Forman, Polanski, Szabó, Makavejev* (1994).

Susan Hayward is Professor of French at the University of Exeter and author of *French National Cinema* (1993) and co-editor of *French Film: Texts and Contexts* (1990).

Andrew Higson is a Senior Lecturer in Film Studies at the University of East Anglia in England. He is the author of *Waving the Flag: Constructing a National Cinema in Britain* (1995), editor of *Dissolving Views: Key Writings on British Cinema* (1996) and co-editor of *'Film Europe' and 'Film America': Cinema, Commerce and Cultural Exchange, 1920–1939* (1999).

John Izod is Professor of Screen Analysis in the Stirling Media Research Institute at the University of Stirling in Scotland. He is the author of *Reading the Screen* (1984), *Hollywood and the Box Office* (1988), *The Films of Nicolas Roeg: Myth and Mind* (1992) and, with Richard Kilborn, *An Introduction to Television Documentary* (1997). He has completed a theoretical book, *Myth, Mind and the Screen*, adapting Jungian theory to the analysis of film and television and is currently working on a study of the films of Bernado Bertolucci.

Elizabeth Jacka is Professor of Communication Studies and Dean of the Faculty of Humanities and Social Sciences at the University of Technology, Sydney. She is co-author of *The Screening of Australia* (2 vols., 1987/8), *The Imaginary Industry* (1988) and *Australian Television and International Mediascapes* (1996) as well as co-editor of *New Patterns in Global Television* (1996).

Richard Kilborn is a Senior Lecturer in the Department of Film and Media Studies at the University of Stirling in Scotland. He is the author of *The Multi-Media Melting Pot* (1986), *Television Soaps* (1992) and, with John Izod, *An Introduction to Television Documentary: Confronting Reality* (1997).

Laura Kipnis is an Associate Professor of Radio/Television/Film, Northwestern University, Evanston. She is the author of *Ecstasy Unlimited: On Sex, Capital, Gender and Aesthetics* (1993) and *Bound and Gagged: Pornography and the Politics of Fantasy in America* (1999) and is an independent video-maker whose work is exhibited and broadcast internationally.

N. K. Leung works for Satellite Asian Region Ltd. in Hong Kong.

Martin McLoone is a Senior Lecturer in Media Studies at the University of Ulster. He is co-editor of a number of publications including *Television and Irish Society* (1984), *Culture, Identity and Broadcasting in Ireland* (1991), *Border Crossing: Film in Europe, Britain and Ireland* (1994) and *Big Picture, Small Screen: The Relations Between Film and Television* (1996).

Armand Mattelart is a Belgian sociologist who worked in Chile from 1962 to 1973 and is now Professor of Sociology at the University of Paris. His publications include *Mapping World Communication: War, Progress, Culture* (1994) and *The Invention of Communication* (1996), and, with Michèle Mattlelart, *The Carnival of Images: Brazilian Television Fiction* (1990) and *Rethinking Media Theory: Signposts and New Directions* (1992).

Simona Monticelli completed an M.Phil. thesis on gender and national identity in Italian Neo-Realist cinema at the University of Warwick where she has also been a part-time lecturer in film.

Michael O'Pray is a Reader in Visual Theories at the School of Art and Design at the University of East London and has written widely on film, the avant-garde, and animation. He is editor of *Andy Warhol: Film Factory* and *Into the Pleasure Dome: the Films of Kenneth Anger* (co-edited with Jayne Pilling, 1989) and author of *Derek Jarman: Dreams of England* (1996).

Ashish Rajadhyaksha is a freelance writer and researcher and co-editor of the *Encyclopaedia of Indian Cinema* (1994).

Keith Reader is Professor of French at the University of Newcastle. His books include *Cultures on Celluloid* (1981), *The May 1968 Events in France* (1993) and *Regis Debray* (1995).

Bérénice Reynaud teaches in the School of Film/Video and the School of Critical Studies at the California Institute of Arts and has written on Chinese cinema for *Cahiers du cinéma*, *Liberation*, *Sight and Sound* and *Cinemaya, the Asian Film Quarterly*. Her book, *Nouvelles Chines/nouveaux cinemas*, about cinema in the three Chinas since 1984, was published in 1999.

Ulrike Sieglohr is a Senior Lecturer in Media Studies at Staffordshire University. She has published on aspects of New German Cinema and has completed a Ph.D. on the German filmmaker Werner Schroeter.

Murray Smith is a Senior Lecturer in Film Studies at the University of Kent at Canterbury. He is the author of *Engaging Characters: Fiction, Emotion and the Camera* (1995) and co-editor of *Film Theory and Philosophy: Aesthetics and the Analytical Tradition* (1997).

Will Straw is Associate Professor within the Graduate Program in Communications at McGill University, Montreal. He has published widely on popular music, film, and cultural studies and is co-editor of *Theory Rules: Art as Theory/Theory and Art* (1996).

Stephen Teo, originally from Malaysia, works as a critic and film-maker in Hong Kong and lives part of the year in Australia. For a number of years he has been editor of the Hong Kong Cinema Retrospective catalogues published annually by the Hong Kong International Film festival and is the author of *Hong Kong Cinema* (1997).

N. Frank Ukadike teaches film and cultural studies at the University of Michigan, Ann Arbor. He is the author of *Black African Cinema* (1994) and *A Questioning of Cinema: Conversations with Black African Filmmakers* (1997).

Ginette Vincendeau is Professor of Film Studies at the University of Warwick. She has written extensively on French cinema and is the editor of the *Encyclopaedia of European Film* (1995) and author of *Pépé le Moko* (1998). She is currently completing a study of 1930s French cinema, entitled *The Art of Spectacle: Popular French Cinema in the 1930s*.

List of illustrations

General Introduction

John Hill

In 1995, the cinema celebrated its centenary. Since 1895, the cinema has grown and spread globally and, despite an actual decline in cinema attendances worldwide, the watching of films is now more popular than ever thanks to television and video. Although new communication technologies and forms of entertainment have undoubtedly affected the social and cultural role of cinema, the cinema nonetheless retains a huge importance as an economic, cultural, and artistic activity. As such, film continues to attract enormous critical attention and commentary in both popular discourses and academic fields of study and it is the ways in which film has been studied, and accounted for, which is the central concern of this book and its two companion volumes: *Film Studies: Critical Approaches* and *American Cinema and Hollywood: Critical Approaches*.

World Cinema: Critical Approaches is the third volume in the series and is designed to provide an overview of the main *theoretical frameworks*, *critical concepts*, and *debates* involved in the study of world cinemas rather than detailed factual information. As such, it is intended to complement, rather than duplicate, *The Oxford History of World Cinema* (1996) which has already undertaken an ambitious mapping of the historical development of 'world cinema'.

What is meant by 'world cinema' also requires some explanation in this context. Since the end of World War One, the U.S. film industry has been the dominant cinema in the world and this has also meant that it has enjoyed a pre-eminent position within film studies. For this reason, a separate volume has been devoted to the study of American cinema and Hollywood. As a result, *World Cinema* is devoted to non-Hollywood cinemas, both in the sense of films that are made geographically outside Hollywood and films which have adopted a different aesthetic model of filmmaking from Hollywood. However, although the cinemas discussed in the book are united by their difference from Hollywood models, they do not constitute a homogeneous filmmaking practice. On the contrary, non-Hollywood, 'world' cinemas have been characterized by considerable aesthetic, cultural, and ideological diversity and have generated a whole range of critical discussion and debate. As a result, the book seeks not only to explore the historical and geographical variety of world filmmaking but also the range of theoretical, critical, and cultural perspectives which its study has involved.

However, while *World Cinema: Critical Approaches* is designed to be wide-ranging in scope, it does not claim to be exhaustive in either its coverage of topics or critical positions. Inevitably, there has had to be a degree of selection and readers will no doubt find both more or less on certain cinemas than they might have expected. The strategy of the book, in this respect, has been to opt for case-studies of particular cinemas and filmmakers rather than to attempt a full coverage of all 'world' cinema. However, although certain countries and filmmakers are not dealt with, it is intended that the critical concepts and issues raised in relation to particular countries and films should still have some critical purchase beyond the circumstances of their immediate application. Thus, it can be seen from the discussion of different national cinemas contained in the book how certain debates—relating to industrial strategies, aesthetic models and cultural attitudes—recur across different contexts.

The structure of the book is as follows. The first two sections—'Redefining cinema: international and avant-garde alternatives' and 'Redefining cinema: other genres'—look at filmmaking traditions outside of the Hollywood mainstream. As various contributors to the book point out, the dominance of Hollywood has meant that other cinemas have often had to define themselves by differentiation from, or opposition to, Hollywood norms. The various ways in which cinema has sought to come to terms with Hollywood, and the critical debates which these have engendered, are examined in a series of discussions on national cinema, the avant-garde, third cinema, documentary and animation.

This is followed by a series of area studies of cinemas in Europe, Asia, South America and Africa. These seek not only to familiarize readers with the relevant critical debates concerning non-Hollywood cinemas but also to put to the test some of the theories and critical approaches which have been adopted in relation to mainstream films. As different contributors to the book indicate, the study of Indian, Chinese, Japanese, and African cinemas has rendered problematic many of the assumptions (about filmic conventions or spectatorship, for example) which have traditionally governed the study of film in the West and has required the employment of new and different forms of explanation. This question of critical perspective is further developed in the concluding section of the book which reviews the changing character of cinema in an era of new technologies and delivery systems and assesses what implications these changes have had for our traditional understanding of the workings of cinema.

Each chapter is intended to lay out and assess the history and meaning(s) of key critical terms, issues, and debates involved in the study of different cinemas. In some cases, there are also additional 'readings' of individual films which are designed to illustrate how different theories or critical perspectives have been applied to particular examples. The bibliographies which accompany each chapter include full details of the material referred to in each chapter as well as certain texts which may not actually be cited but are nonetheless significant texts of relevance to the area. Particularly useful texts, recommended for further reading, are accompanied by an asterisk.

As such, the book is designed to provoke thought, encourage debate, and stimulate further reading and research. The excitement of film studies is that, despite a growing institutionalization, it remains a field in which a variety of approaches coalesce and compete and in which basic questions remain 'unsettled'. This seems particularly so of the study of 'world cinema' where the sheer variety of filmmaking demands a plurality of critical perspectives. If this volume can communicate some of this excitement amongst its readers (be they students, teachers, or those with a general interest in the serious study of film) then it may be judged a success.

Redefining cinema: international and avant-garde alternatives

1

Concepts of national cinema

Stephen Crofts

Prior to the 1980s critical writings on cinema adopted common-sense notions of national cinema. The idea of national cinema has long informed the promotion of non-Hollywood cinemas. Along with the name of the director-auteur, it has served as a means by which non-Hollywood films—most commonly art films—have been labelled, distributed, and reviewed. As a marketing strategy, these national labels have promised varieties of 'otherness'—of what is culturally different from both Hollywood and the films of other importing countries. The heyday of art cinema's 'new waves' coincided with the rise of anglophone film-book publishing in the mid-1960s. Later, 1960s radical politics extended the range of territories covered to those engaged in post-colonial struggles. The ideas of a national cinema underpinning most of these studies remained largely unproblematic until the 1980s, since which time they have grown markedly more complex. Prior to this period, ideas of national cinema tended to focus only

on film texts produced within the territory concerned while ideas of the nation-state were conceived primarily in essentialist, albeit if in sometimes anti-imperialist, terms.

Problematizing the nation-state

Key publications in the rethinking of the nation-state and nationalism have been Anderson (1983), Gellner (1983), Hobsbawm (1990), Smith (1991), and Hutchinson (1994). These have all advanced non-essentialist conceptions of the nation-state and national identity, arguing for both the constructedness of the 'imagined community' (Anderson) which constitutes the nation-state, and its historical limits as a post-Enlightenment organizer of populations, affected particularly by the huge migrations and diasporas resulting from post-

1

Second World War processes of decolonization. Such ideas have informed recent accounts of national cinemas which seek to resist the homogenizing fictions of nationalism and to recognize their historical variability and contingency, as well as the cultural hybridity of nation-states (so that US culture, for example, is seen to be a part of most 'national' cultures and to interact with them). In Philip Rosen's words, 'identifying the . . . coherences [of] a "national cinema" [and] of a nation . . . will always require sensitivity to the countervailing, dispersive forces underlying them' (1984: 71).

Historically, the 1980s and 1990s have put further pressure on the national, with the global spread of corporate capital, the victory of finance over industrial capital, the consolidation of global markets, the speed and range of electronic communications, and the further weakening of national cultural and economic boundaries which has followed the disintegration of Soviet communism and Pax Americana. Half a century after 1945 it is difficult to imagine a nation-state retaining the congruence of polity, culture, and economy which characterized most nation-states before then. Arjun Appadurai's (1990) model for accounting for these developments emphasizes the deterritorialized character of the supranational imagined communities which displace those of the nation-state. He pinpoints the accelerating transnational flows of people (tourists, immigrants, exiles, refugees, guest workers), of technology (mechanical and informational), of finance and media images (all moving ever faster through increasingly deregulated markets), and of ideologies (such as the global spread of Western rhetorics of democracy), and the disjunctions amongst these flows: 'people, machinery, money, images and ideas now follow increasingly non-isomorphic paths . . . the sheer speed, scale and volume of each of these flows is now so great that the disjunctures [rather than overlaps] have become central to the politics of global culture' (1990: 297–301).

This conceptualization of the post-national does, however, have weaknesses. Shohat and Stam (1994) note that 'discernible patterns of domination channel the "fluidities" even of a "multipolar" world; the same hegemony[ies] that unifies[y] the world through global networks of circulating goods and information also distribute[s] them according to hierarchical structures of power, even if those hegemonies are now more subtle and dispersed' (1994: 31). Nevertheless, Appa-

durai's model has many implications for the study of national cinemas, some taken up later, some now. One consequence of the disjunctive relationships he identifies 'is that the state and the nation are at each other's throats' (1990: 304). The former Yugoslavia—with its five nations, three religions, four languages, and two alphabets—stands as a grim emblem of the historical role of the state in suppressing ethnic, religious, and cultural differences. In view of the growing lack of congruence between nations and states, I therefore propose to write of states and nation-state cinemas rather than nations and national cinemas, while clearly differentiating states within a *federal* system, and without of course collapsing all into totalitarian states.

Problematizing nation-state cinema studies: categories of analysis

Nation-state (or 'national') cinema studies until the 1980s focused almost exclusively on the film texts produced within the territory, sometimes seeing these—in a reflectionist manner—as expressions of a putative national spirit. Typically, a historical survey would construct its chosen films as aesthetically great works (usually seen as made by great directors) and as great moments (the longest film, most expensive film, and so on). Such studies rarely analysed the industrial factors enabling the films to be produced.

Since the 1980s new categories of analysis have begun to emerge. A number of these are summarized in Andrew Higson's 'The Concept of National Cinema' (1989), one of the first general considerations of nation-state cinema, based on generalizations around the British case. Higson argues that nation-state cinemas should be defined not only in terms of 'the films produced by and within a particular nation state', but also in terms of distribution and exhibition, audiences, and critical and cultural discourses. Textual and generic questions, however, are strange lacunae in his (industrially oriented) account; for texts do, after all, mediate between exhibition and audiences. The factors which analyses of nation-state cinemas involve, therefore, may be identified as follows:

Production. David Bordwell, Janet Staiger, and Kristin Thompson's monumental *The Classical Hollywood Cinema* (1985) redresses the lack of attention to the industrial which has been characteristic of film studies. They reject any simple reflectionist thesis of text–

context relations and argue how the economic, technological, and ideological factors affecting Hollywood production act as mutually interacting determinations which are irreducible to one another (Lapsley and Westlake 1988: 117). Hollywood's mode of film practice, they conclude, 'consists of a set of widely held stylistic norms sustained by and sustaining an integral mode of film production' (Bordwell et al. 1985, p. xiv). Most subsequent analyses of production have adopted a similarly post-Althusserian model. Crisp's (1993) account of the production of French cinema between 1930 and 1960, for example, develops the Americans' mode of analysis, breaking down the heading of production into various components: political economy and industrial structure, plant and technology, personnel and their training, discursive endeavours to form audiences, authorial control in relation to the mode of production, and work practices and stylistic change.

Distribution and exhibition (these two are taken together because of their virtual interconnectedness). Higson argues that categories of analysis of nation-state cinemas should include 'the range of films in circulation within a nation-state' (1989: 44). One of the few analyses of imported films and their audiences is Paul Swann's *The Hollywood Feature Film in Postwar Britain* (1987), but attention towards 'imported' cinemas is becoming more common in nation-state cinema studies as in Thomas Elsaesser's *New German Cinema* (1989). Given Higson's concern that nation-state cinemas should not be defined solely in terms of production, it is fair to note that many states actually have no production industry. Poor states, especially in Africa, cannot afford it unless, like Burkina Faso—one of the world's most impoverished states—foreign funding sustains an art cinema offering exotic representations to foreign audiences. Some states principally watch films in a language they share with other states, for instance Tunisia and Uruguay. Other states, such as in South Asia and the South Pacific, have no audiovisual production and no cinemas, but do have flourishing video distribution.

Audiences. This remains an under-researched category. It is arguably to the benefit of film studies that it has not followed media studies in its massive investment in empirical audience research. Film studies has thus largely avoided the latter's effective collusion with global consumerisms since the 1980s (see Willemen 1987b). Largely, but not entirely: see John Hill's critique of Higson's willingness to allow Hollywood's popularity in Britain 'to blur the arguments for film *production* which is specifically British rather than North American' (1992: 13–14). Unlike the approach to the audience in media studies, however, nation-state cinema studies has in the main analysed audiences in terms of box-office statistics. Discussion of audiences has been particularly significant in studies analysing the problems which locally produced cinemas experience when faced with transnational domination by Hollywood (Hill 1994), or in sustaining an indigenous 'art cinema' as in Elsaesser's (1989) analysis of the audience desperately sought by the state-funded practitioners of the New German Cinema.

Discourses. The discourses in circulation about film, as well as wider cultural discourses in the nation-state, clearly affect industry and audiences, and also inform—and are articulated within—film texts. Given cultural hybridity, these will of necessity include foreign-originated ideas. Hence, since the 1980s nation-state cinema studies have less commonly treated films as objects for the exercise of aesthetic judgement than as instances of (national-)cultural discourses. Hill (1986), for example, analyses British cinema's ideological articulations—and repressions—of class, gender, youth, consumerism, and related categories in films from the period 1956–63. Marsha Kinder's (1993) account of Spanish cinema gives central attention to 'its distinctive cultural reinscription of the Oedipal narrative, that is, the way Oedipal conflicts within the family were used to speak about political issues and historical events that were repressed from filmic representation during the Francoist era and the way they continue to be used with even greater flamboyance in the post-Franco period after censorship and repression had been abolished' (1993: 197–8). In a similar vein, some scholars have adopted the idea of a national or social imaginary (Elsaesser 1980; Dermody and Jacka 1988: 15–23).

Textuality. Rather than see nation-state cinemas in terms of 'great works', writers have increasingly identified systems of textual conventions, principally generic ones, as characterizing 'national' cinema. Dermody and Jacka, for example, employ a quasi-generic taxonomy to identify the 'aesthetic force-field' of Australian cinema between 1970 and 1986. Genres, in this respect, are seen less in industrial terms than as codifications of socio-cultural tendencies.

National-cultural specificity. National-cultural specificity may be differentiated from both nationalism, and definitions of national identity. As Paul Willemen argues: 'The specificity of a cultural formation may be

Antonio das mortes (1969)—
Latin American counter-
cinema

marked by the presence but also by the absence of preoccupations with national identity . . . the discourses of nationalism and those addressing or comprising national specificity are not identical . . . the construction of national specificity in fact encompasses and governs the articulation of both national identity and nationalist discourses' (1994: 210). Nationally specific cinema, then, is not bound to the homogenizing myths of nationalism and national identity. Hill uses Willemen's example of black British cinema to illustrate the point, arguing how such films display a 'sensitivity to social differences (of ethnicity, class, gender and sexual orientation) within an identifiably and specifically British context' (Hill 1992: 16) and that this is strikingly different from the nationalistically 'successful . . . marketing and packaging [of] the national literary heritage, the war years, the countryside, the upper classes and elite education' noted by Elsaesser (1984: 208) as characterizing dominant British cinema. In contrast, the international co-production can often be seen to erase cultural specificity: as Geoffrey Nowell-Smith observes of *Last Tango in Paris* (Bernardo Bertolucci, 1972), it 'had no nationality in a meaningful sense at all' (1985: 154).

The cultural specificity of genres and nation-state cinema 'movements'. A nation-state cinema's capacity to produce culturally specific genres depends on whether it can sustain production in sufficient volume to support the requisite infrastructures and audience familiarity; on the power of its local cultural traditions; and on how strongly these are articulated by film relative to other artistic practices. The generation and/or survival of local genres has been a gauge of the strength and dynamism of nation-state cinemas, but this may be less so in the 1990s as genres diversify, fragment, and recombine. Local cultural traditions and their articulation through film rather than other artistic practices have likewise underpinned the best-known nation-state cinema 'movements'. These have frequently arisen at historical moments when nationalism connects with genuinely populist movements to produce specifically national films that can claim a cultural authenticity or rootedness (Crofts 1993). Some of these—Italian Neo-Realism, Latin American Third Cinema, and Fifth Generation Chinese Cinema—arose on the crest of waves of national-popular resurgence. The French Nouvelle Vague marked a national intellectual and cultural recovery in the making since the late 1940s. However, cultural hybridity is often a characteristic as well. As Kinder (1993: 6) notes, such movements regularly borrow from elsewhere formal 'conventions to be adapted to the [importers'] own cultural specificity': Italian Neo-Realism from French poetic realism, the Nouvelle Vague from Hollywood and Rossellini, the Fifth Generation from Chinese and foreign painting traditions.

The role of the state. The idea of nation-state cinema needs to be conceptualized in terms not only of the categories above, but also of the state's own involvement. The state retains a pivotal role. For all the much-vaunted 'disintegration' and/or 'supersession' of the state under the forces of globalization and cyber-hype, and alongside the more realistic recognition of its fragmentation under sub- and suprastate pressures, it is still state policies and legislation (or lack of them) which substantially regulate and control film subsidies, tariff constraints, industrial assistance, copyright and licensing arrangements, censorship, training institutions, and so on. Individual states desiring to restrict Hollywood imports, for instance, do at the least have the power to decide whether or not they *want* to risk a trade war, as can be seen in the case of South Korea in 1990, when it battled with the Motion Picture Export Association of America to reduce Hollywood imports to roughly 5 per cent per year (Lent 1990: 122–3).

The global range of nation-state cinemas. In an argument also applicable to film, Geoffrey Hartman argues that every literary theory is 'based on experience of a limited canon or generalised strongly from a particular text/milieu' (1979: 507). In a similar fashion I have argued previously that '[f]ilm scholars' mental maps of world film production are often less than global . . . Sadoul (1962), informed by French colonialism, knows more of African cinema than of Latin American,

while an American scholar, informed by the US imperium and substantial Hispanic immigration, knows more of Latin American cinema than of African cinema' (Crofts 1993: 60–1). Such limited understandings of the cross-cultural have severe implications for canon formation as well as for global politics. Even in 1962 Sadoul took note that Third World production was more plentiful than North American and European combined (1962: 530–1). It is this global range of nation-state cinemas that the following section aims to cover.

Varieties of nation-state cinema production

Table 1 presents a model for differentiating types of nation-state cinema that takes into account the three main industrial categories of production, distribution and exhibition, and audiences as well as those of textuality and national representation (this account distils and substantially reworks Crofts 1993: 50–7). As in most taxonomies, these varieties of nation-state cinema are highly permeable. Individual films can be cross-bred between different varieties. And a given state may host different varieties by sustaining different modes of production, most commonly the industrial and cultural modes. Moreover, the export of a given text may shift its variety, as in the common recy-

TABLE 1. **EIGHT VARIETIES OF NATION-STATE CINEMA PRODUCTION**

	Mode of production as regulated and controlled by the state			
	Minimal ('market economy')	Mixed economy	Maximal, centrally controlled economy	Other or outside state provision
Industrial	1. United States cinemas 2. Asian commercial successes	3. Other entertainment cinemas	4. Totalitarian cinemas	
Cultural	5. Art cinemas:			
	American art	Art	Art for socialist export	
		6. International co-productions		
Political (anti-state)				7. Third Cinemas 8. Sub-state cinemas

cling of films from Third and totalitarian cinemas as art cinema.

The eight varieties of nation-state cinema shown in the table can be briefly summarized as follows:

1. *United States cinema.* It is so called to include the recent medium-budget 'independent' films associated with, say, the Sundance Institute as well as Hollywood. Hollywood's domination of world film markets since as early as 1919 is so well known (Guback 1976; Thompson 1985) that Western nation-state cinemas are habitually defined against Hollywood. It is hardly ever spoken of as a national cinema, perhaps because of its transnational reach. This has been further consolidated since the 1980s by its increased domination of West European screens, and the substantial inroads it has made into East European and other new markets.

2. *Asian commercial successes.* With large domestic and reliable export markets, Indian and Hong Kong cinemas can afford to ignore Hollywood, while Japanese production sometimes outstrips Hollywood imports at the local box-office (Lent 1990: 47).

3. *Other entertainment cinemas.* These include European and Third World commercial cinemas which adopt genres such as melodrama, thriller, and comedy. They customarily depend more on private than state investment, but mostly fail to dominate their local markets (except in rare cases such as Egypt, which supplies other Arab states). This variety of nation-state cinema includes anglophone (Australian, Canadian) imitations of US cinema and Bangladeshi imitations of Indian cinemas.

4. *Totalitarian cinemas.* These include those of fascist Germany and Italy, communist China, and the Stalinist regimes of the Soviet bloc.

5. *Art cinemas.* These vary somewhat in the sourcing of their finances, and in their textual characteristics. Bordwell (1979, 1985) describes the textual characteristics of art cinema in their heyday and Smith (Part 3, Chapter 2) summarizes its features.

6. *International co-productions.* Like offshore productions, these films exemplify the mobility of capital and personnel, as well as the international merging of media images noted by Appadurai (1990) above.

7. *Third Cinemas.* This term originally referred to the anti-imperialist cinemas of Latin America, but its definition has been expanded, especially by Willemen, to cover films with 'a historically analytic yet culturally specific mode of cinematic discourse' (1987a: 8). Directors such as the Indian Mrinal Sen, the Filipino Kidlat Tahimik, the Africans Ousmane Sembene and Souleymane Cissé, as well as black British filmmakers have been included in this category (Pines and Willemen 1989).

8. *Sub-state cinemas.* These may be defined ethnically in terms of suppressed, indigenous, diasporic, or other populations asserting their civil rights and giving expression to a distinctive religion, language, or regional culture. Catalan, Québecois, Aboriginal, Chicano, and Welsh cinemas are examples.

While the categories of state regulation and control on the horizontal axis of Table 1 are self-explanatory, the three modes of production may require some clarification. The industrial mode is that which characterizes Hollywood and applies similarly to the Hong Kong and Indian industries. The cultural mode of production is distinguished from Hollywood by state legislation overtly supporting production subsidy—increasingly via television—and quotas and/or tariffs on imported films. In its anti-state politics, the political mode of production is characterized by artisanal modes of filmmaking, and in its purest form—for example, *Hour of the Furnaces* (Argentina, 1969)—is conducted clandestinely and at risk to the film workers involved.

Under its two axes, Table 1 subsumes nine categories analysable in nation-state film industries. These allow us to expand upon the categories of analysis described in the preceding section:

(a) Mode of production effectively subsumes:

(b) the mode of audience address targeted through distribution and exhibition of texts of the mode of production involved; and

(c) the kinds of genre which it typically produces. Similarly, state regulation of production and distribution–exhibition comprises the following three categories:

(d) state subvention and regulation or control of production (or not);

(e) state intervention in and regulation or control of distribution and exhibition (or not)—in the case of the 'free market' option, the lack of regulation is nevertheless an active state policy decision; and

(f) the implicitly or explicitly nationalist, or indeed anti-nationalist representations—if any (for, as seen above, there need be none)—encouraged by the mode of production concerned.

Three further categories, concerning audiences, are implicit in the table and will be explicated below:

(g) the success or otherwise of the variety of state cinema within its local market;

(h) its success in exporting to other territories; and

(i) the range of competing entertainment forms available within the state concerned.

Under the industrial mode of production there is an almost complete correlation between categories (a) to (c): between, that is, the industrial mode of production, entertainment modes of address in distribution and exhibition, and entertainment genres, with the inflexion of the entertainment mode of address towards the didactic in the case of totalitarian mode. Similarly, there is a strong correlation between the cultural mode of production, the modes of address of the art film—to the cultured, film-literate viewer—which characterizes art cinemas' distribution and exhibition channels, and art film genres. The bulk of international co-productions also conform to these criteria, with the main exceptions being the higher-budget samples of 'Euro-pudding'. Much as the political mode of original Third Cinema production is clandestine, fugitive, and makeshift, so its politicized mode of address endangers its target audiences, and its typically agit-prop documentary genres serve its anti-state politics. Later versions of Third Cinema are less life-threatening. With variable production levels and degrees of access to mainstream distribution and exhibition, the substate cinemas are also instances of this mode of production but are less co-ordinated in their strategies of production, mode of address, and genre.

The horizontal dimension covers categories (d) to (f): state regulation and intervention in the sectors of production and distribution and exhibition, and the explicit or implicit nationalisms advanced by the cinemas involved. Most varieties of state film production exhibit a strong correlation between these three categories. The minimal government subsidy to production which characterizes Hollywood, Asian commercial successes, and to a lesser extent other entertainment cinemas finds echoes in the general lack of intervention in the distribution and exhibition sectors in the territories involved, and in the usually implicit forms that any nationalistic representations adopt. This contrasts with totalitarian cinemas, whose states control production—with the exceptions of fascist Italy and pre-1938 Nazi Germany—and which intervene strenuously in distribution and exhibition with censorship scrutiny of local and foreign product, and which urge expressly, and usually explicitly, nationalistic representations.

The most familiar art cinemas (i.e. of the European model) differ again in that while their production depends largely on state subsidy, their distribution and exhibition operates largely *without* state intervention (post-Second World War France being the conspicuous exception) and their representations are aesthetically constructed before they are nationalistic. American art cinema differs in the lack of state production support, while socialist states subsidize their art cinemas in both production and export distribution. International co-productions function in the same way as art cinemas, except that any nationalisms may disappear in the bland mix (while those of the Fifth Generation Chinese Cinema post-Tiananmen seriously *question* the nationalisms of the People's Republic of China). Original Third Cinema enjoys state support for neither production nor distribution, and its practitioners would argue that their states' abuse of freedoms of speech and assembly justify—indeed necessitate—its anti-state representations. Later versions enjoy less brutal, if still less than comfortable, state patronage. Third Cinema representations overlap with substate cinemas' interests in regions, ethnicities, religions, and/or languages which are non-hegemonic within the state. These latter rarely benefit from state support in production or distribution and exhibition unless from states within a federal system such as the Québecois.

Audiences, conceived in box-office terms, figure under headings (g)–(i): the films in predominant circulation in the state concerned, the success or otherwise of its exports, and the range and popularity of competing entertainment forms available within the state concerned. The last of these is a factor for consideration in nation-state cinema studies. As regards the first two, nation-state cinemas can be categorized as net importers and net exporters. Hollywood, Indian, Hong Kong, and big totalitarian cinemas dominate their local markets, through market and/or regulatory means, and garner varying degrees of additional revenue from foreign markets. Smaller totalitarian cinemas (the Soviet Union's European satellite states) and the other five varieties of nation-state cinema production fight over the remainder, their principal enemy being Hollywood, which dominates most anglophone markets and exerts considerable influence through the United States' world-wide strategic, economic, and cultural links. Indian and Hong Kong cinemas export to their ethnic diasporas, Hong Kong also throughout East Asia, and big totalitarian cinemas to their colonized and satellite territories. Art cinemas of all kinds distribute themselves broadly world-wide, but also thinly, within the limits, that is, of art film distribution and exhibition channels. Third and substate cinemas rarely break out in the mainstream (an exception is the Québecois *Jesus of Montreal* (Denys Arcand, 1989) which was in fact a Canadian–French co-production). Given their predominant anti-state politics, circulation is sorely limited, and sometimes wider—because less policed—outside their country of origin.

Recent cultural issues and debates

Politically critical national cinemas

Perched on the edge of Table 1, the space for anti-state cinemas is very limited, emerging from the political underground in the case of the original Third Cinemas, from the interstices of the contradictions of liberal pluralist funding regimes, from the capacity of production units with progressive heads to cross-subsidize funding in the Fifth Generation Chinese case, or, in the case of those same directors post-Tiananmen, from their ability to raise non-PRC international co-production finance on the strength of their names as auteurs. Willemen has noted the growing pressures on politically unorthodox cinema:

The capital-intensive nature of film production, and of its necessary industrial, administrative and technological infrastructures, requires a fairly large market in which to amortise costs, not to mention the generation of surplus for investment or profit. This means that a film industry [other than Third, substate, and poor cinemas] must address either an international market or a very large domestic one. If the

latter is available, then cinema requires large potential audience groups, with the inevitable homogenising effects that follow from this . . . a cinema addressing national specificity will be anti- or at least non-nationalistic, since the more it is complicit with nationalism's homogenising project, the less it will be able to engage critically with the complex, multi-dimensional and multidirectional tensions that characterise and shape a social formation's cultural configurations . . . the marginal and dependent [politically critical] cinema is simultaneously the only form of national cinema available: it is the only cinema that consciously and directly works with and addresses the materials at work within the national cultural constellation. (Willemen 1994: 211–12)

In terms of the table, internationalizing economic interests force their way downwards and to the right; cultural, national ones struggle upwards and to the left!

Arguing for the cultural

While box-office dollars increasingly drive the industry globally, this should not preclude our attending to cultural issues—indeed, it should demand it. Europe in the 1990s provides some key debates. Even French cinema, which has probably been the world's most successful in meshing industrial and economic concerns with cultural discourses, is feeling the pressure of global commodification in the 1990s. In the case of Britain, Hill elegantly advances cultural against economic arguments in seeking to influence policy and practice on nation-state cinemas, critiquing in particular the policy endorsement of 'the operations of the market place (and its domination by transnational conglomerates) and, hence, the restricted range of cultural representations which the market provides' (1992: 18). This returns the argument to the issue of cultural specificity set out above. The Celtic poor cinema for which Colin McArthur campaigns poses acute problems for the realizability of acceptable culturally specific representations. Given centuries of English othering of Celtic Scotland, Ireland, and Wales as 'uncivilized' and 'backward', he offers this 'axiom to Celtic film-makers: the more your films are consciously aimed at an international market, the more their conditions of intelligibility will be bound up with regressive discourses about your own culture' (1994: 118–20). In the context of the much more powerful West German state, Elsaesser still has occasion to urge the importance of commitment to 'the politics of culture, where independent cinema is a protected enclave, indicative of a will to create and preserve a national film and media *ecology* amidst an ever-expanding international film, media and information *economy*' (1989: 3).

Export and cultural difference

As observed above, a given film can shift its variety of nation-state cinema when exported, depending on the distribution and exhibition parameters of the importing state and its political relationships with the exporter. Cross-cultural readings are more of a worry for art and substate cinemas than for Hollywood, the world's biggest producer of largely undifferentiated product for export. Elsewhere I distinguish three levels of critical response to imported films:

(*a*) blank incomprehension, which is mostly preempted by distributors' not importing culturally specific materials such as the films of Werner Schroeter or Alexander Kluge, or most social realist and poor cinemas;

(*b*) the subsumption of the unfamiliar within depoliticizing art cinema discourses of 'an essentialist humanism ("the human condition"), and complemented by a tokenist culturalism ("very French") or an aestheticizing of the culturally specific ("a poetic account of local life")'; and

(*c*) ethnocentric readings, such as in US accounts of *Crocodile Dundee* (Peter Faiman, 1986) which use the film to inscribe American frontier myths and to rediscover an age of innocence (Crofts 1992, 1993: 58–9). This last mode of reading Willemen calls a 'projective appropriation' (1994: 212).

Theorizing the culturally specific

Besides 'projective appropriation', which includes the 'imperial and colonising strategy' of universalist humanism (Willemen 1994: 210), Willemen distinguishes two other ways of analysing cultural specificity. 'Ventriloquist identification' has the speaker 'immersed in some ecstatic fusion with the others' voices . . . the monopolist-imperialist's guilty conscience' (213). The move beyond these complicit stances is based on Bakhtin's dialogic mode, and is 'not simply a matter of engaging in a dialogue with some other culture's products, but of using one's understanding of another cultural practice to re-

perceive and rethink one's own cultural constellation at the same time . . . a double-outsideness' whereby the analyst relates both to her or his situation and to the group 'elsewhere' as an other (214, 216–17). Rajadhyaksha and Willemen's (1994) encyclopaedia of Indian cinemas represents a realization of that goal. In a similar vein Chow argues for the relevance of the Western theoretical discourse of psychoanalysis to the examination of Chinese social and cultural repressions (1991, p. xiv). And later positioning herself outside both Western and Eastern readings of China, she challenges the notion of an authentic cultural identity as any more than an ideological construct (Chow 1995).

Future projections

Will the wash of globalization rinse out cultural differences between states? If nation-state cinemas and their marketing constitute a point of resistance to the growing pressures against the state from within and without, many argue that they cannot resist for long: 'the concepts "cinema", "nation" and "national cinema" are increasingly becoming decentred and assimilated within larger transnational systems of entertainment' (Kinder 1993: 440). The accelerating flows of people, technologies, images, and ideas combine with the intensifying search of film producers for multiple international markets to imply growing homogeneity in nation-state film production. And the possibility of distinguishing product with nation-state cinema labels is threatened not just by the increasing number of international co-productions, but also by developments in electronic and fibre-optic delivery systems with their encouragement of indiscriminate channel-zapping and image-mixing. On the other hand, art film sectors world-wide offer new hopes of interest in cultural specificity, even if only in the form of finding new foreign sets on which to inscribe old scenarios of innocence and nostalgia. Growing attendances at film festivals in many parts of the West hold out hopes for raised interest in cultural specificities. And the emergence in the 1990s of 'cross-over' distribution successes and of the American 'independent' production sector holds out some promises for growing consumer discrimination, at least in the West, against the typically Hollywood mainstream fare.

BIBLIOGRAPHY

Anderson, Benedict (1983), *Imagined Communities: Reflections on the Origin and Spread of Nationalism* (London: Verso).

*****Appadurai, Arjun** (1990), 'Disjuncture and Difference in the Global Cultural Economy', in Mike Featherstone (ed.), *Global Culture: Nationalism, Globalisation and Modernity* (London: Sage).

Bordwell, David (1979), 'Art Film as a Mode of Film Practice', *Film Criticism*, 4/1.

—— (1985), *Narration in the Fiction Film* (London: Methuen).

—— **Janet Staiger,** and **Kristin Thompson** (1985), *The Classical Hollywood Cinema: Film Style and Mode of Production to 1960* (New York: Columbia University Press).

Chow, Rey (1991), *Woman and Chinese Modernity: The Politics of Reading between East and West* (Minneapolis: University of Minnesota Press).

*****—— (1995), *Primitive Passions: Visuality, Sexuality, Ethnography and Contemporary Chinese Cinema* (New York: Columbia University Press).

*****Crisp, Colin** (1993), *Classic French Cinema 1930–1960* (Bloomington: Indiana University Press).

Crofts, Stephen (1992), 'Cross-Cultural Reception Studies: Culturally Variant Readings of *Crocodile Dundee*', *Continuum*, 6/1.

*****—— (1993), 'Reconceptualising National Cinema/s', *Quarterly Review of Film and Video*, 14/3: 49–67.

Dermody, Susan, and **Elizabeth Jacka** (1988), *The Screening of Australia*, ii: *Anatomy of a National Cinema* (Sydney: Currency Press).

Elsaesser, Thomas (1980), 'Primary Identification and the Historical Subject: Fassbinder and Germany', *Ciné-Tracts*, 11 (Fall), 43–52.

—— (1984), 'Images for England (and Scotland, Ireland, Wales . . .)', *Monthly Film Bulletin* (Sept.), 267–9.

*****—— (1989), *New German Cinema: A History* (London: Macmillan).

Gellner, Ernest (1983), *Nations and Nationalism* (Oxford: Blackwell).

Guback, Thomas (1976), 'Hollywood's International Market', in Tino Balio (ed.), *The American Film Industry* (Madison: University of Wisconsin Press).

Hartman, Geoffrey (1979), 'A Short History of Practical Criticism', *New Literary History*, 10/3.

*****Higson, Andrew** (1989), 'The Concept of National Cinema', *Screen*, 30/4 (Autumn), 36–46.

Hill, John (1986), *Sex, Class and Realism: British Cinema 1956–1963* (London: British Film Institute).

*****—— (1992), 'The Issue of National Cinema and British Film Production', in Duncan Petrie (ed.), *New Questions of British Cinema* (London: British Film Institute).

—— (1994), 'The Future of European Cinema? The Economics and Culture of Pan-European Strategies', in John Hill, Martin McLoone, and Paul Hainsworth (eds.) *Border Crossing: Film in Ireland, Britain and Europe* (Belfast: Institute of Irish Studies; London: British Film Institute).

Hobsbawm, E. J. (1990), *Nations and Nationalism since 1780: Programme, Myth, Reality* (Cambridge: Cambridge University Press).

Hutchinson, John (1994), *Modern Nationalism* (London: Fontana).

Kinder, Marsha (1993), *Blood Cinema: The Reconstruction of National Identity in Spain* (Berkeley: University of California Press).

Lapsley, Rob, and **Mike Westlake** (1988), *Film Theory: An Introduction* (Manchester: Manchester University Press).

Lent, John (1990), *The Asian Film Industry* (Austin: University of Texas Press).

McArthur, Colin (1994), 'The Cultural Necessity of a Poor Celtic Cinema', in John Hill, Martin McLoone, and Paul Hainsworth (eds.), *Border Crossing: Film in Ireland, Britain and Europe* (Belfast: Institute of Irish Studies; London: British Film Institute).

Nowell-Smith, Geoffrey (1985), 'But do we Need It?', in Martin Auty and Nick Roddick (eds.), *British Cinema Now* (London: British Film Institute).

Pines, Jim, and **Paul Willemen** (1989), *Questions of Third Cinema* (London: British Film Institute).

Rajadhyaksha, Ashish, and **Paul Willemen** (1994), *Encyclopaedia of Indian Cinema* (London: British Film Institute and Oxford University Press).

Rosen, Philip (1984), 'History, Textuality, Nation: Kracauer, Burch, and Some Problems in the Study of National Cinemas', *Iris*, 2/2: 69–84.

Sadoul, Georges (1962), *Histoire du Cinéma* (Paris: Flammarion).

Shohat, Ella, and **Robert Stam** (1994), *Unthinking Eurocentrism: Multiculturalism and the Media* (London: Routledge).

*****Smith, Anthony D.** (1991), *National Identity* (London: Penguin).

Swann, Paul (1987), *The Hollywood Feature Film in Postwar Britain* (London: Croom Helm).

Thompson, Kristin (1985), *Exporting Entertainment: America in the World Film Market 1907–1934* (London: British Film Institute).

Willemen, Paul (1987a/1994), 'The Third Cinema Question: Notes and Reflections', *Framework*, 34: 4–38; repr. in *Looks and Frictions* (London: British Film Institute).

—— (1987b), Review of John Hill, *Sex, Class and Realism: British Cinema 1956–1963*, *Framework*, 34: 114–20.

*****—— (1994), 'The National', in *Looks and Frictions* (London: British Film Institute).

2

Modernism and the avant-gardes

Murray Smith

The avant-garde and other alternatives

The types of cinema that I will be discussing are extremely varied, and it might be argued that the only thing that unites them all is their status as 'other' to orthodox narrative filmmaking. Another index of this heterogeneity is the cluster of distinct, if overlapping, terms denoting the filmic practices to be discussed here: art, avant-garde, experimental, independent, and underground, to name the most widespread. Initially, it is useful to bracket these terms and to frame the discussion more generally in terms of modes of film practice. Such a practice is defined by an integrated set of economic, institutional, and aesthetic norms (Bordwell *et al.* 1985, pp. xiii–xv, 378–5).

From our point of view, the most pertinent modes of film practice are art cinema and the avant-garde, both of which contrast with the classical Hollywood mode of film practice. While the latter is characterized by its commercial imperative, corporate hierarchies, and high degree of specialization and division of labour, the avant-garde is an 'artisanal' or 'personal' mode. Avant-garde films tend to be made by individuals or very small groups of collaborators, financed either by the filmmakers alone or in combination with private patronage and grants from arts institutions. Such films are usually distributed through film co-operatives, and exhibited by film societies, museums, and universities

(consequently, such films can only usually be seen in urban centres—and only in a handful of those with any regularity). Importantly, this alternative system of production, distribution, and exhibition is not driven by profit. Avant-garde films rarely break even, let alone make a profit, through the markets of either the mass commodity or the luxury item. There is no market in the negatives of avant-garde films, and truly famous practitioners of avant-garde film have made their fame and fortune either through other activities (Andy Warhol), or through moving into the realm of the art film (Warhol, Derek Jarman, Peter Greenaway), discussed below. Most avant-garde filmmakers make a living as teachers, technicians within the film industry, or through other day-jobs. In this respect, the filmic avant-garde is markedly different from the avant-garde in music, literature, and especially painting—a fact which is obscured by the tendency of critics to talk of *the* avant-garde, as if its conditions of existence were identical from discipline to discipline.

Within the domain of cinema, the avant-garde differs not only from Hollywood cinema, but from that other mode of film practice known as art cinema (even if there have been many practical and aesthetic cross-overs, from Fernand Léger and Germaine Dulac to Chantal Akerman, Jarman, and Sally Potter). Art films are typically characterized by aesthetic norms that are different from those of classical narrative films; they are made within a somewhat less rationalized

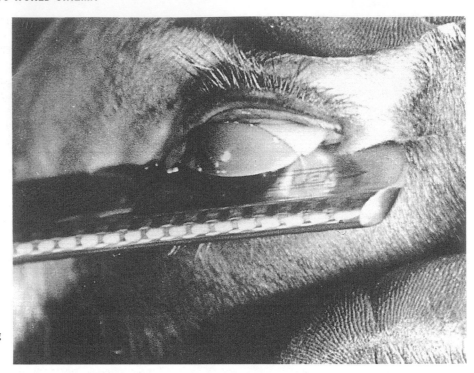

The aggressivity of the avant-garde—the eye-slicing scene in Buñuel's *Un chien andalou* (1928)

system of production; and they are often supported by government policies designed to promote distinctive national cinemas. But art cinema is still a commercial cinema, which depends for its existence on profits, rather than the more ethereal rewards of status and prestige.

So much for the economic and institutional nature of the avant-garde; what of its cultural and aesthetic character? If mainstream cinema is governed by an ethos of entertainment—with all the associations of escapism and leisure implied by that term—the avant-garde, by contrast, aims to challenge and subvert. At its most radical, the avant-garde asks us to rethink fundamentally our preconceptions about cinema. The tone of this challenge may vary widely, from the aggressive stance of *Un chien andalou* (Luis Buñuel and Salvador Dali, France, 1928) (the notorious eye-slicing scene being an apt emblem of its attitude towards the spectator), to the wit and playfulness of Robert Breer's work. An evening of avant-garde films ought to be thought-provoking and stimulating, but offers no guarantee of being pleasurable or beautiful in the conventional senses.

The 'otherness' of the avant-garde has been conceived in two distinct ways—as a *parallel* phenomenon and as a *reactive* phenomenon. P. Adams Sitney

argues that the relationship of the avant-garde to commercial cinema is one of 'radical otherness', in which each operates 'in different realms with next to no influence on each other' (Sitney 1974, p. viii). Although Sitney's study is the classic work on the American avant-garde, this has become an unusual perspective. More typical is the view of David James (1989), who sees the avant-garde as a 'reactive' or 'critical' phenomenon, continually challenging and undermining both the established values of mainstream society and the norms of orthodox aesthetic practice. Doubtless there have been individual avant-garde filmmakers who have had little knowledge or interest in commercial cinema, and thus in intentional terms were forging a parallel aesthetic. But looked at from a social perspective, even the work of such filmmakers becomes bound up in the larger rhetoric of the institutions of the avant-garde.

But from where, one might ask, do these cultural and aesthetic attitudes come from? A full sociological exploration of this question is still to be undertaken, and is certainly beyond the scope of this chapter. One widespread view, articulated in different contexts by the art critic Clement Greenberg (1939) and the philosophers Theodor Adorno and Max Horkheimer (1947/1979), is that the subversive strategies of the avant-garde are a reaction to the rise of mass culture. Such 'kitsch' culture—to use Greenberg's term—relentlessly reduces art to stereotyped patterns incapable of arousing active, intelligent responses. The formulaic nature of mass culture offers only a debased sentimentality, providing nothing more than a temporary respite from the regimentation of work. The fundamentally stagnant nature of mass culture is masked, however, by a continual striving for superficial novelty, and to this end the 'culture industry' (Adorno's phrase) co-opts every genuine cultural expression to its own ends. And it is this that gives rise to the avant-garde, the difficulty and obscurity of which is a deliberate act of resistance to such recuperation. The preservation of a sphere of *autonomous* artistic practice—that is, one guided by internal processes of development, not by the demands of the socio-political order—becomes, paradoxically, a political gesture. It functions—or so Adorno and Greenberg, in their different ways, argue—as a form of resistance to a society which attempts to rationalize, commodify, and so degrade every aspect of life; in the words of Adorno, to reduce even the 'purposelessness' of art to the 'purpose' of commerce.

Of the many things that such 'alternative practices' have challenged, narrative and 'realism' have often been prime targets because of their perceived dominance in commercial filmmaking. What counts as 'realism' is an immensely complex issue, but what is objected to is the claim to realism on the basis of an accurate rendering of the perceivable aspects of the world—continuity of time and space, for example—while equally real, if not directly visible, social and psychological processes are either ignored or mystified. Narrative, or more particularly the kind of traditional narrative form associated with the nineteenth-century novel and the Hollywood film, has been blamed for a variety of evils, but once again a constricting realism is central. 'Classic realism', it is argued, presents a contingent view of the world as if it were a necessary, inevitable one, and so inhibits both psychic freedom and any impetus towards progressive social change. Films conforming to such 'realism' are thought to induce a kind of passivity in the spectator, while anti- or non-realist texts demand a much more active response. The German dramatist Bertolt Brecht is one of the most influential sources for the critique of 'surface realism' and the contribution of traditional narrative to it, though kindred attacks can be found in Surrealism, the French *nouveau roman*, and the circle of writers associated with the journal *Tel quel*, all of

which have fed into alternative filmmaking at some point. A recurrent motif in the history of avant-garde cinema is the idea that cinema need not have become a narrative form at all, but could rather have modelled itself on other art forms, especially painting and music. In his book *Abstract Film and Beyond* (1977), Malcolm Le Grice constructs a history of avant-garde cinema in just these terms, counterposing the origins of orthodox narrative cinema in literature and theatre with the painterly, poetic, and musical origins of the first avant-garde experiments. In doing this, Le Grice was elaborating a gesture made earlier by, among others, Léger, Dulac, Maya Deren, and the art historian Élie Faure: 'There will some day be an end of the cinema considered as an offshoot of the theater, an end of the sentimental monkey tricks and gesticulations of gentlemen with blue chins and rickety legs' (1923/1967: 4). The most extreme statement of this 'anti-narrative' sentiment may be found in the work of the 'structural-materialist' filmmakers of the 1960s and 1970s (to whom we will return). But surveying the history of the avant-garde as a whole, it would be more accurate to say that narrative has been displaced, deformed, and reformed, rather than simply expunged altogether.

Modernism and the avant-garde

The concept of the avant-garde is intimately related to those of modernity and modernism. 'Modernity' refers to the network of large-scale social, economic, technological, and philosophical changes wrought by the Enlightenment and the Industrial Revolution. 'Modernism' is usually used to denote the period of dramatic innovation in all of the arts, from around the end of the nineteenth century (Symbolism and Aestheticism) up to the Second World War, when the sense of a fundamental break with inherited modes of representation and expression became acute. Modernism is thus above all associated with a pervasive formal self-consciousness, though many would also identify a thematic preoccupation with the modern city and its technologies—with the exhilaration of speed and rapid development, but also the potential for physical, social, and emotional dislocation (the latter erupting amidst the former in Walter Ruttmann's *Berlin: Die Sinfonie der Großstadt* ('Berlin: Symphony of a City', Germany, 1927).

Renato Poggioli has described the avant-garde as a 'culture of negation' (1968: 107–8). This commitment to ceaseless (self-)critique may be seen as a prime instance of the modernist emphasis on the new (although, as we shall see, the relationship between modernism and the avant-garde is a matter of considerable controversy). While Poggioli's study *The Theory of the Avant-Garde* pays little attention to film, it analyses the very notion of the avant-garde and relates its history. The term 'avant-garde' is military in origin, referring to the 'advance party' who interrogate the terrain ahead of the main army. (The military basis of the metaphor is sustained by titles like 'Film: The Front Line' (e.g. Rosenbaum 1983) a series of books on contemporary avant-garde filmmaking begun in the 1980s.) In mid-nineteenth-century France, the term was applied metaphorically to revolutionary political groups (in just the way that one speaks in English of 'vanguardist' politics). Towards the end of the century the term's use was extended so as to encompass the idea of, in Robert Hughes's phrase, 'social renewal through cultural challenge'—rather than overtly political activity. This leads Poggioli to talk of 'two avant-gardes'—a political and a cultural avant-garde, which sometimes walk hand in hand but by no means always do. This phrase was later used by Peter Wollen in a very similar fashion to discriminate what he argued were two rather different currents of 'avant-gardism' within film history (Wollen 1975/1982a). First, there is the apolitical avant-garde, concerned more with developing a purist film aesthetic, running from Léger and others in France in the 1920s through the co-operative movements in post-war Europe and the United States. Second, there is a political avant-garde, running from

the Soviet montage directors in the 1920s through to the work of such directors as Jean-Luc Godard and Miklós Jancsó from the 1960s onwards. While Wollen's account has the virtue of giving us a broad perspective on the history of avant-garde practice and in making connections across that history that may not be obvious, its vice lies in its over-simplification of specific phases of avant-garde filmmaking. Some avant-gardists were apolitical, some overtly political, some only implicitly so. Many were members or fellow travellers of the leftist parties, but some avant-gardists, notably in Italy and pre-revolutionary Russia, aligned themselves with the far right. As David James has argued, the positing of a 'single, transhistoric, self-regulating avant-garde' occludes important differences in the economic, cultural, and aesthetic character of superficially similar movements. James argues rather that there is a 'spectrum of alternative practices which develop and decay with historically specific needs and possibilities' (1989: 22).

Moreover, Wollen's use of the phrase 'avant-garde' cuts across the one we began with—that is, as a mode of film practice—in that his two avant-gardes share the 'critical' stance, but otherwise differ dramatically in terms of their institutional and economic foundations. We can see this by comparing the Surrealists (part of what Wollen terms the apolitical avant-garde) with the Soviet montage filmmakers (the first manifestation of an overtly political avant-garde), both active in the 1920s and early 1930s. The Soviets—chiefly Alexander Dovzhenko, Sergei Eisenstein, Lev Kuleshov, V. I. Pudovkin, and Dziga Vertov—began their careers in the early years of the new communist state. Like Soviet artists in other fields—the Constructivist painters, for example—they were concerned to harness radical formal strategies to Bolshevik rhetoric. Until the 1930s such experimentation was supported by the state (though not without controversy). Eisenstein's *Strike* (1925), Pudovkin's *Mother* (1926), and Dovzhenko's *Arsenal* (1929) all relate tales of revolution drawn from Soviet history, organized around either a typical, 'positive' hero, or the 'mass hero' (the proletariat in general), or both. These narratives form the basis of an agitational aesthetic, in which editing—as the label 'montage' implies—plays a crucial role. Whether conceived primarily in terms of architectural construction (Kuleshov), dialectical conflict (Eisenstein), or the musical interval (Vertov), montage aimed to infuse the narrative with a conceptual interplay out of which a revolutionary argument would emerge. The brutal

'Modernism' is usually used to denote the period of dramatic innovation in all of the arts, from around the end of the nineteenth century (Symbolism and Aestheticism) up to the Second World War, when the sense of a fundamental break with inherited modes of representation and expression became acute. Modernism is thus above all associated with a pervasive formal self-consciousness.

The political avant-garde—montage imagery in *Arsenal* (1929)

inequalities of the Tsarist regime, for example, are forcefully rendered in the opening montage of *Arsenal*. Shots of the Tsar writing a stupefyingly dull diary entry ('Today I shot a crow') are intercut with shots of an old woman collapsing from exhaustion as she sows a field, and others depicting frustrated factory workers, hungry children, and a man beating a scrawny horse in desperation.

France provides us with the first example of a fully fledged avant-garde film community in a liberal democracy. Over the course of the 1920s a set of institutions developed through which non-commercial films were made, distributed, exhibited, and discussed critically (Abel 1984). While there were certainly tensions and disputes within the French avant-garde, and many of them centred on political issues, it is not possible to boil them down to a political and an apolitical strain. Ian Christie (1979) has proposed a tripartite division. First, there were the filmmakers associated

with the notion of 'Impressionism': Abel Gance, Louis Delluc, Jean Epstein, Marcel L'Herbier, and the early Germaine Dulac. These filmmakers generally made narrative films which dwelt upon subjective experience, and experimented with the ways in which cinema could render aspects of that experience (e.g. Epstein's *La Glace à trois faces*, France 1927). Many of these films were feature-length and exhibited commercially; in other words, they really constitute an early effort to forge a national art cinema. The second strand Christie picks out is that associated with the notion of 'cinéma pur' (akin to Élie Faure's 'cineplastics'), in which the formal and often abstract exploration of cinematic possibilities dominated. Léger's *Ballet mécanique* (France, 1924) mixes such exploration with other tendencies; later films by Henri Chomette and Germaine Dulac were 'purer' still. The abstract experiments of cinéma pur have come to be thought of as the quintessential modernist aesthetic.

Many authors regard the terms 'avant-garde' and 'modernism' as essentially synonymous. Others, such as Peter Bürger in his *Theory of the Avant-Garde* (1984), Thomas Crow (1981), and (writing specifically on cinema) Paul Willemen (1984), treat them as overlapping but distinct. For them, modernism most appropriately describes a certain kind of formal innovation in the arts (above all, autonomous, reflexive strategies, rooted in the Aestheticism of the late nineteenth century) while avant-gardism implies something more radical, namely an attack on the very institutions and definitions of established practice (including the notion of artistic autonomy, that is, of a complete separation of art from socio-political life). (It should also, perhaps, be noted that some commentators, like John Harwood (1995), argue that the term 'modernism', originally nothing more than an umbrella term for the whole range of experimental artistic practices during the period, now carries a spurious explanatory and evaluative force, implying as it does that radically different artists were all in the grip of an underlying, unified *Zeitgeist*. The same could be said of the term 'avant-garde'.)

If we accept the definition argued for by Bürger and Willemen, then the honorific 'avant garde' is most aptly applied to the third grouping of alternative filmmakers in France identified by Christie, the Surrealists—even if, in a rhetorical gesture utterly typical of the avant-garde, the Surrealist poet Robert Desnos lambasted the notion of the 'avant-garde', associated as it was for him with the Impressionists and the Aestheticism of

Jean Cocteau. The dynamic of 'negation' is not restricted to a criticism of mass culture by everything outside it, but operates within the field of avant-garde artistic practice as well. Nothing is more characteristic of the avant-garde than disputes within its ranks about which subgroup is most deserving of the epithet.

Surrealism was born out of the ashes of an earlier movement, Dada. Dada had been founded in 1916 by a group of expatriate artists in Zurich, but the movement became an international one, with practitioners adopting the banner in Berlin, Cologne, and New York. Tristan Tzara, the Romanian poet who became the leader of the movement, moved to Paris, which became the major centre for Dada, as it was later for Surrealism. Dada is a nonsense word, and as such is a clue to the nature of the movement, which was anarchic, violently anti-traditional, and vociferously anti-bourgeois—at least rhetorically. Many of the Dada artists had been involved in the First World War, and the Dada movement has been understood as a reaction of disgust at a society which could sustain such a barbaric war. If the war was the end-product of a society supposedly built on the principles of rationality espoused by Enlightenment philosophers, then the means of protest against this society would have to be irrational. This is the context in which Marcel Duchamp began to exhibit his 'ready-mades'—ordinary objects, like bicycle wheels and the urinal he named 'Fountain', signed 'R. Mutt', and presented as a sculpture. In doing so, Duchamp offended not only the assumption that art involves creative effort, but also the assumption that only certain objects are appropriate subject-matter for art, and this does not include utterly utilitarian ones. In the words of Thomas Elsaesser, Dada sought 'ways of radically short-circuiting the means by which art objects acquire financial, social, and spiritual values' (Elsaesser 1987: 17), thus fulfilling Bürger's definition of the avant-garde as an attack on the foundations of artistic institutions.

Several artists associated with Dada made films, including Hans Richter and Man Ray. The most accomplished Dada film—completed some time after the movement had disintegrated—was René Clair's *Entr'acte* (France, 1924). Two aspects of the film stand out. First, while the outlines of a narrative can be found—involving the shooting of a man and his subsequent funeral—the energies of the film are invested in a variety of non-narrative strategies which cut across and often completely submerge its progress. Since narrative is a form of rationality—we explain ourselves

through stories revealing our reasons for doing things—it becomes an object of attack, along with standards of propriety (scattered across the film are 'crotch-shots' of a ballerina, ultimately revealed to be a bearded man in drag). Narrative logic is replaced by an unpredictable mix of associative and abstract links. Second, the film was originally conceived and projected as a part of a larger performance: the film acted as an intermission (the literal meaning of 'entr-acte') within the Dada ballet *Relâche* ('Cancelled'). The scenario for the film was the creation of the painter Francis Picabia, who wrote the ballet with the composer Erik Satie (the two of them also 'star' in the film). Thus, although the film was directed by a figure who was to sustain a career as a film director, it emerged very much out of collaboration with artists working in the plastic and musical arts. This was typical of avant-garde film production in the 1920s, and to a lesser degree continued to be so throughout its history.

Surrealism was a more formal movement, with a dominant leader (André Breton) and a more elaborate theory, but which nevertheless continued the Dada interest in the irrational. This was now buttressed by explicit appeals to Freud's theory of the unconscious. In an article from 1927, Breton identified two 'methods' of Surrealist composition: automatism (the attempt to relinquish conscious control of design in the actual creation of the art object), and the controlled depiction of dream and unconscious imagery. What the two methods share is the depiction of chance and 'marvellous' juxtapositions, creating an impression of randomness and irrationality for the viewer, and thus a rejection of the idea that art must cling to the representation of an everyday visible reality.

Another notable feature of Dada and Surrealism was a fascination with popular culture: the Surrealist canon of filmmakers includes Georges Méliès, Buster Keaton, Charlie Chaplin, and the popular French serial *Fantômas* (Smith 1999). This was a fascination shared by many other modernist and avant-garde artists: an animated 'Charlot' (Charlie Chaplin) figurine introduces Léger's *Ballet mécanique*, while *Entr'acte* juxtaposes its ballerina with a host of references to popular attractions—fairground shooting-ranges, chase films, and roller-coasters. This suggests that the 'culture of negation' is a little more complicated than it at first appears, for what we have here are approving references to the very mass culture which the avant-garde is said to negate. Pierre Bourdieu, in his monumental sociology of culture, class, and taste, *Distinction*, provides a clue: 'the avant-garde defin[es] itself in a quasi-negative way, as the sum of the refusals of all socially recognized tastes: refusal of the middle-of-the-road taste of the big shopkeepers . . . refusal of bourgeois taste . . . refusal of the teachers' pedantic taste . . . And so the logic of double negation can lead the artist back, as if in defiance, to some of the preferences characteristic of popular taste' (1979/1984: 294). This attitude is delightfully and succinctly expressed in a slogan used by the German Dadaist Georg Grosz: Chaplin beats Rembrandt!

These textual strategies were echoed by the viewing habits that the Dadaists and Surrealists adopted, at least apocryphally. Breton claims that groups of them would drift in and out of cinemas, disregarding the beginnings and endings of particular films, and break out picnic hampers and champagne while they watched. The effect of such fleeting and broken attention would be to undermine narrative unity and turn fragments of narrative films into prompts for an oneiric, associative spectatorship. Such behaviour also evinced a nostalgia for an earlier era of 'primitive' cinema, when attending the movies shared more with the boisterous atmosphere of the fairground and vaudeville than with bourgeois theatre or opera. The historical accuracy of such an image of early cinema is less at stake here than the fact that such an image was used to upset more 'refined' conventions of spectatorship. What emerges in France of the 1920s is a dialectic, rather than simple negation, of avant-garde and popular culture: the avant-garde may oppose what it takes to be bourgeois taste, but in doing so it frequently embraces and transforms aspects of popular culture.

The Surrealists had been inspired by the Russian Revolution to believe in the possibility of a radically new society, and for a period in the late 1920s they formally allied themselves with the French Communist Party. There was always a tension, though, between Surrealist aesthetics and the demands of direct political agitation. The alliance with the Communist Party eventually broke down in 1935, when 'socialist realism' was adopted as the official aesthetic of the Communist Party, first in the Soviet Union and then in Western Europe. In the Soviet Union itself, Eisenstein, Vertov, and the other montage directors increasingly attracted criticism—for the alleged exclusivity and élitism of their innovative work—in spite of its explicit Bolshevik commitments. Experimental montage was curtailed when socialist realism became mandatory in the Soviet Union in 1934. Thus, for all the differences between the Soviet montage movement and the Surrealists, there is an important parallel between them in their incompatibility with unalloyed and unadorned political agitation, manifest in the events of 1934–5 in both France and the Soviet Union. That said, state repression of the avant-garde was much more obvious under the totalitarian regimes of the Soviet Union and Germany, where avant-garde practice was denigrated as, respectively, 'formalist' and 'degenerate'. In both cases, avant-gardism was stamped out because it conflicted with, or merely failed to serve, official state policy. The dramatic decline of the European avant-garde in the 1930s is thus connected with a paradoxical feature of the avant-garde ethos discussed by Poggioli (1962/1968). Avant-garde artistic practice can only flourish under liberal political regimes, which are willing to tolerate vigorous expressions of dissent against the state and society more generally. In this respect the avant-garde bites the hand that feeds, or, in Poggioli's words, it pays 'involuntary homage' (1968: 106) to the bourgeois liberal democracies it attacks.

Post-war art cinema, political modernism, and Third Cinema

The rise of fascism and the arrival of war definitively broke up the pre-war avant-garde movements in the most literal sense: an entire generation of artists was geographically displaced, politically silenced, or co-opted. After the war, three forms of cinema developed with links to the pre-war experiments. First, within the institutions of the international art cinema, filmmakers like Godard, Jean-Marie Straub and Danièle Huillet, Glauber Rocha, Nagisa Oshima, Gillo Pontecorvo, Janscó, Dušan Makavejev, Rainer Werner Fassbinder, and Raúl Ruiz produced feature-length works which integrated radical-left politics with varying degrees of aesthetic experimentation. Second, in Europe and more visibly in the United States, a new generation of 'artisanal' avant-gardists emerged, whose interests were extremely diverse, ranging from a continuation of the abstract experiments of the 1920s to political satire. In the 1960s a third type of radical cinema emerged, reviving and developing the agitational practices of the Soviet Union in the 1920s. This militant, 'engaged' cinema shared with the artisanal avant-garde small-scale production and co-operative distribution, and the leftist political agenda of some art cinema directors; but it disdained the stress in both art and avant-garde cinema on authorship and aesthetics in favour of agitation and political intervention on specific issues.

Although the notion of an art cinema had existed since at least the formation of the Film d'Art company in France in 1908, it was not until after the Second World War that European art cinema became firmly established, with the succession of movements such as Italian Neo-Realism, the French Nouvelle Vague, and the New German Cinema. A number of factors account for its rise at this point: new legislation in many of the European countries to promote indigenous film cultures, combined with new opportunities for foreign films within the American film market as a result of the dismantling of vertical integration.

The 'art' in 'art cinema' is differentiated from the art of other cinemas in two ways. First, art films are usually expressive of national concerns, even if these concerns are ones that, ironically, make them internationally marketable (for example, it is partly the perceived 'Englishness' of *My Beautiful Laundrette* (Stephen Frears, GB, 1985) that makes it of interest to American audiences). Second, art films attempt to conform with canons of taste established in the existing 'high' arts. That is, art films are generally characterized by the use of self-consciously 'artful' techniques designed to differentiate them from 'merely entertaining', popular cinema, these techniques frequently drawing on nationally specific legacies within the established arts (Expressionist painting in Robert Wiene's *The Cabinet of Dr Caligari* (Germany, 1920), the *nouveau roman* in Alain Resnais's *Hiroshima mon amour* (France, 1959) and *Last Year at Marienbad* (France, 1961), Italian opera in Bernardo Bertolucci's *The Spider's Stratagem* (Italy, 1970)). These 'native' cultural markers are often commingled with allusions, critical or affectionate, to American popular culture, this internal contrast further highlighting the national specificity of such films.

This strategy enables the art film to be viewed at home as part of a national culture, and abroad as exotic or sophisticated—or both—and therefore as worthy of the attention of an educated audience. In the United States in particular, simply being European gives a film an edge in this regard, because of the view of Europe as the 'Old World', repository of Art and Wisdom. For this reason, art cinema still tends to be thought of as European art cinema, even though a substantial proportion of art-house material has for some time come from Asia, South America, Australia, and (less fre-

> **The 'art' in 'art cinema' is differentiated from the art of other cinemas in two ways. First, art films are usually expressive of national concerns, even if these concerns are ones that, ironically, make them internationally marketable. Second, art films attempt to conform with canons of taste established in the existing 'high' arts.**

quently) Africa. 'Art cinema', then, is partly a matter of the marketing and consumption of films outside their countries of production, and the circumstances of *production* of 'art' films varies widely depending on the peculiarities of particular national film industries.

In aesthetic terms, 'art cinema' encompasses a diverse range of options, from the tradition of 'quality', literary adaptations of Merchant–Ivory, to the genre reworkings of Claude Chabrol, to the experiments of Godard. Within this diversity, however, some consistent trends and patterns stand out. David Bordwell (1979) has argued that by the 1960s a distinctive art cinema 'mode of narration' had emerged. Where the Hollywood film typically featured a sympathetic protagonist pursuing his or her goal until an unambiguous conclusion was reached, the art film dwelt upon characters with less clearly defined and singular desires. This produced a narrative less clearly structured by explicit temporal markers like deadlines, and enabled the self-conscious use of style to evoke atmosphere and ambiguity. In general, the art film foregrounds narration (the process of storytelling) as much as narrative (the action itself, assumed to be the locus of attention in the classical film). Distinctive uses of style and idiosyncratic narrational stances in turn become associated with individual directors, around which the marketing of art films centre (a Chabrol film is marketed primarily as a Chabrol film, not as a thriller).

Bordwell sees this form as a modification of classical norms of narration and style, not a radical departure from them. Although the art film director has more freedom to explore stylistic options, a story with recognizable characters must still be told, generally within a screening time of between 80 and 180 minutes, since these are commercial films which must be exhibited in the art-house circuit. For these reasons, Bordwell characterizes art cinema narration as a 'domesticated modernism', and contrasts it with the more radical departures from classical form found within the artisanal avant-garde. The key here, once again, is the freedom of artisanal filmmakers to explore spatial and temporal form in the cinema outside any obligation to tell a story; and to make films—with or without any traces of narrative—of any length, ranging from a few seconds to many hours.

Bordwell's description certainly applies to many art films of the 1960s and 1970s, and captures many of the features of art cinema which differentiate it from straightforward Hollywood-style fare. It is a description, however, only of the typical form of art films during a specific historical phase, and for this reason particular art films and directors will fall outside its ambit. These include not only more conservative filmmakers like Merchant–Ivory, where the 'art' usually amounts to little more than a national picturesque 'gloss' applied to classical narrative form, but also those filmmakers who use the feature-length format for more radical ends—aesthetically, politically, or both.

Chief among these are directors such as Godard, Straub and Huillet, and Oshima, for whom a radical political agenda must be articulated within and by radical, anti-realist form—a trend often identified as political modernism or, in Peter Wollen's terminology, 'counter-cinema'(1982b). Wollen sums up the tendencies of such filmmaking through seven contrasts with orthodox narrative filmmaking, such as those between 'identification' and 'estrangement', and 'transparency' and 'foregrounding'. The revolt and protests by French students and workers in May 1968 have come to symbolize this convergence of radical politics and experimental form, but this was the culmination of developments throughout the 1960s. In West Germany in 1963 Jean-Marie Straub and Danièle Huillet made their first film, the short *Machorka-Muff*. Like their first feature, *Nicht versöhnt* ('Not Reconciled', West Germany, 1965), it explored the history and legacy of fascist politics in Germany. *Not Reconciled*—subtitled 'Only Violence Serves where Violence Reigns'—traces the history of a family across three generations, from the First World War to the time of the film's making. The continuity of fascist beliefs and behaviour across the generations is rendered by a patchwork of flashbacks which moves us back and forth between different times without the usual transitional markers (dissolves, music, and so forth). The title thus evokes at least two connotations: the lack of reconcilia-tion among various social groups in Germany, represented by different members of the family; and the refusal of the film to provide a resolution—a reconciliation—of the conflicts among agents and interests in the film's narrative. The film thus executes Brecht's dramaturgy in its narrative of 'leaps' and 'curves' rather than simple linear development, as it does in its muted performance style, both techniques seeking a 'distanciated' rather than highly emotive, putatively uncritical, response.

Other important instances of the convergence between experimental form and radical left politics were evident outside Europe. Oshima's *Nihon no yoru to kiri* ('Night and Fog in Japan', Japan, 1960) depicted opposition to the US–Japan Security Treaty, using stylized tableaux and an intricate flashback structure to explore conflict among different generations of protesters. In Brazil the Cinema Nôvo filmmakers—among them Glauber Rocha and Ruy Guerra—exhibited a formal inventiveness and diversity akin to the Nouvelle Vague filmmakers who had inspired them, but used them in treating overtly political narratives. In Cuba Julio García Espinosa published in 1969 his manifesto calling for an 'Imperfect Cinema'—one responsive to popular needs rather than the high production values of either Hollywood or most European art cinema. In the same year in Argentina Fernando Solanas and Octavio Getino argued for a 'Third Cinema'—a cinema of militant and interventionist 'film acts' aimed at undermining the neo-colonial status quo—which would be an alternative to both Hollywood (First) and art (Second) cinema. Developing a model similar to the Soviet *agitki* (short propaganda films, often disseminated by trains and trucks to rural areas lacking screening facilities), and the similar use of film by the Vietcong in the Vietnam conflict, Third Cinema advocated the exhibition of films on immediate issues by activist, student, and worker groups, to be used as the basis of political discussion. As Solanas and Getino (1969/1976) note, a kindred movement had already developed in the United States, represented by the Newsreel collectives, and the work of such filmmakers as Robert Kramer and Emile de Antonio (a practice sustained and developed in the 1970s by Christine Choy and Third World Newsreel). Although the enthusiasm for such a project has waned or at least mutated in North America and Europe—an issue we will return to in the final section—the notion of a Third Cinema continues to be of relevance to Third World and diasporic filmmakers in Europe and North America.

The connections between European and Third World radicalism were explicitly represented in a scene in Godard's *Weekend* (France, 1967), in which two black immigrant workers declare a programme of militant resistance to economic and political oppression by the West through guerrilla warfare. Within this apocalyptic film, which views European culture and cinema as profoundly decadent—the film ends with the title 'fin du cinéma'—this dialogue represents the only vital political programme. Godard's arrival at this moment was not a straightforward one, however. His films from the beginning were marked by an unparalleled formal playfulness in which Eisenstein and Brecht were both obvious sources of inspiration. But in contrast to these earlier figures, Godard's formal inventiveness in the first phase of his career was only occasionally yoked with political radicalism. From 1964 onwards, however, an interest in socialist politics comes to occupy an ever-more central role in Godard's work. Spurred on by the events of May 1968, Godard pushed the radicalism of *Weekend* still further and formed with Jean-Pierre Gorin the Dziga–Vertov Group—named after an earlier master of political modernism, and one of a number of film cadres which formed in the wake of May 1968. The political 'essays' made by the group represented a synthesis of ideas drawn from European modernism with others derived from the activist and agitational tradition extending from the Soviets to the Vietcong (an influence cited in the black workers' speech in *Weekend*) and the followers of Third Cinema. In the late 1970s, however, Godard again reoriented himself, moving away from the heavily politicized films of the early and mid-1970s, opting for a more poetic—and commercially viable—form. Godard's retreat from an overtly radical political cinema is emblematic of the fate of political modernism in Europe as a whole.

The post-war avant-garde

Along with better-known figures such as Fritz Lang, Bertolt Brecht, and Jean Renoir, Hans Richter was among the leftist intelligentsia who fled Nazi Europe for the United States. The Second World War was a turning-point not only in the individual lives of so many artists and intellectuals, but in the history of the avant-garde as a whole. If the centre of avant-garde activity between the wars had been Europe (with Paris often identified as playing the leading role), this role passed to the United States, or, more particularly, New York, after the war. Just as Abstract Expressionism emerged in the post-war years as the first style of avant-garde painting geographically rooted in the United States, so a vigorous avant-garde film community began to develop. By 1962 a cohesive non-commercial system of production, distribution, exhibition had been created, with its centres in New York and San Francisco; a critical establishment was not long coming.

The presence of *émigrés* like Richter also played a role in these developments. Richter took up a position teaching film at New York's City College Institute of Film Technique in 1943, and in 1947 attempted to bring the aesthetics of the film avant-garde to a wider audience with the feature-length film *Dreams that Money can Buy*. Funded by the art patron Peggy Guggenheim, the film was comprised of a series of episodes, each of which represents a dream being sold by a dream salesman. Obviously enough, the film is a metaphor for commercial cinema—the dream factory. The style of each episode, however, was anything but commercial, since each was made by an established avant-garde artist (e.g. Max Ernst) and accompanied by avant-garde compositions (e.g. John Cage). Many of the episodes were reprises of avant-garde works from the 1920s. However, Richter framed these episodes with a narrated voice-over which motivates each episode as a dream designed for each client and their particular neuroses. Narrative coherence was to be the bridgehead between avant-garde aesthetics and a wider audience. But the film found little favour with the embryonic American avant-garde, perhaps because it was in the process of establishing its own institutions, and in its aesthetics reaffirming that suspicion of narrative so apparent in the pre-war European avant-garde (Maya Deren, for example, complained that 'narrative pattern has come to completely dominate cinematic expression in spite of the fact that it is, basically, a visual form'; 1946/1988: 318). Richter had recognized that the avant-garde was 'blessed in its liberty and cursed in its alienation' (Poggioli 1968: 109) but discovered that the avant-garde community were not at this point interested in trading in any part of their aesthetic liberty for the sake of reaching a broader audience.

Of the indigenous figures in the nascent American film avant-garde, Deren is among the most significant—not just for making one of the most influential films of the tradition, but for her activities as a promoter and proselytizer of the avant-garde. Her first and most well-known film is *Meshes of the Afternoon*, made in 1943 in collaboration with her husband Alexander Hammid (another European *émigré*). The film depicts a series of narrative loops, in which a dreaming woman (played by Deren) sees herself in a number of menacing confrontations with a husband (played by Hammid), a mysteriously cloaked figure, and several *doppelgängers*. Parker Tyler (1960), and later P. Adams Sitney, saw the film as a precursor of a major 'genre' of the American avant-garde: the 'trance' film or 'psychodrama', in which a 'protagonist wanders through a potent environment toward a climactic scene of self-realization' (Sitney 1979: 21).

Sitney situates this concern with 'self-realization' within the Romantic tradition, that is, the dominant intellectual and literary legacy deriving from European philosophers and artists of the eighteenth-century. Expression of feeling and the transformative power of the imagination are the factors which link these twentieth-century filmmakers with earlier artists; Sitney's history is titled *Visionary Film*, stressing the powerful, shaping force of the individual artistic imagination. Other critics have disputed the appropriateness of Romantic thought as the context in which the American avant-garde is examined. While there are limitations to the approach, however, two factors weigh in Sitney's favour. First, it is hard to conceive of avant-garde culture in general without Romanticism. In its stress on innovation and the continual violation of convention over the values of tradition and the observation of rules, the avant-garde is the apotheosis of Romantic thought. Second, Sitney was in part taking his cue from practitioners who cited ideas drawn from the Romantic tradition. Chief among these was the most prolific filmmaker in avant-garde history, Stan Brakhage.

Many of Brakhage's early films, like *Reflections on Black* (USA, 1955), were trance films. As his work developed, though, Brakhage massively expanded the scale and visual vocabulary of such films and intensified their subjective character. The Romantic character of Brakhage's project emerges most clearly in his collection of writings *Metaphors on Vision* (originally published as issue 30 of the journal *Film Culture*). In Brakhage's view, the human subject loses its authentic identity as it learns language, the conventions of pictorial perspective, and narrative—in other words, as it becomes socialized. By 'wrecking' these conventions, as they are embodied in narrative filmmaking, film can render an 'untutored' perception and consciousness. In *Window Water Baby Moving* (USA, 1959), which depicts his wife Jane giving birth to their first child, Brakhage pursues this effect by counterpointing the sequential development of the birth with repetitive abstract and rhythmic patterns.

By the early 1960s two new notions had entered circulation within this milieu: the New American Cinema and underground cinema. A central figure in these developments was Jonas Mekas. Writing of the 'Cinema of the New Generation' in 1960, Mekas saw promising parallels between the European art cinema (Mekas 1960). In a fashion somewhat similar to Richter in the late 1940s, Mekas envisaged a cinema reconciling self-conscious aesthetic seriousness with popular accessibility, and incorporated under this rubric everything from Brakhage, Breer, and Marie Menken to early direct cinema and independent feature narratives. In 1960 credence was given to this argument by the formation of the New American Cinema Group, comprised of filmmakers, producers, performers, and the catalyst Mekas himself. In 1961 the group published a statement in the journal *Film Culture* which, in its rejection of the 'product film' and 'official cinema', used that rhetoric of negation so typical of the avant-garde (Mekas 1961). However, the positive strategies which were to replace the 'product film' were too diverse to hold together for very long, resulting in a split between the 'purist' artisanal ethos, and a modified commercial practice. Mekas promoted the former, which, increasingly inflected by the post-war youth and counter-cultures, became known as 'underground cinema' (Mekas 1972).

Kenneth Anger's *Scorpio Rising* (USA, 1963) is probably the most well-known icon of the underground cinema—partly because of its early notoriety, partly because it combines superficial accessibility with a formidable density of form. Structured by thirteen contemporaneous pop songs, the film follows the actions of a biker and his associates, dressing and preparing for a climactic race in which one of the bikers is killed. By juxtaposing the songs with the hedonistic and nihilistic activities of the biker gang, the film continually draws out of the pop songs the painful and perverse implications within them, but easily overlooked in their original context.

Another feature of *Scorpio Rising* representative of broader activities within the underground was its use of collage or assemblage—the creation of new works through found or 'quoted' material. Anger's film juxtaposes original footage with rephotographed television and cartoon material (and, of course, the soundtrack, which is also created in collage fashion). The purest form of film collage is the compilation film: a film entirely comprised of footage lifted from other films, as in the work of Bruce Conner (and much earlier, Joseph Cornell's *Rose Hobart*, USA, 1936).

In *Scorpio Rising*, Anger's collage works by a process of 'reverse metaphor', in which the traits and qualities of the counter-cultural bikers are projected onto mainstream figures we would normally regard as virtuous or at least innocuous: children's cartoons and images of Christ (Peterson 1994: 160–1). Bruce Conner's work is similarly subversive and ironic. His film *Report* (USA, 1963–7) explores the Kennedy assassination through a radio broadcast relating the build-up to and aftermath of the event, against which are placed repeated shots of the motorcade, countdown leader, and other filmic detritus, and a furious climactic montage intercutting various shots of Kennedy with (among others) shots of a bullfight, a light bulb being shattered in slow motion, and an advertisement for a fridge. All of this is found footage, re-edited to suggest new meanings: the bulb becomes a metaphor for Kennedy's shattered skull, the bullfight suggesting first Kennedy's status as hero (the matador), then his descent into the role of publicly slaughtered victim (the bull), and finally his status as a commodity to be sold, like the fridge. At the most general level, the film heightens its attention to public spectacles of violence—a theme also explored by Conner's *A Movie* (1958)—by pointedly denying us a direct visual image of the moment of assassination itself.

Films like *Report*, and many other collage films, give the lie to the argument that the avant-garde in America is wholly apolitical. In addition to the artisanal works discussed so far, there also appeared in the United States in the 1960s some politicized narrative films which form a parallel with Wollen's 'political avant-garde'. Some of these were formally conventional features like *Nothing but a Man* (Michael Roemer and Robert Young, USA, 1964), which dealt with black oppression in the American south. The closer parallel is with Jon Jost, who has managed to sustain an idiosyncratic career as a 'guerrilla filmmaker' from the mid-1960s to the present day. Involved early in his career with the founding of a Newsreel office in Chicago, Jost went on to combine familiar art cinema strategies with more unusual ones. *Speaking Directly* (USA, 1974), for example, is an essay on the relations between individual, private existence, political power, and forms of representation. The film combines diary footage of Jost's everyday existence with staged, almost allegorical demonstrations of the film's main thesis (that all filmmaking is intrinsically political, no matter how 'personal' or 'subjective' it appears to be), and collage sections using in one case documentary footage of Vietnam, and magazine advertisements in another.

A rather pointed absence in my discussion of the American avant-garde so far is the name Andy Warhol. Warhol's early filmmaking (1962–6) can be seen as a kind of hinge between the 1960s underground and the avant-garde movement which was to command critical attention in the late 1960s and early 1970s in both Europe and America: structural filmmaking. The most obvious connection between Warhol's films and the underground is the explicit representation of sexuality—straight, gay, and polymorphous—in films like *Kiss* and *Blow Job* (both 1963), *Couch* (1964), and *My Hustler* (1965). But films like *Sleep* (1963) and *Empire* (1964) (eight hours of footage of the Empire State Building, projected at sixteen frames per second) exhibit a different form of outrageousness: the refusal to provide even the most minimal dramatic or visual development.

It is in this respect that Warhol's early filmmaking adumbrates structural aesthetics. Structural films empty themselves of apparent 'content' in order to draw our attention to the functioning of a particular aspect of film technique. The most famous example is Michael Snow's *Wavelength* (USA, 1967), a film comprised of a gradual zoom shot across a loft apartment, interrupted by coloured frames, and accompanied by the sound of an ever-rising tone. Characters involved in a murder narrative stray into this space, but none of this action deflects the zoom from its continual cropping of the space or the sound from its relentless ascent through the frequencies. In Warhol's *Couch*, the use of fixed camera positions and the overt use of the length of film reels (the flare at the beginning and end of each reel is not edited out) give the film an obvious, minimal structure, and emphasize the material features of filmmaking almost in resistance to the 'scandalous' sexual actions which are depicted.

Sitney viewed Snow's work as a further development within 'visionary' cinema. If Brakhage had produced a cinema of vision, Snow's achievement was to create a cinema of the mind, in which the films metaphorically represent or explore features of human consciousness. This view of Snow's work, first proposed by Annette Michelson (1971/1978), has been lucidly elaborated by Sitney and William Wees (1982). But objections to

Sitney's argument have been more common. The most important of these seek to situate structural filmmaking within modernism rather than Romanticism (where it is assumed that modernism, while evolving from Romanticism, makes a decisive break with it). In *Abstract Film and Beyond* (1977), Malcolm Le Grice presents an alternative history of the avant-garde to that proposed by Sitney. Le Grice situates the avant-garde within modernism, in his case drawing implicitly on the influential account of modernism associated with Clement Greenberg. For Greenberg, modernism represents the phase in the history of an art when it reflects upon its materials and undergoes a kind of purification (Greenberg 1961/1973). Similarly, Le Grice traces efforts through the history of cinema to focus on the peculiar properties of film. To this is added the implication that such work is *politically* radical—an argument more explicitly made by Peter Gidal (1989)—in so far as it demystifies the means by which films are made. Le Grice's own films from this period, like *Berlin Horse* (GB, 1971), exemplify this aesthetic; but one of the purest examples of this form of reflexive filmmaking is David Crosswaite's elegant *Man with the Movie Camera* (GB, 1973), which manipulates mirrors and focus to create a series of enigmatic images of a film camera, explained as the film itself reveals progressively more parts of the apparatus. 'Structural-material' film—as it came to be known in the British context—represented the moment at which these 'specifist' concerns fully realized themselves.

Structural film dominated critical attention, and perhaps practice, for at most ten years, but it seems pivotal for a variety of reasons. It was heralded, particularly in its British manifestation, as an ultimate and pure manifestation of modernism within film. This as accompanied by attacks on other trends within the avant-garde made with even more than the usual vigour. In criticism, one consequence of Le Grice's view is the marginalization of a great deal of avant-garde practice—much of the work of the Surrealists and the underground—on the grounds that the incorporation of 'dramatic' elements undermines a film's radical and oppositional status. In filmmaking practice, this purity consisted of a more rigorous—or, to its detractors, rigid—expulsion of all vestiges of narrative. Consequently, viewers unfamiliar with the avant-garde find structural filmmaking the most puzzling and 'difficult' of its many trends. The structural phase of the avant-garde is also important in institutional terms. Although certain filmmakers had occasionally held teaching positions from the 1940s

onwards, the emergence of structural film coincided with a much greater integration of the avant-garde community with art schools, universities, and museums. Structural film, it might be argued, represents at once the apogee and the end of the avant-garde—an idea most usefully discussed in relation to the notion of postmodernism later in this chapter.

Feminism and the avant-garde

The importance attributed to structural film should not obscure other significant developments in the wake of the 1960s underground. One of these is the emergence of a more self-conscious feminist presence within the avant-garde. To some degree, avant-garde filmmaking has always provided opportunities for women's expression denied them in the mainstream, just as it has for gays. Dulac in the 1920s and Deren in the 1940s were important both as theorists and as practitioners, and both made films of proto-feminist import: *La Souriante Madame Beudet* (France, 1923) and *Meshes of the Afternoon*. There have clearly also been other women filmmakers—such as Marie Menken, a major early influence on Stan Brakhage, and later figures such as Shirley Clarke and Joyce Wieland—whose significance has been underestimated in many avant-garde histories (Rabinovitz 1991). But it is only with the emergence of the post-war women's movement in the 1960s that 'woman' as such becomes a major focus within the avant-garde.

Underground cinema embodies the notion of 'Sixties liberation', but as often as not underground films echoed, rather than challenged, the constraining representations of women found in the mainstream. Robert Nelson's exuberant neo-Dada *Oh Dem Watermelons* (USA, 1965) may subject racial stereotypes to parodic distension, but its footage of a naked woman caressing herself with a watermelon hardly subverts the sexual economy of the mainstream film, in which women are usually the object and rarely the subject of the erotic gaze. A number of women filmmakers, however, turned underground aesthetics to feminist ends, including Barbara Rubin, Anne Severson, and Carolee Schneemann. Schneemann's *Fuses* (USA, 1967) is a diary film concerned with the detail of her erotic life with James Tenney, and was made partly out of dissatisfaction with two films made by Brakhage about this relationship. The film breaks with patriarchal conventions of the representation of women not by denying the female body as an object to look at, but by placing it in a fuller context. In addition to love-making, we see unerotic, domestic action. The naked female body is not idealized through soft focus and modelled lighting. Moreover, Schneemann is presented as an initiator in the sexual act, and shots of Tenney are just as frank and frequent as those of her.

This strategy was not welcomed by many in the women's movement at the time, because of the at least superficial resemblance between *Fuses* and porno-graphic films, which by the early 1970s had become a target for many feminists (as did earlier, apparently liberating representations of women, such as Brak-hage's *Window Water Baby Moving*). A very different type of film, drawing heavily on feminist theory, emerged in the 1970s. In 'Visual Pleasure and Narrative Cinema' (1975) British critic and filmmaker Laura Mul-vey argued that the narrative and visual construction of orthodox narrative films embodied a patriarchal ideo-logy in which women were either idealized or punished, but either way diminished. Her call for the 'destruction' of the pleasures derived from such cinema—prefi-gured by Claire Johnston's (1973) discussion of 'women's cinema as counter-cinema'—inspired her own filmic practice (e.g. *Penthesilea*, GB, 1974, and *Riddles of the Sphinx*, GB, 1977, both made with Peter Wollen), as well as influencing that of Yvonne Rainer in the United States. Rainer's *The Man who Envied Women* (USA, 1985), for example, is structured around a female protagonist who is never visible; she is ren-dered only through voice-over. Her husband, the man in the title, is by contrast doubly visible, in that he is played by two actors. So the film reverses the polarity that, according to Mulvey, structures Hollywood cinema, by exempting the main female character entirely from the look of the camera and spectator. In this, as in her other films, however, Rainer does not simply adopt Mulvey's or anybody else's thesis; rather, the film interweaves a great multitude of theories, and types of footage and imagery, around a narrative core, tending to play them off one another rather than endorsing any one. In addition, the film questions the sexual politics not only of Hollywood, but also of the avant-garde itself. The film 'quotes' the opening of *Un chien andalou* and implies that the slicing of the woman's eye is not merely a provocative 'shock' image, but another manifestation of misogyny.

In their efforts to create a feminist cinema in formal—not merely thematic—terms, the work of Mulvey and

Rainer echoed that of European filmmakers like Mar-guerite Duras and Chantal Akerman. Such films shared with structural aesthetics a profound suspicion of con-ventional narrative—Rainer once talked of the 'tyranny' of narrative—but as the influence of structural film waned, narrative returned with a vengeance, becom-ing a major object of concern for both feminists and others within the avant-garde. Several factors moti-vated this renewed attention to narrative. Paul Wille-men questioned the idea that there was a stable relationship between a particular kind of form (like structural form) and an 'avant-garde' or critical effect. The functioning of different strategies had to be re-addressed in each new context. Willemen argued that the investigation of historical questions was a priority, and that narrative was essential to such a project. Other filmmakers became concerned about the exclusivity of the avant-garde, a problem highlighted by structural filmmaking, and one that both Richter and Mekas had tried to solve. Sally Potter turned to narrative form and familiar narrative types in *Thriller* (GB, 1979)—albeit in a novel way—in order to connect with the pleasures of conventional narrative cinema and so address a poten-tially larger audience.

Along with this return to narrative came a renewed attention to expressivity in various ways. Some femin-ists, like Schneemann, had always found themselves out of tune with the detachment of structural filmmak-ing. Similar remarks were made by younger women filmmakers whose careers began in the 1980s, such as Vivienne Dick and Su Friedrich. Friedrich's *Gently down the Stream* (USA, 1981) constitutes a particularly interesting case because of the way it returns to the highly expressive mode of the trance film, while reshaping it for feminist and lesbian ends. Here, the dreams of the implied protagonist concern anxieties over her lesbian desires and religious allegiances. The gradual and painful passage to a new sexual identity is suggested by a progression of water images, each one suggesting greater control over the water than the last. Like Brakhage, Friedrich scratches words onto the sur-face of the film, but where Brakhage uses this as a way of underlining the personal nature of the film, in Fried-rich's film scratched intertitles vie with images for domination of the film in a most un-Brakhagean man-ner. Identity, it is implied, will occur partly through language, not by transcending it. And like *Window Water Baby Moving*, the film is filled with birth imagery, but rather than being rendered as a natural process to be experienced in the most 'untutored' fashion possible, here it is presented as a metaphor for the dreamer's difficulty in attaining selfhood.

The return of interest in narrative and expressivity has been evident in a diverse range of practices since the mid-1970s: New Narrative, New Talkie, Cinema of Transgression, and most recently, New Underground. In contrast to the heyday of the structural films, there is little critical consensus about which mode or style of filmmaking is most important. As in the avant-garde more widely, stylistic pluralism has been a feature of avant-garde film over the last twenty years. There have been moments of such pluralism before—in the 1920s for example—but it is widely held that the contemporary situation is qualitatively different from earlier phases of avant-garde and modernist practice. This is the shift denoted by the term 'postmodernism'.

Postmodernism and the paradox of tradition

The term 'postmodernism' has come to assume a bewildering variety of connotations, but for our purposes these can be reduced to three. In the first use it refers to the stylistic pluralism noted above. In architecture, where this version of the phrase has been particularly important, it refers to the eclectic mixing of various historical styles in the design of buildings (a dominant trend in post-war architecture). The problem with this definition, at least as it is extended to film history, is that the mixing of radically different styles was already evident in the work of many 1920s avant-gardists (as we have seen). A more sophisticated version of the postmodern argument claims that it is not the mere presence of eclecticism, but its cultural position and use, that has changed. Rather than functioning within an avant-garde ethos in which the gesture of mixing styles constituted a typical attempt to occupy the position of most advanced and subversive trend, in postmodern culture stylistic pluralism marks an exhaustion of the subversive energies and ambitions associated with the avant-garde. In Fredric Jameson's words, 'all that is left is to imitate dead styles, to speak through the masks and with the voices of the styles in the imaginary museum' of the past (1991: 115).

Writing more than a decade before Jameson, and reworking the military metaphor underpinning the notion of avant-gardism, Harold Rosenberg argued that we have entered a period in which the culture of negation is replaced by a 'demilitarized zone, flanked by avant-garde ghosts on one side and a changing mass culture on the other' (1972: 219). The once subversive styles of the avant-garde have been assimilated by mass culture, so that the gap between nominally avant-garde products and popular, mass cultural ones is greatly reduced. Is there such a difference, one might ask, between Sadie Benning's *Jollies* (USA, 1990), which explores the filmmaker's passage into lesbianism with hand-held, pixelvision video footage and a soundtrack of rock tunes, and any number of music videos which place imagery ransacked from the avant-garde under the song being marketed? The avant-garde has become nothing more than a posture of aggression and defiance; postmodernism represents a kind of disenchantment with its high ideals. Indeed, in what is perhaps the ultimate indignity, the very phrase 'avant-garde' has now become a marketing device itself, as the name of a new line of deodorant in 1994.

Parallel with the absorption of once-subversive styles within the lexicon of mass culture, the objects of the avant-garde have become useful commodities for the 'Establishment', in the fullest sense of that sometimes vague word. 'Avant-garde' paintings and sculptures adorn the walls of major corporations and wealthy individual clients. They at once constitute useful market investments, and signify a supposed commitment to culture, education, and refinement transcending the materialism of the market. If the Cologne Dadaists had once subverted the polite conventions of the art gallery by forcing patrons to enter an exhibition through a mock lavatory, the institutions of gallery and museum have had the last laugh by simply continually expanding the objects which could accrue value by being exhibited within them (urinals, bricks, latterly dead sheep and heads sculpted from frozen blood). Peter Bürger writes of the emergence of a 'Neo-avant-garde' in the 1960s—an *institutionalized* avant-garde which, by definition, undercuts its own rhetoric of subversion (Bürger 1980/1984: 58). More

> **Parallel with the absorption of once-subversive styles within the lexicon of mass culture, the objects of the avant-garde have become useful commodities for the 'Establishment', in the fullest sense of that sometimes vague word.**

bluntly, Christopher Butler states: 'Aesthetic subversion has . . . become revolutionary pantomime' (1980: 122).

The notion of postmodernism has proven to be compelling to many, but a host of questions can be raised about its legitimacy. A common complaint is that it overlooks the presence within modernism of the defining traits of 'postmodernism' (e.g. Crow 1981: 257). One might also question whether the idea of the avant-garde ever had the power which we assume was ascribed to it before the Second World War; perhaps this is merely a symptom of an ongoing nostalgia for an idea which was always regarded as utopian. (Rosenberg notes that doubts about the continued existence of the avant-garde have been voiced almost as long as the avant-garde has existed—not least by members of the avant-garde.) Similarly, one can question the assumption that there was a moment when avant-garde practice stood wholly outside, or successfully challenged, the operations of the art market. This is true even in the case of the filmic avant-garde, in spite of its displaced position in relation to arguments about a general, cross-media avant-garde. Avant-garde filmmaking has never been embraced by corporations and collectors (notwithstanding the support of Peggy Guggenheim in the 1940s and 1950s, and the brief flirtation of the Ford Foundation with grants to Anger, Conner, and ten other filmmakers in the 1960s). But the filmic avant-garde has become an established part of art schools and many museums, and in Britain has increasing ties with television (for which the avant-garde is another supplier of material for its ever-expanding broadcast hours). More generally, many of the stylistic practices of the filmic avant-garde—especially collage—have been adopted by music videos, TV advertising, and credit sequences (think of Michael Moore's TV Nation, USA/GB, 1994–5). If it did once maintain a more authentically avant-garde status—relative to similar practices in the other arts—it surely no longer does.

J. Hoberman argues that the moment of postmodernism can be described as the moment when the 'oxymoronic tradition of the new'—Rosenberg's description of the avant-garde—'had truly become a tradition' (1991: 117). The sceptical view would hold that, paradoxically, the avant-garde has always in practice 'truly' worked as a tradition. In the words of James Peterson, 'The American avant-garde community trumpets the ideal of aesthetic revolution, but lives a reality of refinement and revision' (1994: 186). The rhetoric of negation has always existed alongside the practice of imitation; the dream of a 'total liberation' from all prior conventions is just that—an unattainable fantasy.

Taking all of this into account, it might be argued that reports of the death of the cinematic avant-garde have been premature, at least if we operate with a more realistic perspective regarding the ambitions and achievements of the historical avant-gardes. There are still filmmakers who work outside commercial structures, depending on their own resources and grants, and who see their work as continually challenging the stylistic and attitudinal norms of the mainstream. When we survey the contemporary scene, we can recognize descendants of all the various strains of avant-garde practice I have discussed: collage in Lewis Klahr's Tales of the Forgotten Future (USA, 1988–91), for example, or the fusion of Surrealism and the underground in The Deadman (Peggy Ahwesh and Keith Sanborn, USA, 1991). Even the goals of political modernism have survived, in the form of a politicized postmodernism in which the role of representation in politics is as central as it was for political modernism. Laura Kipnis (1986), for example, advocates the 'refunctioning' of pre-existent texts in such a way as to realize their oppositional potential, as in the re-editing of popular television shows in Dara Birnbaum's work. Here, however, the focus on politics and ideology is combined with both a suspicion of universal or 'totalizing' claims (e.g. those of Marxist class analysis), as well as the more relaxed attitude to narrative and its pleasures noted above (for example, Potter's Thriller, and some of the films associated with the 'New Queer Cinema', such as Todd Haynes's Poison, USA, 1990). And so it is that some critics talk of a 'postmodern avant-garde' (e.g. Sayre 1989)—a contradiction in terms for the version of postmodernism I began with—in which the critical, subversive, and utopian aspirations of the historical avant-gardes are sustained. The status and value of the avant-garde thus remains a contested issue, as, in different ways, it has been through most of its history.

BIBLIOGRAPHY

Abel, Richard (1984), *French Cinema: The First Wave, 1915–1929* (Princeton: Princeton University Press).

Adorno, Theodor, and **Max Horkheimer** (1947/1979), 'The Culture Industry', trans. John Cummings in *Dialectic of Enlightenment* (London: Verso).

Arthur, Paul (1986–7), 'The Last of the Machine?: Avant-garde Film since 1966', *Millennium Film Journal*, 16–18 (Fall–Winter), 69–97.

*Bordwell, David (1979/1985), 'The Art Cinema as a Mode of Film Practice', *Film Criticism*, 4/1 (Fall), 56–64; repr. rev. in *Narration in the Fiction Film* (Madison: University of Wisconsin Press).

—— **Janet Staiger,** and **Kristin Thompson** (1985), *The Classical Hollywood Cinema: Film Style and Mode of Production to 1960* (New York: Columbia University Press).

Bourdieu, Pierre (1979/1984), *Distinction: A Social Critique of the Judgement of Taste*, trans. Richard Nice (London: Routledge & Kegan Paul).

Bürger, Peter (1980/1984), *Theory of the Avant-Garde*, trans. Michael Shaw (Minneapolis: University of Minnesota Press).

Butler, Christopher (1980), *After the Wake: The Contemporary Avant-Garde* (Oxford: Clarendon Press).

Christie, Ian (1979), 'French Avant-Garde Film in the Twenties: From "Specificity" to Surrealism', in Phillip Drummond, Deke Dusinberre, and A. L. Rees (eds.), *Film as Film: Formal Experiment in Film 1910–1975* (London: Hayward Gallery).

Crow, Thomas (1981), 'Modernism and Mass Culture in the Visual Arts', in Benjamin Buchloh, Serge Guilbaut, and Daniel Solkin (eds.), *Modernism and Modernity* (Halifax: Press of the Nova Scotia College of Art and Design).

Curtis, David (1971), *Experimental Cinema: A Fifty-Year Evolution* (New York: Delta).

Deren, Maya (1946/1988), 'Cinema as an Art Form', in VèVè A. Clark, Millicent Hodson, and Catrina Neiman (eds.), *The Legend of Maya Deren: A Documentary Biography and Collected Works*, vol. i, part 2 (New York: Anthology Film Archives and Film Culture).

Dwoskin, Stephen (1974), *Film is . . . The International Free Cinema* (London: Peter Owen).

Elsaesser, Thomas (1987), 'Dada/Cinema?', in Rudolf E. Kuenzli (ed.), *Dada and Surrealist Film* (New York: Willis Locker & Owens).

Faure, Élie (1923/1967), 'The Art of Cineplastics', in Dan Talbot (ed.), *Film: An Anthology* (Berkeley: University of California Press).

García Espinosa, Julio (1969/1979), 'For an Imperfect Cinema', *Jump Cut*, 20: 24–6.

Gidal, Peter (1989), *Materialist Film* (London: Routledge).

Greenberg, Clement (1939), 'Avant Garde and Kitsch', *Partisan Review*, 6 (Fall), 34–9.

—— (1947), 'Towards a Newer Laocoon', *Partisan Review*, 7 (Fall), 296–310.

—— (1961/1973), 'Modernist Painting', in Gregory Battcock (ed.), *The New Art* (New York: E. P. Dutton).

Harwood, John (1995), *Eliot to Derrida: The Poverty of Interpretation* (London: Macmillan).

Hoberman, J. (1991), *Vulgar Modernism: Writings on Movies and Other Media* (Philadelphia: Temple University Press).

Horak, Jan-Christopher (ed.) (1995), *Lovers of Cinema: The First American Film Avant-Garde 1919–1945* (Madison: University of Wisconsin Press).

Hughes, Robert (1980), *The Shock of the New: Art and the Century of Change* (London: British Broadcasting Corporation).

James, David E. (1989), *Allegories of Cinema: American Film in the Sixties* (Princeton: Princeton University Press).

Jameson, Fredric (1991/1993), 'Postmodernism; or, The Cultural Logic of Late Capitalism', in Thomas Docherty (ed.), *Postmodernism: A Reader* (London: Harvester-Wheatsheaf).

Johnston, Claire (1973), 'Women's Cinema as Counter-Cinema', in Johnston (ed.), *Notes on Women's Cinema* (London: Society for Education in Film and Television).

Kaplan, E. Ann (1983), *Women and Film: Both Sides of the Camera* (London: Macmillan).

Kipnis, Laura (1986), '"Refunctioning" Reconsidered: Towards a Left Popular Culture', in Colin MacCabe (ed.), *High Theory/Low Culture: Analysing Popular Television and Film* (Manchester: Manchester University Press).

*Le Grice, Malcolm (1977), *Abstract Film and Beyond* (Cambridge: Mass.: MIT Press).

MacDonald, Scott (1989), *A Critical Cinema*, i (Berkeley: University of California Press).

—— (1992), *A Critical Cinema*, ii (Berkeley: University of California Press).

Mekas, Jonas (1960), 'Cinema of the New Generation', *Film Culture*, 21: 1–19.

—— (1961), 'First Statement of the Group', *Film Culture*, 22–3: 131–3.

—— (1972), *Movie Journal: The Rise of a New American Cinema 1959–1971* (New York: Collier Books).

Michelson, Annette (1971/1978), 'Toward Snow', in P. Adams Sitney, *The Avant-Garde Film: A Reader of Theory and Criticism* (New York: Anthology Film Archives).

Mulvey, Laura (1975), 'Visual Pleasure and Narrative Cinema', *Screen*, 16/3 (Autumn), 6–18.

Neale, Steve (1981), 'Art Cinema as Institution', in *Screen*, 22/1: 11–39.

Peterson, James (1994), *Dreams of Chaos, Visions of Order: Understanding the American Avant-Garde Cinema* (Detroit: Wayne State University Press).

Poggioli, Renato (1962/1968), *The Theory of the Avant-Garde*, trans. Gerald Fitzgerald (Cambridge, Mass.: Harvard University Press).

Rabinovitz, Lauren (1991), *Points of Resistance: Women, Power and Politics in the New York Avant-Garde Cinema 1943–1971* (Urbana: University of Illinois Press).

Rosenbaum, Jonathan (1983), *Film: The Front Line–1983* (Denver: Arden Press).

Rosenberg, Harold (1972), *The De-definition of Art: Action Art to Pop to Earthworks* (New York: Horizon Press).

Sayre, Henry M. (1989), *The Object of Performance: The American Avant-Garde since 1970* (Chicago: University of Chicago Press).

Sitney, P. Adams (1979), *Visionary Film: The American Avant-Garde 1943–1978*, 2nd edn. (New York: Oxford University Press).

Smith, Murray (1999), 'Superfiends, Surrealism and Sublation: On the Dialectic of Avant-garde and Popular Culture', *Film Studies: An International Review* 1 (Spring), 14–31.

Solanas, Fernando, and Octavio Getino (1969/1976), 'Towards a Third Cinema', in Bill Nichols (ed.), *Movies and Methods* (Berkeley: University of California Press).

Tyler, Parker (1960), *The Three Faces of the Film* (New York: Yoseloff).

Wees, William C. (1982), *Light Moving in Time: Studies in the Visual Aesthetics of Avant-Garde Film* (Berkeley: University of California Press).

*Willemen, Paul (1984), 'An Avant Garde for the Eighties', *Framework*, 24: 53–73.

*Wollen, Peter (1975/1982a), 'The Two Avant-Gardes', in *Readings and Writings: Semiotic Counter-Strategies* (London: Verso).

*—— (1982b), 'Godard and Counter Cinema: *Vent d'Est*', in Wollen (1982a).

3 Realism, modernism, and post-colonial theory

Ashish Rajadhyaksha

'When was "the post-colonial"?', asks Stuart Hall. 'What should be included and excluded from its frame? Where is the invisible line between it and its "others"—colonialism, neo-colonialism, Third World, imperialism—in relation to whose termination it ceaselessly, but without final supersession, marks itself?' (Hall 1996). Does 'post-colonial' refer to some people, or some societies, and not others, as something like a 'badge of merit' (Hulme 1995, quoted in Hall 1996)—or does it signal something more abstract? Bill Ashcroft, Gareth Griffiths, and Helen Tiffin effectively include all nations which have once been colonized in order to 'cover all the culture affected by the imperial process from the moment of colonization to the present day' (1989: 2). In doing so, however, they designate as equally 'post-colonial' 'very different national-racial formations—the United States, Australia and Canada, on the one hand, and Nigeria, Jamaica and India, on the other' (Shohat 1992). Ruth Frankenberg and Lata Mani's (1993) rejoinder to this has been to claim that, while these are all indeed post-colonial societies, they are not so 'in the same way'. A further difficulty with the concept of the 'post-colonial' is that it seems to suggest a period that follows the demise of colonialism. As has often been pointed out, this is a misnomer since colonialism certainly does not end with the arrival of national independence in formerly colonized states. This in turn has lead to charges that post-colonial theory has 'managed to obfuscate some of the enduring legacies of colonialism, including the pauperization of the Third World in the age of late capitalism' (Majid 1995–6). Efforts, sometimes acrimonious, have been made, in this context, to bring to light what post-colonialism is 'actually' all about. Thus, Kwame Anthony Appaiah suggests how post-colonial theory may be seen as the political theory of the diasporic Third World intellectual, who is part of 'a relatively small, Western-style, Western-trained, group of writers and thinkers who mediate the trade in cultural commodities of world capitalism at the periphery' (1991: 348) while Arif Dirlik begins an essay on post-colonialism with the—avowedly facetious—statement that the 'post-colonial' begins 'when Third World intellectuals have arrived in First World academe' (1994: 329).

The seeming shambles that is current post-colonial theory is caused partly, as a number of writers have pointed out, through uncertainty as to whether the concept of post-colonialism is a chronological or an epistemological one. Hall goes further and argues that post-colonial theory is faced with a choice of epistemologies: a 'rational and successive logic or a deconstructive one' (Hall 1996: 255). The way out of this, he suggests, is to agree that, whatever our location, post-colonial theory allows us to reconceptualize colonialism itself, in the light of our current knowledge of global capitalism.

29

Colonization, from this 'post-colonial' perspective, was no local or marginal sub-plot in some larger story (for example the transition from feudalism to capitalism in Western Europe . . .) In the re-staged narrative of the post-colonial, colonization assumes the place and significance of a major, extended and ruptural world-historical event . . . signifying the whole process of expansion, exploration, conquest, colonization and imperial hegemonization which constituted the 'outer face', the constitutive outside, of European and then Western capitalist modernity after 1492. (Hall 1996: 249)

This needs to be said. However, once said, it is worth adding that we cannot simply speak of only *one* 're-staged narrative of the post-colonial'. First, in the designation of the site of the restaging act: it would be my experience, living and working in India, that the route by which issues such as these arrive on my doorstep constitutes them less as issues with an autonomous import than as a staging-ground of numerous binary oppositions. It is precisely this staging context—rather than the debate—that is in turn replicated and restaged in other, typically 'nationalist' contexts which then appear free to introduce to it their own subject-matter. Second, in the (dominant) deconstructionist version of the role of narrative in the post-colonial, there is an assertion that post-coloniality is not one of the *grands récits* of modernity but a baggage of 'narratives' which, because they are narratives, leave out things, have limits, and do not present themselves as 'solutions for the future' (Spivak, in Harasym 1990: 18–19). When I try to situate this kind of argument in India, in some of the most violent, as well as politically contentious, events that have addressed caste (the Mandal Commission), religion (the rise of a Hindu right), and gender (the Uniform Civil Code debates)—none of which, unfortunately, can feature in a brief survey of this kind—I find myself arguing that 'rational and successive logic' is not an epistemological either–or in relation to deconstructionism. It is, rather, that the two alternatives always live in some kind of negotiated relationship to each other, and this in itself is one of the reasons why the sphere of an objective, 'political' arena is so difficult to designate.

This is perhaps best revealed in the crisis of the cinema itself in relation to post-colonial theory. Until the early 1980s the cinema was at the forefront of post-colonial theory but has now virtually disappeared from recent debates on post-coloniality. The very construction of the filmic image, through editing, sound recording and mixing, and the process of projecting that image to an audience, had a relationship with the structuring of various kinds of modernist 'public-ness' which has, in the relocated status of colonialism, lost out to larger, less controllable impulses and to the range of technologies that mediate such 'autonomous social impulses' (to use Spivak's term). In this context, it is worth looking at the three-decade history of post-colonial relations between national cinemas in the 'Third World' and independent film movements in the West.

> **Until the early 1980s the cinema was at the forefront of post-colonial theory but has now virtually disappeared from recent debates on post-coloniality. The very construction of the filmic image, through editing, sound recording and mixing, and the process of projecting that image to an audience, had a relationship with the structuring of various kinds of modernist 'public-ness' which has, in the relocated status of colonialism, lost out to larger, less controllable impulses and to the range of technologies that mediate such 'autonomous social impulses' (to use Spivak's term).**

The Western avant-garde

In 1972 Peter Bürger's influential book *Theory of the Avant-Garde* was first published in German, reflecting, as he wrote later, 'a historical constellation of problems that emerged after the events of May 1968 and the failure of the student movement in the early 70s' (1994: 95). That book in many ways launched a series of theoretical interventions to resuscitate the concept of an avant-garde which Bürger saw as challenging bourgeois notions of aesthetic autonomy. Most of the contributors to this debate agreed that the 'historical avant-garde', which Bürger located mainly in Dadaism, Surrealism, and the post-revolutionary Russian avant-garde, had met its demise following the Second World War, with the institutionalization of modernism in the

United States. Thereafter, while the term survived, it was increasingly 'overpowered by conformism' (in Walter Benjamin's (1973/1979) widely quoted phrase). For Rosalind Krauss (1986) this conformism was identified with a valorization of originality, while Andreas Huyssen (1986) sought to find avant-garde impulses (amongst other places) within mass culture. Several of these debates in New York occurred specifically in the context of the rise of a European 'trans-avant-garde', a set of Neo-Expressionist movements mainly in Germany (Georg Baselitz, Markus Lupertz, A. R. Penck) and Italy (Sandro Chia, Clemente), which were extensively debated in Europe and the United States, and attacked (notably by Buchloh 1981) for their aggressive assertion of a neo-nationalist élitism, 'reflect[ing] and dismantl[ing] the ideological impact of growing authoritarianism' (Wallis and Tucker 1984: 108).

It was within this broad context that Peter Wollen in 1975 wrote his classic essay 'The Two Avant-Gardes', which identified two parallel movements in the West (see Smith, Chapter 2). The first avant-garde emphasized formal experimentation and was deeply suspicious of 'programmatic' political activism; the second was more aggressively political, but still preoccupied with 'the whole process of signification out of which a world view or an ideology is constructed'. In drawing this distinction, Wollen drew the debate into the ambit of modernism proper, emphasizing the 'critical semiotic shift' represented by the avant-gardes: the 'change of emphasis from the problem of signified and reference, a classic problem of realism, to that of signifier and signified within the sign itself'.

It is perhaps only in retrospect that Wollen's essay reveals just why it proved so influential: it was not the two specific vanguard movements that made the essay significant so much as the virtually global resonances of his paradigm. The paradigm spoke of a modernist model in which two (or more) movements were presented as being on different sides of a divide, with each side in some sense staked onto historical precedents which were reprised, reinvented, or re-enacted in order to address the present.

It was characteristic of the time (the 1970s–1980s) that none of the theorists mentioned above, dealing with theories of the avant-garde, were familiar with, or even seriously interested in, what was going on outside the Euro-American context. Nevertheless, I think the model itself remains useful, even as we include those other contexts here. In doing so, I will revert to the original opposition which preceded the concept of the 'two avant-gardes'—that of realism versus modernism—and add a third term: that of nationalism.

Nationalist realism–modernism

A second history can be inscribed into this battle of two avant-gardes. From the 1950s and the Brazilian Cinema Nôvo, 'new cinema' movements swept through large parts of Latin America, Europe, Africa, and Asia. Many of the filmmakers associated with these movements addressed issues similar to those of the Western avant-garde, and were, indeed, in some kind of dialogue with it: most celebratedly in the meeting between Godard and Glauber Rocha (emblematically presented in Vent d'est (1969), where Rocha appears in a brief sequence). Indeed, in this phase many of those active in the 'Third World' were possibly unaware of their counterparts in similar situations, and often came together as a consequence of having common Western referents.

In many countries New Cinema movements were constituted through direct state intervention, and were intended to establish indigenous film infrastructures in the context of political independence. To put it bluntly, in several countries, for example in Africa, there was literally no cinema before the New Cinema. In many of these movements, a commitment to institutionalization went alongside a commitment to the promotion of indigenous realisms. This can be seen in Cinema Nôvo's commitment to GEICINE (the Grupo executivo da indústria cinematográfica, set up by the government to examine the Brazilian film industry in 1961), and later, more significantly, Embrafilme, the Brazilian state organization for funding cinema; the Cuban cinema and ICAIC (the Cuban Institute of Cinematographic Art and Industry, started in 1959, within three months of the success of the revolution); the FEPACI (the Fédération panafricaine des cinéastes) in Africa; the NFDC (National Film Development Corporation) in India; and a host of others (such as the Sri Lankan State Film Corporation and the Royal Nepal Film Corporation).

Thus, it is possible to see several nationalist reconstruction agendas adopting economic programmes based on the principles of scientific rationalism and its aesthetic counterpart of realism. As Fredric Jameson argues, 'realism designates an active, curious,

The Nouvelle Vague meets counter-cinema—Glauber Rocha at the crossroads in Godard's *Vent d'est* (1969)

experimental, subversive—in a word scientific—attitude towards social institutions and the material world; and the "realistic" work of art is therefore one which encourages and disseminates this attitude, yet not merely in a flat or mimetic way or along the lines of imitation alone' (Jameson 1977: 205). Thus, in India the report of the Patil Enquiry (Film Enquiry Committee 1951), the first major state initiative after Independence to address and reform the film industry, embodies several key tenets of this aesthetic of realism, in advocating a cinema of 'social purpose', denigrating the mass-cultural industry as 'gamblers' who work 'often at the cost of both the taste of the public and the prosperity of the industry', and recommending that numerous state institutions be started, including the Film Finance Corporation, the National Film Archive of India, and a film training institute. Between 1945 and 1975, which Aijat Ahmad identifies as the 'high period of decolonization' (1992*b*: 39–40), indigenous realism played a crucial role in nation-building. In the words of Gyanendra Pandey, realism—or rather, various national realisms—were important in writing up the 'biography of the emerging nation-state' (1991: 560), and creating the authoritative self-image of the nation.

During this same period, one particular strand of 'author cinema' from the 'Third World' also came to critical prominence and was associated with artists whose major virtue, it appeared, was the fact that they 'straddled two cultures'. Roy Armes's (1987) book on the subject is exemplary in its identification of this category. In a chapter entitled 'Cinema Astride Two Cultures', he lists a small number of 'first generation' film-authors—Satyajit Ray, Youssef Chahine, Glauber Rocha, Yilmaz Güney, Ousmane Sembene, and Jorge Sanjinés—who are seen as contributing simultaneously to Western modernism as well as to their 'own native tradition' (Armes 1987: 229–30). (We might also add the names of Lester James Peries, Lino Brocka, Nelson Pereira dos Santos, and maybe even Akira Kurosawa.) Most of these filmmakers have consistently been showcased in Western film festivals as exemplars of modernist 'author cinema'. This has led to the virtual exclusion of all knowledge about the contexts in which the filmmaking practices of these very names occur—as well as the work of others who explicitly aligned themselves to (or opposed) a socialist avant-garde internationalism. Furthermore, it has resulted in the elision of any argument that might assign to the mass-cultural mainstream of newly independent 'Third World' nations their own vanguardist initiatives (for example, in creating audiences, or in shaping their own anti-colonial indigenous mass culture).

The Third Cinema and the avant-garde

In 1969 the famous manifesto of Fernando Solanas and Octavio Getino was published, heralding the new concept of a 'Third Cinema' which, for the first time, allowed a second, more explicitly avant-garde position to emerge in opposition to the one of modernist 'author-cinema'. The manifesto, which was followed by several other texts and films hitherto unknown outside their local contexts (see Chanan 1983), was premissed on a replacement of nationalism with 'the development of a worldwide liberation movement whose force is to be found in Third World countries'. According to Solanas and Getino's typology, First Cinema was represented by Hollywood; the Second Cinema by the 'so-called "author's cinema", "expression cinema", "nouvelle vague", and "cinema novo"'; while Third Cinema was seen as using 'films as a revolutionary tool', and radically relocating the practices of viewing and the industrial–economic designation of cinema itself.

It is worth noting that the Third Cinema manifesto was, among other things, in dialogue with a post-May 1968 European–American film avant-garde, and the work of Jean-Luc Godard in particular (see Godard and Solanas 1987: 82–9). Indications of this engagement include the years of Salvador Allende's Popular Unity government, when European filmmakers as diverse as Chris Marker (who helped complete Patricio Guzmán's *Battle for Chile*, 1973–9) and Roberto Rossellini contributed in their own ways to the Chilean filmmakers' famous call for 'national liberation and the construction of socialism' (quoted in Fusco 1987: 118). Indeed, it is clear that Wollen is indebted, in part at least, to Solanas and Getino for his own manifesto statement written six years later and that there are evident continuities between Solanas and Getino's characterization of 'Second' and 'Third' Cinemas and Wollen's identification of two avant-gardes. It is therefore possible to see in Wollen's (1975) essay a relocating of the two concepts of authorship and political activism into more explicitly semiotic and narrative pratices, not only in this essay itself but more schematically in an earlier essay on 'Godard and Counter-Cinema', where he marks the divide in terms of narrative transitivity versus intransitivity, identification versus estrangement, and fiction versus reality (Wollen 1972).

Among the consequences of this manifesto in film—

which accompanied a literary 'boom' that followed the arrival of Latin Americans Gabriel García Marquez, Mario Vargas Llosa, and Julio Cortazar, and the African Ngũgĩ wa Thiong'o on the Western literary scene of the 1960s–1970s—was the excavation of a vastly more complex history, and existing contemporary practice, than allowed by the modernist engagement with 'Third World' film-authors. Senior 'first-generation' filmmakers—notably Ousmane Sembene and Med Hondo (see Diawara 1992; also Jameson 1986 and Mulvey 1991), Nelson Pereira dos Santos, Ritwik Ghatak, and Lino Brocka—were now seen as involved in a far more complex practice than had been earlier allowed to them, and as refusing to offer in opposition to 'the values of colonial or imperial predators' a simplistic notion of 'national identity or of cultural authenticity' (Willemen 1989: 4). On the other side, younger filmmakers from all three continents emerged, and introduced not just filmmaking practice but theory, with a far more explicitly critical post-colonial awareness of their national histories than had previously been possible. In this respect, we could mention (following Willemen), Amos Gitai (from Israel; see Willemen 1993), Haile Gerima (Ethiopia; see Gerima 1989), Kumar Shahani (India; see Shahani 1986), Edward Yang (Taiwan), Chen Kaige and the 'Fifth Generation' (China), and the remarkable avant-garde movement in the Philippines in the early 1980s, gathered at the Mowelfund Film Institute, working mainly in Super-8 and video and involving filmmakers like Raymond Red and Nick Deocampo (see Deocampo 1985).

This phenomenon has gone alongside one in literature: as in Africa, for instance. Appaiah (1991), for example, argues that whereas the first generation of modern African novels (Chinua Achebe's *Things Fall Apart*, Camara Laye's *L'Enfant noir*) were 'written in the context of notions of politics and culture dominant in the French and British university and publishing worlds in the 1950s and 60s' (348) when it was 'held to be obvious both by these writers and by the high culture of Europe of the day . . . that new literatures in new nations should be anti-colonial and nationalist (in the tradition of Sir Walter Scott)' (348–9), a second generation emerged with radically different perceptions.

Ouologuem's novel [*Le Devoir de violence*, 'Bound to Violence'] is typical of novels of this second stage in that it is not written by someone who is comfortable with and accepted by the new elite, the national bourgeoisie. Far from being a celebration of the nation, then, the novels of the second, postcolonial, stage are novels of delegitimation: they reject not only the Western *imperium* but also the nationalist project of the postcolonial national bourgeoisie. (Appaiah 1991: 353)

As many writers have pointed out, the 'end' of anticolonial developmentalist nationalism also coincides with the rise of post-structuralism. Ahmad, for instance, writes that

. . . the national-bourgeois state partly basked in the reflected glory of the wars of national liberation, hence in the greater valorization of nationalism as such. . . . Now, as the stagnation of that type of post-colonial state has become more obvious in more recent years, and as the perception of that stagnation coincided chronologically with the ascendency of post-structuralism in literary theory, cultural nationalism itself is currently in the process of being discarded as illusion, myth, totalizing narrative. (Ahmad 1992*b*: 41)

Post-colonial theory and internationalism

It is possible to list a three-way split in the directions that post-colonial theory has broadly taken since the early 1980s—all three differently informed by post-structuralism and the work of Edward Said, especially *Orientalism* (1978). The first, we might broadly characterize as an investigation into nationalism itself: the best-known work being, in the West, Benedict Anderson's remarkable book *Imagined Communities* (see also Gellner 1983) and, outside the West, the influential writings of the Subaltern Studies Collective (see Guha 1982–9), and those of Partha Chatterjee (1986, 1994) in particular. A second track sought mainly to shift erstwhile 'Third World' nationalism into a theory of the 'Third World' itself: effectively transforming the more subtle divides along the fault lines of modernism–realism, as these impacted upon the construction of citizenship, into more straightforwardly 'First-World'–'Third World' opposites. While this was introduced into film theory by Teshome Gabriel's *Third Cinema in the Third World* (1982), with its prescriptive listing of how 'First World' films differed from those of the 'Third World', later developments have taken place almost entirely outside the ambit of film, and would be, in some respects, the dominant trend in US academia today. The third track, in which cinema did (and still does) feature, albeit on the margins, was a more explicit effort to deploy post-colonial theory to address the

condition of immigrant minorities in the West, and it is mainly in this area that cultural studies has made its most significant impact on post-colonial theory.

Two seminal essays by Fredric Jameson—'On Magic Realism in Film' and the more controversial 'Third World Literature in the Era of Multinational Capital' (1986*a, b*)—attempt to link, on the one side, the Brecht-Lukács debate concerning realism with, on the other, a new literary categorization of the 'Third World' in post-colonial theory that might address all the three alternatives stated above. The trajectory that both essays assume is the one that began with nationalist 'Third World' efforts to translate the realism–modernism divide into their own terms, and ended with the redesignation of nationalism itself within post-colonial theory. On the way, they make indirect reference to Third Cinema theory, and more pertinently seem to designate the place where that theory came to reside in its post-colonial versions of the 1980s.

Both essays are premised on questions of narrative—on structures that seemingly resemble, but do not eventually play the part of, more familiar narrative conventions in the West (as in the resemblance, at times, between magic realism and the American nostalgia film). The first essay seeks, it seems to me, to address the poignant question of Kwame Anthony Appaiah's (1991) text 'Is the Post- in Postmodernism the Post- in Postcolonial?' Jameson chooses to compare a Polish film (Agnieszka Holland's *Fever*, 1981) with a Venezuelan production (Jacobo Penzo's *La casa de agua*, 1984) and a Colombian production (Francisco Norden's *Condores no entierran todos las días*, 1984) to argue that the very location of narrative—the 'shock of entry into narrative—departs from the 'consumed . . . visual commodity' of the nostalgia film in the way that the 'permutations of the gaze, which irritate and intensify it, do not . . . as in postmodernism and the nostalgia film, transform its objects into images in the stronger sense of that word'. Although both genres deal with history, the magic realist film is a 'history-with-holes', where a 'whole range of subtle or complicated forms of narrative attention, which classical film . . . laboriously acquired and adapted from earlier developments in the novel, are now junked and replaced . . . Narrative here has not been subverted or abandoned, as in the iconoclasm of the experimental film, but rather effectively neutralised, to the benefit of a seeing or a looking in the filmic present.' All of this is presented in contrast to the 'enfeebled'—both in terms of history and class—post-modernism of the industrialized West.

The second essay takes this argument further: narrative, in non-canonical 'Third World' literatures, is not only woven in more complex and subtle ways into history and political action than its seeming resemblance to Western conventions would reveal, but plays a different role altogether even in its position in civil society. The key (and intensely controversial, as we shall see) paragraph goes: 'All third world texts are necessarily, I want to argue, allegorical, and in a very specific way: they are to be read as what I will call *national allegories*, even when, or perhaps I should say, particularly when their forms develop out of predominantly Western machineries of representation, such as the novel.' Jameson goes on to argue that whereas 'the culture of the Western realist and modernist novel' involves 'a radical split between the private and the public', Third World texts—'even those which are seemingly private and invested with a properly libidinal dynamic'—'necessarily project a political dimension in the form of national allegory: *the story of the private individual destiny is always an allegory of the embattled situation of the public third world culture and society*'.

Jameson's avowed intention is to 'rethink our [i.e. the US academic] humanities curriculum' and to do so in a way that avoids simply embracing non-canonical texts by proving that these are 'as great as those of the canon itself', a self-defeating exercise which 'borrows the weapons of the adversary'.

There is, however, a second history that feeds into this intervention, contributing to Jameson's somewhat deliberately provocative tone. This history constitutes, in one spectacular moment of the 'end of nationalism',

> **Jameson goes on to argue that whereas 'the culture of the Western realist and modernist novel' involves 'a radical split between the private and the public', Third World texts—'even those which are seemingly private and invested with a properly libidinal dynamic'— 'necessarily project a political dimension in the form of national allegory'.**

a literal migration of Third Cinema into the 'West', notably into the United States, and thereby also into post-colonialism. In 1973 the Allende government fell in Chile and through the 1970s state repression in several Latin American countries increased massively. Jorge Sanjinés and Mario Arrieta, members of the Ukamau group, went into exile following the *coup d'état* in Bolivia in 1971; the Third World Cinémathèque in Montevideo was ransacked by the police in 1972, who confiscated all films, equipment, and records; while elsewhere organizations like the Argentine Anti-communist Alliance (AAA) were on the rise. The AAA killed Julio Troxler, an actor, while working on a Fernando Solanas production. In 1976, in an epochal statement, Leopoldo Torre Nilsson, when in Spain, vowed never to return to his native Argentina as long as his films were banned there.

To a great extent, this caused the very concept of the Third Cinema, along with its key protagonists, to go into exile (in the United States and in Europe) or turn to Cuba, its only major support in Latin America still to be intact. In 1976 the Emergency Committee to Defend Latin American Filmmakers, based in New York, was supported by Hollywood stars like Candice Bergen, Francis Ford Coppola, Jane Fonda, Jack Nicholson, and Martin Scorsese. A decade later, the Fundación del nuevo cine latinoamericano (New Latin American Film Foundation, FNCI) was founded in 1985, with Marquez as chairman and with major—if radically different from the past—ambitions, including owning movie theatres in every Latin American country and several cities in Europe, and even installing their own satellite. But it was soon forced to resort to a political–aesthetic survival strategy addressed mainly towards garnering support within the 'First World'. In 1986 the FNCI started the Escuela internacional de cine y TV (International School of Cinema and TV), with Fernando Birri as its first director. The school constituted one important statement of this intention with its barely concealed effort to export 'revolutionary film' to the capitalist world. Apart from Latin American connections (the Instituto Nacional de Cinematográfia (INC) Argentina, Embrafilme, the Colombian Ministry of Communication), the only 'exchange link' this school had was with Robert Redford's Sundance Film Institute. Birri, in his inaugural speech, provided a virtual recipe for the by-now vastly broadened concept of the Third Cinema when he debunked 'marginalism' versus 'professionalism' as a false option, promising to provide students with filmmaking that included possibilities 'that go from pure political cinema to pure experimental cinema, taking into account all the possible alternatives: clandestine, militant, denunciation, resistance, social, didactic, independent, vocational, underground, marginal, diverse, off and off-off cinema' (Birri 1986: 5).

During much of this time, the contribution of writers like Julianne Burton and Julia Lesage, as well as journals like *Jump Cut*, was perceived even by people as eminent as Tomás Gutiérrez Alea as providing a virtual lifeline to the Cuban cinema in familiarizing and popularizing their work with US audiences. This issue was for a while extensively debated, notably in an encounter between Burton and Teshome Gabriel in the pages of *Screen* (Gabriel 1983, 1986; Burton 1983, 1985). Fredric Jameson himself saw the three films he discusses in his 'magic realism' essay (1986*a*) at the Latin American Film Festival in Havana, 1984, and dedicates the essay to the Cuban Revolution. This essay, written at the same time as the Burton–Gabriel debate, suggests that the Western critic, in the current situation, could—indeed, had to be—'critic and interpreter' within certain new terms of globalization requiring new kinds of political responsibility to be addressed.

Aijaz Ahmad's (1987) attack on Jameson's (1986*b*) 'Third World Literature' essay constitutes a seminal launch of post-colonial theory into one of its current positions. Ahmad begins by questioning Jameson's very intention: in seeking a 'cognitive aesthetics of third world literature', he argues, Jameson suppresses the multiplicity of significant differences to create a simple, binary opposition between 'First' and 'Third World' literatures. Much of Ahmad's critique stems from his argument that the 'Third World' itself consists of several independent nation-states, with developed social formations and with their own well-established literary canons. He therefore recommends the abolition of the 'three worlds' concept, and its replacement by the 'radically different . . . proposition that we live not in three worlds but in one; that this world includes the experience of colonialism and imperialism on both sides of Jameson's global divide . . . that societies in formations of backward capitalism are as much constituted by the division of classes as are societies in advanced capitalist countries' (Ahmad 1992*a*: 103).

Post-colonial theory: political–deconstructionist

By the 1990s post-colonial theory had clearly carved for itself a distinct disciplinary 'area', as is evident in the appearance of several 'readers' and anthologies (see especially Williams and Christman 1994; Prakash 1995; Chambers and Curti 1996). Virtually all of these, in their choice of authors as well as their category distinctions, embody a new contest between efforts to find political modes of addressing 'Otherness', versus a more deconstructionist initiative featuring, mainly, the writings of Trinh T. Min-ha, Gayatri Chakravorty Spivak, and Homi K. Bhabha.

Homi K. Bhabha's influential work began in the 1980s as a deliberate confrontation with such themes of 'Third Worldist' resistance. At the Edinburgh Third Cinema conference he presented what he saw as a false and disabling opposition.

Between what is represented as the 'larceny' and distortion of European 'metatheorizing' and the radical, engaged, activist experience of Third World creativity, [he argued,] one can see the mirror image (albeit reversed in content and intention) of that ahistorical nineteenth century polarity of Orient and Occident which, in the name of progress, unleashed the exclusionary imperialist ideologies of self and other. This time round, the term 'critical theory', often untheorized and unargued, is definitely the 'other', an otherness that is insistently identified with the vagaries of the depoliticised Eurocentric critic. (Bhabha 1994: 19)

He argued, instead, for theory as negotiation: 'the event of theory becomes the negotiation of contradictory and antagonistic instances that open up hybrid sites and objectives of struggle' (Bhabha 1989/1994: 25). Bhabha's insistence on discovering, within colonial discourse, those spaces where 'hybridity' starts shifting away from strait-jacketed oppositions and into 'a heterogeneity that the existing dichotomies themselves make simultaneously possible and impossible' (Prakash 1992: 17) revitalized the very terrain on which theory could now operate, seemingly overcoming the shambles of 'multiple subjects of fragmented histories' that post-colonial theory had become in the late 1980s. As Gyan Prakash puts it, 'at these moments of indeterminacy, when the discourse can be seen to veer away from the implacable logic of oppositionality, the critic can intervene, and, using historical work as a license for a strategy of critical reading, re-negotiate the terms of discourse' (17).

Crucial to Bhabha's work has been his formulation of 'colonial mimicry', or the 'desire for a reformed, recognisable Other, as a subject of a difference that is almost the same, but not quite . . . the discourse of mimicry is constructed around an ambivalence; in order to be effective, mimicry must continually produce its own slippage, its excess, its difference' (Bhabha 1987). Such terms as 'slippage', 'excess', and the crucial one, 'difference', or the ones that circulate extensively in Trinh T. Min-ha's work—'hybridity, interstices, voids, intervals, in-betweenness' (cited in Chambers and Curti 1996)—opened a new space, veritably a flood, of theory for what still goes broadly under the title 'deconstructionism'.

Perhaps the most significant contribution contextualizing both the political as well as discursive constitution of the 'subject' of theory—including crucially the colonial subject—is Gayatri Spivak's essay 'Can the Subaltern Speak?' (1988). Working with a triangular grid of 'power, interest, desire', Spivak distinguishes between two concepts of representation: representation, in the sense in which the 'people', an absent collective consciousness often dispersed and dislocated as 'subjects', find a category of representatives (who sometimes betray them), versus re-presentation: the space for rhetoric, realism, the 'scene of writing'; radical practice should attend to this 'double session of representations rather than reintroduce the individual subject through totalizing concepts of power and desire'.

It is on this terrain, of the tragic, eternally silenced subaltern figure whose own voice is always lost in the tumult of an invoked subject of oppression, that Spivak seems to bring together two until then incompatible intellectual positions: the Derridean and the explicitly stated anti-élitist historiography of the Subaltern Studies group. Both effectively work on their resistance to the constitution of the undifferentiated, textualized subject.

Gyan Prakash's contribution to this debate has been to suggest, controversially, a need to move beyond 'foundational histories'.

The subaltern is a figure produced by historical discourses of domination, but it nevertheless provides a mode of reading history different from those inscribed in elite account . . . these historians seek to uncover the subaltern's myths, cults, ideologies and revolts that colonial and nationalist elites sought to appropriate and conventional historiography has laid to waste by their deadly weapon of cause and effect. (Prakash: 1992: 9)

The importance of the link between Derridean–Spivakian deconstructionism and Subaltern historiography is, however, less related to its linguistic designation of the subaltern voice (or its absence) than it is to a consequent validation of the status of a new kind of history-writing, which Prakash calls 'Post-Foundational history'. Work by the Subaltern Studies historians 'disrupts . . . the nationalist narrative that considers all colonial revolts as events in the becoming of the . . . nation and contests the older Marxist accounts which see these episodes as preludes to the emergence of full-fledged class-consciousness' (Prakash 1990: 399–400).

The most contentious of Prakash's statements was an apparent dismissal of capitalism itself on the grounds that capitalist narratives, being by definition homogenizing and therefore foundational, cannot therefore thematize post-colonial history, since it is precisely histories emphasizing heterogeneity—rather than mere documentation of how capitalism becomes dominant—that will allow us to contest capitalist homogenization. Two major attacks followed: one by Rosalind O'Hanlon and David Washbrook (1992), who argued that, for Prakash, capitalism becomes a 'disposable fiction', and a second by Dirlik (1994), who argued, effectively, that this entire trend of argumentation (represented by Spivak, Bhabha, Prakash et al.) constitutes a deliberate 'obfuscation of its own relationship to what is but a condition of its emergence, that is, to a global capitalism that, however fragmented in appearance, serves as the structuring principle of global relations' (331).

Post-colonial theory and diaspora: negritude to immigritude

Politically, there is a straightforward problem with the very approach of deconstructionism: a problem that Stuart Hall sums up as the 'fantasy of a powerless utopia of difference. It is only too tempting to fall into the trap of assuming that, because essentialism has been deconstructed theoretically, therefore it has been displaced politically' (1996: 249). There is however a different sense in which one can, perhaps more fruitfully, contextualize Spivak's and Bhabha's work: as an interrogation of the colonial encounter in the context of, and addressing the condition of, immigrant minorities in the West. In his effort to shift the emphasis of identity politics away from its burden upon the slave, the colonized, the immigrant, to the colonial authority itself, Bhabha (and generally deconstructionist politics) intervenes, along with major writers mainly from Africa, the Caribbean, and the black community in Britain and the United States, in the shift away from colonial ethnography and into a new terrain of ethnic cultural politics.

> There is however a different sense in which one can, perhaps more fruitfully, contextualize Spivak's and Bhabha's work: as an interrogation of the colonial encounter in the context of, and addressing the condition of, immigrant minorities in the West.

The inversion of ethnography, a colonial discipline to tackle the problems of studying alien cultures, into an assertive politics premised on identity is a key part of this history. An early inversion of colonial identity was the concept of 'negritude', originating in the work of Aimé Césaire and Leopold Sedar Senghor. In its original form, negritude claimed black culture as 'emotional rather than rational' with 'a distinctive African view . . . separated from the supposedly universal values of European taste and style' (Ashcroft et al. 1989: 21–2). Although extensively critiqued by African writers— most notably by Wole Soyinka, who declared 'a tiger does not proclaim its tigritude'—negritude as a concept was transformed by and survived in various subsequent efforts, through this century, to posit a black aesthetics. Senghor's work traces an influence to the Harlem Renaissance, to Langston Hughes and Richard Wright, and, subsequently to Black Power movements. In the 1980s it was once again addressed, via black musical structures as these related to literary style, in Henry Louis Gates's influential compilation *Black Literature and Literary Theory* (1984) while Gates's own book *The Signifying Monkey* (1988) attempted 'to identify a theory of criticism that is inscribed within the Black vernacular tradition'.

The double problem—how to assert ethnicity and at the same time combat the essentializing imperialist ethnography on which that identity has, all too often, been based—bedevils a great deal of black theory on the subject. There has also been a certain discounting of 'nativism', of whatever kind, in the face of what Vivek Dhareshwar has called 'immigritude'—the 'whole narrative of displacement which has become a normative experience in metropolitan politics' (1989: 143). If 1970s–1980s Latin America saw in its right-wing takeovers one spectacular end of anti-colonial nationalism, clearly it was on a scale nowhere near the experience of Black Africa's own experience, of having to comprehend an earlier 'global' economy of the slave-trade. The descendants of those enslaved, and later immigrants, some of whom emigrated through choice, experienced the end of nationalism within the heartlands of globalized capital, even as they were forced to acknowledge the impossibility of return.

Some of the richest interventions into political theory, and indeed the cutting edge of post-colonial theory itself, have taken place at this particular frontier. Frantz Fanon's work in positing black identity as first and foremost a political one clearly shifted negritude into a different terrain (see notably Fanon 1967). E. K. Braithwaite's emphasis on a pan-African nationalism, alongside his interests in forming a new cultural thrust for creolization (Braithwaite 1984), informed a new effort to understand the phenomenon of racism, especially following the realization that 'by defining "race" and ethnicity as cultural absolutes, blacks themselves and parts of the anti-racist movement risk endorsing the explanatory frameworks and political definitions of the new right' (Gilroy 1987: 13). Gilroy points to the 'social movements which have sprung up in different parts of the world as evidence of African dispersal, imperialism and colonialism' as providing a 'global perspective from the memories of slavery and indenture which are the property of the African diaspora' (156–7).

Perhaps the most useful way of reading the African American and black British theory mentioned would be in its address of nationalism itself, but from the outside, and in the process its transformation of the very terrain on which 'the national' operates as a phenomenon. If, as Gilroy has argued, an effort to understand racism requires a new understanding of class, then, by extension, an effort to understand the conditions of immigrant ethnic, minorities equally requires a new understanding of nation.

At any rate a new area was opened up for theory itself within this broad field when in 1964 the Centre for Cultural Studies was started in Birmingham. Interestingly, black cultural theory and politics were not on the centre's agenda in much of its initial work. The thrust was mainly around culture—the space it occupied on the terrain of a public arena. Ethnography was, however, a key area, anticipating much of what came later to be known as 'ethnic studies', and underpinned the centre's early interest in working-class subcultures. For Cohen (1972) all subcultures correspond to a 'parent' culture, and attempt to work out, express, and resolve, 'albeit magically, the contradictions which remain hidden or unresolved in the parent culture' or which are 'inserted' into the subculture by the parent culture. Placed on the realm of the symbolic, the 'parent culture' could discursively extend into both an understanding of the state—in Britain, crucially the Thatcherite state—as well as the numerous communitarian institutions that constitute, as well as oppose, 'state apparatuses'.

Gilroy's *There Ain't No Black in the Union Jack* (1987) comes out of this tradition, but remains one of the first works to remap the 'parent' symbolic—here the symbolic of racial identity—onto questions of class and nation (in the sense in which British 'patriotic' nationalism crucially depends on mobilizing racial factors), and eventually onto what he calls an 'affirmative' culture of syncretism. This mass upsurge had its component in a 'dimension of diaspora', a 'back to Africa' move, which saw its culmination in the Rastafari, a pan-African, Ethiopianist movement (see Gilroy 1987: 187–92), and inaugurated numerous cultural forms, in dress, music, and the very formation of what Gilroy, quoting Said, calls an 'interpretative community'.

Those outside the debates encapsulated above (which includes myself) are nevertheless aware of some of the impact made by this entire history onto the cinema: notably, in the first phase, the revaluation of first-generation black filmmakers from Africa (Sembene and Souleymane Cissé), and, later, black cinema's efforts to enter both the mass-cultural mainstream (notably Spike Lee) as well as create an independent sector which nevertheless relates to the cultural repositionings that the later theoretical history took (e.g. Charles Burnett in the United States, the Black Audio, Sankofa, and Ceddo collectives in the United Kingdom).

Conclusion

Although Gilroy's later book *The Black Atlantic* (1993) has attempted to address the shift in the space occu-pied by identity politics—the shift towards imaginary constructs, discourse theory, and the broad terrain of constructing Subjects-as-the-Other of deconstructionism—it is clear that several of the areas I have tried to map in this chapter, quite simply, do not talk to each other. A great deal more work still needs to be done before we can clearly identify 'post-colonial theory' and before—in the words of Spivak—'power, desire and interest' can come together to offer large patterns of what has happened and what is likely to happen.

BIBLIOGRAPHY

Ahmad, Aijaz (1987/1992a), 'Jameson's Rhetoric of Otherness and the "National Allegory"', in *In Theory: Classes, Nations, Literatures* (London: Verso).

—— (1992b), 'Literature among the Signs of our Time', in *In Theory: Classes, Nations, Literatures* (London: Verso).

—— (1996), 'Postcoloniality: What's in a Name?', in Roman de la Campa et al. (eds.), *Late Imperial Culture* (London: Verso).

Anderson, Benedict (1983), *Imagined Communities: Reflections on the Origin and Spread of Nationalism* (London: Verso).

Appaiah, Kwame Anthony (1991/1996), 'Is the Post- in Postmodernism the Post- in Postcolonial?', *Critical Inquiry*, 17 (Winter); repr. in Padmini Monga (ed.), *Contemporary Postcolonial Theory* (London: Arnold).

—— (1992), *In my Father's House: Africa in the Philosophy of Culture* (New York: Oxford University Press).

Armes, Roy (1987), *Third World Film Making and the West* (Berkeley: University of California Press).

Ashcroft, Bill, Gareth Griffiths, and **Helen Tiffin** (1989), *The Empire Writes Back: Theory and Practice in Post-Colonial Literatures* (London: Routledge).

Benjamin, Walter (1973/1979), 'Theses on the Philosophy of History', in *Illuminations*, ed. Hannah Arendt (London: Fontana/Collins).

Bhabha, Homi K. (1987), 'Of Mimicry and Man', in *October* (Boston, Mass.: MIT Press).

—— (1989/1994), 'The Commitment to Theory', in Pines and Willemen (1989); Babha (1994).

—— (1994), *The Location of Culture* (London: Routledge).

Birri, Fernando (1986), 'Acta de Naciniento de la Esquela Internacionale de Cine y TV'.

Braithwaite, E. K. (1984), *History of the Voice: The Development of Nation Language in Anglophone Caribbean Poetry* (London: New Beacon Press).

Buchloh, Benjamin H. D. (1981), 'Figures of Authority, Ciphers of Regression: Notes on the Return of Representation in European Painting', *October*, 16 (Spring), 39–68.

Bürger, Peter (1972/1994), *Theory of the Avant-Garde*, trans. Michael Shaw (Minneapolis: University of Minnesota Press).

Burton, Julianne (1983), 'The Politics of Aesthetic Distance: Sao Bernando', *Screen*, 24/2: 30–53.

—— (1985), 'Marginal Cinemas and Mainstream Critical Theory', *Screen*, 26/3–4: 2–21.

Chambers, Iain, and **Lidia Curti** (eds.) (1996), *The Post-Colonial Question: Common Skies, Divided Horizons* (London: Routledge).

Chanan, Michael (ed.) (1983), *Twenty-Five Years of the New Latin American Cinema* (London: British Film Institute and Channel 4).

Chatterjee, Partha (1986), *Nationalist Thought and the Colonial World: A Derivative Discourse* (New Delhi: Oxford University Press).

—— (1994), *The Nation and its Fragments: Colonial and Postcolonial Histories* (New Delhi: Oxford University Press).

Cohen, Phil (1972/1980), 'Subcultural Coflict and Working-Class Community', in Stuart Hall *et al.* (eds.), *Culture, Media, Language* (London: Routledge).

de la Campa, Roman, E. Ann Kaplan, *et al.* (eds.) (1996), *Late Imperial Culture* (London: Verso).

Deocampo, Nick (1985), *Short Film: Emergence of a New Philippine Cinema* (Communication Foundation for Asia).

Dhareshwar, Vivek (1989), 'Towards a Narrative Epistemology of the Postcolonial Predicament', in James Clifford and Vivek Dhareshwar (eds.), *Travelling Theories, Travelling Theorists*, Inscriptions.

—— (1995), 'Postcolonial in the Postmodern; or, The Political after Modernity', *Economic and Political Weekly*, 30/30, 29 July, 104–11.

Diawara, Manthia (1992), *African CInema: Politics and Culture* (Bloomington: Indiana University Press).

Dirlik, Arif (1994), 'The Postcolonial Aura: Third World Criticism in the Age of Global Capitalism', *Critical Inquiry*, 20 (Winter), 328–56.

Fanon, Frantz (1967), *Toward the African Revolution* (Harmondsworth: Pelican Books).

Film Enquiry Committee (1951), (Chairman, S. K. Patil), *Report of the Film Enquiry Committee* (New Delhi: Government of India Press).

Frankenberg, Ruth, and **Lata Mani** (1993), 'Crosscurrents, Crosstalk: Race, "Postcoloniality" and the Politics of Location', *Cultural Studies*, 7/2: 292–310.

Fusco, Coco (ed.) (1987), *Reviewing Histories: Selections from New Latin American Cinema* (Buffalo, NY: Hallwallis Contemporary Arts Center).

Gabriel, Teshome H. (1982), *Third Cinema in the Third World: The Aesthetics of Liberation* (Ann Arbor, Mich.: UMI Research Press).

—— (1983), 'Teaching Third World Cinema', *Screen*, 24/2:

—— (1986), 'Colonialism and "law and Order" Criticism', *Screen*, 27/3–4: 140–7.

Gates, Henry Louis (ed.) (1984), *Black Literature and Literary Theory* (London: Methuen).

—— (1988), *The Signifying Monkey: A Theory of African-American Literary Criticism* (New York: Oxford University Press).

Gellner, Ernest (1983), *Nations and Nationalism* (Oxford: Blackwell).

Gerima, Haile (1989), 'Triangular Cinema, Breaking Toys and Dinknesh vs. Lucy', in Pines and Willemen.

Gilroy, Paul, (1987), 'There Ain't No Black in the Union Jack': The Cultural Politics of Race and Nation (Chicago: University of Chicago Press).

—— (1993), *The Black Atlantic: Modernity and Double Consciousness* (London: Verso).

'Godard on Solanas/Solanas on Godard: An Interview', in Fusco (1987).

Guha, Ranajit (ed.) (1982–9), *Subaltern Studies*, i–vii (New Delhi: Oxford University Press).

*****Hall, Stuart** (1996), 'When was "the Post-Colonial"? Thinking at the Limit', in Chambers and Curti (1996).

Harasym, Sarah (ed.) (1990), *Gayatri Chakravorty-Spivak: The Post-Colonial Critic: Interviews, Strategies, Dialogues* (New York: Routledge).

Hulme, Peter (1995), 'Including America', *Ariel*, 25/1.

Huyssen, Andreas (1986), *After the Great Divide: Modernism, Mass Culture, Postmodernism* (Bloomington: Indiana University Press).

Jameson, Fredric (1977/1980), Reflections in Conclusion', in Theodor Adorno *et al.*, *Aesthetics and Politics*, London (trans. Ronald Taylor, Verso 1977).

—— (1986a/1992), 'On Magic Realism in Film', *Critical Inquiry*, 12/2 (Winter); repr. in *Signatures of the Visible* (New York: Routledge).

—— (1986b), 'Third World Literature in the Age of Multinational Capital', *Social Text*, 15 (Fall), 65–88.

—— (ed.) (1993), 'Postmodernism: Center and Periphery', *South Atlantic Quarterly*, 92/3 (Summer), 417–22.

Krauss, Rosalind (1986), *The Originality of the Avant-Garde and Other Modernist Myths* (Cambridge, Mass.: MIT Press).

McClintock, Anne (1992), 'The Angel of Progress: Pitfalls of the Term Post-Colonial', *Social Text*, 31–2: 84–98.

Majid, Anouar (1995–6), 'Can the Postcolonial Critic Speak? Orientalism in the Rushdie Affair', *Cultural Critique*, (Winter), 5–42.

Mongia, Padmini (ed.) (1996), *Contemporary Postcolonial Theory* (London: Arnold).

Mulvey, Laura (1991/1996), 'The Carapace that Failed: Ousmane Sembene's *Xala*', *Fetishism and Curiosity* (London: British Film Institute).

Ngũgĩ wa Thiong'o (1986), *Decolonizing the Mind: The*

Politics of Language in African Literature (London: James Currey).

O'Hanlon, Rosalind, and David Washbrook (1992), 'After Orientalism: Culture, Criticism and Politics in the Third World', *Comparative Studies in Society and History*, 34/1 (Jan.).

Pandey, Gyanendra (1991), 'In Defence of the Fragment: Writing about Hindu–Muslim Riots in India Today', *Economic and Political Weekly*, 26/11–12, Annual Number, 559–72.

*Pines, Jim, and Paul Willemen (eds.) (1989), *Questions of Third Cinema* (London: British Film Institute).

Prakash, Gyan (1990), 'Writing Post-Orientalist Histories of the Third World: Perspectives from Indian Historiography', *Comparative Studies in Society and History*, 32/2 (Apr.), 383–408.

—— (1992), 'Postcolonial Criticism and Indian Historiography', *Social Text* 31–2: 8–19.

—— (ed.) (1995), *Imperial Histories and Postcolonial Displacements* (Princeton: Princeton University Press).

Prasad, Madhava (1992), 'On the Question of a Theory of (Third World) Literature', *Social Text*, 31–2: 57–93.

Rajadhyaksha, Ashish, and Paul Willemen (eds.) (1994–5), *Encyclopaedia of Indian Cinema* (London: British Film Institute and Oxford University Press).

Said, Edward (1978), *Orientalism* (London: Routledge & Kegan Paul).

Shahani, Kumar (1986), 'Dossier: Kumar Shahani', *Framework*, 30–1. 67–111.

Shohat, Ella (1992), 'Notes on the Post-Colonial', *Social Text*, 31–2: 99–113.

*Solanas, Fernando, and Octavio Getino (1969), 'Towards a Third Cinema', in Fusco (1987).

Soyinka, Wole (1975), 'Neo-Tarzanism: The Poetics of Pseudo-Tradition', *Transitions*, 48.

Spivak, Gayatri Chakravorty (1987), *In Other Worlds: Essays in Cultural Politics* (New York: Methuen).

—— (1988), 'Can the Subaltern Speak?', in Cary Nelson and Lawrence Grossberg (eds.), *Marxism and the Interpretation of Culture* (Urbana: University of Illinois Press).

Wallis, Brian, and Marcia Tucker (eds.) (1984), *Art after Modernism: Rethinking Representation* (New York: New Museum of Contemporary Art).

Willemen, Paul (1989), 'The Third Cinema Question: Notes and Reflections', in Pines and Willemen (1989).

*—— (ed.) (1993), *The Films of Amos Gitai* (London: British Film Institute).

*Williams, Patrick, and Laura Christman (eds.) (1994), *Colonial Discourse and Post-Colonial Theory* (New York: Columbia University Press).

Wollen, Peter (1972/1982), 'Godard and Counter-Cinema: Vent d'est', in Wollen (1982).

—— (1975/1982) 'The Two Avant-Gardes', in Wollen (1982).

—— (1982), *Readings and Writings. Semiotic Counter-Strategies* (London: Verso).

4

The documentary

John Izod and Richard Kilborn

Looking back on the achievements of a century of moving images, critics often remark on two contrary tendencies. On the one hand, there is the tradition of narrative, or fictional, film in which the primary object is to divert or entertain, and, on the other, there is that of documentary whose main aim, it has been said, is to instruct or inform (Kracauer 1960). Historically this division into fictional and factual modes of filmmaking is seen to be classically exemplified in the work of the early French film pioneers Georges Méliès and the Lumière brothers. While the work of Méliès regularly transported viewers into mythic and fantastical realms (Christie 1994), the main appeal of the actuality of the Lumière brothers lay in the camera's ability to reproduce scenes from everyday life that were instantly recognizable by those who flocked to see them. In the subsequent history of cinema, and later in television, this factual–fictional typology has been maintained, even though it is generally recognized that it is over-simplistic, disguising the degree to which these opposing tendencies coexist in practice.

Defining 'documentary'

The term 'documentary' itself seems to have been coined in 1926 by John Grierson, the man usually considered to be the founding father of British documentary. Grierson not only outlined what he saw as the defining features of documentary, but also reflected on the purposes to which documentary could be put. For him, whilst every documentary is bound to present evidence or information about the socio-historical world, it must be more than a quasi-scientific reconstruction of reality. The documentarist must deploy a whole range of creative skills to fashion the 'fragments of reality' into an artefact that has a specific social impact: that is educationally instructive or, in some measure, culturally enlightening. This account must be, in Grierson's phrase, a 'creative treatment of actuality', being aesthetically satisfying while also having a clearly defined social purpose (Hardy 1979: 35–46).

> **The term 'documentary' itself seems to have been coined in 1926 by John Grierson, the man usually considered to be the founding father of British documentary.**

Many critics have regarded Grierson's definition as a useful starting-point for debating the form and function of documentary, but his concept of 'creative treatment' is by no means unproblematic. It attempts to bring together two elements that are not easily reconciled: a commitment to construct an account based on observable reality and, in contrast, the recognition that to produce the desired impact on an audience always requires a good deal of artifice (Nichols 1991). Arising out of this dilemma, there has always been a lively debate amongst documentarists and critics over the legitimacy of certain techniques in the shaping of the documentary account. What indeed is the status of works bearing the documentary label, when so many are structured in much the same way as the fictional works to which they are said to be diametrically opposed? Even some of the short actuality films of the Lumière brothers are marked by conventional storytelling procedures. Furthermore, doesn't the fact that documentaries are made up of 'fragments of reality' which are carefully assembled and edited according to established narrative principles make them an essentially fictional construct? Doesn't the declared or undeclared presence of the documentarist during the recording process mean documentaries are authored pieces much like any other feature film? And do the commercial imperatives, which are so influential in moving-image production, mean that documentaries will always be assessed as much for their entertainment value as for their educational or consciousness-raising potential? Especially in the last few decades, with television's increasing influence on the form that documentary has taken, the debate has remained alive, and ensured that it is impossible to come up with a definition of the genre more watertight than Grierson's.

Recent theoretical work, particularly by Edward Branigan (1992), draws a clear distinction between narrative, as a means used by journalists as well as feature film writers for structuring information, and fiction, as a way of describing the truth-claims of a text. For instance, while it is widely agreed that narrative underlies much documentary, there has been heated controversy over the legitimacy of certain types of dramatic re-enactment (Kilborn 1994b). In the early days of cinema, documentarists were often forced to use dramatic reconstruction. For example, in *Night Mail* (Harry Watt and Basil Wright, GB, 1936) the sequences in which postal workers sort the mail as the train runs through the night were shot on a studio set because the equipment then available was too cumbersome to use on location. Today's generation of filmmakers, with the help of lightweight, go-anywhere cameras, have few such technical problems and dramatic reconstructions tend to be used for different reasons: to re-enact events where camera access has been denied (as is usually the case in the British courts of justice) or to enhance the film's commercial appeal by including a strong dramatic element. Predictably enough, the disagreements have tended to centre on the concern that this blurring of fact and fiction might mislead audiences. Can they distinguish sufficiently well those parts of a work which are based on surmise from those which are more solidly substantiated? Could audiences be duped into taking something to be factual which in fact has its origins in the creative imagination of the drama-documentarist? There is, however, one principal difference between the reconstruction done out of technical necessity and today's drama-documentary that critics often seem to forget: reconstructions in drama-documentaries such as *Who Bombed Birmingham?* (Granada for ITV, 1990) are explicitly signalled as such.

A further issue which has featured prominently in the critical discourse surrounding documentaries centres on questions of realism. Right from the outset documentary's special claim on an audience's attention has been its capacity to provide a seemingly objective window on the world. Much has been made, for instance, of the so-called 'indexical bond' which allows viewers to make a clear connection between on-screen representations and events in the historical world. Whilst there has been widespread acceptance of documentary's referential or indexical qualities, there has

Classic British documentary—*Night Mail* (1936)

been far less agreement about the significance of this defining feature: documentaries may well give us privileged access to empirically observable reality, but this is far from suggesting that they can reveal important truths about that reality (Nichols 1991). Brecht was always keen to remind us, that to capture what is going on beneath the surface of empirically observable reality is far more challenging than accurately to record the surface itself (Brecht 1938/1980). By the same token, documentarists have always had to be careful not to make too grand a claim about how representative of the wider reality is a specific detail they have captured on film.

Critics of documentary have always been aware that all attempts to represent reality carry with them important ideological implications. The photographic realism of the documentary, for instance, can easily conceal the extent to which it often actively constructs a particular view of the world. This view is determined, among other things, by the filmmaker's own preconceptions, by the perspective from which the events are witnessed, and by the structuring principles according to which the material is edited. In other words, documentaries can never be wholly objective; they will always involve a greater or lesser degree of intervention on the part of the documentarist. This is always painfully obvious when one looks at documentaries

from eras gone by. For example, the narration of *Industrial Britain* (GB, 1931) tells us that Robert Flaherty and John Grierson meant to celebrate the craftsmanship of the shop-floor worker. To our ears, however, the fruity accent of the narrator and the heavily value-laden language of the script suggest the patronizing curiosity of the educated middle classes facing an unfamiliar working-class culture.

The very act of documenting an event implies intervention, of course, and there has always been argument about the extent to which the (mere) presence of

> **The photographic realism of the documentary, for instance, can easily conceal the extent to which it often actively constructs a particular view of the world. This view is determined, among other things, by the filmmaker's own preconceptions, by the perspective from which the events are witnessed, and by the structuring principles according to which the material is edited.**

a documentary camera team will influence the course of events. Filming events in the public arena might influence them only minimally, but, where the documentarist is operating in a more confined domestic or institutional setting, the impact of the camera's presence can be quite considerable.

Modes of documentary

While advances in camera and microphone design have made it possible for the documentarist to be less obtrusive than in the past, the intervention issue has remained a matter of intense debate. It might even be said that distinct modes of filmmaking have developed out of the manner in which documentarists indicate their role in the filmmaking process: whether they appear on camera in the presence of their documentary subjects; whether they tell their audience how the documentary material has been gathered; or even whether they go as far as to reflect on other ways in which the project might have been handled.

Discussion of the various modes in which filmmakers might work has been a feature of debates about documentary since the mid-1980s (see Nichols 1991), and for the purposes of critical analysis the idea of modes is attractive as a means of dividing the subject. If we think of documentary as a vast genre as substantial as fiction or journalism, then it is tempting to see the modes as representing the parts of that genre. However, unlike subgenres, they differ from one from another primarily in the manner in which they represent the historical world, and only after that in the nature of their subject-matter. At their most distinctive, the modes are themselves so different in appearance that they make it possible to conceive of a neat formula whereby the many functions that documentary can fulfill are paralleled by a variety of formats in which they can be constructed.

Unfortunately, the matter is not quite so simple. On the one hand, discussion of the modes of filmmaking practice has brought a measure of clarity of thought concerning the various ways in which documentary can construct its discourses and address its audiences; it has thus also drawn attention to the discursive richness of the genre. On the other hand, the debate has given rise to expectations of critical precision where, because of the very nature of the modes, precision is not always to be found. Symptomatic of this is the problem theorists have had in distinguishing one

mode from another. For the fact is that they are no more tidily delineated than the genre in its entirety. Just as we have had to learn to recognize that documentary has permeable boundaries, with fiction on one side and journalism on another, so we have to understand that the modes are equally ill-defined. What is more, some of them (the reflexive one, described below, is an obvious case in point) readily absorb some of the main characteristics of other modes. Therefore, when observers of documentary form refer to its modes, it is probably best to understand them as having in mind the dominant formal characteristics that shape a film.

The evolution into mainstream practice of each of the modes tends to be associated with technological advance, which is usually said to lie in the improvement and miniaturization of sound- and picture-recording equipment. However, most theorists would not regard technology as the sole determining factor; institutional constraints and opportunities are also seen as highly significant in the development of new modes, as becomes clear when we look at the way they are described.

The *expository mode* addresses its audience directly, usually through a narrator who interprets what we see, in effect telling us what we should think of the visual evidence before our eyes. Because the limited sound-recording technology of the 1930s made it easier to dub in an unseen speaker, narration of this type became known as the 'voice-of-God' mode, which describes so well the implicit claim of narrators in this mode to speak with authority. I have already referred to the narration of the film *Industrial Britain*, and it was rare for a documentary of the 1930s and 1940s to be made in any other mode (see Barnouw 1974; Ellis 1989). Television production technology overcame these restrictions on sound long ago, and it is now almost as easy to record the narrator on- as off-screen, but the expository mode is still in use (for example, in almost all natural history and scientific documentaries), but its innate tendency to authoritarianism is softened by using people with gentle voices and by offsetting interviews against the commentary, which seems to give the subjects of the film their own voice.

The *observational* mode, or *direct cinema*, is often referred to as a product of the new technology of the late 1950s, and it is true that without lightweight equipment, large magazines, and audiotape machines with the facility for synchronous sound recording, it would not have been possible to get extended footage of people going about the routine business of their lives. This is the single most obvious characteristic of observational films (Barnouw 1974). However, the more sensitive historians of cinema have noted that even these films, with their claim simply to observe reality as it unfolds, are both the vehicles of a distinctive ideology and the product of institutional pressures and opportunities. Allen and Gomery (1985) show how the philosophical implications of direct cinema fitted the dominant liberal values of the Kennedy era. Indeed, Kennedy himself was ready to allow observational cameras to accompany him on more than one occasion (for example, on the campaign trail in the film *Primary* (D. A. Pennebaker and Richard Leacock, USA, 1960). Where these films provided insights into chronic social problems, it was assumed they would be politically effective: the state would be able to relieve social malaise just so long as it had been recognized. Allen and Gomery also demonstrate how, in its early days at the start of the 1960s, it was hoped that the new format would boost the audience for the US television network ABC, which at the time was trailing its competitors. When it failed to do this, the direct film was dropped from the schedules.

Also dependent on the new equipment of the late 1950s was the *interactive mode*. Partly because it can also use long takes recorded in the field, it is sometimes confused with the direct mode. However, at its most distinct, the mode is characterized by the film crew interacting with the people in front of the lens (see Nichols 1991). In general this will occur via an on-camera interview, but sometimes it can be achieved in the editing process, for instance by constructing the facsimile of a dialogue from fragments of recorded statements by people who have not actually met. In this way the main procedures of the interactive mode resemble those of the journalistic interview, which is why interactive documentary has become routine television practice (Lockerbie 1991). Since it gets round one of the disadvantages of the direct documentary—that the latter can only eavesdrop on what is said in front of the camera—the interactive mode suits that current of television discourse that claims to get the truth from the horse's mouth (as it were). It is a form that familiarity has rendered seemingly natural to viewers; but it too is redolent with cultural associations, including the very idea that 'truth' can be uncovered in this way.

The *reflexive mode* is found where the manner in which the historical world is represented itself becomes the topic of cinematic representation. It makes not only the film's subjects, but also its own formal qualities, the object of questioning and doubt. Such films frequently discourage spectators from accepting that a single point of view is an adequate representation of the whole truth on any topic (see Nichols 1991; Renov 1993). The reflexive mode has aroused greater interest among observers of documentary than among most members of the public. This is probably because reflexive films accommodate theoretical goals of the kind that Brecht or Godard might have advocated for documentary. To a whole generation of critics and theorists weaned in the 1970s on *Screen* and the cultural debates of the left, the reflexive documentary was a concept whose time had come even before it had hit the screen. And, indeed, in its re-visioning of the world, the reflexive documentary often does have a political goal, undermining the certainties of a political leader or a business executive by refusing the visible or epistemological bases upon which certainty is founded. Nick Broomfield's pursuit of Margaret Thatcher, *Tracking down Maggie* (Channel 4, GB, 1994), and Michael Moore's hunt for the Chief Executive of General Motors, *Roger and Me* (USA, 1989), are good examples.

The political dimension of the reflexive project lies partly in the way such films imply that people's memory, perception, and interpretation of events are distorted by the stereotypes (largely screen-based) that circulate in our culture. More emphatically, the deconstructive methods these films deploy undermine realism, which term, as we have seen, is usually taken by documentarists to refer to an unproblematic access to the world through traditional mimetic representation. In reflexive films such as *The Thin Blue Line* (Errol Morris, USA, 1987), the viewer begins to question whether the images and sounds of the text could possibly represent the world adequately, since they are plainly a construction of the filmmakers.

> **In reflexive films such as *The Thin Blue Line* (Errol Morris, USA, 1987), the viewer begins to question whether the images and sounds of the text could possibly represent the world adequately, since they are plainly a construction of the filmmakers.**

The Thin Blue Line (1987)—deconstructive methods used to undermine realism

Whereas the norm in other forms of documentary is to concentrate attention on the filmmaker's encounter with the world in the reflexive mode the encounter between viewer and filmmaker is emphasized. The viewer comes to expect the unexpected, designed not so much to shock or surprise as to raise questions about the film's own status and that of documentary in general (Nichols 1991; Renov 1993). As Lockerbie argues, a text is likely to switch constantly between different forms of representation in a typically Brechtian fashion: 'Snatches of song or dance, clips from other films, sequences of animation, and other film forms, are mixed in with documentary material' (1991: 228).

Categorizing such a large corpus of work according to particular documentary modes, as outlined above, has proved to be a useful starting-point for discussing *some* of documentary's characteristic forms of address.

Nevertheless, it is important to remember that this taxonomy is by no means exhaustive. Throughout the history of documentary, for instance, there has been a clearly discernible strand of work to which one might attach the label *poetic* (Nichols 1991; Loizos 1993). Here the filmmaker will, typically, gather together recorded sights and sounds of the natural or social world and mould them in such a way as to evoke a particular mood or atmosphere. Such documentaries will more often than not eschew the guiding commentary or narration in favour of musical or diegetic sound accompaniment. Often, as in the case of the city symphonies of the 1930s, but also in the more recent work of filmmakers like Werner Herzog, the documentarist will use an incremental montage technique to evoke an emotional rather than intellectual response from the viewer. These poetic accounts clearly bear the marks of a shaping and sensitive intelligence. For similar reasons some critics have suggested that it might be appropriate to establish a further category, that of *authored documentary* to characterize work where the individual creative input, and even personality, of the filmmaker has manifestly become an important factor in determining its appeal (Winston 1995; Crawford and Turton 1992).

In the 1990s in the output of television channels yet other forms of documentary have emerged which may well warrant description as modes, although they have not yet been identified as such in the critical literature. They include the *video diary*, or first-person documentary. It is yet another product of the confluence of new technology (especially the development of high-quality camcorders) and institutional pressure (in this case for novel and comparatively inexpensive programming material). It carries the documentary inwards, being able to do directly things at which other documentaries have to labour. It can do this by revealing an individual's personality both from the inside, through interior monologue in which the filmmaker reflects upon the nature of his or her own life, and also from the outside, via the opinions and actions of others directed towards the filmmaker. A compelling example is Willa Woolston's *My Demons: The Legacy* (Video Diaries, BBC, 1992), in which a journey back to the land of her birth becomes both a recovery of autobiographical history and a self-administered therapy.

Another emergent mode is that known as *reality programming*, in which television packaging makes the most sophisticated intervention in actuality-based production, as it seeks to highlight the sense of shared experience or lived reality. Such programming uses a wide range of television techniques to enhance the entertainment value of the material. Indeed, many such programmes are entirely devoted to prime-time entertainment bearing a close relationship to tabloid journalism and having no meaningful connection with documentary. But even where they do resemble documentaries, the emphasis is on capturing the vibrancy of real-life events in short packages, each with its unmissable emotional climax. The whole is linked into programme format by a celebrity presenter who typically builds audience anticipation so as to focus it on the sequence of emotional impacts—which arrive regularly every three or four minutes. It follows that each series has its own characteristic and tightly defined themes, and these are usually identified by a dramatic series title: *999* (BBC), *Rescue 911* (CBS), *Crimewatch UK* (BBC), *Cops* (Fox), and *America's most Wanted* (Fox). Reality programming has been introduced to the schedules in response to institutional pressure simply because it is popular and brings large audiences (see Kilborn 1994a).

When we add to these emergent modes another well-established one that has already been mentioned, namely *drama-documentary*, we have to recognize that documentaries exist in many forms, and may often be a hybrid of several of them. They perform multiple functions which tend to change with the passing of the years and as this brief look at their history suggests, the rise and fall of grand new projects accounts in part for the way in which each mode rises to prominence and is superseded by others.

BIBLIOGRAPHY

Allen, Robert, and **Douglas Gomery** (1985), *Film History: Theory and Practice* (New York: Alfred A. Knopf).

Barnouw, Erik (1974), *A History of the Non-Fiction Film* (New York: Oxford University Press).

Bloch, Ernst, et al. (1980), *Aesthetics and Politics* (London: Verso).

Branigan, Edward (1992), *Narrative Comprehension and Film* (London: Routledge).

Brecht, Bertolt (1938), 'Against Georg Lukács', in Bloch *et al.* (1980).

Christie, Ian (1994), *The Last Machine* (London: British Film Institute).

Crawford, Peter, and **David Turton** (eds.) (1992), *Film as Ethnography* (Manchester: Manchester University Press).

Ellis, Jack C. (1989), *The Documentary Idea* (Englewood Cliffs, NJ: Prentice-Hall).

Hardy, Forsyth (ed.) (1979), *Grierson on Documentary* (London: Faber & Faber).

Kilborn, Richard (1994a), 'How Real can you Get?: Recent Developments in "Reality" Television', *European Journal of Communication*, 9: 421–39.

—— (1994b), 'Drama over Lockerbie: A New Look at the Drama-Documentary Debate', *Historical Journal of Film, Radio and Television*, 14/1: 59–76.

Kracauer, Siegfried (1960), *Theory of Film* (New York: Oxford University Press).

Lockerbie, Ian (1991), 'The Self-Conscious Documentary in Quebec: *L'Emotion Dissonante* and *Passiflora*', in Peter Easingwood et al. (eds.), *Probing Canadian Culture* (Augsburg: AV-Verlag).

Loizos, Peter (1993), *Innovation in Ethnographic Film: From Innocence to Self-Consciousness 1955–1985* (Manchester: Manchester University Press).

Lovell, Alan, and **Jim Hillier** (1972), *Studies in Documentary* (New York: Viking).

*Nichols, Bill** (1991), *Representing Reality: Issues and Concepts in Documentary* (Bloomington: Indiana University Press).

*Renov, Michael** (ed.) (1993), *Theorizing Documentary* (London: Routledge).

Rosenthal, Alan (1988), *New Challenges for Documentary* (Berkeley: University of California Press).

—— (1990), *Writing, Directing and Producing Documentary* (Carbondale: Southern Illinois Press).

Winston, Brian (1995), *Claiming the Real* (London: British Film Institute).

5

The animated film

Michael O'Pray

Definitions and theoretical approaches

The animated film is an enormously wide and heterogeneous category, traditionally understood as film that is shot frame by frame and by which drawings and objects are given the appearance of moving. However, it ranges from Hollywood cartoons to abstract modernist animation, from puppet films to types of special-effects cinema to computer-generated moving imagery, and so on. This promiscuity of forms is bewildering, and unique in cinema and this is one of the main reasons why animation has suffered theoretical and critical neglect for so long. Another is the low status it has derived from its massive use in children's entertainment and in advertising.

Another major and related reason for its neglect is animation's use of a broad array of image-making materials and techniques—drawings, paint, cels, clay, plasticine, puppets and marionettes, dolls, computers, sand, glass, film footage, paper cut-outs, pins, special effects. Inevitably this technical and material eclecticism has marginalized it from current film theory and analysis (Kotlarz 1995). For some, the massive introduction of special effects and computer-generated imagery in contemporary mainstream cinema, as in *Robocop* (USA, 1987) and *Terminator II* (USA, 1991), has radically complicated the matter (Cholodenko 1991).

Understandably, animators themselves propose varied definitions, ranging from Norman McLaren's 'the art of movements-that-are-drawn' (Gordon 1977) to Jan Svankmajer's refusal of the term 'animation' (Hames 1995). Definitions are complicated by the differences between two-dimensional animation, primarily identified as drawing animation, and all its derivatives (painting, cel, collage, and so forth), and three-dimensional animation using real objects, puppets, or clay models. A further complication, though one shared with live-action film, is that animation is divided between narrative and non-narrative. The story-telling charm of Disney can be contrasted to the abstract rhythms of the 1920s graphic cinema of Hans Richter and Walter Ruttmann (Lawder 1975), even if the two traditions merge fleetingly in films like Disney's experimental film *Fantasia* (USA, 1940).

Thus the question of the definition of film animation remains acute in so far as its resolution nearly always excludes certain kinds of filmmaking. Crafton (1984), for instance, sees animation as a subspecies of film in general. On the other hand, Cholodenko (1991) understands animation, perhaps unhelpfully, as that which pervades all film as a result of the latter's origins in the 'persistence of vision' of pre-cinematic optical toys and its 'illusion of life'. In contrast, Klein (1993) conceives of the American cartoon as at least primarily a graphic art form.

One of the most sustained and rewarding studies of animation is to be found in the Soviet filmmaker Sergei

Eisenstein's writings on Disney. Written in the 1940s, they focus on the 'protoplasmatic' (O'Pray 1997) of Disney's pre-sound cartoons. Connected with his concept of ecstasy and the primitive notion of an omnipotent fluid 'form' which is pre-imagistic, Eisenstein's 'protoplasmaticism' stresses the versatility of the formal line of the drawing, suggesting that its creation is an expression of the artist's unconscious and its transformational powers are omnipotent in character.

Eastern Europe remains the source of fairly abstract inquiry into animation. For example, Yuri Lotman (1981) suggests that the basic property of animation is the operation of 'signs on signs' so that the animated representation is an image of an image (Yampolsky 1987). In other words, the screen image with its sign system represents the images produced by drawings, cels, puppets, clay models, and so on, and their sign system of dynamic plasticity. The interplay between these two systems lies at the core of any aesthetic understanding of a particular animated film. Endemic to animation is the dominance of the plastic sign system in terms of its versatility, control, and mastery (O'Pray 1997), what Klein (1993) calls the *machina versatilis* of animation.

Roland Barthes's (1982) essay on the painter Giuseppe Arcimboldo suggests that the way in which he deals with levels of meanings—using the natural objects (trees, flowers, books, and so on) that make up a portrait of a face which is also a painting—is similar to animation. So animation could be divided into three systems: (1) that of the means of representation—drawings, cels, clay, objects; (2) that of the representation—Mickey Mouse, a Svankmajerian collage figure, Grommit, and so on; and (3) that of the representational system of film with its close-ups, zooms, pans, edits, superimpositions, sound, and colour.

Studies of computerized imagery with a strong realist aesthetic imitating live action, as in *Toy Story* (USA, 1995), has given it the rather far-fetched, characterization of 'postmodernist' for its intertextual referencing (Cholodenko 1991). Digital imaging, totally generated by a computer whilst marketed as animation, mimics the realist aesthetic of mainstream live-action film. The fascination, and perhaps for some confusion, of such films lies in the ambiguity of whether or not they are animation at all. Such an effect is to be likened perhaps to *trompe-l'œil* painting, where we thrill to the virtuosity of the means of representation itself (O'Pray 1997).

The American animated cartoon

Undoubtedly, the major area of serious research has been into the American cartoon (notably Maltin 1987; Klein 1993; Crafton 1984). In particular, this research has been undertaken from the historical perspective of the major cartoon studio systems like Disney (Finch 1973) and Warner Bros. (Schneider 1988; Maltin 1980), emphasizing the animation studio as part of the American film industry complex. However, there have been exceptions, with studies of the role of racism (Kotlarz 1983), genre (Thompson 1976), auteurism (Thompson 1976), and the political function of Disney (Dorfman and Matellart 1975; Smoodin 1993).

By definition, the American cartoon is grounded in drawing, and this allows it great flexibility so that, through scale and perspective, it can imitate the camera's movements and angles; whereas in object-animation the camera must operate in three-dimensional space with pans, tracks, and zooms, as in live-action narrative cinema. Thus drawing frees animation from the denotative qualities of film and photography. Prior to sound, with its demand for dialogue and therefore more orthodox narrative structures, cartoons were intrinsically graphic, dealing with line, rhythm, and surface (Klein 1993) and thus indebted to comic strips, vaudeville (Crafton 1984), and madcap silent comedies (Klein 1993). Mimicry of the camera was minimal. In many ways this early period of late 1920s Disney, Max Fleischer, and the creator of Felix the Cat, Otto Messmer, reflects Eisenstein's (1949) notion of the ideogram and the hieroglyphic using the early, more graphically based notion of montage. The introduction of sound established a tendency in cartoons away from a modernist anti-realism, with its stress on the picture plane, and towards a deep-space naturalism-cum-realism.

The arrival of sound undoubtedly led to highly developed plot lines and characterization, which lent themselves to the auteurist approaches and genre analyses found in the literature on the American cartoon. The literal creation and control of particular characters (such as Roadrunner and Bugs Bunny), even within the heavy division of labour of the Hollywood animation studios between the late 1920s and 1950s, made cartoons more amenable to auterist analyses, which have been usefully applied to Tex Avery, Chuck Jones, and others from the Hollywood cartoon classical period (Thompson 1976). In more recent years filmmakers such as Svankmajer have also received auteurist accounts of their work (Hames 1995).

Cartoons especially have been more open to a genre reading (Thompson 1976) although the idea of cartoon *per se* being a genre rather makes the idea of subgenre within it—the chase film, the dotty individual, or whatever—more problematic. In fact the subgenre is most understood in terms of long-standing characters such as Tom and Jerry, Bugs Bunny, and Donald Duck. Animation itself is a type of filmmaking, rather than a genre with its shared thematic and institutional coherence.

The relationship between animation and fairy- and folk-tales has been well recognized and suggests an approach to narrative analysis (Propp 1928) in which narrative functions and elements are identified and relationships between them established. Analysis in terms of paradigmatic and syntagmatic elements and their functions provides a formal basis for cartoon theory. In the case especially of post-1930 Hollywood cartoons, this has been done by Klein (1993) in terms of the nuisance, over-reactor, and controller.

Three-dimensional animation

The revived popularity of object-animation using three-dimensional space, as practised by Svankmajer, the Quay brothers, Aardman, and others, establishes close connections with mainstream film and divides the ontological basis of animation. The animation of actual objects could be understood within the notion of a realist mode and self-generating two-dimensional work within a more semiotic one. However, the most sustained semiotic analyses have been of drawing animation (Yampolsky 1987; Lotman 1981), although semiotics has been applied to puppetry (Jurkowski 1988) and thus by implication to the works of Svankmajer and the Quay brothers.

Loman's (1981) argument that animation is essentially 'an image of an image' and is constituted by signs of signs accompanies discussion of the disquiet of images moving at all. This latter idea can be related to Freud's (1919/1960) concept of the 'uncanny', which has been applied to East European object-animation (O'Pray 1989), which has been associated with psychoanalysis, surrealism, and notions of fantasy (O'Pray 1989; Hammond 1987; Cardinal 1995). 3-D or object-animation has been largely identified with East Euro-pean traditions, as manifested in the puppet and marionette tradition of Czechoslovakia and Poland, where it has had a strong cultural and historical significance as a part of popular culture and as a political allegorical system (Hames 1995; Holloway 1983; Jurkowski 1988). Jiři Trnka was the most important of these animators. As susceptible to Proppian analysis as Hollywood cartoons, given their siting in European folk-tales and myths, they have at times also been influenced by art movements, especially surrealism in the case of Svankmajer (O'Pray 1995; Cardinal 1995) and Walerian Borowczyck.

Theories of surrealism in recent years (Forster 1993), in which the role of the automaton in surrealist photography has been identified with issues around the 'uncanny', have led to a more psychoanalytical approach. Both Forster (1993) and Todorov (1975) use the surrealist uncanny in their differing theories of fantasy. With its links to castration anxiety and fantasies linked with death through the animation of inanimate objects, the uncanny became a fertile ground for theorizing in animation. The links between the uncanny and surrealism are also strong in the use of mannequins and dolls by such artists as Man Ray and Hans Bellmer (Krauss 1986) and by animators like the Quay brothers and Svankmajer.

That such an approach is largely appropriate to object-animation also suggests that the genre of the fantastic could be applied creatively to certain animation films—possibly three-dimensional films, and not just cartoons *per se*. In the case of the Quay brothers, for instance, who use both live action and object-animation, the distinctions between animation and live-action narrative become blurred. Any analysis of such films is not entirely separable from those applicable to such special-effects films as *The Fly* (USA, 1986), *Edward Scissorhands* (USA, 1990), and *Robocop* (USA, 1987). The profound difference lies in the narrative role of such special-effects animata in most special-effects films (Robocop is a robot) and the juxtaposing and quite transparent use of animated figures in their own right, as found in the films of the Quay brothers. This emphasis on the means of representation as being part of the representation itself seems central to much animation and lends it an uncanny air at times. There seem to be conscious elements of versatility and the marvellous in animation which are not shared in the same way by live-action film. The idea of taking an animated figure (whether cartoon or three-dimensional) for its own sake links with

Jan Svankmajer modelling

notions of psychical omnipotence and control (Freud 1919; O'Pray 1997). Of course, this cannot be generalized over all instances of animation, but it is probably one way of making initial, if tenuous, distinctions.

The fascination of audiences for anthropomorphic models and puppets in recent years (as in Nick Park's *Creature Comforts* (GB, 1989), Tim Burton's *The Nightmare before Christmas* (USA, 1989) and Henry Selick's *James and the Giant Peach* (USA, 1996)), with their elements of satire, social humour, and nightmare, suggests both the influence of Svankmajer and the longstanding tradition of the grotesque and the carnivalesque (Bakhtin 1968; O'Pray 1989) flowing out of caricature, fairy-tales, and newspaper cartoons whereby 'difficult' material finds a cultural space often abetted by the safety-net of humour (Kris 1964).

Avant-garde and abstraction

Paradoxically, the pre-sound cartoons were often more modernist in their acceptance of the screen surface than the so-called abstract graphic cinema of the 1920s of Richter, Ruttmann, Oskar Fischinger, and Viking Eggeling, (Le Grice 1977). Like its cartoon counterparts, it was rarely silent (Eggeling's classic *Diagonalsymphonien/Diagonal Symphony* (Germany, 1925) was an exception). Often using cut-out paper manipulation, it worked with movement of shapes through space, and at times had anthropomorphic tendencies. Marcel Duchamp's *Anemic Cinema* (France, 1925), also used text with obscene visual puns as part of a Dadaesque project. Again the impetus was graphic as opposed to filmic (Sitney 1974). This abstraction was developed by James and John Whitney, who in the 1960s developed a high-technology computer aesthetic in the United States (*Permutations*, USA, 1967).

Len Lye's camera-less, partially hand-painted films of the 1930s (*Colour Box*, GB, 1935; *Trade Tattoo*, GB, 1937) owed much to modernist ideas of collage and abstraction intermixed with ideas culled from 'primitive' Maori art. McLaren's films of this period were also modernist, but with a strong political agit-prop in the case of *Hell Unlimited* (USA, 1936). In the period after the Second World War Robert Breer began his career with similar experiments with shape and space but moved onto anarchic Dadaesque montages of drawings, the result of tracing from live-action film (rotoscoping), object-animation with free-wheeling domestic allusions which owe more perhaps to Émile Cohl and pre-sound cartoons than to a pure modernist aesthetic.

In the case of abstraction in animation, critical approaches are filtered through notions of avant-gardism and modernism within the fine arts in general. Richter's and Ruttmann's work can be seen as responses to abstract painting, using music as an analogy (Lawder 1975). In the case of experimental animators like Breer, there are connections to be made both to the commercial animation film, especially that of the early pioneers Cohl (Crafton 1990) and the Fleischers, and to Dada and surrealism and notions of collage, montage, and modernism. In other words the institutional context of such work is importantly wider than that of mainstream cinema and some of its aims arise from issues in other art forms.

Part of European avant-gardism, but standing closer to notions of art cinema in their psychological exploration and sexual and political radicalism, are the early European animation films of Borowczyk (Pierre 1968), Trnka, and Jan Lenica (Holloway 1983), who used techniques and materials of many kinds, but especially the puppet, to explore themes of sexuality, political allegory, and surrealist symbolism.

Futures

There are many areas within animation studies crying out for serious thought and analysis. One of the dangers of focusing too much on animation as such is that the complexity and imaginative qualities of a particular film can be too easily cut off from other kinds of cinema. The Quay brothers, Burton, and Svankmajer are good examples of filmmakers who straddle many kinds of film—children's animation, art cinema, avant-gardism, and of course mainstream 'entertainment'. Animation's traditional formal and material promiscuity and hybridity are its strength at a time when new technologies like computerization are beginning to saturate the broad spectrum of cinema. To this extent, definition is probably inappropriate; rather, we should be using the Wittgensteinian model of the 'family resemblance'. A film is often simply more than 'animated'; it bears a family resemblance to many other kinds of filmmaking and an analytical approach that is rigorous but broad-minded is more likely to produce critical and theoretical analyses that escape reductionism and do justice to the density of the work in hand.

BIBLIOGRAPHY

Afterimage (1987), 13, Special Issue: *Animating the Fantastic*, (Autumn).

Bakhtin, Mikhail (1968/1984), *Rabelais and his World* (Bloomington: Indiana University Press).

Barthes, Roland (1982/1991), 'Arcimboldo; or, Magician and Rhetoriqueur', in *The Responsibility of Forms: Critical Essays on Art, Music and Representation* (Berkeley: University of California Press).

***Bendazzi, Giannalberto** (1994), *Cartoons: One Hundred Years of Cinema Animation* (London: John Libbey).

Canemaker, John (ed.) (1988), *Storytelling in Animation: The Art of the Animated Image*, 2 vols., ii (Los Angeles: American Film Institute).

Cardinal, Roger (1987), 'Stirrings in the Dust', *Afterimage* (1987).

—— (1995), 'Thinking through Things: The Presence of Objects in the Early Films of Jan Svankmajer', in Hames (1995).

Ceram, C. W. (1965), *Archaeology of the Cinema* (London: Thames & Hudson).

Cholodenko, Alan (ed.) (1991), *The Illusion of Life: Essays on Animation* (Sydney: Power Publications).

Crafton, Donald (1984), *Before Mickey: The Animated Film 1889–1928* (London: MIT Press).

—— (1990), *Émile Cohl, Caricature, and Film* (Princeton: Princeton University Press).

Dorfman, Ariel, and **Armand Mattelart** (1975), *How to Read Donald Duck: Imperialist Ideology in the Disney Comic* (New York: International General).

Eisenstein, Sergei (1949/1977), 'The Cinematographic Principle and the Ideogram', in *Film Form: Essays in Film Theory* (London: Harvest/Harcourt Brace Jovanovich).

—— (1988), *Eisenstein on Disney* (London: Methuen).

Finch, Christopher (1973/1995), *The Art of Walt Disney: From Mickey Mouse to the Magic Kingdoms* (rev. London: Virgin Books).

Forster, Hal (1993), *Compulsive Beauty* (London: MIT Press).

Freud, Sigmund (1913/1985), 'The Uncanny', in *Art and Literature: The Pelican Freud Library* (Harmondsworth: Penguin).

—— (1919/1960), *Totem and Taboo* (London: Routledge & Kegan Paul).

Gordon, Lindsay (1977), *Norman McLaren* (Edinburgh: Scottish Arts Council).

Hames, Peter (ed.) (1995), *Dark Alchemy: The Films of Jan Svankmajer* (Trowbridge: Flicks Books).

Holloway, Ronald (1983), 'The Short Film in Eastern Europe: Art and Politics of Cartoons and Puppets', in David W. Paul (ed.), *Politics, Art and Commitment in the East European Cinema* (London: Macmillan).

Jurkowski, Henry K. (1988), *Aspects of Puppet Theatre* (London: Puppet Centre Trust).

Klein, Norman M. (1993), *Seven Minutes: The Life and Death of the American Animated Cartoon* (London: Verso).

Kotlarz, Irene (1983), 'The Birth of a Notion', *Screen*, 24/2 (Mar.–Apr.) 21–9.

—— (1995), 'In Betweening: An Interview with Irene Kotlarz', *Art History*, 18/1 (Mar.), 24–36.

Krauss, Rosalind (1986), 'Corpus Delicti', in *L'Amour fou: Photography and Surrealism* (London: Arts Council of Great Britain).

Kris, Ernst (1964) in collaboration with **Ernst Gombrich**, 'The Principles of Caricature', in *Psychoanalytic Explorations in Art* (New York: Schocken Books).

Lawder, Standish (1975), *The Cubist Cinema* (New York: New York University Press).

*__Le Grice, Malcolm__ (1977), *Abstract Film and Beyond* (London: Studio Vista).

Lotman, Yuri (1981), 'On the Language of Animated Cartoons', in *Russian Poetics in Translation*, 8: 36–8.

Maltin, Leonard (1980/1987), *Of Mice and Magic: A History of American Animated Cartoons* (rev. New York: Plume Printing).

Moritz, William (1979), 'Non-Objective Film: The Second Generation', in *Film as Film*, exhibition catalogue (London: Hayward Gallery).

Noake, Roger (1988), *Animation: A Guide to Animated Film Techniques* (London: Macdonald).

O'Pray, Michael (1989), 'Surrealism, Fantasy and the Grotesque: The Cinema of Jan Svankmajer', in James Donald (ed.), *Fantasy and the Cinema* (London: British Film Institute).

—— (1995), 'Jan Svankmajer: A Mannerist Surrealist', in Hames (1995).

—— (1997), 'Eisenstein and Stokes on Disney: Film Animation and Omnipotence', in Pilling (1997).

Peary, Gerald, and **Danny** (1980), *The American Animated Cartoon: A Critical Anthology* (New York: Dutton).

Pierre, Sylvie (1987), 'The Theatre of Monsieur Borowczyck', *Afterimage* (1987).

Pilling, Jayne (1997a), *Women and Animation: A Compendium* (London: British Film Institute).

—— (1997b), *A Reader in Animation Studies* (Luton: University of Luton Press/John Libbey Media).

Propp, Vladimir (1928/1977), *Morphology of the Folk Tale* (rev. London: University of Texas Press).

Russett, Robert, and **Cecile Starr** (1976/1988), *Experimental Animation: Origins of a New Art* (New York: Da Capo Press).

Schneider, Steve (1988), *That's all Folks: The Art of Warner Brothers Animation* (New York: Henry Holt).

Sitney, P. Adams (1974/1979) *Visionary Film: The American Avant-Garde 1943–1978* (Oxford: Oxford University Press).

Smoodin, Eric (1993), *Animating Culture: Hollywood Cartoons from the Sound Era* (Oxford: Roundhouse).

Solomon, Charles (ed.) (1987), *The Art of the Animated Image* (Los Angeles: American Film Institute).

Thompson, Kristin (1980), 'Implications of the Cel Animation Technique', in Teresa de Lauretis and Stephen Heath (eds.), *The Cinematic Apparatus* (London: Macmillan).

Thompson, Richard (1976), 'Meep Meep', in Bill Nichols (ed.), *Movies and Methods*, 2 vols., i (London: University of California Press).

Todorov, Tzvetan (1975), *The Fantastic: A Structural Approach to a Literary Genre* (New York: Cornell University Press).

Yampolsky, Mikhail (1987), 'The Space of the Animated Film: Khrzhanovsky's *I Am With You Again* and Norstein's *The Tale of Tales*', *Afterimage* (1987).

6

Issues in European cinema

Ginette Vincendeau

European cinema has always been recognized as aesthetically and culturally important and yet, as a branch of film studies, it was, until recently, underdeveloped. This is a problem of both terminology and concept. Since it has traditionally been defined in terms of 'high art'—as opposed to Hollywood—and of originality and diversity, European cinema has tended either to be reduced to the work of a few auteurs, under the concept of 'European art cinema', or to be split between studies of national cinemas, movements, and individual filmmakers. Only since the early 1990s has it emerged as a topic in its own right, for reasons which I will examine at the end of this chapter. But first I will chart the more established ways in which European cinema has been approached.

European art cinema

The dominant concept in studies of the cinemas of Europe has been that of 'art cinema'. Arising from the avant-garde works of the 1920s, the films of prominent figures such as Jean Renoir, Ingmar Bergman, and Federico Fellini, and the post-war movements of Italian Neo-Realism and the French New Wave, the essence of European cinema has been defined as residing in works that are, to various degrees, aesthetically innovative, socially committed, and humanist in outlook. To these features are often added the auteurist notions of originality and personal vision—all characteristics which define, and promote, European art cinema as fundamentally different from the industrially based and generically coded Hollywood. Although the French critics of the 1950s claimed the possibility of authorship and artistry in Hollywood films—Alfred Hitchcock, Howard Hawks—the sense of art as being the defining characteristic of European film has remained.

In the 1970s and 1980s European art cinema was further defined, as an institutional (Neale 1981) and aesthetic (Bordwell 1979) phenomenon designed to counter Hollywood's invasion of European film markets. European art films, it was claimed, propose a different spectatorial experience—loose, ambiguous narratives, characters in search of meaning rather than action, overt directorial expression, a heightened sense of realism (including depictions of sexuality), and a slower pace— and therefore require a different viewing context. Hence, the films are exhibited in 'art cinemas' and at film festivals and they receive a special kind of critical attention.

> **The dominant concept in studies of the cinemas of Europe has been that of 'art cinema'. Arising from the avant-garde works of the 1920s, the films of prominent figures such as Jean Renoir, Ingmar Bergman, and Federico Fellini, and the post-war movements of Italian Neo-Realism and the French New Wave, the essence of European cinema has been defined as residing in works that are, to various degrees, aesthetically innovative, socially committed, and humanist in outlook.**

While these are observable facts, this approach involves three dangers. One is a flattening-out of differences between individual films and filmmakers. The second is of reducing a vast and diverse European production to what is—or at least has been for many decades—only one section of the market. The third is to reinforce American-centrism: if a variety of diverse practices, some of which pre-date Hollywood, are reduced to an 'alternative', then Hollywood is reinforced as for ever 'the norm'. Ultimately, the notion of European art cinema is a useful polemical and marketing tool and a guide to an aesthetically rich tradition of European filmmaking, but it should be no more than that.

'The national' in European cinema

The cinemas of Europe have traditionally been considered 'national' in a way which Hollywood has rarely

been. For instance, most reference works and film history books (e.g. Cook 1985; Allen and Gomery 1985; Nowell-Smith 1996) classify Hollywood under headings relating to genre, industry, and technological developments, while they subsume European cinemas under 'national cinemas'. In the United Kingdom and the United States this is reflected institutionally in the fact that European cinemas—except the British cinema, which is always in an ambiguous position *vis-à-vis* continental cinema— are often studied within foreign-language departments, as opposed to film and media departments.

Many of the seminal film histories were studies of national European cinemas or of world cinema organized along nationalist lines, especially British (Rotha 1936), French (Bardèche and Brasillach 1935; Sadoul 1953), and German (Kracauer 1947; Eisner 1952). Soviet cinema also attracted attention from an early age, thanks to the writings of its practitioners (Eisenstein 1942, 1949) and to the communist bias of formative French film history (Sadoul 1953). The dominance of these 'major' countries in scholarly studies of European cinema has continued to the present day, with the addition of Italy in the wake of Neo-Realism. The rest of Europe tends to be considered in regions— Central Europe, Nothern Europe—while 'minor' countries remain in isolation if not oblivion: Belgium, Holland, Greece, Portugal, Austria, Switzerland. In this respect, one remarkable development of the 1990s has been the rise of Spanish cinema, attributable to the post-Franco liberalization of the country, but especially, as José Arroyo points out, to the enormous success of director Pedro Almodóvar (Chapter 13*d*).

While European national cinemas are generating a regular flow of books and university courses, the limited availability of subtitled film prints or videos hinders their comprehensive study. In most cases—even in the 'major' countries—only a narrow canon of work is known outside that country. As Ian Christie says of the 1920s, 'the bulk of the mainstream cinema . . . remains little known in comparison with the handful of Soviet, French, and German avant-garde classics that dominate the decade's image' (Chapter 7); Simona Monticelli makes a similar comment in relation to Neo-Realism (Chapter 8). Truly comprehensive histories of national European cinemas in the English language still remain to be written.

A contributing factor is that, unlike Hollywood (the 'dream factory'), European cinemas, globally and individually, have been treated with little reference to their industrial context. There are complex reasons for this, which include the international promotion of European 'art' cinema, but also the nature of the European film industries. With some notable exceptions—Pathé and Gaumont in early twentieth-century France, UFA in Germany in the 1920s and 1930s, Cinecittà in post-war Italy, the Central and East European countries under socialism—European production has been small-scale, fragmented, and disorganized. Since the 1950s there have been few integrated distribution or exhibition systems, and most studios have worked on a hire basis. Empirical studies of the industry therefore tend to be localized—studies of the Film Europe movement, of the coming of sound, of funding (the latter especially during and since the 1993 GATT negotiations; see Mattelart, Chapter 12). There are few large-scale studies of European production, distribution, and exhibition in the English language; two exceptions are Crisp (1993) and especially Finney (1996). Work on audiences is equally underdeveloped and localized (for example, studies of reception in early German cinema and 1950s Britain). Studies of film culture are mostly restricted to the British context (Higson 1993) and the French cinéphile environment (Hillier 1985, 1986; Roud 1983). There is no pan-European study of industrial practices in relation to film aesthetics on the lines of David Bordwell, Janet Staiger, and Kristin Thompson's, *The Classical Hollywood Cinema* (1985). Salt (1983) and Crisp (1993) consider such matters, but are restricted, for the former to a small selection of filmmakers and for the latter to one country. As mentioned earlier, the dominant concept informing studies of the national cinemas of Europe remains that of 'European art cinema', a largely aesthetic category.

The sense of 'the national' has been most pervasive in studies of national cinemas that are concerned with a cultural and social contextualization: Siegfried Kracauer's From *Caligari to Hitler* (1947), Millicent Marcus's *Italian Films in the Light of Neo-Realism* (1986), Alan Williams's *Republic of Images* (1992), Thomas Elsaesser's *New German Cinema* (1989), Susan Hayward's *French National Cinema* (1993), Andrew Higson's *Waving the Flag* (1995), to name a few. Although there has been, over the years, a shift in these studies towards a more self-conscious examination of the concept of 'national cinema' (Hayward, Higson), all take national boundaries as the defining factor of their study. In different ways, their project is to match the

stylistic and representational strategies of a national film production with the cultural, social, and political events and climate of the country from which the films emerge.

While some national surveys have suffered from the problems outlined above—especially the reduced canon on which they are often based—the matching of texts and contexts has been variously productive or reductive. For instance, Daniel Goulding remarks of Central European cinema that there is a tendency among Western critics 'to stress the political messages of the films and to celebrate the most controversial and provocative of them'. Goulding's point can be extended to most studies of national cinemas produced outside their country of origin. As a result of a bias towards art films and/or politically 'subversive' films, the entirety of a national production can be very sketchily examined. For example, it is only recently that the German cinema of the Nazi period has begun to be properly examined (Rentschler 1996). Conversely, as we will see, a few 'privileged moments' in each national cinema continue to dominate public perception.

The difficulties in conceptualizing national film industries are compounded by their international nature. Cinema personnel have always crossed national boundaries: the French Pathé and Gaumont operators went all over Europe, Russians came to Germany and France in the 1920s, Germans to France in the 1930s, and many went back and forth between these countries as well as to Britain and Italy on a regular basis. A more individual form of emigration has continued to take place, with such figures as Luis Buñuel, Jean Vigo, Roman Polanski, Chantal Akerman (Fowler, Chapter 13c), while in the post-war period co-production deals became a major element in the reconstruction of national European cinemas. American funding, the increased part taken by television companies since the 1970s, and more recently the role of the European Union (Horrocks 1995), have further problematized the notion of 'national' cinemas in Europe. What determines the national identity of a film when funding, language, setting, topic, cast, and director are increasingly mixed? How can we classify films such as Louis Malle's 1992 film *Damage* (French director, Franco-British cast, English settings), Krzysztof Kieślowki's *Three Colours* trilogy (*Blue*, 1993; *White*, 1993; *Red*, 1994; made by a Polish director with French funds and a Franco-Polish cast), and Lars von Trier's 1996 film *Breaking the Waves* (Danish director, Norwegian–

The 'allegorical medievalism' of *The Seventh Seal* (1957)—European art-house staple and success of the 1950s

European funds, British cast, Scottish setting)? However, despite the fluidity of national boundaries, the majority of European films are perceived as having a clear national identity, especially when it comes to particular movements and filmmakers.

Movements and moments

The selection and canonization of privileged 'moments' in national cinemas is a method derived from art and literary history. It informs the structure of history books, the planning of film courses and art cinema retrospectives, and the spatial organization of film museums, such as the Museum of the Moving Image in London. Based on recent film history surveys and encyclopaedias (Bordwell and Thompson 1979; Cook 1985; Vincendeau 1995; Nowell-Smith 1996), the canon of such movements includes: Soviet cinema,

Weimar cinema and German Expressionism, the British documentary movement, French poetic realism, Italian Neo-Realism (Monticelli, chapter 8), the French New Wave (Forbes, Chapter 9), New German Cinema (Sieglohr, Chapter 10). Others, such as Early Scandinavian cinema, the British and Czech New Waves, and the Polish Cinema of Moral Concern (Goulding, Chapter 11) appear as more specialized interests. Recently, pre-Soviet Russian cinema, Nazi cinema, French cinema of the occupation, post-Franco Spanish cinema, French *cinéma beur* (or 'film de banlieue') have emerged as new areas of study and the canon may be enlarged.

The benefits of isolating movements are obvious; they help us make sense of a mass of otherwise unmanageable material and, in so far as scholarship has any impact on distribution, it helps ensure the continued availability of films on video and through television and cinema retrospectives. The analogy with art and literary movements also gave these pockets of European cinema cultural legitimacy and media identity, and it continues to do so in marketing films which do not have the benefit of a well-known auteur (for instance, the French 'films de banlieue' in the wake of *La Haine*, Mathieu Kassovitz, 1995). The drawbacks are equally obvious: the wood of a national cinema becomes invisible behind the trees of a small number of canonical movements. This is true both of the gaps between the movements (what happens between Weimar and New German Cinema?), and of the rest of the production at the time of the movements (how does the French New Wave relate to the mainstream production of its time?). The concept of 'influence' equally pervades film history, which tends to relate subsequent films to an earlier, 'golden' movement—the documentary tradition for British cinema, poetic realism and then the New Wave in France, and so on. Finally, the desire to bracket films together inevitably homogenizes a collection of diverse works. A close study of films belonging to a movement reveals at least as many stylistic and ideological differences as it reveals similarities, a point made by both Sieglohr about New German Cinema and Monticelli about Italian Neo-Realism.

Despite these problematic aspects, the concept of film movements is a useful one, if only because it is so controversial. As critical constructions, European film movements make sense, and yet they are almost without exception rejected or challenged by filmmakers. Furthermore, they are subject to change. The fate of Neo-realism as a critical category first constructed and then deconstructed (Monticelli) is, in this respect, exemplary.

Authorship in European cinema: the canon and how to challenge it

The figure of the director has always been central to European cinema. Powerful directorial figures arose as in Hollywood from the mid-1910s (e.g. Abel Gance, Victor Sjöström), but unlike their American counterparts, decision-making rested primarily with them. Concurrently, early theoretical writing in 1920s France identified the director as the main source of artistic creativity (Abel 1984, 1988), preparing the grounds for the more comprehensive theorization of the *politique des auteurs* in the 1950s (Hillier 1985, 1986). This claimed the director's personal vision as paramount,

transcending the team-work of filmmaking while also unifying a filmmaker's *œuvre* across time, through a body of stylistic and thematic motifs.

Over the decades, a canon of 'great European directors' has arisen, which has fluctuated (as exemplified by the *Sight and Sound* critics' polls made every ten years since 1952), but which has nevertheless established a pantheon. The selective list below, which parodies that published in *Movie* in June 1962, is simply meant to identify the canon as well as ways of challenging it. It is based on critical opinion rather than personal taste (though absolute objectivity is impossible).

The great: Angelopoulos, Antonioni, Bergman, Bresson, Buñuel, Clair, Dreyer, Eisenstein, Fassbinder, Fellini, Godard, Kieślowski, Lang, Murnau, Oliveira, Ophuls, Pabst, Pasolini, Renoir, Resnais, Rohmer, Rossellini, Sjöström, Tarkovsky, Tati, Vertov, Vigo, Visconti, Wajda.

The good: Bardem, Becker, Bertolucci, Blasetti, Carné, Chabrol, De Sica, Dupont, Duvivier, Feyder, Forman, Frears, Grémillon, Herzog, (European) Hitchcock, Ivens, Jancsó, L'Herbier, Loach, Lubitsch, Malle, Mikhalkov, Munk, Passer, Pudovkin, Saura, Stiller, Szabó, Tavernier, Truffaut, Varda, Wenders.

The interesting: Almodóvar, Bava, Borowczyk, Cohl, Demy, Dulac, Ferreri, Feuillade, Franju, Gance, Greenaway, Guitry, Jarman, the Kaurismäki brothers, Kusturica, Leigh, Leone, Makavejev, Marker, Méliès, Melville, Moretti, Pialat, Polanski, Powell and Pressburger, Reisz, Riefensthal, Rivette, Rouch, Ruiz, Schroeter, Svankmajer, Syberberg.

The rest . . .

First of all, the lists are overwhelmingly male, reflecting not so much the male bias of cinema, since European cinema has nurtured the highest number of women directors, but the male bias inherent in ideas of genius. A counter, all-female European canon might read:

The great: Akerman, Chytilová, Dulac, Duras, Mészáros, Muratova, Sanders-Brahms, Varda.

The good: Audry, Balasko, Box, Dorrie, Gogoberidze, Jakubowska, Kaplan, Kurys, Miró, Osten, Serreau, Toye, von Trotta.

The interesting: Breillat, Gorris, Guy, Isserman, Notari, Ottinger, Potter, Sander, Schub, Treut.

They are also significantly art-cinema-oriented. As discussed at the beginning of this chapter, art cinema has dominated critical constructions of European film, and this is reflected in the canon of 'great auteurs'. Yet, European cinema also produced rich traditions of popular films, some of which are identified—at least in their own country—by their director alongside genre and star. Thus the category of the 'popular auteur' is an important one in European cinema, though critically unrecognized. Names in this particular canon would include some 'cross-overs'—e.g. Tavernier, Serreau, Reisz, Almodóvar—as well as mainstream film-makers—Annaud, Attenborough, Balasko, Beineix, Berri, Besson (see Hayward, Chapter 13e), Lean, Schünzel, Matarazzo, May, Pagnol, Verneuil—to name a few.

Though the canon is largely international, national variations occur. For example, Sacha Guitry figures under 'interesting', but in France many see him as one of the 'greats'. The canon thus also bears the marks of availability problems for non-English-language films.

Closely allied to the 'masterpiece tradition' (Allen and Gomery 1985), the idea of a canon of great directors, like that of movements, derives from art and literary history. Directors deemed geniuses tower above the production of their country (Ivens for the Netherlands, Wajda for Poland, Jancsó for Hungary) or even world cinema (Bergman, Lang, Fellini, Renoir: see Reader, Chapter 13a). Some stand for the entire production of their 'small' country (Angelopoulos for Greece, Bergman for Sweden). Some were celebrated in the pre-war period (Eisenstein, Hitchcock, Sjöström, Renoir), but the critical practice of auteur canons developed mainly in the 1950s and 1960s, in the wake of the *politique des auteurs*, provoking a boom in monographs on individual directors. Subsequently, auteurism has been the most contested critical approach. Throughout the 1970s a severe critique of authorship was conducted, displacing it in favour of the structuralist analysis of narratives and of close textual studies (Cook 1985). At the same time, the critical revaluation of Hollywood and the rise of cultural studies produced a (critical) devaluation of art cinema and European auteurs, and arguably of European cinema altogether.

The 1980s and 1990s saw a 'return to the auteur' for two main reasons. One is the renaissance of film history after the 'theoretical 1970s', which sparked off an interest in neglected areas such as early cinema, and in the process some early cinema auteurs (Crafton 1990). The

other has to do with gender studies. Feminist studies polemically reclaimed the notion of authorship for women and, although this work has been predominantly on American cinema, important studies of European women directors have also come out (Flitterman-Lewis 1990; Portuges 1993). Some established male filmmakers have been reappraised in the light of feminism (Mulvey 1996) and more work of this kind is under way. Similarly, gay studies have generated an interest in gay directors such as Pedro Almodóvar (Smith 1994) and in rereading the work of classic figures such as Marcel Carné (Turk 1989).

The concept of the auteur, like that of movements, has fluctuated in the light of changing critical discourse and increased availability of material. If understood in an industrial, social, and cultural context, as opposed to just as an expression of genius, it can still illuminate areas of European film history that remain unknown—for example, the popular auteurs alluded to above—leading us to the most uncharted terrain of European film studies, that of genre and stardom.

The forgotten categories: genre and stardom

Genre and stardom, the twin foundations of popular cinema, have always existed in European cinema. However, the fact that both operate in an unsystematic way compared to Hollywood, and the unavailability of subtitled versions of much popular European cinema, have created enormous scholarly difficulties. I will briefly sketch out the main trends in popular European genres (concentrating, as a case-study, on heritage cinema) and stardom.

Most European countries have produced national inflexions to universal genres, and in particular comedy, melodrama, horror, and the musical (Dyer and Vincendeau 1992; Vincendeau 1995). The critically ignored genre of pornography should be added to this list. Even the archetypal American western has had European variations, especially in Italy and Germany—though these are numerically small. On the other hand, the other genre thought of as uniquely American, the thriller, has a rich following (and antecedents) in Europe—in Britain and especially in France, where the *policier* is one of the mainstays of post-war cinema (along with comedy). There are many reasons why these genres, which have been—and in France still are—numerically important, are critically virgin territory. One is the art cinema bias. Popular European genres (unless personalized by an auteur, such as Sergio Leone's 'spaghetti' westerns and the comedies of Claude Chabrol and Jacques Tati) simply do not correspond to the international *idea* of European cinema. In addition, national agencies promote art cinema and are somehow embarrassed by their popular films. Ironically perhaps, popular genres require more complex decoding than art cinema, because of their closeness (through language, character's gestures, topical references) to popular culture. Thus the international nature of high culture helps the exportability or art cinema, while the cultural 'noise' around popular films renders them more or less 'inexportable' (Jeancolas 1992). However, the eminent exportability of popular American cinema points to the single most important reason for the lack of export (as opposed to inexportability) of popular European cinema, that is the American monopoly of world distribution circuits in Europe, and the European failure to develop its own (Finney 1996). As the number of European films shown on the world market keeps decreasing (under 2 per cent in the mid-1990s), only two 'genres' of European cinema still travel relatively well: art cinema and heritage films.

European 'heritage' cinema describes popular costume films made in Europe since the 1970s, usually with high production values and often based on a canonical literary source. Typical examples include *Babette's Feast* (Denmark 1987), *Cyrano de Bergerac* (France, 1990), *A Room with a View* (UK, 1985), *Emma* (UK, 1996). As a European genre which exports well, heritage films are worthy of interest. They also raise interesting issues of definition. For instance, how different are they from earlier costume films? How close to the present does a 'heritage' film come? The Second World War? The 1960s? As films that re-present national history and myths to their audience, they have often been rejected by critics as conservative (Higson 1993), but are being re-assessed (Dyer 1995;

> **Ironically perhaps, popular genres require more complex decoding than art cinema, because of their closeness (through language, character's gestures, topical references) to popular culture.**

Higson 1996). Finally, heritage films are classic narrative films which on the whole do not display the self-conscious stylistic marks of European art authorship, and thus provide a good terrain to study classical *European* film style.

Heritage films' high production values include the use of stars; indeed some European stars (Emma Thompson, Gérard Depardieu) are increasingly associated with the genre, which has given them an international profile, where their predecessors traditionally attained international status through Hollywood (Marlene Dietrich, Greta Garbo) or their association with art cinema (Jeanne Moreau, Marcello Mastroianni, Liv Ullman). A few others gained global fame in their own national cinema, among them Max Linder, Jean Gabin, Sophia Loren, Brigitte Bardot (Vincendeau, Chapter 13f), Totò, Alain Delon, and Catherine Deneuve. Academic star studies (Dyer 1979, 1987; Gledhill 1991), however, have conceptualized stardom as intrinsically linked to Hollywood. And yet, there are many important European stars beyond those mentioned above who have, in Dyer's formulation, crystallized social and ideological values, have enjoyed enormous popularity in their own country, but are virtually unknown outside. Examples include: Lida Baarová (Czechoslovakia), Annabella, Bourvil, Martine Carol, Micheline Presle, and Louis de Funès (France), Zarah Leander, Willi Fritsch, and Hildegard Knef (Germany), Lola Flores and Sara Montiel (Spain), Gino Cervi and Alberto Sordi (Italy), Paula Wessely (Austria), Regina Linnanheimo (Finland).

The difficulties in studying European stars resemble the difficulties in studying European cinema. They start with the material problem of getting hold of films as well as other resources: letters, press books, popular film journals. On the other hand, these hurdles point to the originality and interest of such studies. There are three other main issues raised by the study of European stars. The first one relates to the fragmentation of the European film industry, making it difficult to identify with precision this dimension of stardom; for example, the construction by the industry of the star's image and the determinants of a 'star vehicle'. Meanwhile, budgets and detailed box-office figures are hard to get, especially for the pre-war period. The second one relates to aesthetics. In mainstream cinema, a study of a particular star needs to be aware of the genre(s) in which (s)he works. So, for instance, a study of Martine Carol needs to have a good understanding of the French costume dramas of the 1950s. As far as auteur cinema is concerned, the most interesting issue is that of the interaction between star and directorial voices. Here the relatively low attention given to European stars is in direct (inverse) relation to the attention lavished on auteurs, who in a sense *are* the stars of European cinema. Another interesting issue is the differential value a star acquires at home as opposed to internationally; for example, Mastroianni was both a popular and art cinema star at home, but only an art cinema star abroad, while Moreau, predominantly an art cinema star, has a consequently much higher reputation outside France than inside. Finally, the greatest impediment, but also the greatest reward, in studying European stars is to gain an understanding of their relationship with social, historical, and ideological values. Here, the most 'inexportable' are potentially the most interesting.

The international canon of European stars is still very narrow, and there is, correspondingly, much scope for innovative and revealing work in this area of film studies.

'European cinema': a new category

As alluded to at the beginning of this chapter, a recent expansion of studies of 'the European' in relation to the cinema has taken place, which can be understood within three contexts. The first is a boom in theoretical and historical studies of national cinema(s) and national identity. The second is the topicality of Europe on the social and political scene and the prominent role now played by the European Union *vis-à-vis* the cinema (Horrocks 1995; Finney 1996). The third relates to the severe difficulties experienced by film industries throughout Europe, due to the fiercer than ever competition from Hollywood since the mid-1980s. This has produced a sense of a beleaguered (perhaps even doomed) cinema, the condition of which needs to be documented.

With the publication of Pierre Sorlin's *European Cinemas, European Societies* (1991), of Duncan Petrie's *Screening Europe* (1992), and of Richard Dyer and my *Popular European Cinema* (1992), an area of academic study emerged. Other books followed, such as my *Encyclopedia of European Cinema* (1995), Wendy Everett's *European Identity in Cinema* (1996), and Angus Finney's *The State of European Cinema* (1996). These books adopt different methodologies: Finney's is an industry study while the others concen-

trate on aesthetics. But while Petrie (1992), Sorlin (1991), and to a large extent Everett (1996) concentrate on auteur films, Dyer and Vincendeau (1992) address popular genres. All, however, share a major concern with the nature of European cultural identity: does it exist as an entity, or is it no more than a patchwork of discrete national identities? There is a tension between a search for common features—'the European'—and a desire to isolate or preserve national specificity. New European cinema studies have reclaimed important pan-European genres and themes, for example heritage cinema and comedy, and the representation of the Second World War. Ultimately, though, national differences keep resurfacing. Even such a systematic attempt at characterizing the European film industry as an entity as Finney's frequently breaks down into national specificities ('the French case', 'the British case' . . .). At the same time, most pan-European statistics (e.g. film production) need to be broken down into national units to be meaningful. Thus scholars and viewers are thrown back on to the rich diversity of national industries, individuals, and films that constitutes European cinema.

BIBLIOGRAPHY

Abel, Richard (1984), *French Cinema: The First Wave 1915–1929* (Princeton: Princeton University Press).
—— (1988) *French Film Theory and Criticism*, 2 vols. (1907–1929, 1930–1939) (Princeton: Princeton University Press).
Allen, Robert C., and **Douglas Gomery** (1985), *Film History: Theory and Practice* (New York: Alfred A. Knopf).
Armes, Roy (1976), *The Ambiguous Image: Narrative Style in Modern European Cinema* (London: Secker & Warburg).
Balski, Grzegorz (1992), *Directory of Eastern European Film-Makers and Films 1945–1991* (Trowbridge: Flicks Books).
Bardèche, Maurice, and **Robert Brasillach** (1935), *Histoire du cinéma* (Paris: Denoël & Steele).
***Bordwell, David** (1979), 'Art Cinema as a Mode of Film Practice', *Film Criticism*, 4/1: 56–64.
—— and **Kristin Thompson** (1979/1993), *Film Art: An Introduction* (New York: McGraw-Hill).
—— **Kristen Thompson,** and **Janet Staiger** (1985), *The Classical Hollywood Cinema: Film Style and Mode of Production to 1960* (London: Routledge & Kegan Paul.
Cook, Pam (ed.) (1985), *The Cinema Book* (London: British Film Institute).
Cowie, Peter (1992), *Scandinavian Cinema: A Survey of Film and Film-Makers in Denmark, Finland, Iceland, Norway and Sweden* (London: Tantivy Press).

Crafton, Donald (1990), *Émile Cohl, Caricature and Film* (Princeton: Princeton University Press).

Crisp, Colin (1993), *The Classic French Cinema 1930–1960* (Bloomington: Indiana University Press).

Dyer, Richard (1979), *Stars* (London: British Film Institute).

—— (1987) *Heavenly Bodies: Film Stars and Society* (Basingstoke: Macmillan).

—— (1995), 'Heritage Cinema in Europe', in Vincendeau (1995).

*—— and **Ginette Vincendeau** (eds.) (1992), *Popular European Cinema* (London: Routledge).

Eisenstein, Sergel (1942), *The Film Sense*, ed. and trans. Jay Leyda (London: Faber & Faber).

—— (1949), *Film Form*, ed. and trans. Jay Leyda (New York: Harcourt Brace).

Eisner, Lotte (1952/1969), *L'Écran Démoniaque*, trans. Roger Greaves as *The Haunted Screen: Expressionism in the German Cinema and the Influence of Max Reinhardt* (London: Thames & Hudson).

Elsaesser, Thomas (1989), *New German Cinema: A History* (London: British Film Insitutue and Macmillan).

Everett, Wendy (1996), *European Identity in Cinema* (Exeter: Intellect Books).

Finney, Angus (1996), *The State of European Cinema* (London: Cassell).

Flitterman-Lewis, Sandy (1990/1993), *To Desire Differently: Feminism and the French Cinema* (Bloomington: Indiana University Press; repr. New York: Columbia University Press).

Gledhill, Christine (ed.) (1991), *Stardom, Industry of Desire* (London: Routledge).

Goulding, Daniel J. (1989) *Post New Wave Cinema in the Soviet Union and Eastern Europe* (Bloomington: Indiana University Press).

—— (1994), *Five Filmmakers: Tarkovsky, Forman, Polanski, Szabó, Makavejev* (Bloomington: Indiana University Press).

Hayward, Susan (1993), *French National Cinema* (London: Routledge).

Hewitt, Nicholas (ed.) (1989), *The Culture of Reconstruction: European Literature, Thought and Film 1945–1950* (Basingstoke: Macmillan).

Higson, Andrew (1993), 'Re-Presenting the National Past: Nostalgia and Pastiche in the Heritage Film', in Lester Friedman (ed.), British Cinema and Thatcherism (London: University College London Press).

—— (1995), *Waving the Flag: Constructing a National Cinema in Britain* (Oxford: Oxford University Press).

—— (1996), 'The Heritage Film and British Cinema', in Higson (ed.), *Dissolving Views: Key Writings on British Cinema* (London: Cassell).

Hill, John, Martin McCloone, and **Paul Hainsworth** (eds.) (1994), *Border Crossing: Film in Ireland, Britain and Europe* (Belfast: Institute of Irish Studies; London: British Film Institute).

Hillier, Jim (ed.) (1985), *Cahiers du cinéma*, i: *The 1950s* (London: Routledge & Kegan Paul).

—— (1986), *Cahiers du cinéma*, ii: *The 1960s* (London: Routledge & Kegan Paul).

Horrocks, Simon (1995), 'The European Community and the Cinema', in Vincendeau (1995).

Jeancolas, Jean-Pierre (1992), 'The Inexportable: The Case of French Cinema and Radio in the 1950s', in Dyer and Vincendeau (1992).

Kracauer, Siegfried (1947), *From Caligari to Hitler* (Princeton: Princeton University Press).

Liehm, Mira, and **J. Antonin** (1977), *The Most Important Art: East European Film after 1945* (Berkeley: University of California Press).

Marcus, Millicent (1986), *Italian Film in the Light of Neo-Realism* (Princeton: Princeton University Press).

Mulvey, Laura (1996) 'The Hole and the Zero', in *Fetishism and Curiosity* (London: British Film Institute).

***Neale, Stephen** (1981), 'Art Cinema as Institution', *Screen*, 22/1: 11–39.

Nowell-Smith, Geoffrey (ed.) (1996), *The Oxford History of World Cinema* (Oxford: Oxford University Press).

Petrie, Duncan (1992), *Screening Europe* (London: British Film Institute).

Portuges, Catherine (1993), *Screen Memories: The Hungarian Cinema of Márta Mészáros* (Bloomington: Indiana University Press).

Rentschler, Eric (1996), *The Ministry of Illusion, Nazi Cinema and its Afterlife* (Cambridge, Mass.: Harvard University Press).

Rotha, Paul (1936) *Documentary Film* (London: Faber & Faber).

Roud, Richard (1983), *A Passion for Films: Henri Langlois and the Cinémathèque Française* (London: Secker & Warburg).

Sadoul, Georges (1953), *French Film* (London: Falcon Press).

Salt, Barry (1983), *Film Style and Technology: History and Analysis* (London: Starword).

Smith, Paul Julian (1994), *Desire Unlimited: The Cinema of Pedro Almodóvar* (London: Verso).

***Sorlin, Pierre** (1991) *European Cinemas, European Societies* (London: Routledge).

Turk, Edward Baron (1989), *Child of Paradise: Marcel Carné and the Golden Age of French Cinema* (Cambridge, Mass.: Harvard University Press).

***Vincendeau, Ginette** (ed.), (1995) *The Encyclopedia of European Cinema* (London: Cassell and British Film Institute).

Williams, Alan (1992), *Republic of Images: A History of French Filmmaking* (Cambridge, Mass.: Harvard University Press).

7

The avant-gardes and European cinema before 1930

Ian Christie

The 1920s golden age of avant-garde film might be said to have culminated in an international conference held at La Sarraz in Switzerland in 1929. Here film-makers from a dozen countries gathered to discuss possible forms of co-operation in production and distribution. They also made a collective film, *Storm over La Sarraz*, which is lost—or perhaps was never completed (Montagu 1968). For, despite its resolutions and plans, La Sarraz left little trace, except the idea of an independent cinema, both avant-garde and international, which would soon fragment and retreat in the face of political confrontation in the 1930s. Its legacy, however, would prove powerful. For when synoptic histories of cinema first began to be written in that decade, a handful of Soviet, French, and German avant-garde classics—the films of Sergei Eisenstein, Dziga Vertov, René Clair, G. W. Pabst, Walter Ruttman—came to occupy a disproportionate space compared with the bulk of the mainstream cinema of this period, an anomaly which has largely persisted.

Although the earliest instances of modernist artists planning and making films were in Russia and Italy in the 1910s, it was in the 1920s that the term 'avant-garde' began to be applied to film, as part of a new kind of discourse about cinema (Elliott 1986; Kirby 1971). What proved crucial was the self-definition of a group of French filmmakers, who were also active as critics and theorists. Louis Delluc and Jean Epstein, together with Abel Gance, Marcel L'Herbier, Germaine Dulac, and Henri Chomette, all subscribed to a preoccupation with film's 'specificity', in order to demonstrate the legitimacy of cinema as an art in its own right. Their films ranged from short experiments, like Chomette's *Five Minutes of Pure Cinema* (1925), to Gance's six-hour epic *Napoléon* (1927), but they shared a common interest in exploring the optical and psychological power of the film image, focusing on the concept of *photogénie* (Willemen 1994). They also spawned a support system of film clubs, specialized cinemas, and magazines, all devoted to the promotion of film as a modern art; and this network soon spread beyond France, creating a sympathetic context for innovative work from elsewhere.

By the end of the 1920s more mainstream critics had institutionalized the avant-garde as a kind of 'R & D' department, present to a greater or lesser degree in most major national schools of filmmaking. Thus Paul Rotha, in his pioneering world survey *The Film till Now* (1930), defended the French avant-garde as 'an excellent grounding for the young film director' (211), providing 'object lessons in cinematic values', which in turn 'should be of the utmost interest to the big-scale director' (227). And when discussing the limitations of British cinema, he noted as a factor that 'there has never been any school of *avant-garde* in England', The critic C. A. Lejeune invoked a similar rationale: 'the value of the experimental film lies less frequently in achievement than in suggestion, in the fact that it precedes mature work' (1931: 205). She also maintained that experimental films could help free movies from their 'one great obsession' with the human figure.

But if the avant-gardes were gaining mainstream acceptance, they had also already come under fire from a number of positions which equally could be—and often are—considered avant-garde. First came the attack of the Soviet left, also composed of filmmaker-critics, and led by Eisenstein. In a polemical reply to a 1926 German article, Eisenstein challenged the claim that Soviet montage films, like all serious cinema, depended on the 'figurative quality of the [individual] shot' (1926: 79). Instead of 'literary' or 'pictorial', shots, Eisenstein argued for the 'director's' or 'compositional' shot, which is conceived as an integral part of the montage sequence; and in doing so he dismissed the work of the French avant-garde as 'children's playthings', which merely exploit 'the photographic possibilities of the apparatus'—in terms similar to those he would also use against his equally polemical Soviet contemporary Dziga Vertov.

Neither Eisenstein nor the other new Soviet filmmakers who emerged after 1924 would have accepted the label 'avant-garde', regarding it as symptomatic of a bourgeois conception of art. Yet they were committed to challenging Soviet audiences' conservatism by means of experiment; and such experiments, as Leonid Trauberg argued, would often not be, at first, 'intelligible to the millions' (1929: 250). This may seem broadly similar to the western 'R & D' concept of an avant-garde, but in fact the Soviet left's refusal of avant-garde status and willingness to 'battle with pub-

lic taste' marked a rejection both of the autonomy of aesthetics and of an implicitly élitist view of art. As Eisenstein and Grigori Alexandrov admitted of *The General Line* (1929), 'while rejecting the glitter of external formal searches, it is inescapably an experiment', but one which they hoped would be, 'however contradictory it may sound . . . *intelligible to the millions*' (Eisenstein and Alexandrov 1929: 257).

Another challenge to the self-declared French avant-garde in the late 1920s came from closer to home. The Surrealist movement, composed initially of writers, although with a growing number of visual artists, declared its opposition to all conventional art in the name of a call to revolt. Surrealist activity, in whatever genre, aimed to provoke, to scandalize, and to seek new forms of self-expression and pleasure. As such, it could easily be seen—and was—as yet another faction within the avant-garde. But Surrealists vigorously rejected this conscription, venting their outrage particularly on avant-garde work which seemed close to Surrealism in its themes, such as Dulac's realization of a scenario by the Surrealist Antonin Artaud, *The Seashell and the Clergyman* (France, 1927), or Epstein's adaptation of Edgar Allan Poe's *The Fall of the House of Usher* (France, 1928). When Luis Buñuel and Salvador Dali followed Surrealist precepts to make one of that movement's first authentic films *Un chien andalou* (France, 1929), they proclaimed a break with the French avant-garde tradition, yet the film's shock tactics and its early success clearly owe much to that same tradition.

The Surrealist and Soviet 'anti-avant-gardes' were to have a lasting influence on the cinema at large, far beyond the relatively short duration of the original movements. Their key films became the 'classics' of the 1920s, when histories of cinema began to be written in the following decade, and have largely remained so ever since. The prestige of their leading figures—Eisenstein, Pudovkin, and Vertov; Buñuel, Dali, and Jean Vigo—became linked to the appeal of Soviet montage's dialectic and of the Surrealist belief in the unconscious as cyphers for Marxism and Freudianism respectively. Thanks in large part to these alliances, film was acquiring a new status, which allowed it to engage with the most serious cultural and political issues of the day.

By 1930 the new film culture spawned by the avant-gardes had produced its own radical film clubs, magazines, distribution networks—and an emerging generation of filmmakers and activists already steeped in

The Surrealist and Soviet 'anti-avant-gardes' were to have a lasting influence on the cinema at large, far beyond the relatively short duration of the original movements. Their key films became the 'classics' of the 1920s, when histories of cinema began to be written in the following decade, and have largely remained so ever since.

the ideologies and debates of the rival avant-gardes. Many of these would become leaders of the documentary movements which were typical of the 1930s: figures like John Grierson, Ivor Montagu, Len Lye, and Humphrey Jennings in Britain, Joris Ivens in the Netherlands, and Henri Storck in Belgium. In effect, documentary became an 'applied' avant-garde, inheriting much of its theory and practice from the avant-gardes of the previous decade, while recasting these in instrumental rhetorics of information, revelation, or mobilization, depending on who, if anyone, was the sponsor (Winston 1995).

The fact that much pioneering cinema history was written under the influence of the early Soviet and/or Surrealist positions has meant that the received history of film still echoes many of the original battles, and indeed often follows the contours of these highly polemical movements. A good example of this kind of 'engaged' history is an account of the French avant-garde of the 1920s by the Surrealist critic and filmmaker Jacques Brunius, who remained in Britain after the war and was prompted to write his essay by rumours of a new avant-garde emerging in America (Brunius 1948). Brunius stresses how the French avant-garde emerged from a combination of dissatisfaction with existing French cinema at the end of the First World War and the new stimuli of German Expressionism, American comedy, Swedish mysticism, and Soviet montage. He dismisses much of its output as pretentious, but defends the importance of the aesthetic issues it raised and the need to break 'the routine of a developing academicism', which in turn paved the way for French cinema's great achievements in the more accessible genres of satirical comedy and poetic realism in the 1930s.

This long-term dialectical view of the relationship between avant-garde and mainstream marks an advance on the Rotha–Lejeune laboratory view, and introduces an important historial perspective. But the lasting influence of Surrealism on critical opinion was to reinforce antagonism towards any idea of a distinct

Entr'acte (1924)—Dada meets cinema in this cornerstone of the 'historic avant-garde', which was originally commissioned to be shown during the interval of the ballet *Relâche*

avant-garde, replacing this with a wide-ranging selection of films chosen for their largely unintended qualities of *amour fou*, incongruity, *näiveté*, fantasy, and the like—a selection of 'involuntary Surrealist' works by such as Georges Méliès, Louis Feuillade, Charlie Chaplin, F. W. Murnau, but also by Mack Sennett, Tod Browning, Albert Lewin, Joseph H. Lewis, and many lesser names (French Surrealist Group 1951). Against this pantheon, the Surrealists set a list of filmmakers to *avoid*, which included, as well as the entire French avant-garde of the 1920s, Walt Disney, Carl Theodor Dryer, D. W. Griffith, Ernst Lubitsch, Alexander Dovzhenko, and many who would be regarded by others as 'surrealist' (French Surrealist Group 1951). This also featured two particular Surrealist *bêtes noirs*, Fernand Léger and Jean Cocteau, creators of two of the most remarkable and influential avant-garde films of the 1920s, *Ballet mécanique* (France, 1924) and *Le Sang d'un poète* (France, 1930).

Fairness, of course, was not the point. The grounds for rejection of most deliberately avant-garde work were precisely that it *was* deliberate: 'intellectual' or 'literary' were Surrealist terms of abuse. As an exercise in radical revisionism, the post-Second World War Surrealist intervention was to prove influential far beyond the narrow confines of the group, encouraging interest in many areas of genre cinema and establishing a counter-canon (in opposition to the traditional realist histories of cinema) which is still recognizably the basis of much French and French-inspired criticism. But in doing so, it created a strong antagonism against the non-Surrealist avant-garde which long discouraged many from investigating this at first hand. For example, it was not until the feminist film movement of the 1970s began to research forgotten women directors that Germaine Dulac—effectively stigmatized by the Surrealists—was actually shown and reassessed.

What encouraged a widespread renewal of interest in avant-garde film in the 1970s was no doubt in part a search for ancestry or legitimization by a new generation of critics who were also often filmmakers—and avant-garde either by choice or by economic necessity. The sheer variety and vigour of contemporary avant-garde production in the late 1960s and early 1970s resulted not only from a growing radicalization of the European 'new wave' art cinema of Jean-Luc Godard, Jean-Marie Straub, and Danièle Huillet and Dušan Makavejev, but also from the burgeoning American 'underground' of Jonas Mekas, Jack Smith, and Andy Warhol, and also from the Third World, with the challenging agitational work of the Argentinians Fernando Solanas and Octavio Getino, the Cuban Santiago Alvarez, and the mythopoeic cinema of the Brazilian Glauber Rocha; and from the network of filmmakers' co-operatives which sprang up across Europe.

Against this background, a new historiography began to emerge, articulated first in the United States by way of explaining the ancestry of 'new American cinema' (Renan 1968), then in a more balanced form in David Curtis's *Experimental Cinema* (1971), subtitled 'A Fifty Year Evolution' and in a number of works by UK-based filmmakers. Curtis included in his survey, not only the European avant-gardes of the 1920s and the American post-war 'underground', but also numerous examples of creativity and 'personal' filmmaking in the margins of industrial production, such as the Serbian special-effects expert Slavko Vorkapich working in Hollywood during the 1920s and 1930s. Similar trajectories were followed in two 'participant-observer' accounts, by the filmmakers and teachers Stephen Dwoskin and Malcolm Le Grice, which effectively traced a parallel history to that of narrative cinema (Dwoskin 1975; Le Grice 1977). Le Grice, a leader of the structural school of filmmaking and performance in Britain, naturally saw in much of the Cubist and abstract film of the 1920s the ancestry of his own work.

In the midst of this alternative canon-making, another intervention by a critic-filmmaker, Peter Wollen's influential essay 'The Two Avant-Gardes' (1982) sought to mediate between what seemed to be two polarized traditions within the avant-garde, those of artists' film and radicalized art cinema (see Smith, Part 3, Chapter 2, for another treatment of Wollen's argument). Using a semiotic terminology, Wollen argued that any attempt to distinguish these as 'formal' and 'political' was simplistic, since both traditions included what could be considered work on the signifier and on the signified, although to differing degrees in different periods. His declared aim, 'writing as a filmmaker', was in fact to create a sympathetic climate for new work that would draw on both traditions and create a 'third'—or mixed—avant-garde (Wollen 1981).

But Wollen's appeal for a truce and mutual understanding, although influential in terms of reopening theoretical interest in the historical avant-gardes, did not silence debate. In a move intended to counter the recuperation of the avant-garde, Paul Willemen proposed to 'rearrange' Wollen's celebrated two avant-gardes into 'an opposition between avant-garde and modernism' (Willemen 1984/1994: 148). According to this view, the tradition identified by Wollen as concerned with semiotic reduction and reflexiveness is effectively what modernism has become in the twentieth century—a conservative force seeking to preserve art's traditional autonomy by new formal means—while his 'other' avant-garde, which challenges purism and seeks expansion of the semiotic range, is the true avant-garde, constantly posing problems of reference—to politics and to life.

The idea of an avant-garde cannot, by its nature, be static or agreed. It is perhaps best understood as, in the philosophers' term, an essentially contested concept, always open to dispute or redefinition. As recently as 1968 it was possible for the critic Andrew Sarris to introduce his encyclopaedic survey of American cinema in the sound era with an attack on the idea that 'avant-garde movies point the way for commercial movies' (Sarris 1968). On the contrary, Sarris insisted, avant-garde filmmakers have usually been more conservative about technology than their commercial contemporaries. In terms of meaning, he was even more dismissive: 'few avant-garde mannerisms can stand for long the withering gaze of the camera'. After the debates and the rediscoveries of the 1970s and 1980s, such attitudes seem antediluvian. The 'historic' avant-gardes of the 1920s are still being explored; neglected work comes to light; and the known threshold of avant-garde film activity itself is pushed back to the early years of the century, contemporary with the birth of the seminal Futurist and Cubist avant-gardes out of late Symbolism (Christie 1995).

But even as the historiography of the avant-gardes grows more sophisticated, this prompts new debates. The concept of the avant-garde has seemed intrinsically European—perhaps, indeed, a differentiating feature of European cinema in the post-First World War era, when Hollywood began to consolidate its global domination. But does the specificity of individual avant-garde productions and ideologies not also undermine any overarching concept of 'Europe'? Philip Dodd has suggested, in the context of questioning notions of European identity, that perhaps 'we should no longer think of Buñuel and Dali's *Un Chien Andalou* as a European movie but as a part of Catalan modernism' (Dodd 1992). Similar questions of identity could be posed in any number of cases from the historic avant-gardes: *Ballet mécanique* as a cross between American West Coast modernism, via Dudley

Murphy, and Léger's late Parisian Cubism; Len Lye bringing Oceanic neo-primitivist influences to bear on his work in Britain in the late 1920s and 1930s; or Vorkapich as part of the exiled Serbian Futurist (Zenithist) diaspora. At issue in all such cases, it would seem, is what force, or value, or even topography, we assign to 'Europe'—that Europe is or was the crucial *site* of avant-garde film is not in question.

> **The concept of the avant-garde has seemed intrinsically European—perhaps, indeed, a differentiating feature of European cinema in the post-First World War era, when Hollywood began to consolidate its global domination.**

However, the most fundamental question, implicit in many recent interventions, is whether it makes sense to continue thinking of *any* film as 'avant-garde', instead of as an 'independent' or an artist's film. To the legendary La Sarraz conference more recent scholarship has added another late 1920s focus for the concept of independent cinema, now conceived more as a process and discourse (which was also how the attenders at La Sarraz saw it). This is the linked publishing and production activity of the Pool group, led by Bryher and Kenneth Macpherson, which published the journal *Close Up* between 1927 and 1932 and produced a pioneering psychoanalytic film, *Borderline*, in 1930 (Cosandey 1985; Christie 1996). Meanwhile, as Walter Benjamin noted in the mid-1930s, 'Dadaism attempted to create by pictorial—and literary—means the effects which the public today seeks in the film' (Benjamin 1936). Certainly many of the aspirations which drove avant-garde art in the first quarter of the twentieth century subsequently found expression in film (and later in other moving-image media), and so escaped the aura of avant-gardism. Thus the avant-garde, in Benjamin's sense and perhaps in Curtis's or Wollen's, is all about us, distinguished only by its artisanal point of production and its attack on preconceptions of a what a film, video, or CD-ROM should be.

BIBLIOGRAPHY

Benjamin, Walter (1936/1978), 'The Work of Art in the Age of Mechanical Reproduction', in *Illuminations* (London: Fontana-Collins).

Brunius, Jacques (1948), 'Rise and Decline of an "Avant-Garde"', in *Penguin Film Review*, v (London: Penguin).

Christie, Ian (1995), 'L'Avant-garde internationale et le cinéma', in E. Toulet (ed.), *Le Cinéma au rendez-vous des arts: France, années 20 et 30* (Paris: Bibliothèque nationale).

—— (1996), 'The Odd Couple', in Phillip Dodd and Ian Christie (eds.), *Spellbound: Art and Film* (London: Hayward Gallery and British Film Institute).

Cosandey, Roland (1985), 'On *Borderline*: Reassessing a Lost Film', *Afterimage*, 12 (Autumn).

Curtis, David (1971), *Experimental Cinema: A Fifty Year Evolution* (London: Studio Vista).

Dodd, P. (1992), 'Introduction to Saturday Morning Session, in Duncan Petrie, (ed.) *Screening Europe: Image and Identity in Contemporary European Cinema* (London: British Film Institute).

Dwoskin, Stephen (1975), *Film Is* (London: Peter Evans).

Eisenstein, Sergei (1926/1988), 'Bela Forgets the Scissors', in Taylor (1988).

—— and Grigori Alexandrov (1929/1988), 'An Experiment Intelligible to the Millions', in Taylor and Christie (1988).

Elliott, David (1986), *New Worlds: Russian Art and Society 1900–1937* (London: Thames & Hudson).

French Surrealist Group (1951/1978), 'Some Surrealist Advice' in Hammond (1978).

Hammond, Paul (ed.) (1978), *The Shadow and its Shadow: Surrealist Writings on Cinema* (London: British Film Institute).

Kirby, Michael (1971), *Futurist Performance* (New York: Dutton).

Le Grice, Malcolm (1977), *Abstract Film and Beyond* (London: Studio Vista).

Lejeune, C. A. (1931), *Cinema* (London: Alexander Maclehose).

Montagu, Ivor (1968), *With Eisenstein in Hollywood* (Berlin: Seven Seas).

Renan, Sheldon (1968), *The Underground Film* (London: Studio Vista).

Rotha, Paul (1930), *The Film till Now* (London: Jonathan Cape).

Sarris, Andrew (1968), *The American Cinema: Directors and Directions* (New York: Dutton).

Taylor, Richard, and Ian Christie (eds.) (1988), *The Film Factory: Russian and Soviet Cinema in Documents* (London: Routledge).

Trauberg, Leonid (1929/1988), 'An Experiment Intelligible to the Millions', in Taylor and Christie (1988).

Willemen, Paul (1984), 'An Avant-Garde for the 80s', *Framework*, 24 (Spring), 53–73; repr. as 'An Avant-Garde for the 90s' in Willemen (1994).

—— (1994), *Looks and Frictions* (London: British Film Institute). See esp. 'Photogénie and Epstein'.

Winston, Brian (1995), *Claiming the Real: The Documentary Film Revisited* (London: British Film Institute).

Wollen, Peter (1981), 'The Avant-Gardes: Europe and America' *Framework*, 14, (Spring): 9–10.

—— (1982), 'The Two Avant-Gardes', in *Readings and Writings* (London: Verso).

8

Italian post-war cinema and Neo-Realism

Simona Monticelli

Accounts of the history of Italian cinema are dominated by the critical centrality of a cluster of films made between the mid-1940s and the mid-1950s and commonly described as Neo-Realist. The films themselves are relatively few, constituting no more than eighty or ninety over a period in which domestic film production figures were ten times larger. Yet discussion of these films has been substantial and has encompassed a complex range of theoretical, methodological, and historiographical debates.

The bulk of Neo-Realist films were made at a particularly sensitive time in the history of contemporary Italy, as the country emerged from over twenty years of fascist dictatorship (lasting from 1922 to 1943). In the immediate post-war years, Neo-Realist films provided an immediate response to the desire to wipe out the material and ideological legacies of fascism. They denounced the horrors of the war and/or dealt with themes central to the agency of Reconstruction such as poverty, unemployment, shortage of housing, and social strife. Moreover, in their social and geographical inclusiveness, they represented a bid to redefine the co-ordinates of national and cultural identity uncontaminated by the legacy of fascism.

Central to this discourse was the construction of fascism itself as the antithesis of truth and authenticity. The realism of films like *Roma città aperta* ('Rome Open City', Roberto Rossellini, 1945), and *Ladri di biciclette* ('Bicycle Thieves', Vittorio De Sica, 1948) was perceived as a rejection of the distortions of fascist ideology and the culture it had engendered. As such, Neo-Realism was construed as constituting a radial break from the practices and values which had informed film production during the fascist regime. This, in turn, depended upon the almost wholesale condemnation of the Italian cinema produced during the regime which was mostly dismissed as vacuous entertainment (e.g. 'white telephone' comedies) or bougeois formalism (e.g. 'calligraphic style').

Accordingly, Neo-Realist films may be seen to depart quite radically from the conventions and production values of the studio system of the 1930s. Location shooting and use of available light resulted in more naturalistic photography, closer to the documentary than to the studio-made fiction film. In addition, the contemporary topicality of subject-matter, the focus on the lower-class milieux, and the casting of unglamorous minor stars, or even unknown non-professional actors, further distinguished the films from both indigenous studio productions and those of Hollywood. However, although these developments are characterized as entailing a significant break with pre-war Italian cinema and undoubtedly acquired tremendous poignancy in the post-war period, their use was not entirely new.

Worthy artistic experimentations such as *1860* (Alessandro Blasetti, 1933), or fictionalized documentaries such as *La nave bianca* ('The White Ship', Roberto

'A rejection of the distortions of fascist ideology'—*Roma città aperta* (1945)

Rossellini, 1941) had already made use of similar representational strategies, involving real locations and non-professional performers, while, since the silent era, a range of subgenres rooted in regional theatrical traditions had represented popular milieux with their distinct local character. As a result, it is interesting to note that the first film to be credited as Neo-Realist, *Roma città aperta*, can be seen to draw on both these documentary and subgeneric strands. Trained as a documentary filmmaker, director Roberto Rossellini also cast as his leads two actors, Anna Magnani and Aldo Fabrizi, who had made their names on the Roman vaudeville scene and who had previously duetted in popular film comedies such as *Campo de'fiori* (Mario Bonnard, 1943) and *L'ultima carrozzella* (Mario Mattoli, 1943).

What this suggests is that the Neo-Realist corpus does not display the degree of stylistic coherency that would allow for easy categorization (and, indeed, the definition and selection of films seen to represent 'Neo-Realism' has been a matter of some dispute). The evidence of the films themselves is complicated. Some films may be seen to be clearly indebted to popular forms of entertainment and existing film genres. Other films may be more aptly described as 'art cinema'. In some cases, from *Roma città aperta* to *Riso amaro* ('Bitter Rice' Giuseppe De Santis, 1949), it is simply

not possible to make a clear-cut categorization (and, indeed, a part of their novelty consists of the blurring of distinctions between 'art' and 'popular' cinema). The evidence of the films' commercial success is therefore varied, with a few hugely successful hits and a number of disastrous flops. However, on the whole the box-office performance of Neo-Realist films was respectable, albeit uneven.

These difficulties in identifying a clear set of features specific to Neo-Realist cinema are compounded by the persistence of uncertainties over the origins of the term 'Neo-Realism' and its semantic content. What is clear, however, is that the word cannot be traced back to the consciously thought out and publicly circulated manifesto of a movement. On the contrary, the term 'Neo-Realism' is a descriptive category which has evolved through critical discourse. As a result, the meaning and use of the term have been closely linked to developments in the theory and practice of film criticism and historiography.

It seems that the film editor Mario Serandrei was among the first to use the word when, in a letter to director Luchino Visconti, he employed it with reference to *Ossessione* (Luchino Visconti, 1943) (quoted in Fofi and Faldini, 1979). Indeed, because of its use of real locations and uncompromisingly grim portrayal of the provincial fringes of Italian society during fascism,

Ossessione has generally been regarded as a harbinger of post-war Neo-Realism. Serandrei's use of the term was one of a few isolated instances of its occurrence before the end of the war and was possibly the first instance of its use in relation to an Italian film, rather than to literature or to the French films of Marcel Carné and Jean Renoir.

The context in which *Ossessione* was produced and described as a Neo-Realist film, however, raises some interesting historical issues. Throughout the early 1940s Visconti and the screenwriters of *Ossessione*, Giuseppe De Santis, Mario Alicata, and Gianni Puccini, were writing articles for the specialist film journal *Cinema*, edited by Benito Mussolini's son Vittorio. Their articles, some of which are reprinted in Overbey (1978), insisted on the necessity of using realism in the development of a national film language. In doing so, they suggested models from both an indigenous tradition of high cultural literature and painting and from film styles, such as French poetic realism, and even, on occasions, from Hollywood film genres, such as the 1930s gangster film. The strongest emphasis, however, was placed on the power of landscape—and the human presence within it—to act as signifiers of Italian cultural identity.

Significant though these writings were, they do not fully account for the emergence of Neo-Realism, which must be traced to a much wider range of developments in Italian film production and critical discourse from the pre-war to the post-war period. In terms of critical discourse, moreover, the term 'Neo-Realism' did not acquire wide critical currency until the late 1940s, when it was also invested with a new range of meanings. Indeed, during the post-war years, it was the international critical acclaim with which some Italian films were recieved on the fast-growing art-house circuit which was to play a decisive role in shaping the canon of films and authors to which the term 'Neo-Realism' was applied.

What is clear, however, is that the word cannot be traced back to the consciously thought out and publicly circulated manifesto of a movement. On the contrary, the term 'Neo-Realism' is a descriptive category which has evolved through critical discourse.

It was the French critic André Bazin, in particular, who was to express highly influential views regarding the essence of the Neo-Realist phenomenon (Bazin 1971). Bazin's concern with the definition of an ontology of film language, and his belief that genuine film art derives from a phenomenological rather than analytical approach to the real, was strongly linked to his appraisal of Neo-Realism. He particularly valued a number of formal traits found in Rossellini's films such as elliptical narrative structure, the rejection of plot-enhancing detail, unpredictability of character motivation, use of long takes, and the preference for medium and long shots and rejection of close-ups. As a result of Bazin's influence, these formal traits became common terms in the description of the Neo-Realist style. This was not without its problems, however. Indeed, Bazin himself faced some difficulty in reconciling his enthusiasm for Rossellini's phenomenological approach with his own praise for *Ladri di biciclette*, which displayed a much more conventional use of camera style and continuity editing.

Moreover, while Bazin acknowledged the importance of the historical circumstances in which Neo-Realism had emerged, he did not see them as an essential part of its novelty or significance. In contrast, it was precisely a concern with these historical circumstances which structured the debate on Neo-Realism taking place in Italy. There, it was the construction of Neo-Realism as a movement with specifically national roots which defined the parameters of the term's currency in the critical discourse of leftist intellectuals. These writers were particularly concerned with placing Neo-Realism at the very core of the cultural reconstruction of post-war, post-fascist Italy. Indeed, it was in the late 1940s, when the Cold War was beginning and the anti-fascist political front was breaking down, that the most intense period of debate around Neo-Realist cinema took place.

The parties of the left, and in particular the Communist Party (PCI), had been at the forefront of the anti-fascist Resistance; the PCI enjoyed considerable popular support, but soon after the war it was marginalized from the institutional political mainstream occupied by the conservative Christian Democrats (DC). The championing of Neo-Realism on the part of leftist intellectuals was consistent with the aim of reasserting the credentials of the left as the 'true' representative of a genuine national-popular tradition against both the persisting legacies of fascism and overwhelming American influence in the life and politics of the country.

This is not to say, however, that the conceptualizations of Neo-Realism inside and outside Italy were entirely incompatible. For what was shared was an unqualified support for the absolute artistic and moral value of realist aesthetics. The equation of realism with film art and the opposition of realism to the standardized conventions of entertainment film therefore figure prominently in all the writings of this period. There were, none the less, differences and disagreements over the scope and aims of the commitment to realism as well as conflicting concepts of what constituted the 'essence' of the real.

Perhaps the most compelling definition of Neo-Realism in this period remains the one formulated by Cesare Zavattini, the screenwriter who teamed up regularly with Vittorio De Sica to produce such key Neo-Realist works as *Ladri di biciclette* and *Umberto D* (Vittorio De Sica, 1952). Zavattini maintained that the greatest achievement of Neo-Realist cinema was that it brought onto the screen the lives of ordinary people. This contrasted with more conventionally constructed fictions which fascinated their audiences but bore no relation to their experience outside of the cinema. For Zavattini, the aim of Neo-Realism had to be to rediscover, without embellishment or dramatization, the 'dailiness' of people's lives. He argued that the most minute and apparently insignificant detail of these lives was full of poetry as well as the 'echoes and reverberations' of the human condition (Zavattini 1953).

> **For Zavattini, the aim of Neo-Realism had to be to rediscover, without embellishment or dramatization, the 'dailiness' of people's lives. He argued that the most minute and apparently insignificant detail of these lives was full of poetry as well as the 'echoes and reverberations' of the human condition.**

Other critics and filmmakers such as Luigi Chiarini, Giuseppe De Santis, Carlo Lizzani, and the editor of the Marxist journal *Cinema nuovo*, Guido Aristarco, were more explicit in placing the representation of social reality at the very core of the aesthetic and ethical commitments of Neo-Realism. From their perspective, the roots of the phenomenon in the socially progressive ideals of the Resistance represented its innermost essence. Thus, the promotion of a democratic sense of collective identity for the Italian people, and more specifically for the working classes, was considered the primary aim of Neo-Realism.

Writing in the 1950s, Guido Aristarco insisted that, to remain faithful to its original impulse, Neo-Realism had to evolve, making the leap from 'chronicle to history', from 'short story to novel' (Aristarco 1975). Only in making this leap, he argued, would the films produce a thorough understanding of the conflicts and dynamics of social and historical processes. In doing so, Aristarco favoured the novelistic narrative structure and sense of clear character development characteristic of nineteenth-century literary realism. However, as Nowell-Smith (1976–7) observes, Aristarco's choice of artistic models was anachronistic even for the time when he was writing. Moreover, the line adopted by Aristarco and others at *Cinema nuovo* also exemplified a more general failure to take into full account the material modes of production, distribution, and consumption of film texts. This, in turn, had consequences for the way the development of Neo-Realism was critically assessed in the 1950s.

The critical discourse of the 1950s was dominated by a concern with the commercial and political bastardization of Neo-Realism. From the late 1940s onwards, new generic strands of the sentimental comedy (i.e. 'pink Neo-Realism') and melodrama (i.e. 'popular Neo-Realism') were at the forefront of the commercial resurgence of the domestic product. These films incorporated elements of mise-en-scène and thematic motifs from their worthier Neo-Realist predecessors, but they were generally denounced by critics, who saw in them a victory for commercialism and escapism over art and engagement (views which then necessarily reinforced a split between *cinema d'autore* (auteur or art cinema), on the one hand, and genre production, on the other). However, the attachment of many critics to criteria of Neo-Realist purity also complicated the discussion of the films made by those authors who had originally been most closely identified with Neo-Realism.

In diverse ways *Riso amaro*, *Stromboli terra di Dio* ('Stromboli', Roberto Rossellini, 1951), *L'oro di Napoli* ('Gold of Naples', Vittorio De Sica, 1954), *Senso* (Luchino Visconti, 1954), and *La strada* (Federico Fellini, 1954), to name only a few of the most controversial cases, all departed from understood Neo-Realist orthodoxies. Throughout the 1950s Rossellini and Fellini defended the integrity and coherence of their work against what they saw as an imposition of ideological restrictions on the development of a 'new way of seeing' (see Overbey 1978; Bondanella 1978). In 1956, in a letter to Guido Aristarco, André Bazin reiterated this point, arguing that Rossellini and Fellini had remained faithful to the spirit of Neo-Realism in their aesthetic approach to the wholeness of human reality, its ambiguity and resistance to analysis (Bazin 1971). Aristarco, on the other hand, admired the formal accomplishments of the two authors' films, but, in branding them spiritualistic and individualistic, emphatically rejected the idea that they were truly realist or free from ideological considerations.

While these debates revealed differences regarding the relationship between form and content, and between art and ideology, in Neo-Realism there was none the less a shared belief in the value of a realist aesthetic. From the early 1960s onwards, however, a series of challenges were waged against existing definitions of Neo-Realism as an inherently innovative and progressive phenomenon. One of the most serious of these challenges stemmed from the reassessment of the historiography of fascism, the Resistance, and the post-war settlement. The radical left developing on the fringes of the Communist Party mounted a harsh critique of the Resistance politics pursued by the PCI, the culture of Reconstruction, and the ways the legacies of fascism had been negotiated in post-war Italy. It was argued that, far from marking a break with the past regime, the culture of Reconstruction was characterized by long-term continuities in the history of Italian culture and politics, continuities to which fascism had itself accommodated. From this point of view, the idealist and humanist core of bourgeois cultural traditions and the perpetuation of the hegemony were viewed as central facets of the post-war organization of consensus and its continuity with the past.

This critique inevitably queried received ideas about Neo-Realism as an innovative practice springing from the rejection of fascist rhetoric and representing a genuine expression of the national-popular character. Instead, new historiographical perspectives suggested that the genesis of Neo-Realism could be traced in discourses and practices already existing within fascist culture and that it had never really challenged the Establishment, nor its post-war reorganization (see Cannella 1973–4; Rohdie 1981). Salutary though such revisionist work has been, its polemical slant has none the less tempted it towards claims and dismissals that are as monolithic in their character as the accounts which they have sought to challenge.

A further challenge to Neo-Realist orthodoxy, however, has come from the theoretical and methodological development of non-realist, or frankly anti-realist, positions in film criticism (see Easthope, Part 1, Chapter 6). As a result of these developments, it has become increasingly difficult to fasten definitions of Neo-Realist aesthetics to an ontology of film language free from ideological determinations (see Micciché 1975; Williams 1973–4; Bettettini 1975).

A positive consequence of this phase of deconstruction, conducted on the two fronts of previous definitions of Neo-Realism, was to open the study of the films to perspectives no longer concerned with identifying Neo-Realism with some kind of 'essence' which then had to be defended against subsequent developments. On the other hand, the effects of this process have often been disorientating, questioning the very need for, and validity of, a distinct descriptive category of Neo-Realism and rendering its contours both conceptually and historiographically nebulous.

More recent work, however, has reinstated some of Neo-Realism's importance for the study of Italian film history by providing a more detailed and exhaustive picture of the modes of production and consumption of film culture in post-war Italy. An important development in this respect has been the renegotiation of the boundaries between film and cultural studies, which has led to a greater emphasis on the role which film plays in relation to a nation's cultural history. Therefore, outside Italy, the area of Italian studies has provided many fresh insights into the position of Neo-Realist cinema in Italian culture (see Hewitt 1989; Baranski and Lumley 1990; Wagstaff and Duggan 1995). In such work, the impact of Neo-Realism on domestic production has been analysed in relation to the viewing habits of Italian filmgoers in the 1940s and 1950s, the structures and institutions which regulated these habits and defined the scope of viewer's semantic competence. Neo-Realist films have also been studied for their relations with a wider spectrum of discursive and iconographical components of Italian culture. And, within this wider network of references, the question of the breaks and continuities which characterize the development of Neo-Realism has also been re-examined (see Dalle Vacche 1991).

What also emerges from this redefinition of the field of study is the necessity to extend knowledge of Italian cinema to include those filmmaking practices and genres which were marginalized by the sustained focus on the dozen or so films which won international acclaim. This does not mean denying the aesthetic specificity of Neo-Realist cinema. Neo-Realist films did contain a challenging aesthetic project and, to this day, they may still be regarded as one of the generative sources of the national film vocabulary.

> Paradoxically, the continuing interest of Neo-Realism lies precisely in that it was neither a straightforwardly homogeneous or unitary phenomenon but successfully crossed the boundaries between highbrow and lowbrow, tradition and modernity, engagement and pleasure.

What the redefinition of the field of study does mean, however, is that it is no longer possible to take for granted the nature of cinematic realism or the ways in which Neo-Realist films have been implicated in often conflicting notions of national and cultural identities. It also suggests the importance of understanding these aesthetic practices in relation to specific historical and production contexts. Paradoxically, the continuing interest of Neo-Realism lies precisely in that it was neither a straightforwardly homogeneous or unitary phenomenon but successfully crossed the boundaries between highbrow and lowbrow, tradition and modernity, engagement and pleasure.

BIBLIOGRAPHY

Aristarco, Guido (ed.) (1975), *Antologia di 'Cinema Nuovo' 1952–1958* (Florence: Guaraldi).

Baranski, Zygmut, and Robert Lumley (eds.) (1990), *Culture and Conflict in Postwar Italy* (London: Macmillan).

*Bazin, André (1971), *What is Cinema?*, 2 vols. (Berkeley: trans. Hugh Gray, University of California Press).

Bettettini, Gianfranco (1975), 'On Neo-Realism', *Framework*, 2: 9–10.

Bondanella, Peter (ed.) (1978), *Federico Fellini: Essays in Criticism* (Oxford: Oxford University Press).

Cannella, Mario (1973–4), 'Ideology and Aesthetic Hypotheses in the Criticism of Neo-Realism', *Screen*, 4/4 (Winter), 5–60.

Dalle Vacche, Angela (1991), *The Body in the Mirror: Shapes of History in Italian Cinema* (Princeton: Princeton University Press).

Fofi, Goffredo, and Franca Faldini (eds.) (1979), *L'avventurosa storia del cinema italiano raccontata dai suoi protagonisti 1935–1959* (Milan: Feltrinelli).

Hewitt, Nicholas (ed.) (1989), *The Culture of Reconstruction: European Literature, Thought and Film* (London: Macmillan).

*Marcus, Millicent (1986), *Italian Film in the Light of Neorealism* (Princeton: Princeton University Press).

Micciché, Lino (ed.) (1975), *Il neorealismo cinematografico: atti del Convegno della X mostra internazionale del nuovo cinema* (Venice: Marsilio).

Nowell-Smith, Geoffrey (1976–7), 'Cinema Nuovo and Neo-Realism', *Screen*, 17/4 (Winter), 111–17.

*Overbey, David (ed.) (1978). *Springtime in Italy: A Reader on Neorealism* (London: Talisman).

*Rohdie, Sam (1981), 'A Note on Italian Cinema during Fascism', *Screen*, 22/4: 87–90.

Wagstaff, Christopher, and Christopher Duggan (eds.) (1995), *Italy and the Cold War: Politics, Culture and Society* (Oxford: Berg).

Williams, Christopher (1973–4), 'Bazin on Neo-Realism', *Screen*, 14/4 (Winter).

Zavattini, Cesare (1953), 'Some Ideas on the Cinema', *Sight and Sound*, 23/2 (Oct.) 64–9.

9 The French Nouvelle Vague

Jill Forbes

The history of French cinema in the 1950s and 1960s is marked by three moments of radical change: the Blum–Byrnes trade agreement of 1946, the birth of the Nouvelle Vague in 1959, and the events of May 1968. Each of these had a profound impact on the way cinema developed in France after the Second World War and on the kinds of film made in that country.

French cinema experienced a 'golden age' during the German occupation of 1940–4, when it was protected from foreign competition. As soon as the war ended, however, the backlog of Hollywood's wartime production flooded into France and was enthusiastically received by audiences fascinated by all aspects of American culture. The flow of American imports was regulated by the Blum–Byrnes Agreement (whose cinema clauses were revised in 1948), which set at thirteen the maximum number of weeks during which cinemas could only screen French films, the remainder being free for American and other imports. This quota probably corresponded, more or less, to the production capacity of the French film industry, which had been badly hit by lack of investment during the war and by damage incurred at the Liberation. However, it was widely condemned as failing to protect French interests. Some of the loudest complaints came from the strongly pro-communist film technicians' union, and these naturally intensified with the advent of the Cold War in 1947. The effect of these protests was to reinforce the corporatism of the French industry, and to

ensure that the administrative structures established to control it under the wartime Vichy regime were continued in peacetime. Equally importantly, they persuaded the government of the need to vote a series of measures designed to give financial assistance to French film production and exhibition. These were: the *loi d'aide* of 1948, under which production and exhibition were automatically assisted by a tax on profits and which, perhaps ironically, was largely funded, at first, by the huge success of *Gone with the Wind* (1939); the *fonds de développement*, established in 1953 specifically to support artistically ambitious productions; and the *fonds de soutien*, created in 1959, which provided for *avances sur recettes*, or interest-free loans, allocated on the basis of a project and which were repayable if a film made a profit. In addition to these three domestic measures, a Franco-Italian co-production agreement signed in 1946, and renewed regularly thereafter, allowed the two film industries to pool resources for ambitious co-productions during the 1950s and 1960s.

These measures are not the only indicators of the cultural significance of cinema in France in the 1950s. For all the combatant powers, the war had brought home film's significance as a means of propaganda and as a way of promoting national cohesion. Cinema attendances were extremely high—often because it was the only entertainment available—and they remained high after the war, especially in France, where television was slow to develop. Popular education movements such as Travail et culture, Peuple et culture, and La Ligue de l'enseignement, organized film screenings followed by group discussions led by luminaries such as André Bazin, who also wrote notes for their programmes. Most literary and arts magazines—*La Nouvelle Revue française*, *Les Temps modernes*, *Arts*—devoted space to serious discussion of the cinema and to film reviews. The specialist film press flourished. Alongside *L'Écran français*, which was clandestinely published during the war and emerged afterwards as the most influential of film magazines, the period saw the founding of *La Revue du cinéma* (1946–9), *Cahiers du cinéma* (1951), *Positif* (1952), and *Image et son* (1951). Many cinemas, like the Ursulines and Studio 28 in Paris, ran 'ciné-clubs' where impassioned discussion of films took place, while the Cinémathèque française, under Henri Langlois, offered unparalleled opportunities for eclectic viewing. France was therefore perhaps the first country in which the cinema was taken seriously as an object of study, and although this was conducted in a decidedly 'counter-cultural' manner, outside the universities by individuals who were often either drop-outs from academic life (Bazin, Eric Rohmer, Jean-Luc Godard) or auto-didacts (François Truffaut), the problematic, the rhetoric, and the range of references of their writings—especially those of Godard and Rohmer—pointed to a concerted and provocative attempt to position the cinema within the mainstream of French and European culture. These issues were explicitly addressed in Godard's film *Le Mépris* ('Contempt' 1963), which tells the story of an American producer's attempt to film *The Odyssey* in the Cinecittà studios in Rome, and they have inspired the evident literariness of virtually all of Rohmer's films.

Among those to benefit immediately from the various measures of support was the so-called Left Bank Group of directors of short films, including Alain Resnais, Chris Marker, and Agnès Varda. With *Nuit et brouillard* ('Night and Fog', 1956), *Lettre de Sibérie* ('Letter from Siberia', 1958), and *Du côté de la Côte* ('On the Riviera', 1958) they evolved a highly personal, often politically committed, style of avant-garde documentary filmmaking characterized by a montage of striking images and a poetic voice-over commentary. Similarly, some fifteen productions a year were mounted as a result of the Franco-Italian agreements. Perhaps not surprisingly, the first of these was Christian-Jaque's *La Chartreuse de Parme* (1947), but many important post-war directors—Jean-Pierre Melville,

Max Ophuls, Marcel Carné, Jean Grémillon for the French, Roberto Rossellini, Federico Fellini, Michaelangelo Antonioni for the Italians—benefited from their provisions. In the same way, the *avance sur recettes* system was often instrumental in the 1960s in determining whether or not a film could be made, and assisted many young filmmakers in raising the capital for their productions. It was, in short, crucial in the creation of a lively art cinema movement.

Two distinct trends are to be observed in French 1950s cinema. On the one hand, 'la tradition de qualité' identified in François Truffaut's devastating critique 'Une certaine tendance du cinéma français', published in *Cahiers du cinéma* in 1954; on the other, the so-called *francs-tireurs*, or independents, who belonged to no identifiable school. Following Alexandre Astruc's seminal article 'Naissance d'une nouvelle avant-garde: La caméra style', published in *L'Écran français* in 1948, Truffaut's polemic, rightly considered the manifesto of the Nouvelle Vague, was a plea for an auteur cinema, one in which the director would control the film and in which the film would be the expression of his personal preoccupations. Truffaut's principal targets of criticism were the writers of screenplays who reduce the role of the director to that of 'the chap who puts the frame round the story'. He particularly attacked the 'psychological realism' of Jean Aurenche and Pierre Bost, whose literary adaptations he accused of distorting the original works so as to derive from them an ideology of anticlericalism and anti-militarism, and of inventing scenes to pursue their ideological points. The respect shown for literature throughout Truffaut's films perhaps explains his outrage at Aurenche and Bost's infidelities, but the main purpose of his article is the search for a new kind of realism based on differently conceived authenticity.

Another less immediately obvious target of Truffaut's criticism of the films of Claude Autant-Lara, Christian-Jaque, and Jean Delannoy seems just as important today. The astonishing homogeneity of their films has, more recently, been attributed to the influence of technicians rather than to that of writers. Indeed, veteran filmmaker Louis Daquin somewhat mischievously attributed the *tradition de qualité* to the German Jewish cinematographers and producers who emigrated to France before the war and who trained an entire generation of French technicians. Their perfectionism and the legacy of Expressionism all contributed to the 'glacis de la lumière', the coldly perfect photography which not only gave mainstream French cinema in the 1950s a studio 'look', which is, indeed, impersonal, but ultimately created a *Weltanschauung* in which style was more important than substance.

Although the *tradition de qualité* was dominant in France in the 1950s, it was not exclusively so. Italian Neo-Realism offered a different model of filmmaking which used authentic locations and non-professional actors, marrying fiction and documentary in a manner that was to influence the Nouvelle Vague, while in France itself there were many directors who bucked the trend: Jacques Tati (*Jour de fête*, 1949; *Les Vacances de Monsieur Hulot*, 'Monsier Hulot's Holiday', 1953) and Melville (*Le Silence de la mer*, 1948; *Bob le flambeur*, 'Bob the Gambler', 1956) because they worked outside the studios, writing and producing as well as directing their own films; Robert Bresson and Jean Renoir because they consistently contrived to subvert the studios even while working within them; Ophuls and Jacques Becker because they assumed the legacy and turned it into a self-referential feature of their movies which are often consciously, and sometimes parodically, expressionist.

Despite this, the Nouvelle Vague represented a significant break with the *tradition de qualité* and brought into filmmaking a large number of younger directors. The phrase 'Nouvelle Vague' was coined by the journalist Françoise Giraud, who was conscious of the birth of 'youth culture' at the end of the 1950s and who wrote a series of portraits of young people and their aspirations for the magazine *L'Express*. In the cinema, however, it refers to the group of directors, Truffaut, Godard, Claude Chabrol, Jacques Rivette, and Rohmer, who had all worked as critics for *Cahiers du cinéma* in the 1950s and who, at the end of the decade, began to make films. Their talent was recognized when Truffaut's first feature film, *Les Quatre Cent Coups* ('The 400 Blows', 1959), was awarded the critics' prize at the 1959 Cannes Film Festival, and the Nouvelle Vague quickly became a marketing slogan in the pro-Gaullist press to promote the idea that with the change of regime in 1958 France had been regenerated and rejuvenated.

Although the directors themselves resisted the idea that they belonged to a 'school' or 'wave', since this would have appeared incompatible with their insistence on making highly personal films, it is indisputable that a series of brilliant first and second features was launched in France in the late 1950s and 1960s: Truffaut's *Tirez sur le pianiste* ('Shoot the Pianist', 1960) and *Jules et Jim* (1961); Godard's *À bout de souffle*

('Breathless', 1959), *Une femme est une femme* ('A Woman is a Woman', 1961), *Vivre sa vie* ('My Life to Live', 1962); Chabrol's *Le Beau Serge* ('Bitter Reunion', 1959) and *Les Cousins* ('The Cousins', 1959); Rivette's *Paris nous appartient* ('Paris Belongs to Us', 1960); and Rohmer's *Le Signe du lion* ('The Sign of Leo', 1959). It is also clear that whatever their many individual differences, collectively these films represented a significant break with the *tradition de qualité* and a revolution not just in the way films were made but also in their social and aesthetic significance.

What these Nouvelle Vague directors had in common was an approach to filmmaking which dispensed with the technical hierarchies required by the *tradition de qualité*. Thus the divisions between producer, director, editor, cameraman, actor, writer, and so on became extremely blurred. Unlike, say, Claude Autant-Lara, who prided himself on visualizing the entire film before he commenced shooting it, Nouvelle Vague directors worked from an idea, frequently improvised, served as the producers and writers for one another's films, cast their wives and girlfriends in starring roles, and used their own or one another's apartments instead of sets. The subject-matter of the films changed too in line with Chabrol's belief that 'small subjects' could be every bit as important as 'big subjects' and with Godard's precept that 'we must begin with what we know'. Thus literary adaptation went out of the window, except for Truffaut's *Jules et Jim*, where it is subverted in a self-conscious manner, and, along with it, the facile morality that was the mainstay of Aurenche and Bost's screenplays. Instead, the moral message of Nouvelle Vague films was to be indistinguishable from their aesthetics because, in Godard's famous phrase, 'les travellings sont affaire de morale'.

The central *topos* of a Nouvelle Vague film is the young heterosexual couple and, more generally, relations between young men and women, exemplified in the long, central sequence between Jean Seberg and Jean-Paul Belmondo in *À bout de souffle*, which is set in and on the bed in a hotel room. The stock characters of *tradition de qualité* cinema which derived ultimately from melodrama were therefore swept aside, and with them the actors they had employed. New actors like Jean-Claude Brialy and Jean-Paul Belmondo, Marie Dubois, Jeanne Moreau, and Anna Karina came to the fore. Godard's penchant for using foreign actresses like Anna Karina and Jean Seberg, whose accents were difficult to understand, showed how little importance was now attached to 'mots d'auteur', the so-called witty dialogue deriving from the theatrical tradition. Above all, in a search for a new kind of realism, *Nouvelle Vague* directors gave their films the 'look' of documentaries by shooting in authentic and recognizable locations instead of in the studio, by using faster film with natural light and lighter cameras which were often hand-held, blurring the distinction between fiction and documentary at the same time as abandoning any pretence that the world depicted was not that of a film. They were profoundly influenced by the French school of ethnographic filmmaking represented by Jean Rouch, whose *Moi un noir* (1958) had received public screening. But they were also assisted by their cameramen, Raoul Coutard and Henri Decaë, whose training had not been in the studios but in documentaries, newsreels, and the army film unit.

The preoccupations of the Nouvelle Vague matched those of more clearly avant-garde directors like Resnais or Varda, whose films explicitly interrogate the relationship between fiction and documentary and between naturalism and formalism. But what they additionally brought into their films was a consciousness of the history of the cinema, and especially of Hollywood movies, which, as critics for *Cahiers du cinéma* in the 1950s, they had analysed at length. As Eric Rohmer put it: 'We didn't attend IDHEC [the film school], but we did spend years at the Cinémathèque'. Nouvelle Vague films are studded with references to American genres, American directors, American actors, and American studios, from the dedication to Monogram Pictures at the opening of *À bout de souffle*, the parodies of Howard Hawks in *Une femme est une femme*, the imitation of Hitchcock in Truffaut's *Baisers volés* ('Stolen Kisses', 1968), to the innumerable *mises-en-abîme* which take the fictional characters to the cinema—almost always, as is the case with *The Harder they Fall* in *À bout de souffle*, to see an American movie. At the same time, however, the Nouvelle Vague brought about a revolution in the history of the cinema by abandoning the 'grammar' of Hollywood films. This is most brilliantly illustrated in Godard's appropriately titled *À bout de souffle*, which, instead of the shot–reverse shot and continuity editing in which bodies are carefully positioned in space, eyelines are matched, and the sources of sound are identified, a more elliptical, faster-moving, and apparently inconsequential narrative based on jump cuts and a montage of sound and images profoundly changed film techniques.

The Nouvelle Vague gave a new lease of life to French cinema, which had survived the 1950s with declining audiences, but which, with the spread of television, was about to lose its mass audience for good. Producers like Georges de Beauregard and Pierre Braunberger saw in this new approach to filmmaking not merely a way of making films with lower budgets, or films which could be designated as 'art movies', thus qualifying for the *avance sur recettes*, but also a way of targeting the audience aged 16–25 which did remain faithful to the cinema. They thus financed the production of a large number of first feature films in the 1960s, bringing about a radical rejuvenation of the film industry.

The final moment of radical change to affect the French cinema was, of course, the revolt of May 1968. Filmmakers were involved in a number of ways. In February 1968 many directors had demonstrated in support of Henri Langlois, the director of the Cinémathèque, and against government proposals to take over the organization. During the events themselves, filmmakers held a States-General of the Cinema, a series of meetings intended to set out what the revolutionary role of film might be, what form of state intervention should suport filmmaking, and how films might be distributed to a wider audience. In addition, many filmmakers like Jean-Luc Godard were involved in making so-called *cinétracts*—or film leaflets. These were film records of events in the streets and public buildings that were intended to serve as a counterweight to the strongly pro-Gaullist ORTF television service, which was hostile to the striking students and workers.

One of the most important longer-term effects of May 1968 was to throw into sharp relief the ideology of the Nouvelle Vague. Until that time it was frequently affirmed that the undoubted aesthetic iconoclasm of the Nouvelle Vague directors was matched by political radicalism. This belief was reinforced by the banning of Godard's *Le Petit Soldat*, made in 1960 and not released until 1963, which appeared critical of the war in Algeria, and of Rivette's *La Religieuse*, made in 1966 and not released until 1967, which not only seemed to adumbrate a different sexual politics but was also highly critical of the Catholic church. However, the transformation of politics itself, brought about by the May events, and especially the way in which gender and race joined class as matters of acute political concern, exposed the extremely reactionary nature of the ideology of some Nouvelle Vague films as well as that of the critics who had hailed 'auteur cinema' as a form of art for art's sake. Thus Chabrol's *Le Beau*

Serge and *Les Cousins* were now reread as right-wing anarchist statements, while Truffaut's refusal to engage in politics was taken as an expression of his conservative views.

However, it was the sexual politics of Nouvelle Vague films that occasioned most re-evaluation. Whether encouraged by Truffaut's misogynistic denunciation of the mother figure in *Les Quatre Cents Coups* or of the predatory female in *Tirez sur le pianiste*, Godard's vision of the contemporary spider-woman in *À bout de souffle*, or of prostitution as the general condition of women in virtually all of his pre-1968 films, or Chabrol's thesis, in the pejoratively entitled *Les Bonnes Femmes*, that sexually active women invite rape, it is certain that the events of May and the birth of the women's movement imposed a rereading of this corpus that placed it in a much less favourable ideological light. Later still, the homophobia evident in many of Truffaut's films, but especially *Baisers volés*, and its echo in Godard's *Masculin–féminin*, became a subject of criticism in its own right.

May 1968 also marked the divergence of the careers of Nouvelle Vague directors and revealed how fragile and temporary the apparent homogeneity of the group had been. Truffaut and Chabrol seemed content to rejoin the mainstream, with the former shooting a series of autobiographical essays (*L'Enfant sauvage*, 1970; *La Nuit américaine*, 'Day for Night', 1973; *La Chambre verte*, 1978), whose morbidity has only recently been noted, while the latter embarked on a series of immensely successful bourgeois comedies and thrillers. Godard, on the other hand, took seriously the politics of May 1968 and, in his attempts to make political and feminist films and to experiment with new technologies of production and distribution, helped to expose the ideological assumptions of the Nouvelle Vague aesthetic (see Smith, Part 3, Chapter 2).

More recent interpretations of the Nouvelle Vague, especially of Godard and Truffaut, have been inspired by postmodernism. Taking their cue from Godard's professed admiration for the double narrative of William Faulkner's *The Wild Palms* (and the admiration echoed by the character Patricia in *À bout de souffle*), critics have emphasized the cultural eclecticism of the early works of these directors as well as their disjunctive narratives. Godard, in *À bout de souffle*, *Le Mépris*, and *Pierrot le fou* (1965), Truffaut, in *Tirez sur le pianiste* and, to a degree, in *Jules et Jim*, mix genres and styles, taking elements from both popular culture and high culture, passing rapidly from cartoon strips to Rimbaud, from Romantic music and painting to agit-prop. This approach to filmmaking might be understood as the inevitable anxiety of influence generated by French cinema's colonial relationship to Hollywood or as the astonishing aesthetic prescience of great artists who abandoned grand narratives and the unitary point of view before the post-industrial society was invented. The very fact that such films continue to lend themselves to reinterpretation suggests that the Nouvelle Vague has not ceased to exercise an influence on contemporary filmmaking and criticism. Whereas the Nouvelle Vague was traditionally held to have invented the low-budget art film and the director as auteur, it is now seen as having introduced a radical approach to narrative and genre, but to have done this without taking any account of the social transformations that have placed gender and race at the heart of aesthetic concerns.

BIBLIOGRAPHY

Armes, Roy (1985), *French Cinema* (London: Secker & Warburg).

Astruc, Alexander (1949/1968), 'Naissance d'une nouvelle avant-garde: La caméra style', trans. as 'The Birth of a New Avant-Garde: La Caméra-Style', in Peter Graham (ed.), *The New Wave* (London: Secker & Warburg).

Austin, Guy (1996), *Contemporary French Cinema* (Manchester: Manchester University Press).

Forbes, Jill (1992), *The Cinema in France after the New Wave* (London: British Film Institute and Macmillan).

Hayward, Susan (1993), *French National Cinema* (London: Routledge).

*Monaco, James (1976), *The New Wave* (New York: Oxford University Press).

Pauly, Rebecca (1993), *The Transparent Illusion: Image and Ideology in French Text and Film* (New York: Peter Lang).

Truffaut, François (1954/1976), 'Une certain tendance du cinéma français', trans. as 'A Certain Tendency of the French Cinema', in Bill Nichols (ed.), *Movies and Methods*, 2 vols., i (Berkeley: University of California Press).

Williams, Alan (1992), *Republic of Images: A History of French Filmmaking* (Cambridge, Mass.: Harvard University Press).

10

New German Cinema

Ulrike Sieglohr

Critical positions

The non-commercial West German cinema of the 1960s and mid-1970s, which brought to international prominence auteurs such as Rainer Werner Fassbinder, Werner Herzog, and Wim Wenders, is one of the most aesthetically eclectic and politically radical national cinemas of the post-war period. Unlike its predecessors and its influential models—Italian Neo-Realist Cinema, British Free Cinema, and the French New Wave—this national cinema did not constitute a coherent grouping with a unifying style. Consequently film historians, such as Thomas Elsaesser (1989), Eric Rentschler (1984), Timothy Corrigan (1983), and James Franklin (1983), have debated the ways in which these films may be regarded as forming a movement and assessing whether their stylistically very different auteurs have, in fact, anything in common.

Their respective books indicate their different perceptions of the German cinema of this period. Whereas Franklin's book concentrates on individual 'star' directors within a chronological framework and Corrigan's work focuses upon the themes and stylistic approaches of the films in relation to art cinema in general, Rentschler's approach traces generic trends which are discussed as part of the wider German cultural–political environment. Elsaesser's multifaceted book of interlocking essays, however, breaks with these earlier,

more linear historical models by emphasizing the discontinuities of German cinema between the 1960s and 1970s and questioning some of the assumptions upon which they were based. He suggests, for example, that aesthetic innovation is often more of an economic necessity than an avant-garde formalist inclination, and that the concept of the self-expressive auteur is better understood as a discursive construction designed to attract media attention rather than the indicator of any creative originating source.

Historical determinants and institutional frameworks

In order to understand what first gave rise to the intellectual formalism of the Young German Cinema in the 1960s, and the subsequently more narratively accessible New German Cinema at the end of the decade, it is necessary to examine the cinema and politics of the 1950s. From the end of the Second World War Germany was an occupied country and America, as one of the occupying powers, indirectly controlled all aspects of the West German cinema industry. This was justified in terms of a denazification process of education-as-entertainment, through which it was intended that German audiences would be shown the error of their ways in narratives of moral example, made by people themselves only recently denazified. The Cold War, however, brought the denazification process to a premature end, and subsequent American anti-communist policies led to the promotion of only the most conservative film personnel, who tended to be those with a Nazi past. These directors and technicians continued to reproduce—albeit ambiguously—an ideology that had its roots in fascism, and West Germany's post-war commercial cinema generally had little to offer but escapist *Heimat* films—clichéd romances, set in some idyllic, pastoral environment—and apologetic war films. At the same time, the industry faced the prevalence of Hollywood films and the rise of television, which, combined with under-investment, brought it to the brink of collapse by the early 1960s.

The bleak prospects for the commercial cinema meant that the West German government could not help but welcome the young filmmakers' *Oberhausen Manifesto* of 1962 arguing for a subsidized non-commercial cinema. This manifesto was instrumental in bringing about legislative changes in the funding institutions and gave rise to a highly complex framework of state subsidies whereby a national cinema was fostered as a 'high' art form. The first films made under this system became known as Young German Cinema and, while they were thematically varied, they tended to share a narrative and formal austerity. As a result, films like Alexander Kluge's *Abschied von Gestern* ('Yesterday Girl', 1966), Edgar Reitz's *Mahlzeiten* ('Mealtimes', 1967), Danièle Huillet and Jean-Marie Straub's *Nicht versöhnt* ('Not Reconciled', 1965), although acclaimed critically, were virtually ignored by audiences.

The Young German Cinema's intense lobbying and the founding of the grant agency Kuratorium junger deutscher Film in 1965 prepared the institutional framework for the more spectator-friendly New German Cinema, and in the late 1960s a new generation started to make their first feature-length films. In 1968 Herzog directed *Lebenszeichen* ('Signs of Life') and in 1969 Fassbinder made *Liebe ist kälter als der Tod* ('Love is Colder than Death'). It is important to note that the films were made in a climate of political upheaval and of marked anti-Americanism due to US involvement in the Vietnam War. In West Germany and throughout the West the years 1967–8 were marked by student rebellion, extra-parliamentary opposition, and anti-authoritarianism, which in turn produced a surge in what were then considered counter-cultural activities, such as huge rock festivals, 'happenings', and the popularization of psychedelic drugs.

Within this larger context, specific cinematic cultural policies gave radical left-wingers the opportunity to make films. The government felt, as Sheila Johnston (1981–2) argues, that the political radicalism of the young filmmakers could be contained and also exploited in terms of an ideological 'pay-off' which would demonstrate its cultural liberalism. As a result, funding—however inadequate—became available for projects that were to some extent critical of the state. This political dimension of the New German Cinema also became a means for the West German government, particularly under Willy Brandt's chancellorship between 1969 and 1976, to prove its ability and readiness for self-criticism both at home and abroad. Internationally, this cinema became a kind of cultural ambassador (the Goethe Institut, a government-funded agency for promoting German culture abroad, exhibited the majority of these films rather than cinemas) that would bear witness to the liberalization brought about by the Social Democrats.

> **In effect, the New German Cinema functioned in West Germany throughout the 1970s primarily as a public sphere—a forum for debating contemporary issues—rather than within the realm of entertainment.**

At home the New German Cinema found its audiences primarily among students. As Thomas Elsaesser (1989: 155) points out, audience and filmmakers had come together through the events of 1967–8, which had politicized them, and this shared political perspective gained the filmmakers a devoted audience. However, the films never attracted a mass audience and were more often screeened at 'special-interest' events, such as trade union meetings, or feminist conferences, where it was quite common for filmmakers to be present to introduce and discuss their work with the audience. In effect, the New German Cinema functioned in West Germany throughout the 1970s primarily as a public sphere—a forum for debating contemporary issues—rather than within the realm of entertainment. This cultural conception of the New German Cinema therefore distanced it from the market values of both Hollywood and the commercial German cinema.

Themes and formal strategies

West Germany's post-war national identity was shaped by the division of Germany in 1949, the largely unacknowledged historical guilt of the Holocaust, and by US cultural–political imperialism. Anton Kaes (1989) and Eric L. Santner (1990) explore in depth how these factors are articulated in the New German Cinema as a steadily growing preoccupation with history and with what it means to be German. Examples are Hans Jürgen Syberberg's 'German Trilogy' *Ludwig—Requiem für einen jungfräulichen König* ('Ludwig—Requiem for a Virgin King', 1972), *Karl May* (1974), and his highly controversial *Hitler—Ein Film aus Deutschland* ('Our Hitler', 1977), Fassbinder's *Die Ehe der Maria Braun* ('The Marriage of Maria Braun', 1978) and Volker Schlöndorff's *Die Blechtrommel* ('The Tin Drum', 1979). However, an engagement with history is not necessarily articulated as an explicit theme, but conveyed as a diffuse sense of alienation, as in Wenders's *Im Lauf der Zeit* ('Kings of the Road', 1976).

Unlike other national cinemas it is more difficult, if not impossible to identify shared formal characteristics amongst the filmmakers of the New German Cinema, since a diversity of stylistic responses to a common historical situation were its hallmarks. Aesthetic strategies range from the documentary realism of Erwin Keusch and Christian Ziewer, through the biting anarchic satires of Herbert Achternbusch, to the outlandish operatic camp and kitsch of Rosa von Praunheim and Werner Schroeter. However, characteristics which *are* common to most of the films are those that David Bordwell (1985: 206–7) has identified as constitutive of art cinema in general: ambling narratives with a lingering on details and seemingly unimportant events; a stress on mood rather than on actions; and an overall sense of ambiguity.

In the German context, however, stylistic diversity can also be understood as an ideological choice, one arising from a desire to invent a new cinematic language uncontaminated by fascism. A concern with history is therefore not confined to thematic treatment but inscribed, albeit obliquely, in notable features of the mise-en-scène, such as, for example, theatricality, excess, and artifice. Fassbinder's *Katzelmacher* (1969) starts with the aphorism by Yaak Karsunke: 'It's better to make new mistakes than to reproduce old ones unthinkingly'. And, similarly, Wenders (1977/1988: 128) notes the unavailability of a native cinema tradition for him and his peers, and the loss of confidence in German images, stories and myth. 'Never before and

A preoccupation with history: *Ludwig—Requiem für einen jungfräulichen König* (1972)

nowhere else have [images and language] been debased so deeply as vehicles to transmit lies.'

New German Cinema's quest for new anti-illusionist styles was therefore centrally motivated by a desire not to reproduce the mode of representation which had contributed to seducing millions of Germans into Nazism. But anti-illusionism can also be seen as a rather more ambivalent rejection, or negotiation, of the dominant cinema's aesthetics and of the role Hollywood had played in US strategies of cultural domination in West Germany: 'The Yanks have colonized our subconscious' (*Im Lauf der Zeit*).

Finally, the non-commercial look of some of the New German films can be attributed to the funding system itself. Insufficient funding frequently meant that producing a seamless classic narrative was beyond the filmmakers' means, even if that had been their intention, which rarely it was. The very name *Autor* for a filmmaker (and, indeed, *Autorenfilm* for the New German Cinema itself) was, therefore, less the product of retrospective critical evaluation than a conscious cultural strategy to identify filmmakers as working almost artisanally, like traditional artists, and to distinguish them from commercial and industrial filmmakers.

Given these determinants it becomes clear why New German Cinema cannot simply be absorbed into an art cinema framework, for to do so would be at the expense of a specific historical and political understanding of a national cinema. Nevertheless, the New German Cinema derives its international acclaim precisely from being constructed by the critics and by the distributors as a national variant of art cinema.

Women filmmakers

Although the New German Cinema was dominated by male filmmakers, the emergence of the women's movement and the broadly liberal policies employed in film funding provided a limited space for women filmmakers. From the mid-1970s an increasing number of women were competing with the already established male auteurs and had to campaign intensively to receive funding and access to the media. In particular, television offered many first-time filmmakers, and therefore women, a chance. Julia Knight (1992) notes that many women filmmakers had a political commitment to the left and were actively engaged in the women's movement. In this respect, political activism rather than auteurist self-expression may be seen

to be the motivating force for many. An autobiographical example of this tendency is Helke Sander's *Die allseitig reduzierte Persönlichkeit—Redupers* ('Redupers', 1977), which shows the struggle of a single parent and professional photographer. In a number of films the characters—fictional and autobiographical—are used to engage with historical processes from a feminist perspective (see Frieden *et al.* 1993): Jutta Brückner's semi-autobiographical film *Hungerjahre—In einem reichen Land* ('Hunger Years', 1979) depicts growing up in the repressive Adenauer era and Helma Sanders-Brahms's internationally acclaimed, but nationally controversial, autobiographical film *Deutschland, bleiche Mutter* ('Germany Pale Mother', 1980) indicts patriarchy for the rise of fascism and the atrocities of war. Margarethe von Trotta, like Fassbinder, uses melodrama as a powerful device for an engaged political cinema. This approach is already evident in her first solo feature film, *Das zweite Erwachen der Christa Klages* ('The Second Awakening of Christa Klages', 1978), a contemporary tale about a morally justified bank robbery. Unlike many of her peers, Ulrike Ottinger rejected a realist treatment of women's issues, preferring exaggeration, artifice, and parody. Her film *Madame X—Eine Absolute Herrscherin* ('Madame X—An Absolute Ruler', 1978), about a band of female pirates, provoked a mostly hostile response from feminists at the time. Although, the majority of women filmmakers could only produce intermittently low-budget films—and thus remained marginal—von Trotta's and Sanders-Brahms's move towards international art cinema paid off in terms of public recognition and paved the way for other successes in the 1980s.

End of the New German Cinema

Increasingly official support for the New German Cinema became restrictive and conservative as the power of the state was undermined and then seriously threatened by a surge of direct confrontational actions from the Baader-Meinhof group in 1977. It is indicative of the changes in government funding policy that *Deutschland im Herbst* ('Germany in Autumn', 1978)—an almost immediate reaction by some of the most notable leftwing filmmakers (Alf Brustellin, Rainer Werner Fassbinder, Alexander Kluge, Maximiliane Mainka, Edgar Reitz, Katja Ruppé, Hans Peter Cloos, Bernhard Sinkel, and Volker Schlöndorff) to the alleged suicides of 'terrorists' in Stammheim prison—was produced and funded by the collectively owned Filmverlag der Autoren rather than by the government. However, the break-up of the support system was not just one-way and a much wider range of determinants needs to be taken into account, including the effectiveness of vigorous commercial lobbying, and indeed the changing political consciousness of the filmmakers themselves. By the early 1980s New German Cinema had no longer institutional, or ideological, support. Instead, state subsidies and international co-productions gave rise to a much more popular and genre-oriented cinema and, in the process, a political drive and national distinctiveness were lost.

Why should we still be interested?

The New German Cinema matters because it clearly embodies the *Zeitgeist* of a period marked by political utopian ideals and then melancholic disillusionment. It is a cinema which foregrounds the struggle over an embattled national identity in the way in which the filmmakers negotiated the past, not as a heritage to be preserved, but as a site for investigation and excavation, and for reconstructing history as histories and her-stories. It is also important for its institutional framework, which granted access to politically underrepresented groups: women, gays and lesbians, and

> **It is a cinema which foregrounds the struggle over an embattled national identity in the way in which the filmmakers negotiated the past, not as a heritage to be preserved, but as a site for investigation and excavation, and for reconstructing history as histories and her-stories.**

ethnic minorities. Finally, it is still one of the most exciting national cinemas, in so far as this body of work encompasses films which range from romantic excess and spectacular visions to documentary realism. The more films one sees, the more interested one becomes in understanding how these diverse films nevertheless bear witness to a particular period and culture rather than merely expressing the outlook of a few talented auteurs—although they may do that too.

BIBLIOGRAPHY

Bordwell, David (1985), *Narration in the Fiction Film* (London: Methuen).

Corrigan, Timothy (1983/1994), *New German Film: The Displaced Image* (Austin: University of Texas Press).

*****Elsaesser, Thomas** (1989), *New German Cinema: A History* (London: Macmillan and British Film Institute).

Franklin, James (1983/1986), *New German Cinema: From Oberhausen to Hamburg* (London: Columbus Books).

Frieden, Sandra, Richard W. McCormick, Vibekke R. Petersen, and **Laurie Melissa Vogelsang** (eds.) (1983), *Gender and German Cinema: Feminist Interventions*, 2 vols., i: *Gender and Representation in New German Cinema*, ii: *German Film History/German History on Film* (Providence, RI: Berg).

Johnston, Sheila (1981–2), 'A Star is Born: Fassbinder and the New German Cinema', *New German Critique* 24–5 (Fall–Winter), 57–72.

*****Kaes, Anton** (1989), *From Hitler to Heimat: The Return of History as Film* (Cambridge, Mass.: Harvard University Press).

*****Knight, Julia** (1992), *Women and the New German Cinema* (London: Verso).

*****Rentschler, Eric** (1984), *West German Film in the Course of Time* (New York: Redgrave).

Santner, Eric L. (1990), *Stranded Objects: Mourning, Memory, and Film in Postwar Germany* (Ithaca, NY: Cornell University Press).

Wenders, Wim (1977/1988), 'That's Entertainment: Hitler'; repr. in Eric Rentschler (ed.), *West German Filmmakers on Film: Visions and Voices* (London: Holmes & Meier).

11

East Central European cinema: two defining moments

Daniel J. Goulding

The fall of the Berlin Wall and the dramatic collapse of communist regimes in East Central Europe and the former Soviet Union during 1989–91 brought to a close a unique chapter in the history of world cinema. In the four decades or so after the end of the Second World War, an attempt was made to forge national cinemas predicated upon and guided by Marxist-inspired aesthetic, ideological, and political doctrines promulgated and enforced by the state. With the exception of Albania, the communist regimes of East Central Europe (Poland, Hungary, Czechoslovakia, Romania, Bulgaria, and the former East Germany, and Yugoslavia) made a deep and unprecedented commitment in their respective countries to building up the material infrastructure of film production, exhibition, and distribution and in subsidizing the development of film education and film culture. Even in difficult economic times, the annual levels of production of feature films, animated films, experimental, and short films in these countries far exceeded what could be sustained in a commercially oriented industry totally or substantially dependent upon box-office returns. On the other hand, the creation of artistically and socio-culturally significant films was often stymied by shifting party lines and the alternations of periods of freer film creativity with periods of crisis, repression, bureaucratic intervention, and what regime authorities euphemistically termed processes of 'stabilization' or 'normalization'.

Because of the diversity and scope of developments in East Central European national cinemas—with their different rhythms of 'reform' and 'repression', cinematic resurgence and decline, and distinct national histories, literatures, and cultures—it is not possible, in a chapter of this length, to cover all of the key movements and moments since the end of the Second World War that have raised important issues of critical interest to students of film. This chapter will focus instead, on the Czechoslovak New Wave of the 1960s and the Polish Cinema of Moral Concern of the late 1970s and 1980s as being among the most significant defining and paradigmatic moments in the development of post-war East Central European cinema. Both of these moments illustrate struggles common to all of the East Central European national, socialist cinemas in striving for greater freedom, diversity, and socio-cultural and political relevance of artistic film expression.

The struggle for greater artistic freedom was waged on several fronts. First, there was the struggle to free film expression from the dogmatic norms of socialist realism. Articulated by Stalin's supreme aesthetic arbiter Andrei A. Zhdanov in the 1930s, this rigid doctrine was imposed on the emergent socialist cinemas of East Central Europe soon after the end of the Second World War, and it never fully relinquished its grip even into the 1970s and 1980s, especially in the ideologically more conservative regimes of East Germany, Bulgaria,

Romania, and the neo-Stalinist period in Czechoslovakia following the fall of Dubček in 1968. At its most rigid, the doctrine of socialist realism emphasized the strict delineation of good and evil, approved genres, and set character types. It combined socialist orthodoxy with classical patterns of film narrative; i.e. film narrative based on directed logical coherence, rationally presented character motivation, and a predictable 'clockwork' functioning of intentions, causes, and effects. The dogmatic application of socialist realist doctrine in the area of film creation led to films that served the explicit, immediate needs of socialist construction by fostering appropriate attitudes and by depicting reality not as it existed but in terms of its 'revolutionary development'. Films were expected to be didactic and clear-cut, avoiding formal and stylistic innovation and providing assessments of situations that were ultimately 'progressive' and optimistic.

The struggle to free film from the confining tenets of socialist realism initially took the form of expanding the range of permissible film genres and challenging the idealized, optimistic representations of socialist 'reality' called for by socialist realist doctrine. Filmmakers claimed for themselves the right to express a more critical 'realism'—including the right to invoke the darker, ironic, and more alienated side of human, social, and political existence. A more radical struggle involved freeing film from the requirements of 'realistic' representation itself, in favour of wide-ranging modernist experimentation with film form and non-linear narrative structures that directly opposed the prescriptions of socialist realism.

In addition to struggling against the confining dogma of socialist realism, East Central European filmmakers fought to reconnect their national film cultures to world-wide film developments. As they succeeded in doing so, their work was especially influenced by Italian Neo-Realism, the French Nouvelle Vague, and the British school of social realism of the 1960s. Even more important was the effort to reconnect film to the filmmakers' own distinctive national histories, folklore, and literary and cultural traditions. These efforts gained increasing momentum after the death of Stalin in 1953, but did not reach full fruition until the 1960s and 1970s.

On a more pragmatic level, intense efforts were made to free film production, distribution, and exhibition from the Stalinist centralized bureaucratic structures set up after the Second World War. The most radical experiments in decentralization, and the placing of greater control in the hands of filmmakers themselves, was carried out in the former Yugoslavia after Tito's dramatic break with Stalin in 1948. As part of Tito's programme of 'self-management socialism', extensive reforms of the film industry were codified into law in 1956 and continually modified through the 1960s and early 1970s. The 1950s witnessed similar, though less radical, developments in Poland, Hungary, and Czechoslovakia—developments that involved the formation of separate small, specialized studios and the reorganization of large, centralized studios into smaller production units headed by creative teams of filmmakers.

As previously noted, the waxing and waning struggles for greater artistic autonomy and freedom of expression that occurred throughout East Central European cinema are nowhere more dramatically etched than in the two defining moments selected for brief discussion in this chapter: the Czechoslovak New Wave (sometimes called the Czech Film Miracle) of the 1960s, and the Polish Cinema of Moral Concern of the late 1970s and 1980s.

The Czechoslovak New Wave

During the brief period from the beginning of the 1960s to the fall of Dubček in 1968 the former Czechoslovakia produced an astonishing number of internationally significant films of great stylistic diversity and creative range. Along with the many critically acclaimed films that received major awards at prestigious international film festivals and achieved limited art-house circulation, there were a significant number that also succeeded in capturing a much wider domestic and international audience. Among the better known of these critically and commerically successful films were *Loves of a Blonde* ('Lásky jedné plavovlásky', 1965) and *The Firemen's Ball* ('Hoři má panenko', 1967) directed by Miloš Forman: *The Shop on Main Street* ('Obchod na korze', 1965), winner of the 1965 Academy Award for best foreign film, directed by Elmar Klos and Ján Kadár; and *Closely Observed Trains* ('Ostře sledované vlaky', 1966), winner of the 1966 Academy Award for best foreign film, directed by Jiří Menzel.

The surge of creative energy from Czech and Slovak filmmakers in the 1960s was paralleled by modernist 'new wave' tendencies in the neighbouring socialist cinemas of Hungary, Poland, and the former Yugoslavia. All of these film movements were tied, in part, to larger political and economic struggles within their respective countries to move away from Stalinism towards a more 'liberal' interpretation of Marxist socialism. In Czechoslovakia, Alexander Dubček led the forces of reform against the more conservative factions of the Communist Party aligned with President Novotný. Dubček's efforts were crowned with triumph in January 1968 with his elevation to party secretary—a triumph, however, that was remarkably short-lived and quickly turned to defeat when the Soviet tanks rolled into Prague in August of the same year. The fall of Dubček ushered in a harsh period of neo-Stalinism characterized by greatly increased censorship, a draconian purge of the film community, and the reinstatement of strict party control.

In the early 1960s Czechoslovakia was favourably positioned to take a leading role among East Central European socialist states in widening and deepening film expression and making its presence felt in world cinema. First, it shared with Hungary the distinction of possessing a sophisticated film tradition that stretched back to the silent period. Second, it was alone among East Central European socialist states to come through the Second World War with its film infrastructure virtually intact. In fact, the well-equipped labs and studios in Prague were improved even further during the war by the Germans, who planned to make Prague a major producing centre in the Third Reich.

At a much deeper level, there existed a close relationship between filmmakers and the related arts of literature, painting, music and theatre. Especially enriching was the direct collaboration of filmmakers with leading Czech and Slovak writers—including several who had already begun to acquire an international reputation. Among the most important of these were Bohumil Hrabal, Josef Škvorecký, Milan Kundera, Ludvík Aškenazy, Alfonz Bednár, Ladislav Fuks, Ladislav Grosman, František Hrubín, Vladimír Körner, Arnošt Lustig, Sergej Machonin, Vladimír Páral, and Jan Procházka. In addition, a group of talented screenwriters specifically trained and experienced in their craft contributed significantly to some of the most important films of the period, including, among others, Jaroslav Papoušek (all of Miloš Forman and Ivan Passer's films), Antonín Máša (*Everyday Courage*, 'Každý den odvadhu', 1964), Pavel Juráček (*Josef Kilián*, 'Postava k podpírání', 1963), and Ester Krumbachová (*The Party and the Guests*, 'O slavnosti a hostech', 1966; *Martyrs of Love*, 'Mučedníci lásky', 1967; *Daisies*, 'Sedmik-

rásky', 1966; *Valerie and her Week of Wonders*, 'Valerie a tyden divů', 1969.

The impressive pre-war Czechoslovak literary tradition also exerted a strong influence. Jaroslav Hašek's satirical masterpiece *The Good Soldier Schweick* was a sophisticated model for the ironic, humorous, and satirical portrayal of unheroic protagonists in the Forman–Passer and Menzel films. Franz Kafka's major works, rehabilitated in Czechoslovakia in the early 1960s, inspired dark and mordant filmic explorations into the labyrinthine complexities of psychological and socio-political tyranny and repression. Several of the 'experimental' or 'fantastic' films of the Czechoslovak New Wave explicitly revealed their linkage to the pre-war poetic Surrealist avant-garde and to the writings of Vadislav Vančura and Vítězslav Nezval. Among the most important theatrical influences on the New Wave was Alfred Radok's experimental *Laterna Magika* with its audacious combination of live action and cinematic projections, and the Semafor Theatre of Jiří Suchý and Jiří Šlitr, whose work revealed parallels to the influential pre-war avant-garde theatrical works of Jiří Voskovec and Jan Werich.

Paradoxically, the most 'unifying' characteristic of the Czechoslovak New Wave was its very lack of a unifying aesthetic and of any attempt to define itself as a collective movement aimed at achieving consciously articulated goals. Breaking through the stale crust of socialist realist dogma and cultural Stalinism, it openly tolerated and encouraged a variety of aesthetic approaches.

> **Paradoxically, the most 'unifying' characteristic of the Czechoslovak New Wave was its very lack of a unifying aesthetic and of any attempt to define itself as a collective movement aimed at achieving consciously articulated goals. Breaking through the stale crust of socialist realist dogma and cultural Stalinism, it openly tolerated and encouraged a variety of aesthetic approaches.**

Among the most influential stylistic and thematic approaches was the critical realism and the ironic anti-heroic cinéma vérité depictions of 'everyday' reality in the films of Forman, Passer, Menzel, Klos and Kadár; the expressionistic and Kafkaesque film portrayal of Juráček (*Josef Kilian; The End of August at the Hotel Ozone*, 'Konec srpna hotel Ozón', 1966; the dream realism of Jan Němec (*Diamonds of the Night*, 'Démanty noci', 1964; *The Party and the Guests; Martyrs of Love*); the feminist absurdist films of Věra Chytilová (*Daisies; The Fruit of Paradise*, 'Ovoce stromů rajaských jíme', 1969); the stylized fantasy and surrealistic films of Vojtěch Jasný (*Cassandra Cat*, 'Až přijede kocour', 1963; and *All My Good Countrymen*, 'Všichni dobří rodáci', 1969), and Jaromil Jireš (*Valerie and her Week of Wonders*); and the films of lyrical social engagement by Evald Schorm (*Everyday Courage; Return of the Prodigal Son*, 'Návrat ztraceného syna', 1966). The leading New Wave filmmakers, of course, combined several complex stylistic influences in their film works. The above schematic categorization is meant to be suggestive only.

In the initial critical assessments of Czechoslovak New Wave films, some Western critics tended to view them primarily as derivative reflections of major West European film movements—most notably vanguard Italian cinema (Neo-Realism and beyond) and French Nouvelle Vague. More complete analyses, however, both by Czech film writers and critics (Josef Škvorecký and Antonín Liehm) and Western film scholars (David Paul and Peter Hames) illuminated the specifically Czech and Slovak historical, socio-political, cultural, and folkloric influences that stamped the films with originality and depth.

There was also a tendency among some Western film critics to stress the political messages of the films and to celebrate the most controversial and provocative of them as anti-regime and anti-communist 'dissident' films. Such critics were especially intrigued by films that delivered their socio-political critiques with irony, subtle allegorical indirection, and Aesopian language. Milan Kundera was one of several leading figures in contemporary Czechoslovak literature and film to speak out eloquently against such critical reductionism. He lamented the tendency of some Western critics to interpret East Central European art in terms of being pro- or anti-communist in its attitudes. He suggested that if Western critics could not view art coming from Prague, Budapest, or Warsaw 'in any other way than by means of this wretched political code, you murder it, no less brutally than the worst Stalinist dogmatists'. He went on to suggest that the importance of this art does

not lie in the fact that it pillories this or that political regime (although it may, in fact, do so with wit and devastating effectiveness) but that, 'on the strength of social and human experience of a kind people here in the West cannot even imagine, it offers new testimony about mankind' (quoted in Hames 1985: 142). Kundera expresses an important insight. The best of the Czechoslovak films transcended the political particularities of the moment to express deeper layers of the unique Czechoslovak historical and cultural experience and such dimensions of human existence as the grotesque, the tragic, the absurd, death, laughter, conscience, and social responsibility.

Some Western leftist critics attempted to measure Czechoslovak New Wave films against contemporary Marxist and neo-Marxist theoretical and aesthetic models in opposition to the distorted, vulgar Marxism of socialist realist dogma. Antonín Liehm and František Daniel have both expressed considerable scepticism regarding the utility of such models. They argue that in East Central Europe, not only did the attempt to apply Marxist models to the active creation of literature and film not succeed, but efforts to elucidate the meaning of arts through a Marxist aesthetic similarly failed to produce worthwhile results (Paul 1983: 149–57). Liehm points to Czechoslovakia's pre-war experience with democratic institutions and cultural humanism as a more valid starting-point for understanding the underlying values expressed in Czechoslovak New Wave films. It is these same democratic and humanistic values that expressed themselves later in the 'Velvet Revolution' of 1989 and in the accomplishment of an orderly and peaceful separation of Czechoslovakia into the Czech Republic and Slovakia in 1993.

The Polish Cinema of Moral Concern

In Poland the richest periods of post-war film expression occurred from the mid-1950s to the early 1960s and again in the mid-1970s and early 1980s. The first, 'New School', period was nourished by a system of decentralized film production 'units' headed by leading film artists, by the steady maturation of the internationally respected Polish film school at Łódź, and by the high artistic, moral, and political status achieved by a gifted community of film directors, scenarists, cinematographers, actors, and other film artists. As in the case of Czechoslovakia and other East Central European cinemas, there was a close relationship of film

Wajda's *Man of Iron* (1981) traces the formation of the Solidarity movement

expression to the deepest and best currents of Polish national literature and the arts as well as to the distinctive shaping influences of Polish history, past and contemporary. Among those shaping historic influences was the Polish Romantic tradition, with its emphasis on nationalism, mysticism, and messianism; the profound consequences of the long years of Polish partition (from the close of the eighteenth century until 1918); the more recent history of war, socialist reconstruction, and cultural Stalinism; and the tradition of the artist as moral agent and participant as well as reflector of socio-cultural and historical forces.

After a comparatively sterile period in the mid-1960s to early 1970s, Polish cinema once again burst onto the world stage in the late 1970s and early 1980s with an impressive outpouring of artistically and socially meaningful films, labelled by the filmmakers themselves as the 'cinema of moral concern'. Andrzej Wajda, who led the way in the first post-war period of Polish film resurgence with his visually sophisticated and emotionally powerful film trilogy of the war years, *A Generation* ('Pokolenie', 1955), *Canal* ('Kanał', 1957) and *Ashes and Diamonds* ('Popiół i diament', 1958), also initiated the 'Cinema of Moral Concern' with his film *Man of Marble* ('Czlowiek z marmaru', 1977), the first film to penetrate the official mythology surrounding the Stalinist years and to expose its propagandistic excesses and grotesqueries. His film *Man of Iron* ('Czlowiek z zelaza', 1981) staked out even bolder territory by mirroring the formation of the Solidarity movement—a film that both reflected and helped to shape its dramatic course.

The new mood of Polish cinema was richly confirmed and enhanced by Krzysztof Zanussi's complex cinematic and philosophical meditations *Camouflage* ('Barwy ochronne', 1976), *Spiral* ('Spirala', 1978), and *The Constant Factor* ('Constans', 1980). These two long-established filmmakers were soon joined by a younger generation of filmmakers (Agnieszka Holland, Krzysztof Kieślowski, Tomasz Zygadło, Piotr Andrejew, Zbigniew Kamiński, Witold Orzechowski, Ryszard Bugajski, Feliks Falk, and others) who rapidly rose to international prominence. Following the crackdown on Solidarity in late 1981, several of these rising talents emigrated to the West, and Polish film production went through a brief period of shock and suspended animation. It was widely assumed by Western film critics that the recently reborn Polish cinema would be strangled in the cradle. Such gloomy prognostications did not take into account the moral and intellec-

tual tough-mindedness of the Polish film community and the unique and complex relationship which existed between the Polish intelligentsia and regime authorities. By 1983–4 Polish filmmakers were once again making artistically interesting films that continued to critique contemporary Polish social and political realities. The films explicitly denounced official corruption, media manipulation, economic failure, social disintegration, lack of political and personal integrity, and the worn-out myths and shabby results of communist ideology and practice—critiques that helped prepare the ground for the eventual fall of communism and the triumph of the Solidarity movement in 1989.

Continuing legacy

The most important defining moments in post-war East Central European cinema have contributed an impressive legacy of critically significant films. They also have raised serious issues concerning the subtle and complex interrelationships of politics, art, and social commitment within a government-subsidized system of film production, distribution, and exhibition. Issues of artistic freedom, censorship, and the economic and ideological determinants of artistic production are brought dramatically to the foreground. Important questions are raised about the various and sometimes conflicting roles of the filmmaker in society: as popular entertainer and celebrity icon; as 'serious'

> **The most important defining moments in post-war East Central European cinema have contributed an impressive legacy of critically significant films. They also have raised serious issues concerning the subtle and complex interrelationships of politics, art, and social commitment within a government-subsidized system of film production, distribution, and exhibition. Issues of artistic freedom, censorship, and the economic and ideological determinants of artistic production are brought dramatically to the foreground.**

artist freed from the dominating influence of box-office success; as propagandist and reinforcer of the established order; or as transgressive provocateur and agent of reform and revolution.

Since the fall of communism in 1989 the cinemas of East Central Europe have been engaged in an often painful and difficult transition towards a mixed system of free enterprise buttressed by modest government subsidies. Whether such a system will result in films that match the artistic and socio-cultural significance of those made during the 'best' moments of the post-war communist past remains to be seen, and to be systematically studied.

BIBLIOGRAPHY

*Goulding, Daniel J. (ed.) (1989), *Post New Wave Cinema in the Soviet Union and Eastern Europe* (Bloomington: Indiana University Press).

*Hames, Peter (1985), *The Czechoslovak New Wave* (Berkeley: University of California Press).

Liehm, Antonín J. (1974), *Closely Watched Films: The Czechoslovakian Experience* (White Plains, NY: International Arts and Sciences).

Liehm, Mira, and **Antonín J. Liehm** (1977), *The Most Important Art: Eastern European Film after 1945* (Berkeley: University of California Press).

*Michałek, Bolesław, and **Frank Turaj** (1988), *The Modern Cinema of Poland* (Bloomington: Indiana University Press).

Paul, David W. (ed.) (1983), *Politics, Art and Commitment in the East European Cinema* (New York: St Martin's Press).

Skvorecky, Josef (1971), *All the Bright Young Men and Women: A Personal History of the Czech Cinema* (Toronto: Peter Martin).

12

European film policy and the response to Hollywood

Armand Mattelart

'Cinema is an art, but it is also an industry', the novelist André Malraux liked to recall in the 1960s, after he had become de Gaulle's Minister for Culture. He had previously used the phrase to round off his *Ésquisse d'une psychologie du cinéma*, published in 1939, and while it must have seemed banal to the Hollywood studio bosses who had, since about 1910, made an industry out of producing films, in the France of the 1960s, this little aphorism was surprisingly bold given the traditional French emphasis upon the 'art' of the film director. Paradoxically, if Malraux's phrase still retains some of its provocative nature, it is not because of the second part but because of the first. The importance of industrialization in the whole process of cultural production, as well as the intimate relationship which links it to the internationalization of markets and products, are now recognized as integral to the shaping of cultures, both present and future. On the other hand, in this conversion to market laws, the idea that cinema is something other than just a product can get lost. In 1993 it was precisely this balance between economics and culture that representatives of the member states of the European Union and those of the United States debated during the final Uruguay Round of negotiations between the members of the General Agreement on Tariffs and Trade (GATT).

Until then, the controversy about the definition and the place of cultural creation in the new commercial order of the world had been lurking just below the surface. When it was debated whether to extend the principles of free exchange to the audiovisual, the problem exploded into the open. 'Creations of the mind cannot simply be assimilated to simple products', was how President Mitterrand expressed it in October 1993. The French position was to call for special treatment of this section of international exchange: a clause entitled 'cultural exception' to exclude the audiovisual from the measures governing the liberalization of commerce in the same way that public health, the environment, and a state's internal security are excluded. After controversies and agitated talks, the parties present decided to exclude 'creations of the mind' from the rules governing other merchandise on 15 December 1993. However, the intensity of the argument obscured the fact that the GATT negotiations were only part of a long history of debates in France, in a wider Europe, and elsewhere about whether or not they needed to protect themselves from an unequal relation of forces in this area. To understand what is really at stake in what is no doubt only the first stage of the 'commercial war of images' on a world-wide level, it is more than ever necessary to trace the genealogy of the problem.

Germany: a pioneer country

The idea that it is essential for a nation-state to safeguard the independence of its production of images appeared for the first time in Europe in the Kaiser's Germany, right in the middle of the First World War, when European companies were losing control of the European film market. Before this, the international film trade was not encumbered by any customs measures or commercial policies specific to this type of production. In 1916–17, however, the German authorities equipped themselves with legal measures to combat the free exchange of films. Thereafter, they exerted a strict control on the importation of foreign films and developed a state policy of constructing a national cinema industry.

Thus, in 1917 the famous Universum-Film-Aktiengesellschaft (UFA) was founded in Berlin thanks to the conjunction of banking groups, the state, and the armed forces, who recognized the role that film could play as a propaganda weapon. The UFA brought together the majority of the existing national businesses, and combined production with distribution and exhibition. The communiqué published on the occasion of the inauguration of the UFA is revealing of the philosophy which inspired its foundation:

We are pleased to note that the general public is increasingly of the opinion that films are not just produced as a diversion for people, but that they must respond to the national educational and economic needs. It is for this reason that it was necessary to give the German film industry a more solid base, particularly in commercial and financial terms, so that when a peace has been concluded, it will be able to compete on an equal footing, both in terms of capital and also in terms of organization, with foreign films whose influence has, until now, been dominating. (Bächling 1947)

This global strategy was in keeping with the philosophy handed down by the economist Friedrich List (1789–1846), one of the spiritual fathers of the *Zollverein* (the customs union) who did not think of the construction of the nation-state and a 'national economy' as separate from an 'educational protectionism', and who was fiercely opposed to the theory of free exchange inspired by the theoreticians of classical economics such as Adam Smith and David Ricardo (Mattelart 1996). Opening up one's national economy to foreign competition is not profitable until it has developed to a level on which it can compete. What resulted was a doctrine which advocated neither total self-sufficiency nor total protectionism, but one which could be varied from case to case depending on the degree of independence achieved by any particular sector of

the industry. As we shall see, this is an argument which was used again by opponents of a totally free market in the debates on the construction of the 'European economy', the ratification of the Maastricht Treaty, and the negotiations between the Twelve and GATT.

The fear of America

During the Great War American cinema took advantage of the gap left by the warring countries in Europe to extend their exportation networks, and in the interwar period they further consolidated their power. At the same time, a number of European countries, in particular France and Britain, organized systems to protect themselves from the influence of Hollywood films in the cinemas. At the end of the Second World War the American government did all that it could to alleviate these restrictions by using the occasion of the Marshall Plan. In the case of France, the Blum–Byrnes Agreement, named after the French representative Leon Blum and the American Secretary of State James Byrnes, was signed in Washington in May 1946 (Guback 1969). In place of an importation quota, this substituted a 'screen' quota which reserved four weeks in every quarter (or 31 per cent) of screen time for French films (compared with 50 per cent before the war) (see Forbes, Chapter 9). This meant that the new quota did not allow enough screen time for the full potential of French production to make it into the cinemas. Thus, whereas before the war France produced about 120 films per year, in 1946, it produced ninety-six and, in 1947, only seventy-four.

This new crisis, which extended across various sections of the industry, pushed French actors, directors, and producers, supported by the press, onto the street and obliged the National Assembly to reconsider the agreement. Negotiations with Washington succeeded in altering it, and a new agreement was signed in September 1948. The system of an importation quota was put back in place, backed up with the control of 'screen' time. Of the 186 foreign films which would be allowed to be screened each year, 121 could come from the United States. The reserved 'screen' time for French films was also increased from four to five weeks (or 31 to 38 per cent). These protective measures were accompanied by a policy of actively encouraging film production at home. The Centre national de la cinématographie (CNC) was at the heart of a new support system and one of its roles was to ensure that part of the receipts received in France from foreign films was rein-vested in the national industry.

France, because of this strategy of protection and production of national films, became one of the few countries, not only in Europe but also in the world, to retain a certain pluralism in its cinemas. Jacques Thibau, the director-general for cultural, scientific, and technical relations of the Ministry of Foreign Affairs, remarked in 1982, in a published report on French policy on cultural matters: 'The lesson of these last twenty years in Europe is clear: there can be no national cinema without a policy of aid to the national cinema. This is true for France, Italy, Germany. . . . The example of Great Britain (which made the opposite choice), is very instructive in this respect: a film industry survives, but British cinema has practically disappeared' (Mattelart *et al.* 1984: 67).

> **The lesson of these last twenty years in Europe is clear: there can be no national cinema without a policy of aid to the national cinema.**

Unequal exchange and the cultural industries

The 1970s mark a historic turning-point in the understanding of both the industrial mechanisms which govern the production and distribution of films and other audiovisual material and the international imbalance of cultural exchange. A concern to diagnose these problems and to propose policies at both national and international levels first sprung up in Third World countries which chose Unesco, the organization representing the community of nations in matters of culture, communication, education, and science, as its main forum. From 1969 this international institution (presided over at the time by the Frenchman Jean Maheu) debatd the idea of 'one-way communication' which characterized the relationship between developing countries and the others, and which, because of its unilateral nature, was in danger of 'causing problems for the mutual understanding of nations'. In 1977 Mr Maheu's successor, Amadou Mahtad M'Bow from Senegal, ordered a report from an international commission to study the problems of communication. The

MacBride Commission's report was published in 1980 and clearly set down the imbalances in the international flow of programmes, films, and other cultural products (MacBride 1980).

A number of factors—such as the intransigence of Reagan's America, which, following free market principles, wanted to impose the argument for the free flow of information at all costs (an argument that would be taken up later during the GATT talks), and a telescoping of the interests of Southern countries who were struggling for national cultural emancipation and the interests of communist bloc countries who knew how to manipulate these legitimate demands to oppose any opening-up of their systems of mass communication—blocked a successful outcome to proposals of a 'new world order of communication and information' (Mattelart 1994).

Despite this, the Unesco debates were the first occasion when concern had been voiced about the unequal exchange of information and images, and these did encourage policies in certain Third World countries for protecting their own cinema market. This was particularly the case in Latin America, where ever since 1967 and 1969, when the first meetings of filmmakers from the Southern continent had been organized at Viña del Mar in Chile, the idea of a 'common market for Latino-American film' had been making headway. In 1977 Embrafilme, the state enterprise for film in Brazil, proposed extending the project to Italy and France and asked its Latin American partners to demand of the various governments a quota policy in favour of national films. In 1985, however, the United States, invoking the drift towards a politicization of the problems of communication, turned their backs on Unesco and were followed shortly after by Mrs Thatcher's Britain. In the 1980s, as a result, the question about the regulation of media networks and exchange slipped into the domain of organizations which were more technical in character (of which GATT was at the forefront).

'Television without Frontiers'

In the 1980s deregulation, the privatization of audiovisual systems, and the increase in the power of the market moved the centre of gravity of both the debates and the players. While the Third World countries, who had supported calls for a 'new world order of communication and information' during the 1970s, deserted the field of debate and rallied around the principle of free exchange of cultural merchandise, Europe was impressing upon its community institutions the question of the unequal exchange of audiovisual material. In June 1984 the EEC published a voluminous report entitled *Television without Frontiers: A Green Paper on the Establishment of the Common Market for Broadcasting especially by Satellite and Cable* and invited the other players in the audiovisual future of Europe to make their opinions known. This was the first shot in the debate that went back and forth between the different authorities in the Community, the government representatives, and the professional organizations concerned. Their aim was to establish a directive on television without borders. The Council of Europe for its part set in motion a convention on the same subject in 1986.

The final version of *Television without Frontiers* was approved by the Twelve on 3 October 1989. Article 4 invites the member countries to reserve the majority of air-time for European productions (films and documentaries) 'whenever possible'. A joint declaration from the European Council of Ministers and the Commission specified that this was a 'political obligation'. In other words, the directive was a legally enforceable document, except in the cases of quotas whose non-observation in a certain country could not in practical terms be punished by the European Court of Justice. Article 4 thus had the status of a 'declaration of intention'. The directive also dictated the frequency of commercial breaks and forced television stations to promote independent production and respect the chronology cinema–video–television in their exposure of works. It also recognized the right of each member country to determine for itself the quota of European productions. In France, for example, channels are obliged to broadcast 40 per cent French productions (60 percent European) and must invest a part of their turnover in film production. The Convention on Television without Frontiers elaborated by the Council of Europe and adopted shortly before was hardly different from that approved a few months later in Brussels. Against its will, France gave its support to these two texts. At the last moment Paris advocated more stringent terms for the quotas. Led by the British delegation, those member states most opposed to the imposition of quotas succeeded in persuading a majority of the Twelve to back them against the French proposition, which was supported by Belgium, Luxembourg, and Spain. France wanted to impose a minimum quota of 60 per cent of air-time, excluding the time given over to the news, sporting events, game shows, advertisements, or teletext services.

Over the five years of confrontation it was clear how much the European governments were split rather than brought together by the very notion of culture. Whilst the neo-liberal government delegation from London jumped at the mention of the word 'cultural' when applied to the audiovisual, the French representatives ardently defended a quota system in the name of a 'European cultural identity'. Others thought this identity to be unlocatable. Portugal could not understand why they had to swap the latest successful Brazilian telenovella for a French soap opera like *Chateauvallon*, merely so as to favour European productions. Smaller countries like Belgium openly criticized both sides for ignoring the intercultural power relations in a Europe composed of national and regional communities whose capacity for audiovisual and advertising production was unequal.

However, despite numerous concessions and compromises, the directive was badly received by those working in the audiovisual environment in the United States, and they announced a recourse to GATT almost immediately. According to them, the directive infringed the obligation made on member states not to discriminate against foreign products. The reception worsened in December 1990, a year after its adoption, when the Council of Ministers of the Twelve took a series of decisions with a view to setting a deadline for a European audiovisual industry: the MEDIA programme. Endowed with a budget of some 220 million ECUs spread over the period 1991 to 1995, and overseen in a decentralized way from the large European cities (London, Hamburg, Barcelona, Brussels, Paris), this programme covered teaching, production, and distribution: help for screenplays, documentaries, and cartoons, and aid for distribution and exhibition.

An overwhelming balance sheet deficit

Throughout the 1980s one fact underpinned the strategy of the European Union: the growing commercial domination of the audiovisual market in Europe by the American cinema, television, and video industries. According to the estimates made in 1990 by the Institut de l'audio-visuel et de télécommunications en Europe (IDATE), American revenue in the EEC countries was as high as $US3.719 billion (of which $1.134 billion was earned in cinema, $1.278 billion in television, and $1.307 billion in video) whilst EEC revenue in the United States only reached $247 million: a deficit of $3.472 billion.

External markets were becoming more and more important for the US major studios. In 1988 these large companies earned 41.6 per cent of their turnover abroad; four years later that figure was almost 47 per cent. In 1991 an average of 72 per cent of cinema takings in Europe went to American films. Although France was the only country that managed to save a substantial percentage for its national cinema, even it had to face the growing proportion of American films, which jumped from 31 to 57 per cent between 1979 and 1993. Steven Spielberg's *Jurassic Park* showed, in 1993, how much power the American cinema has: in the United States and Canada the film earned $345 million while in other countries it earned $538 million. Thanks to utilization rights granted to licensed companies (covering 500 firms and 5,000 products), the film generated more than $1 billion in sales. The film cost $60 million dollars to make, whereas the average French film costs $4 million.

By including services in the commercial negotiations for the first time since its creation in 1947, GATT put the transnational exchange of intangible products, including all the products of the cultural industries, up for debate. Until then, the question of regulating this flow had been a purely European one. Henceforth it would be thrown into the contentious problems of worldwide application. At the end of the Second World War the General Agreement on Tariffs and Trade had been signed by twenty-three countries; in 1993 it brought together 107 nations. The problem was that while GATT underlined the necessity of applying the same general rules of the liberalization of international commerce that governed other goods and services to the audiovisual, this would involve the abolition of the different systems installed by Europe and each European country to protect their own audiovisual space such as financial support for cinema at a national and EU level and the fixing of television transmission quotas for fiction of European or national origin. This was the object of the wrestling-match begun in 1993 between the European Union, represented by Leon Brittan (the commissioner for foreign economic relations), and the United States in the person of the American Mickey Kantor, the special representative for commerce from the White House. The mediator was the director-general of GATT, the Irishman Peter Sutherland, whose brief was to conclude the last phase of the agreement (the Uruguay Round) and to create a new insititution, the World Trade Organization.

In the name of which European cultural identity?

The reason for the scale of the French involvement in the GATT affair is that it has a long tradition of defending national cinema, rooted in a concern both for culture and for the numerous companies in the cinema business who year in, year out, produce between 100 and 120 films, in a sector which has some 70,000 employees. Another important element has been the official fear of seeing French culture lose influence in Europe and throughout the world: a fact which has not escaped African intellectuals and artists given that imported French programmes account for between 23 and 50 per cent of programmes broadcast in French-speaking Africa. This has meant that the way that they have looked at the problem of a threatened cultural identity is very different. Echoing the words of the former French minister of Culture Jack Lang ('Culture and Economy: it's the same struggle'), the Cameroon producer Michael Lobe Ewane summed up the position of African audiovisual workers: '*Dallas* and *The Olive Castle* [a successful French television series]-it's the same struggle!' (*Liberation*, 8 November 1993).

What this suggests is some of the problems involved in mobilizing the concept of 'European culture'. This leitmotif was evident in the appeal, published as a full-page article in the daily newspaper *Le Monde* (18 September 1993) by leading French arts and media organizations when authors and filmmakers gathered in Venice on the initiative of the Fédération européenne des réalisateurs audiovisuels to discuss the GATT question:

A reasonable GATT for a European Culture
. . . Each people benefits from an inalienable right to develop its own culture at the same time as having access to the wealth of other peoples' cultures. They know that in this crisis, which is tearing apart a fin-de-siècle world, it is essential that cinema and other means of audiovisual expression be allowed to contribute to understanding, to a coming together, and to cultural blossoming. The maintaining and reinforcing of a strong cultural identity in the Community is nowadays indispensable if the European construction is to succeed . . . [We wish] European negotiators to demand unconditionally that the rules laid down in the

agreement have no hold over the audiovisual sector in Europe. The clause for a cultural exception, a rule only designed to protect our identities, must be included in the GATT agreement without any concession.

However, the declaration does not indicate that there was unanimity among French filmmakers on this question. Some of them openly demonstrated their reservations and showed how difficult it was to defend the interests of independent creators at the heart of this debate. As the filmmaker Marcel Hanoun was to write later in the newspaper *Libération* (6 March 1995):

'Cultural exception' is the tree that hides the forest of cultural exclusion . . . For some people, 'cultural exception' is only a struggle between markets. For others it is the silent, permanent exploration of the immense field of writing for the audiovisual, the field of research, of innovation, of discovery. . . . The vociferous supporters of the cultural exception cannot and will not accept the alternative of alterity, difference, right here at home in France.

In this respect, we should note the real absence of any probing interrogation into what a 'European cinematographic and audiovisual identity' might or should be.

> **We should note the real absence of any probing interrogation into what a 'European cinematographic and audiovisual identity' might or should be.**

We should also note another important complication. For, if the professionals—and in particular the organizations of authors, directors, and producers—were at the vanguard of mobilization against the initial GATT plan, the large communications groups claiming to be European, both in France and elsewhere, did not display the same anxieties. Despite the growing sense of confrontation between France and America, French groups such as Canal plus and the Chargeurs réunis were signing agreements with the conglomerate Time Warner with the aim, particularly in the case of the Chargeurs réunis, of creating a cinema network on the European mainland whilst the NBC network took control of the European cable channel Superchannel. As for the broadcaster TF1, the old 'voice of France', which had been privatized in 1986, it was content

merely to reiterate its hostility towards any policy of quotas.

The partners in the European Union, estimating that they did not have the same interests (nor the same conception of culture) to defend as the French, were also reluctant to support the idea of the 'cultural exception' fully and only the Belgian government and those of southern Europe initially rallied behind it. However, when the outcome of negotiations was announced, the cultural sector was successfully excluded from the GATT agreement. There was not long to wait for the reactions of those representing the American film industries. Jack Valenti, president since 1963 of the Motion Picture Association of America, whose statements throughout the previous two years had surprised a number of European directors and producers, made the following statement on the night of the announcement of the verdict:

The greatest negotiations of our age have come to an end. The EEC, our biggest market, leaves us with no cause for hope. . . . Their final offer is, in fact, lamentable . . . These negotiations had nothing to do with culture (unless we are to believe that every television series or game show from Europe considers itself to be the cultural equivalent of a Molière comedy). The only thing that really mattered was money, and what avarice there was! (Valenti, 1993).

Towards the digital super highway: White Paper, Green Paper

Hardly had the GATT problems been concluded than more appeared on the horizon: the great projects for an infrastructure of information networks in Europe. These were 'information superhighways', a deployment of networks for new multi-media services, mixing sound, text, and images, either still or animated. This hybridization of televisions, computers, and telephones signalled the beginning of communication in which the user has the possibility of participating, thanks to intelligent consoles, and plugging into interactive services (films, games, catalogues, video conferences, education, banking, medicine, and so on).

The send-off for these projects was given in the White Paper prepared by Jacques Delors and adopted by the European Union Council of Ministers in December 1993. This official report describes the technological leap as a 'change comparable to the first industrial revolution', and the digital networks are seen as right at the heart of a reorganization of the modes of production and distribution within society, their 'growth', their 'competitiveness', and 'employment' (three terms included in the title of the White Paper). With this, another difference between Europe and America came into play. At least, that is how Jack Valenti understood matters in February 1994: 'The development of satellites, number compression and transmission by telephone will multiply tenfold, a hundred fold, the capacity of a cable network. And not in the year 2000 but tomorrow. Each individual will be able to choose from between 5,000 and 10,000 programmes, and that sort of power will render the very idea of quotas absurd!' (Valenti 1994.) Thus will begin the period of the 'audiovisual superhighway', to take up Mr Valenti's phrase.

It was with these new technological stakes in mind that in April 1994, in the wake of the White Paper, Jacques Delors and João de Deus Pinheiro (the Portuguese commissioner in charge of culture and the audiovisual) presented a Green Paper on the audiovisual. Its title was *Strategy Options to Strengthen the European Programme Industry in the Context of the Audiovisual Policy of the European Union*. Its goal was to construct a well-defined framework and a credible financial basis for European audiovisual businesses in order to exploit the 'potential of the digital revolution' and to prevent the Single Market from becoming solely for American companies. Directly linked to the preoccupations elaborated in the White Paper, there is a promise for the future, to create 2 to 4 million jobs by the year 2000 in a Europe which has 18 million unemployed. Even if the figures that make this report sparkle are, in the eyes of many economists, deceptive, one thing is certain: the spectre of a crisis henceforth projects the discussion about employment (and unemployment) to the heart of the concerns about identity and the relations between 'art' and 'industry'.

On the centenary of the cinema

In 1995 the European Union Council of Ministers for Culture and Communication met to discuss the revision of the 1989 Directive on Television without Frontiers. On this occasion France proposed strengthening the quotas imposed on European channels, hoping to have the clause which obliged stations to transmit a majority of European works 'whenever possible' removed. According to them, the lack of legal clarity in this wording allowed the clause to be abused. The

French delegation found itself practically isolated in defending this revision, and most of the European partners refused any rewording that would tighten the existing constraints on television. France's European partners remained dug into their minimalist position.

Also in 1995 the group of the world's most industrialized nations, G7, met in Brussels for a summit on new communications technology, and more specially to discuss information highways. For the first time, representatives from the large American, European, and Japanese firms in the communications sector were invited to a meeting of this type. They stressed the pressing necessity to hasten the deregulation of the telecommunications services and to suppress public monopolies in order to accelerate the development of future electronic arteries. They were all agreed that 'private initiatives must drive the global information society' (Bangemann 1994).

So the G7 representatives parted, recommending a rapid liberalization of telecommunications. Employment and cultural diversity, however, were either excluded from the agenda or treated as marginal issues. A tacit agreement had prompted the seven great industrialized nations not to tackle such questions, which were 'by nature too polemical'. The representatives of Hollywood have also been pragmatic and have avoided any open polemic. They wait for the future deployment of these highways so that they will be proved to have been right about what they still insist on interpreting as a sign of European (and French) chauvinism in the era of 'global' media.

BIBLIOGRAPHY

Bächlin, P. (1947) *Histoire économique du cinéma* (Paris: La Nouvelle Édition).

Bangemann, M. (chairman) (1994), *Europe and the Global Information Society: Recommendations to the European Council* (Brussels: EC).

Delors, J. (1993), *Livre blanc. Croissance, compétitivité et emploi: les défis et les pistes pour entrer dans le vingt et unième siècle* (Brussels: European Economic Community).

European Commission (1984), *Television without Frontiers: A Green Paper on the Establishment of the Common Market for Broadcasting especially by Satellite and Cable*, Com (84) 300 final (Brussels: EC).

—— (1994), *Strategy Options to Strengthen the European Programme Industry in the Context of the Audiovisual Policy of the European Union* (Brussels: EC).

*Guback, T. (1969), *The International Film Industry: Western Europe and America since 1945* (Bloomington: Indiana University Press).

MacBride, S. (1980), *Many Voices, One World* (Paris: Unesco).

Malraux, A. (1939), *Esquisse d'une psychologie du cinéma* (Paris: Nouvelle Revue française).

Mattelart, A. (1994), *Mapping World Communication: War, Progress, Culture*, trans. S. Emanuel and J. Cohen. (Minneapolis: University of Minnesota Press).

—— (1996), *The Invention of Communication*, trans. S. Emanuel (Minneapolis: University of Minnesota Press).

*—— X. Delcourt, and M. Mattelart (1984), *International Image Markets: In Search of a New Perspective*, trans. D. Buxton (London: Comedia and Methuen).

Pinheiro, J. D. (1994), *Green Paper on Audiovisual Policy* (Brussels: EC).

Valenti, J. (1993), 'La CEE tourne le dos à l'évenir', *Le Monde* 16 Dec.

—— (1994), 'Le Concurrence stimule le qualité', *Le Monde*, 15 Feb.

13

Directors and stars

(a) **Jean Renoir**   KEITH READER

Very few filmmakers, paradoxically, arouse so little critical debate, in the negative sense of the term, as Jean Renoir. His two best-known films are *La Grande Illusion* (1937), acclaimed as one of the true masterpieces of humanist cinema, and *La Règle du jeu* ('The Rules of the Game', 1939), which consistently vies with *Citizen Kane* (USA, 1941) in *Sight and Sound*'s critics' poll for all-time best film. One major reason for this is Renoir's status as auteur. Leo Braudy writes of how he was 'fascinated to find that each of the films of Jean Renoir stayed whole, establishing its continuity with other films, at the same time that it refused to lose its individual artistic identity' (1977: 17). His iconic status for the French New Wave stems largely from this continuity, often articulated around a number of key themes: the theatre (clearly a metaphor for cinematic mise-en-scène), nature in general and water in particular, the importance of location shooting, and the elusive balance between order and improvisation.

That these thematic continuities should have been perceived across a range of genres that is exceptionally wide for a European art filmmaker—from political drama (*Le Crime de Monsieur Lange*, 1936) to literary adaptation (*La Bête humaine*, 1938), from social farce

(*Boudu sauvé des eaux*, 'Boudu Saved from Drowning', 1932) to near-musical (*French Can-Can*, 1955)—makes Renoir in many respects the archetypal European auteur. This is not, however, to say that his career forms an entirely homogeneous whole, and the major critical debates around his work centre around both its socio-political relevance and the quality and status of the films he made between fleeing to the United States at the outbreak of the Second World War and the end of his filmmaking career in 1969.

'The auteurist obsession with the transhistorical wholeness of art and the artist' (Faulkner 1986: 6–7) long obscured the acute social relevance of Renoir's pre-war work. The propaganda film he made for the French Popular Front, *La Vie est à nous* (1936), was given one of the 'classic' analyses of *Cahiers du cinéma*'s Marxist period (Bonitzer *et al.* 1970), but for the rest he was often seen, by Truffaut and by Beylie (1975) among others, as the timeless humanist *par excellence*. That quality has often been seen as distilled in the remark made by Octave, the character he himself plays in *La Règle du jeu*: 'Everybody has their reasons.' Yet the remark is prefaced by: 'on this earth, there is one thing which is terrible', which is borne out by the violent, and ultimately tragic, social conflicts in the film.

In the wake of the influence of Marxism on film theory, more recent work on Renoir (Serceau 1981; Faulkner 1986; Vincendeau and Reader 1986) has placed much more stress on how his 1930s work is imbued with a savagely satirical socio-political awareness that goes well beyond his whole-hearted but brief commitment to the French Popular Front. *Le Crime de Monsieur Lange* asserts Renoir's commitment to a precarious, but necessary, social solidarity not only through its subject-matter (it is about a workers' publishing co-operative), but, as Bazin (1971) masterfully demonstrates, through the circularity of its mise-en-scène, culminating in the 360° pan around the courtyard immediately before Lange kills the exploitative Batala.

La Grande Illusion's humanist qualities are not in doubt, but to overstress them is to risk obscuring the fact that the film, although set during the First World War, is also a fierce social anatomy of the France that was about to plunge into the Second (see Faulkner 1986: 85–7). From 1939 until his death in 1979, although he returned regularly to film in France, his main residence was in California, and for François Poulle (1969) this isolation from the mainstream of French society has a deleterious effect on his work. The majority of critics, not necessarily for reasons as overtly political as Poulle's, would agree with this, and *La Règle du jeu*'s status as cinematic myth doubtless owes much to its being widely perceived as the summit of Renoir's 'real' career, after which the rest could not but be an anticlimax.

Yet *Le Carrosse d'or* ('The Golden Coach', 1953) was the film whose title Truffaut chose for his production company (Les Films du carrosse), and *Cahiers du cinéma* found no difficulty in getting prominent directors and critics to write favourably about every one of the post-1939 films in their special Renoir issue (July–August 1994). The most stalwart and articulate defender of the later films is Daniel Serceau—one of the first critics to analyse the social importance of the earlier period—for whom they represent a supreme refinement of Renoir's art and the articulation of an ethic of renunciation, beginning with *The River* (1950) (Serceau 1985).

Renoir was also, for André Bazin above all, one of the masters of cinematic realism—a term defined not by plausibility of subject-matter, but by the organic qualities of the mise-en-scène. For Bazin, the fact that 'pan-

ning and lateral dollying became his two main camera techniques' (Bazin 1971/1973: 21) goes beyond stylistic observation to constitute an aesthetic and ontological—even an ethical—judgement. But film theory, in its pomp, systematically eschewed ethics and ontology (though emphatically not judgement), so that, while the importance of Bazin's views was always recognized, they did not influence later critics in the way that might have been expected.

Renoir's own comments on his work, collected in interviews and television programmes, may seem at first sight inconsequential. Yet an observation such as 'realism is not realism at all. It is simply another way of translating nature' (Renoir 1989: 57) has much in common with more overtly theoretical and semiological approaches, and his stress on the importance of material and technological change in art is scarcely consonant with a timeless or transcendental view of his work. Perhaps what almost all commentators would agree is that Renoir's mise-en-scène, his collaborative style of working with actors, his use of the cinematic medium to articulate the coexistence of the comic and the tragic, make him, for all his lack of overt theoretical pretensions, one of the cinema's major innovators.

BIBLIOGRAPHY

*Bazin, André (1971/1973) *Jean Renoir*, trans. W. W. Halsey II and William H. Simon (Paris: Éditions Champ Libre; New York: Simon & Schuster).

Bertin, Célia (1994), *Jean Renoir* (Monaco: Éditions du Rocher).

Beylie, Claude (1975), *Jean Renoir: le spectacle, la vie* (Paris: Éditions Seghers).

Bonitzer, Pascal, Jean-Louis Comolli, Serge Daney, and **Jean Narboni** (1970), '"La Vie est à nous, film militant', *Cahiers du cinéma*, 218 (Mar.), 44–51.

*Braudy, Leo (1977), *Jean Renoir: The World of his Films* (London: Tobson Books).

*Faulkner, Christopher (1986), *The Social Cinema of Jean Renoir* (Princeton: Princeton University Press).

Poulle, François (1969), *Renoir 1936; ou, Jean Renoir pour rien?* (Paris: Éditions du Cerf).

Renoir, Jean (1989), *Renoir on Renoir* (Cambridge: Cambridge University Press).

Serceau, Daniel (1981), *Jean Renoir, l'insurgé* (Paris: Le Sycomore).

—— (1985) *Jean Renoir: la sagesse du plaisir* (Paris: Éditions du Cerf).

Vincendeau, Ginette, and **Keith Reader** (eds.) (1986), *La Vie est à nous! French Cinema of the Popular Front 1935–1938* (London: British Film Institute).

(b) **Ingmar Bergman** CHRIS DARKE

The case of Ingmar Bergman indicates that neither the longevity of a director's career nor the breadth of his influence guarantee his reputation. Although Bergman directed forty films between 1944 and 1982, his critical profile has declined from 1960s auteur cinema supremacy to present-day neglect. The popular memory of Bergman today is a kind of pale parodic photocopy, exemplified by Woody Allen's homages, where the Swedish director is stylistically invoked as a reference for European art cinema *gravitas* and to generate a kind of profundity-by-proxy (acutely analysed by the American critic Jonathan Rosenbaum 1993). But this fate is itself highly revealing of the shifts that have taken place in film criticism since the late 1950s. Indeed, Thomas Elsaesser (1994) has studied the process of Bergman's steady disappearance from the canon, as well as his centrality in defining the outlook of 1960s cinephile.

'The first critical articles I struggled with—as reader and writer—were on Bergman', recalls David Thompson (1994). He was not alone. For many film critics in the late 1950s, and throughout the 1960s, Bergman was the central figure of European art cinema. When writing for *Cahiers du cinéma*, the future French New Wave directors recruited him as an inspirational figure. Bergman's 1953 film *Sommaren med Monika* ('Summer with Monika'), released in Paris in 1957, provoked Jean-Luc Godard's eulogy 'Bergmanorama', in which he claimed that Bergman was the most original filmmaker of the European cinema and a stylistic inspiration (Godard 1958).

In Britain too, where the film magazine *Movie* was reappraising and promoting Hollywood cinema along auteurist lines, critics were cutting their teeth on the emergent European cinema of directors such as Bergman, Michelangelo Antonioni, Alain Resnais, and Godard. This was the heyday of auteur-based criticism, with close textual analysis serving to reveal the continuity of themes and style across the body of a director's work. Exemplary of this critical approach is the work of the British critic Robin Wood (1969), who devoted a book-length study to Bergman's films. Wood's study is a model of the sort of criticism—serious, humanistic, and text-based—that led to Bergman becoming synonymous with the idea of art cinema. With the

allegorical medievalism of *The seventh Seal* (1957) and the complex narrative time-schema of *Wild Strawberries* (1957), Bergman's first internationally successful films marked the director as being equally preoccupied with symbolism and psychology and therefore ripe for extensive critical exegesis and interpretation.

The cycle of more intimate 'chamber dramas' including *The Silence* (1963), *Persona* (1966)—one of the key films of the 1960s—and *Cries and Whispers* (1973) saw Bergman's focus narrow but become increasingly refined and austere, concentrating on intimate relationships, family breakdown, and the foregrounding of female characters. If art cinema can be seen to address its audience in such a way that audience identification shifts from characters to author (Cook 1985: 116), these films capitalized on this mode of address in their repeated casting of a troupe of performers, most notably the actresses Ingrid Thulin, Liv Ullmann, and Bibi Andersson, as well as Bergman's preferred actors, Max von Sydow and Gunnar Björnstrand. This family of performers lent Bergman's films an increasingly personal, autobiographical tone—a mode that perhaps reached its peak with *Fanny and Alexander* (1982)—and served to underline the authority of the director's control over his characters. Bergman's fascination with his female characters led Wood to assert: 'If one were to name the cinema's greatest director of women, the automatic response would probably be George Cukor. But on further reflection one might be tempted to retract this and say "No—Ingmar Bergman"' (Wood 1969).

In the 1970s feminist critics began to question the 'greatness' that Wood attributes to the director. In her essay 'Bergman's Portrait of Women: Sexism or Subjective Metaphor' (1979), Birgitta Steene critiques this characterization of Bergman. While she acknowledges that, in his 'chamber dramas', Bergman focused predominantly on female characters, she nevertheless identifies these films as conforming to a conventional artistic male perspective on female subjectivity that identifies femininity with hysteria.

That Bergman was to become the focus of alternative critical tendencies was to be expected, whether that perspective was feminist or one contextualizing the director within his national culture (Bergom-Larsson 1978); that he was unable to remain as central a figure to film studies, or even to film criticism, as Hitchcock is testimony to the way in which a commitment to art cinema was jettisoned in the 1970s, and faith was increasingly placed in an idea of 'the popular'. Bergman might be said to have been both occulted by academic fashions and a victim of his own art cinema success. Whatever the emphasis one chooses to place, it is to the disadvantage of academic film studies that such a crucial European director should remain quite so sidelined.

BIBLIOGRAPHY

Bergom-Larsson, Maria (1978), *Ingmar Bergman and Society* (London: Tantivy).

Cook, Pam (ed.) (1985), *The Cinema Book* (London: British Film Institute).

Elsaesser, Thomas (1994), 'Putting on a Show: The European Art Movie', *Sight and Sound*, 4/4 (Apr.), 22–7.

Godard, Jean-Luc (1958/1972), 'Bergmanorama', *Cahiers du cinéma*, 85 (July), in *Godard on Godard*, trans. Tom Milne, ed. Jean Narboni and Tom Milne (London: Secker & Warburg).

Rosenbaum, Jonathan (1993), 'Notes towards the Devaluation of Woody Allen', in *Placing Movies: The Practice of Film Criticism* (Berkeley: University of California Press).

Steene, Birgitta (1979), 'Bergman's Portrait of Women: Sexism or Subjective Metaphor', in Patricia Erens (ed.), *Sexual Stratagems: The World of Women in Film* (New York: Horizon Press).

Thompson, David (1994), *Biographical Dictionary of Cinema* (London: André Deutsch).

Wood, Robin (1969), *Ingmar Bergman* (London: Studio Vista).

(c) Chantal Akerman CATHY FOWLER

When, in 1981, Peter Wollen revised his initial definition of two avant-gardes, he also suggested that some work straddled the two. One body of work, he suggested, was that of Chantal Akerman, whom Wollen positions at some point between the two avant-garde traditions of New York and Paris. Although Akerman has since moved away from this mid-way position, her work retains that initial sense of hybridity, so that, while her films have a place in discussions of avant-garde cinema, art cinema, and (women's) auteur cinema, they do not fit neatly into any one of these categories.

For Anglo-American film theory, the value of Akerman's early films in the mid-1970s lay in their careful interrogation of film language at a time when film theory itself was trying to come to terms with the workings of the cinematic apparatus and cinema's textual operations. However, what distinguished Akerman's project from that of other 'modernist' directors such as Jean-Luc Godard and Michael Snow was the fact that she interrogated without actually interrupting the fictional world. Instead of a Godardian 'counter-cinema' in which Brechtian strategies ensure the distance and unpleasure necessary for a critical viewing, Akerman offered a different way of seeing and of making meaning. Although each of Akerman's films can be said to have a 'story', it is in the telling of that story that emphasis is shifted from narrative to other aspects such as time, space, ritual, and repetition. The result of this shift of focus is that attention is given to what would normally be considered 'minor' subjects. Thus *Jeanne Dielman, 23 quai du commerce, 1080 Bruxelles* (1975) depicts the quotidian rituals and routine of the eponymous widow over the course of three days, while in *News From Home* (1976), set in New York, we see not the meta-cinematic image, but those parts of the city which have been overlooked.

The 'difference' of Akerman's cinema, though, is primarily located in what can be seen as her stylistic signature. From her early films to her most recent work, Akerman has favoured the use of a low-angle static camera which sees its world through a tableau frame. This static framing is coupled with a denial of camera angles and movements, point-of-view shots and close-ups. Such a style could be read in terms of art cinema's 'objective realism' (Bordwell 1979), in which meaning is made according to the rules of reality rather than those of classical narrative. However, Akerman also enforces a denial of the conventional modes of

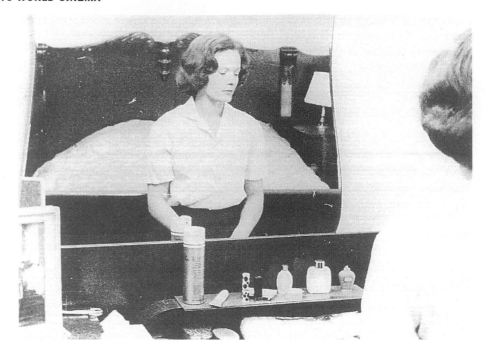

'Feminist film practice' and 'female aesthetic'—*Jeanne Dielman, 23 quai du commerce, 1080 Bruxelles* (1975)

identification and involvement, which lie uneasily within art cinema's mode of address.

Akerman's style is more usually read as promoting a liberation of the gaze: rather than examining the image in terms of narrative information, the spectator is allowed, and indeed encouraged, to let his or her gaze wander within the frame. In *Les Rendez-vous d'Anna* (1979) the lack of expression through camera movement and cutting would at first seem to echo the passive wandering of Anna. However, once the different gaze is in action, new levels of expression and meaning emerge. On one level Akerman's strategies could be seen as a response to Mulvey's call in her famous article 'Visual Pleasure and Narrative Cinema' to 'free the look of the camera into its materiality in time and space' (1975: 18), but on another level this style illustrates the 'cinema of attractions', theorized by Tom Gunning (1986) as one part of early cinema which he suggests finds its way into certain aspects of the avant-garde.

These connections with Mulvey and Gunning also refer us to the two key discourses within which Akerman's work has figured: feminist film theory and debates around avant-garde and alternative filmmaking. Akerman's unmoving camera offered a cinema which was neither ruled by narrative (having other priorities) nor regimented by a voyeuristic impulse. Both of

these aspects proved attractive to film feminism, which was seeking out ways of denying the spectacular objectification of woman which it saw as axiomatic of dominant cinema. *Jeanne Dielman*, released the same year as Mulvey's article, was seized upon as the key illustration of a 'feminist film practice' and 'female aesthetic' (Bergstrom 1977; Kuhn 1982: 173–4). Equally, as Wollen's reference to Akerman proves, her reintroduction of narrative and characters into the avant-garde's otherwise de-humanized world led the way for an alternative practice which would challenge mainstream cinema on its own ground.

If Akerman's denial of identification with characters opens the way for other ways of reading, then one of the strongest of these is via the 'auteur' Akerman. Yet, as with Akerman's use of avant-garde and art cinema strategies, important differences from conventional (read: male) auteur cinema should be noted. Though Akerman would deny any associations with a 'women's' auteur cinema, her films inevitably assert a different desire (which must be expressed through a different form) from the model which originated in the 1950s with *Cahiers du cinéma*.

The task of tracing Akerman's female authorship across all twenty-eight years of her filmmaking has yet to be undertaken, as film theory generally lost interest after her 1970s work. This lack of attention to her more recent work has meant an ignorance of the shifts these films make towards genre (melodrama in *Toute une nuit*, 1982, and the musical in *Golden Eighties*, 1986) and the spectacular elements of cinema. What is more, it has left Akerman associated almost wholly with 1970s discourses around the deconstruction of narrative for formal or political (feminist) purposes.

Other more important questions raised by her films of both the 1970s and later have also been ignored. Thus Akerman's place in French cinema was assured by her move to Paris in the mid-1980s and her subsequent dallying with 'French' subjects, actors, and inter-texts. However, this embracing of France has obscured Akerman's Belgian ties, and work is lacking on her 'Belgianness', whether through her relation to Belgian cinema (which is also relatively critically ignored), her place among a Belgian school of auteurs (other examples being André Delvaux, Jean-Jacques Andrien, and Marion Hänsel), or the ways in which her films explore this identity (specifically through *Toute une nuit*, which is set in Brussels).

Finally, Akerman's reintroduciton of genre, spectacle, and ultimately narrative pleasure into her work is echoed by feminist film theory's sudden fascination with these very same elements. It is here, then, that the critical connection could be renewed, and Akerman's work examined once more for the rigorous interrogation and, most recently, play with film language which it offers.

BIBLIOGRAPHY

Bergstrom, Janet (1977), '*Jeanne Dielman, 23 Quai de Commerce, 1080 Bruxelles* by Chantal Akerman', *Camera Obscura*, 2: 115–21.

Bordwell, David (1979), 'The Art Cinema as Mode of Film Practice', *Film Criticism*, 4/1 (Fall), 56–64.

Gunning, Tom (1986), 'The Cinema of Attractions', *Wide Angle*, 8/3–4 (Fall), 63–77.

Kuhn, Annette (1982), *Women's Pictures* (London: Routledge & Kegan Paul).

Mulvey, Laura (1975), 'Visual Pleasure and Narrative Cinema', *Screen*, 16/3 (Autumn), 6–18.

Wollen, Peter (1981), 'The Avant-Gardes: Europe and America', *Framework* 14: 9–10.

—— (1982), 'The Two Avant-Gardes', in *Readings and Writings* (London: Verso).

(d) **Pedro Almodóvar**   JOSÉ ARROYO

Pedro Almodóvar is the most successful film director of the post-Franco period in Spain and the best-known Spanish film director abroad since Luis Buñuel. His success is such that in Spain it is referred to as the 'Almodóvar phenomenon'. From *Pepi, Luci, Bom, y otras chicas del montón* ('Pepi, Luci, Bom, and Other Girls on the Heap', 1980), his first feature, each of his subsequent films outdid the box-office success of the previous one, a rise that climaxed with *Mujeres al borde de un ataque de nervios* ('Women on the Verge of a Nervous Breakdown', 1988), the most financially successful Spanish film ever. Abroad, Almodóvar's films have also succeeded: the films are international box-office hits; they have garnered excellent reviews and festival prizes; and, in English-language academic film studies, literature on Almodóvar represents a large and disproportionate amount of literature on Spanish film studies in general. Critical discussion of Almodóvar's work has focused on interrelated (though often decontextualized) issues of representation (gender, homosexuality, the nation) and on aesthetics (postmodernism).

Since *Pepi, Luci, Bom, y otras chicas del montón*, Almodóvar's films have centred on a gallery of complex women (housewives, nuns, lawyers, singers, actresses, writers, mothers, and daughters) who seek to fulfil their sometimes socially transgressive emotional and sexual desires: Luci (Eva Siva) is a masochist who wants to get beaten up; Sexilia (Cecilia Roth) in *Laberinto de pasiones* ('Labyrinth of Passion', 1982) is a nymphomaniac; the Mother Superior (Julieta Serrano) in *Entre tinieblas* ('Dark Habits', 1983) is a lesbian drug addict; Maria (Assumpta Serna) in *Matador* (1986) gets turned on by killing her sexual partners during orgasm.

However, these social transgressions are narrated as perfectly moral within the films' terms, and audiences are asked to identify with the transgressor. The women in Almodóvar's films have provided career-making roles for what amounts to a repertory company of actors which includes some of the biggest stars of Spanish cinema (Carmen Maura, Victoria Abril, Verónica Forqué) and some of the most able and appealing supporting players (Chus Lampreave, Maria Barranco, Rossy de Palma).

The male characters in Almodóvar's films are often rooted in the melodramatic clichés of Spanish popular culture: bullfighters, detectives, priests, brutal or adulterous husbands, escaped prisoners, sons dominated by their mothers. Many of the male characters in Almodóvar's films may be interpreted as failed attempts at hegemonic notions of masculinity or a *machista* ideal. For example, in *Matador* the bullfighter (Nacho Martinez) has been gored, the policeman (Eusebio Poncela) is gay, and the youth (Antonio Banderas) faints at the sight of blood. These three archetypes of Spanish machismo are subverted by the story and are also structurally subservient to their female counterparts in the film.

While the representation of men in Almodóvar's films has been largely downplayed if not downright ignored, the representation of women has received a great deal of attention. Women are so associated with Almodóvar's *œuvre* that the repertoire of actresses who appear in his films is often referred to as 'las chicas Almodóvar', a patronizing moniker that highlights their association with Almodóvar while obscuring their distinguished bodies of work in the theatre and in other films. Almodóvar is considered a 'women's director' and his representation of women has generally been lauded. However, the release of *¡Atame!* ('Tie Me Up! Tie Me Down!' 1990), a story of a former porn star who falls in love with her kidnapper, led to accusations of misogyny which have not quite abated. These accusations have been culturally specific. According to Paul Julien Smith, 'English- and German-speaking viewers attack Almodóvar for the "negative" political content of his images and Spanish and French critics absolve those images of any content, displace them wholly into ironic humour or pastiche' (1994: 112). Debates around the representation of gender and sexual orientation in Almodóvar's work have also raised questions about film criticism *per se*: should critics measure these films by 'universal' criteria or should cultural context be taken into account?

The question of sexual orientation has also been a key one in discussions of Almodóvar's work. The director is known to be gay and all of his films up to *La ley del deseo* ('The Law of Desire', 1987) featured homosexual characters. Lesbian characters featured prominently in *Pepi* and *Entre tinieblas*. Gay male characters featured in *Laberinto*, *¿Que he hecho yo para merecer esto?* ('What have I Done to Deserve This?', 1984), and *Matador*. *La ley*, up to now the only Almodóvar film to focus on a gay relationship, was a breakthrough for its director. Within Spain it was considered his first 'personal' film, in which subject-matter and what was known about the director's personal life finally coincided, and thus Almodóvar could finally be bestowed auteur status by critics. Outside Spain *La ley*'s publicity addressed a gay audience as well as the traditional art cinema audience for foreign films, and gay culture was instrumental in making of Almodóvar arguably the most popular auteur of 1980s international art-house cinema.

The representation of gender and sexual orientation in Almodóvar's films are of crucial importance in considering how his films came to represent post-Franco Spain at home and abroad. Basically these representations would not have been allowed before censorship was abolished in Spain in 1977. Gender was one of the certainties of Franco's Spain, whereas Almodóvar's films continually highlight its constructedness (as, for example, when he has Bibi Andersson, a well-known Madrid transsexual, play Ada's biological mother in *La ley*, while Carmen Maura plays a transsexual in the same film). However, Almodóvar's films also signified the 'new' Spain in other ways. *Pepi* and *Laberinto* were seen in Spain as almost documents of the Movida madrileña, a diverse group of young underground artists who aimed to test the limits of the new freedoms in various arts. Almodóvar's films stress their 'modernity', i.e. their commonalities with the rest of Europe, and by doing so distance themselves not only from the privations of the Franco years but also from contemporary Spanish cinema, which in the 1980s seemed to be obsessively trawling through those privations. Almodóvar's films are urban, camp, frivolous, sexy, colourful, fun, and free. They epitomize how post-Franco Spain liked to see itself and how it liked to be seen (*La Ley* was the film that most represented Spain in international film festivals in 1987).

Almodóvar's films have lent themselves easily to theories of postmodernism: they can be seen as pastiches, they rely on intertextuality, they de-centre tradi-

'Urban, campy, frivolous, sexy, colourful, fun, and free'—Almodóvar's *Kika* (1993)

tional notions of socio-sexual identity, and, through their uses of television, they seem both to embody and to ironize Jean Baudrillard's notion of the hyper-real. Almodóvar borrows indiscriminately from film history. A case in point is ¿Que he hecho?, which contains direct reference to, or echoes of Neo-Realism, the caper film, *Carrie*, Luis Buñuel, Billy Wilder, Andy Warhol, and John Waters. Moreover, it is clear that Almodóvar's preferred mode of cinema is the melodramatic. It is a mode that cuts across genre, equally capable of conveying the tragic and the comic, eminently emotional, adept at arousing intense audience identification, and capable of communicating complex psychological processes no matter what the character's gender or sexual orientation.

Almodóvar's signature, and a unique contribution to the movies, is the synthesis of the melodramatic mode with a clash of quotations. This combination allows Almodóvar both a quasi-classical Hollywood narrative structure (which facilitates audience identification) and a very self-conscious narration (which normally pro-

duces a sense of alienation. This results in dialectical moments in which the absurd is imbued with emotional resonance (the mother selling her son to the dentist in ¿Que he hecho?). In this way the emotional can be checked with cheek without disrupting identification (superimposing a character's crying eyes with the wheels of a car in *La ley*) and camp can be imbued with depth without losing its wit (the transference of emotions that occurs when we see Pepa dubbing Joan Crawford's dialogue from *Johnny Guitar* in *Mujeres*). At his best (¿Que he hecho?, *La ley*, *Mujeres*), Almodóvar drills a heart into the postmodern and fills it with an operatic range of feeling.

In Spain critical attention has focused more on Almodóvar's films as a sociological phenomenon (on what their popularity, themes, marketing, design, and characters say about contemporary Spain) than on their artistic merits. Abroad, however, Almodóvar's work has been a rich mine to academics involved in various areas including feminism, Hispanic studies, queer studies, and film studies. Critics and scholars have focused on the consistencies of Almodóvar's *œuvre*: his focus on women, his use of boleros and other sentimental music, the insertion of satirical advertisements in the narrative, the urban setting, the characters' search for pleasure, the themes of passion and desire. There is a tendency to narrate his career in terms of his 'underground' work (*Pepi*, *Laberinto*), his work for other producers (*Entre tinieblas*, *¿Que he hecho?*, *Matador*), and the work he produced after setting up his own independent company (from *La ley* to the present). The beginning of the last period is seen as the pinnacle of his success (*La ley*, *Mujeres*) before a gentle but steady decline (*A'tame*; *Tacones lejanos*, 'High Heels', 1991), *Kika* (1993), and then a resurgence (*La flor de mi secreto*, 'The Flower of my Secret', 1995). With few exceptions (Paul Julien Smith's (1992, 1994, 1996) exemplary work; Vernon and Morris's (1995) excellent collection of essays), foreign critics have tended to ignore the films' industrial and cultural context.

BIBLIOGRAPHY

Abaladejo, Miguel et al. (1988), *Los fantasmas del deseo: a propósito de Pedro Almodóvar* (Madrid: Aula 7).

Besas, Peter (1985), *Behind the Spanish Lens: Spanish Cinema under Fascism and Democracy* (Denver: Arden Press).

Blanco, Francisco (pseud. Boquerini) (1989), *Pedro Almodóvar* (Madrid: Ediciones JC).

García de León, Maria, and Teresa Maldonado (1989), *Pedro Almodóvar: la otra España cañi* (Ciudad Real: Biblioteca de Autores y temas Manchegos).

Higginbotham, Virginia (1988), *Spanish Film under Franco* (Austin: University of Texas Press).

Hopewell, John (1986), *Out of the Past: Spanish Cinema after Franco* (London: British Film Institute).

Kinder, Marsha (1993), *Blood Cinema: The Reconstruction of National Identity in Spain* (Berkeley: University of California Press).

Smith, Paul Julien (1992) *Law of Desire: Questions of Homosexuality in Spanish Writing and Film 1960–1990* (Oxford: Clarendon Press).

—— (1994), *Desire Unlimited: The Cinema of Pedro Almodóvar* (London: Verso).

—— (1996), *Vision Machines: Cinema, Literature and Sexuality in Spain and Cuba 1983–1993* (London: Verso).

Strauss, Frédéric (1996), *Almodóvar on Almodóvar*, trans. Yves Baignères (London; Faber & Faber).

Vernon, Kathleen M., and Barbara Morris (1995), *Post-Franco, Postmodern: The Films of Pedro Almodóvar* (Westport, Conn.: Greenwood Press).

(e) Luc Besson   SUSAN HAYWARD

A very anti-establishment director, Besson aims to compete technically with American action films, quoting as his inspiration Sam Peckinpah. His work is visually and sonorifically pulsating and technically brilliant. Dominant themes of loneliness, suffering, and displacement resonate throughout his work. A new moralist of the cinema, in the tradition of Jean Renoir, he exposes the negative connotations of commodity fetishism: consumer goods as signs of death. Against this he opposes his modest protagonists, with their vision of self-fulfilment, the value of which is based in a purely personal aesthetic (for example, the music in *Subway* (1985); deep-sea diving in *Le Grand Bleu* (1988); violence in *Nikita* (1991) and *Léon* ('The Professional', 1994)).

To date Besson has made seven feature films, including *Atlantis* (1991), his homage to the sea; and his most recent film, 'The Fifth Element' (*Le Cinquième Élément*.) However, this relatively young filmmaker says he will go on to make only ten, partly because, much like Constantin Costa-Gavras, it takes him two years to make a film. With the exception of his first feature film, *Le Dernier Combat* (1983), which was liked by all, Besson's work has been acclaimed by popular film critics in journals like *Première* and dismissed by other, more heavyweight critics in journals like *Cahiers du cinéma* and *Positif*. All of his films, none the less, have been huge successes with audiences of the 1980s and 1990s (which consist mostly of 15- to 35-year-olds) in France and abroad—in the United States and particularly Japan.

Besson lays no claim to being an auteur; indeed, he says he does not make art or culture—he tells stories. And the stories he tells are of individuals who experience great difficulty in adapting to society, who are prevented from achieving their goals because they are in a state of 'dis-ease' with society—a society, Besson claims, that has seriously unbalanced the family and thereby created emotional deprivation in young people. His films are his way of fighting against this, and, given the appeal of his work, it is clear that Besson is a filmmaker who makes films that are perceived as signs of their time.

Besson broke into the film scene very young, aged 17, and, from 1976 to 1982 worked across virtually all the film set jobs: from gofer to casting, and from camera assistant to editing assistant. In these early years he also made advertisements, short films, and promotional films for songs. What emerged from these formative years was a filmmaker of deep convictions, particularly in the domain of cinema technology, as is evidenced by his commitment to CinemaScope, designing special lightweight cameras, and use of the Louma crane. These convictions include a deep-rooted non-conformity. Ever since he founded his own production company, Les Films du loup, to finance his first feature film, Besson has fought against the rules and conventions established by producers and distributors. He now owns a second company, Les films du dauphin. But, more significantly, he has shown, through his own filmmaking practices, the way in which the French film industry can compete with the Americans: by co-financing, and shooting in English, but retaining director's control (in short, by making hybrid films that cut across French and American cultures).

All Besson's films have violence at the core of the narrative. But it is not just a case of 'designer violence'. Violence is inscribed onto the body; the body becomes the site of violence. More significantly still, violence is represented not just through any body but through that of the main protagonist. In other words, the site of representation for violence is the star text. The star embodies a tension that melds violence with fragility, be it Christophe Lambert (*Subway*), Anne Parillaud (*Nikita*), or Jean Reno (*Léon*). Nor is this tension restricted to a particular gender, as the eponymous heroine of *Nikita* makes clear. With Besson's films, the star text, in the end, disappears—either literally or through death. And technology functions as an extension of this violence which leads to their disappearance. Cameras, high-powered, long-distance rifles with telescopic lenses, proliferate in Besson's films; even the superficially non-violent *Le Grand Bleu* abounds with camera technology that probes and investigates. In his films, technology is a two-way system. Cameras function as instruments of investigation

and surveillance, and while the star text may well use them to observe and destroy, they are also used to observe and destroy him or her. Technology stands as a metaphor for the conformity and control and the policing of social norms, all of which are institutionally sanctioned. It is against this that Besson's heroes and heroines revolt—first in the form of aggression against the norms, and secondly in the form of violence against the self.

Besson's protagonists, then, fail or are unwilling to adapt to contemporary society. And this partly manifests itself in their regressive nature. Isabelle Adjani erupts like a petulant teenager in *Subway*; Lambert (in the same film) persists in fulfilling his childhood fantasy of starting a rock band at the expense of completing his Oedipal trajectory. Jean-Marc Barr (*Le Grand Bleu*) tops himself deep-sea diving rather than resume 'normal' life with his child-bearing landlubber partner, Rosanna Arquette. Anne Parillaud (*Nikita*) remains stuck as a woman-child robotic hit-woman, only to disappear, and Jean Reno (alias *Léon*) does much the same as a man-child robotic hit-man. Fathers and mothers are massively absent except in substitute form, and when they are present in a film they are as dysfunctional as the adult-child they are purporting to parent.

As a filmmaker, Besson has been described as neo-baroque, post-New Wave, and postmodern. From both the point of view of style and genre he is indeed all of these. His films are highly stylized bricolage, pastiche, and reproduction, and they cut across genres. *Subway*, for example, is a melodrama, a musical, and a thriller. It is also a remake that is as indebted to Jean Cocteau's *Orphée* (1949) as it is to any American television cop series. In this film ugliness is emptied out and atmospheric shots transform the Paris Métro into an attractive, even seductive, space where anything can and does happen. This, coupled with the interplay between illusion and reality, is high baroque at its best.

In terms of the New Wave and the postmodern, Besson—like his antecedents—does play with genre and film style. He also addresses spectator pleasure derived from the foregrounding of generic elements and visual and aural counterpointing, even to the point of excess. Like the New Wave filmmakers, he is a director-producer who is technology-conscious. But he also harks back to earlier times. In his own practices of team filmmaking, he recalls those of filmmakers in the 1930s. Finally, as much as he is in a tradition of French filmmaking, he is also a ground-breaker in that he has managed to marry Frenchness with internationalism: French films with speed and visual brilliance—what could be termed an American edge—something serious critics may find difficult to countenance.

BIBLIOGRAPHY

Austin, Guy (1996), *Contemporary French Culture* (Manchester: Manchester University Press).

Hayward, Susan (forthcoming), *Luc Besson: Filmmaker* (Manchester: Manchester University Press).

(f) Brigitte Bardot   GINETTE VINCENDEAU

Brigitte Bardot, or 'B.B.', is arguably the French film star best known internationally. As in the case of her contemporary Marilyn Monroe, her fame outlasts the period of her main films, the late 1950s and early 1960s. In the mid-1990s she is still a recognizable icon in several areas of popular culture: film and television, fashion, postcards, music, coffee-table books, and even current affairs, for her involvement in animal rights campaigns. Her extraordinary youthful beauty, 'ideal' body, and powerful sexual aura position her as a traditional object of male desire. At the same time, the bold expression of her desire and rebellious stance make her enduringly fascinating for women, including feminists. Her star persona is thus characterized by a series of dualities and paradoxes: she is both traditional sexual object *and* agent of her own sexuality; she can be seen as modern heroine or retrograde version of femininity. Her international fame needs to be studied as part of contemporary (global) popular culture, while her persona needs to be understood within the specific context of French cinema and French culture of the 1950s.

A European star

After appearing in sixteen films, Brigitte Bardot emerged (at the age of 22) as a star in *Et Dieu . . . créa la femme*, directed in 1956 by her then husband, Roger Vadim. The character of Juliette she plays in this film was instantly perceived as a new and *authentic* type, closely connected to Bardot the real person. As Richard Dyer (1979) has shown, the popularity of stars can be ascribed in large part to the way they crystallize and authenticate social values which the audience can relate to. Bardot in this respect is a powerful example of

stardom, as a woman emblematic of a new—and controversial—type of femininity. A beautiful and charismatic performer who was obsessively photographed and imitated and whose life became the object of intense media scrutiny, she was also a star in the film industry sense of the term.

Bardot became a valuable commodity for the French film industry, in terms of export (in the late 1950s she allegedly earned France more foreign currency than the Renault car factory) more than on the domestic market, where she briefly challenged but did not displace the male hegemony: the top ten French stars of the post-war period have all been men. Thus the phenomenon of her popularity is complex. Her films enjoyed box-office success for a short period of time (1956–65) and low critical status, with the exception of *La Vérité* (1960) and *Le Mépris* ('Contempt', 1963), but her *image* appealed to the public on a massive scale, and became associated with a particular vision of French femininity (she modelled for Marianne, the effigy of the Republic). Virtually all writing on Bardot is interested in her global image and her life rather than her films. This is just as true of Simone de Beauvoir's seminal text (1960), Edgar Morin's sociological study of stars (1957), and Catherine Rihoit's excellent analysis of Bardot's 'myth' (1986) as of the numerous coffee-table books (Crawley 1975; Evans 1972; French 1994), biographies (Roberts 1984; Robinson 1994) and Andy Martin's 'romance' (1996). This is as much to do with the extraordinary vividness of Bardot's image as with the fact that most of her films were mainstream French productions and thus suffer from the common lack of critical interest in popular European cinema (Vincendeau). Bardot's own memoirs (1996) have equally little time for her films.

Following *Et Dieu . . . créa la femme*, a series of films

Brigitte Bardot—'sex kitten', cultural icon, feminist role model?

were made that perpetuated, accommodated, or commented on the image developed in that film. Out of the twenty-eight films she subsequently made, *La Vérité*, *En cas de malheur* ('Love is my Profession', 1958), *Vie privée* (1961), *Babette s'en va-t-en guerre* (1959), *Le Mépris* (1963), and *Viva Maria* (1965) constitute the classic Bardot canon. Bardot can be regarded as the 'author' of these films, from both an industry and a theoretical point of view. All post-1956 Bardot films were marketed on her name (now even films such as *Les Grandes Manœuvres* (1955), in which she played a small part, appear in a video collection of her films marketed in the United Kingdom). They built their narrative entirely around her. *La Vérité*, *Vie privée*, and *Le Mépris* are, in addition, commentaries on her stardom. In the French cinema of the 1950s and early 1960s, with no studio in the American sense to 'groom' her, and a diffuse genre system, a star such as Bardot acquired special importance, as a stable element in an otherwise unregulated industry. However, as French directors commanded more decision-making power than in Hollywood, with a few exceptions (most obviously Jean-Luc Godard) Bardot worked with French directors without a strong authorial agenda. Given Bardot's high 'authorial' role and the lack of attention her films have elicited so far, a thorough study of Bardot's function in French mainstream cinema from the mid-1950s to the mid-1960s would be both original and illuminating.

Bardot emerged at a time when European cinema was trying to take advantage of the weakening of the Hollywood studio system and the end of the Hays Code. Female sexuality was a selling-point not lost on Vadim: 'Of course the success of *Et Dieu . . . créa la femme* came from its sexual frankness . . . That is what distributors, and especially American ones, demanded' (Vadim 1976). The European cinema of the late 1940s and 1950s produced successful stars such as Sophia Loren, Silvana Mangano, and Harriet Andersson, noted for their 'natural' sexuality, compared with the overtly manufactured glamour of Hollywood stars such as Monroe. Bardot in this respect is poised half-way between the blonde glamour of Monroe and Diana Dors in the United Kingdom (she had started her career as a brunette) and the 'earthy' sexuality of Loren and Mangano. Later, she would form a contrast with the more 'intellectual' stars of the New Wave, such as Anna Karina and Jeanne Moreau. Bardot's sexuality was her main asset and the most debated area of her persona.

Sexuality: feminist debates

Bardot epitomizes the attributes and paradoxes of the sex goddess. In her films, the camera systematically highlights her face and body in a suggestive manner; her full, pouting mouth and wild mane of hair are picked up by close-ups, while her breasts, hips, bottom, and legs are emphasized by her poses, clothes, and camera angles in a way which frequently evokes strip-tease or pin-up. Her sexuality and its impact are at the core of the narratives. *Et Dieu . . . créa la femme* and *La Vérité* are exemplary in this respect. Bardot's sexuality is a disruptive force which the community (Saint Tropez, provincial France, even Paris's bohemian Latin Quarter) tries to tame, with difficulty. Here, two paradoxes operate. First, there is a dichotomy between mise-en-scène and narrative. The work of the camera clearly 'objectifies' Bardot: in Laura Mulvey's terms, it emphasizes her 'to-be-looked-at-ness' (Mulvey 1975), and her films offer spectacular moments of display (for example, the mambo sequence at the end of *Et Dieu . . .*). At the same time, the narrative point of view gives the spectator more knowledge of her subjectivity than the characters around her possess; in *La Vérité*, the spectator knows long before the jury that she is 'not guilty'. Secondly, like the *femmes fatales* of American film noir, Bardot dominates her films, but is punished at the end: in *Et Dieu . . .* she is denied the man she desires, in *En cas de malheur*, *La Vérité*, and *Le Mépris* she dies brutally.

Bardot's originality, her 'scandal', however, comes from another, more powerful, paradox. In her films, unlike the more 'reactive' Monroe, she takes active pleasure in her body and expresses her own desire. In Simone de Beauvoir's much-quoted remark, in the sexual game, she is 'the hunter, not the prey' (Beauvoir 1960). This feature underlines the films' narratives— she goes after the men she wants, or from whom she wants things—and her performance: her direct gaze, insolent voice, rebellious or *j'men-foutiste* (careless) poses. This was reinforced by her off-screen promiscuous and non-conformist life-style: many lovers, several husbands, a child whom she rejected, as she confirms in her memoirs (Bardot 1996). Many of her songs reiterated this message, for instance her hit *Sidonie* ('Sidonie has more than one lover'). Sex, however, is a double-edged weapon for women; as de Beauvoir also pointed out, the Bardot persona called forth the most reactionary myth of the 'eternal feminine', a fantasy of an identity reduced to sex. As Vadim ineffably put it, she would be 'the impossible dream of married men'. Following Beauvoir, many feminist commentators have debated this paradox, some celebrating Bardot as a role model or a 'force of nature', others voicing more or less stringent criticism of a misogynistic representation. Among those celebrating Bardot's use of sexuality as empowering are Françoise Audé (1979) and Camille Paglia, speaking on the Channel 4 programme *Without Walls* (1994). Others are more critical, emphasizing the misogyny of the Bardot character (Burch and Sellier 1995) and others again concentrate on the ambivalence of the Bardot persona (Rihoit 1986; Vincendeau 1992) as well as her enduring fascination for feminists (Merck 1994). Ultimately, the irreducibility of the paradox is precisely what makes Bardot fascinating: rather than being either pure male fantasy, or affirmation of women's desire, she is both. The force of her star persona is to reconcile these two antagonistic aspects.

> **The paradox is precisely what makes Bardot fascinating: rather than being either pure male fantasy, or affirmation of women's desire, she is both. The force of her star persona is to reconcile these two antagonistic aspects.**

Bardot was truly a 'shocking' figure whose attitude was ahead of what was permitted to women at the time, illustrated by the passion and hostility she provoked (as detailed in her memoirs; Bardot 1996). Her films were banned in many provincial towns, in France and abroad, and her appeal, like the narrative conflicts of her films, arose simultaneously from her sexual aura and from its repression. It is noticeable that the later films in her career, for example *Si Don Juan était une femme* ('Don Juan was a Woman', 1973), made in a more liberal era, increased the display of her naked body—edging towards soft pornography—but lost audience appeal. She had served her purpose. Bardot's sexual persona was crucially connected to her youth and the era of her youth. While a mature sexuality was evoked, she occupied the territory of the sex kitten in her looks and performance style—her initials 'B.B.' ('bébé' in French) stand in for baby in both senses of infant and young woman. Furthermore, one may,

from a feminist point of view, see the limits of her sexual rebellion in the way it was always pitted against mother figures (usually hostile), but aimed at pleasing father figures. And the image of sexual liberation she proposed was, for women too, a fantasy: in 1950s Catholic France dominant sexual mores—especially outside Paris—were oppressive to women (though lenient to men); contraception and abortion were illegal.

The modernity of Bardot

As central as sexuality was to the Bardot phenomenon, it does not exhaust her novelty or interest. Bardot crystallized the importance and sexiness of youth during the wave of modernization that swept through post-war France, especially from the advent of de Gaulle's Fifth Republic in 1958. Bardot both anticipated and epitomized the rise of youth consumer power. Like James Dean in America, she embodied a notion of youthful rebellion, and her films dramatize generational conflicts. The paradox mentioned earlier in relation to her sexuality, of her triumph over the narrative of her films, and yet fateful endings can be reread as expressing an ambivalence towards modernity, desired yet feared. Here, a thorough examination of all her films would especially yield useful information on France's attitude to modernization.

If Bardot became such a model, if her hairstyle and clothes were widely imitated (Mylène Demongeot and Julie Christie are the most obvious examples), it is because she signalled a new era of fashion and behaviour. Compared with the rigid and expensive *couture* clothes of her mother's generation and previous French stars, such as Michèle Morgan and Edwige Feuillère, Bardot proposed a cheap and easy, yet sexy and glamorous, alternative: the famous gingham dresses, Capri pants, and striped sailors' tops, the working overalls wittily unbuttoned. When, in *Et Dieu . . . créa la femme*, she tells Curt Jurgens's rich woman friend that she bought her dress 'on the market', she symbolically signals the end of *haute couture* and the arrival of *prêt-à-porter*. Her 'unkempt' hairstyle equally makes nonsense of the neat perms of her predecessors, from Martine Carol to Danielle Darrieux, and her contemporaries Monroe and Dors. It is fitting that in the nostalgic 1990s her most prominent heiress is supermodel Claudia Schiffer (in the French cinema, one can look to Vanessa Paradis and Béatrice Dalle as latter-day versions of her uppity young sexual rebels).

But Bardot signalled modernity in more profound and ambivalent ways. Emerging at the time when the cinema started putting characters on the streets, the Bardot heroines took women characters from the domestic sphere into public space. True, these spaces tended to be, like Saint Tropez and central Paris, the playground of the rich. But it is also true that the subversiveness of this move can be measured by the frequency with which she was punished. In the eyes of the judge in *La Vérité*, one of her greatest crimes is being attracted to 'the bright lights and shop windows of the Champs-Élysées'. Another is that she is reading Simone de Beauvoir's *Les Mandarins*.

The key to Bardot's appeal, alongside her looks and sexual aura, was her 'naturalness'. It no doubt corresponds to a genuine desire for innocence, transparency, and freedom—very much a leitmotif in her memoirs—but it is a desire which also sums up her era. In this respect, one needs to explore further the emergence of 'the natural' in late 1950s and early 1960s culture, together with Bardot's 'non-performance' style of performance, her on- and off-screen association with children, animals, and what would now be called 'world music'. I would concur with feminist historian Michelle Perrot (1996), who argues that Bardot represented not so much a new woman as the male desire for that new woman. Furthermore, like all sex goddesses, she must not age, as the caricatures and comments that accompany photographs of her ageing show. However, unlike Monroe and Dors, Bardot did not suffer a tragic death. In her memoirs, which must rank as among the best in the genre, she reveals herself to be in turn exasperating, spoilt, and fully of her (bourgeois) class, but equally shrewd, tough, and extremely funny. She proves that there can be life and fun after the sex goddess. Her image, however, like the one she chose for the cover of her memoirs, is bound to remain eternally young and beautiful.

BIBLIOGRAPHY

Audé, Françoise (1979) *Ciné-modèles, Cinéma d'elles* (Lausanne: L'Age d'homme).

Bardot, Brigitte (1996), *Initiales B.B.: Mémoires* (Paris: Bernard Grasset).

Beauvoir, Simone de (1960), *Brigitte Bardot and the Lolita Syndrome* (London: André Deutsch and Weidenfeld & Nicolson).

Burch, Noël, and **Geneviève Sellier** (1995), *La Drôle de guerre des sexes du cinéma français* (Paris: Nathan).

Crawley, Tony (1975), *Bébé* (LSP books).

Dyer, Richard (1979), *Stars* (London: British Film Institute).

Evans, Peter (1972), *Bardot, Eternal Sex Goddess* (London: Leslie Frewin).

French, Sean (1994), *Bardot* (London: Pavilion Books).

Martin, Andy (1996), *Waiting for Bardot* (London: Faber & Faber).

Merck, Mandy (1994), *Perversions, Deviant Readings* (London: Virago).

Morin, Edgar (1957), *Les Stars* (Paris: Éditions du Seuil).

Mulvey, Laura (1975), 'Visual Pleasure and Narrative Cinema', *Screen*, 16/3: 6–18.

Perrot, Michelle (1996), interviewed on *Brigitte Bardot*, Arte, June.

Rihoit, Catherine (1986), *Brigitte Bardot, un mythe français* (Paris: Livre de poche).

Roberts, Glenys (1984), *Bardot: A Personal Biography* (London: Sidgwick & Jackson).

Robinson, Jeffrey, (1994) *Bardot: Two Lives* (London: Simon & Schuster).

Vadim, Roger (1976), *Memoirs of the Devil* (London: Arrow Books).

Vincendeau, Ginette (1992), 'The Old and the New: Brigitte Bardot in 1950s France', *Paragraph*, 15: 73–96.

Anglophone national cinemas

14

British cinema

Andrew Higson

In the late 1960s two prominent British film critics complained that British cinema was an 'unknown cinema' (Lovell 1969), 'utterly amorphous, unclassified, unperceived' (Wollen 1969: 115). What Lovell and Wollen had in mind was not that there wasn't a popular film culture, or that audiences didn't watch British films or know how to make sense of them, but that British films had not been written about extensively by the new generation of critics, historians, and scholars. In the late 1960s little serious critical writing engaged with British cinema, past or present, and certainly not on the scale of the strong body of writing about American cinema that already existed. There were no major studies of key British directors, no influential surveys of the most important genres of the British cinema, no

detailed analyses of the output of individual studios. All this has changed in the last couple of decades with numerous publications classifying the history and present configuration of British cinema from the point of view of the dominant critical discourses of academic film studies. It would be misleading, however, to suggest that no serious attempts had been made to classify British cinema before this period.

Over the years various commentators have constructed their preferred versions of British cinema. Inevitably, this has brought competing definitions of British cinema, its strengths, and its weaknesses into the market-place of ideas. In each period, however, certain key ideas have prevailed over others so that it is possible to talk about the dominant critical discourses of the moment. The films which have the greatest prominence in the history books may occasionally be those which fared best at the box-office. But they are just as likely to be those which most met the approval of the prevailing critical discourse, or which captured the imagination of influential critics and intellectuals. The understanding of British cinema promoted by those discourses has been written into the histories of that cinema so that future generations have also been coloured by the same critical judgements. It is only in recent years that a new revisionist history of British cinema has emerged which both attempts to understand why certain films have appealed to particular critics, and goes behind the discourses mobilized by those critics to reassess, or even rediscover, other traditions of filmmaking.

It is in this spirit that I chart the historical development of the critical discourses which have dominated intellectual debate about cinema in Britain. Which are the films, the filmmakers, and the traditions of filmmaking that have been singled out for attention, and why? Why have other films been neglected? And how is British cinema understood as a national cinema, distinct from Hollywood, its main competitor?

The first efforts at writing about British cinema as a specifically national cinema with its own characteristics and sensibility can be found in the specialist film trade press in the 1910s. Already, some of the problems facing later commentators on British cinema dogged the writers of the 1910s. How could British films comprise a national cinema when American films were so popular with British audiences? If British-made films simply copied American styles and stories, could they really be considered British? And if international standards were defined by the films of the emergent Hollywood studio system, how should one evaluate British films which worked according to different standards? Were they to be seen as primitive, because they lagged behind the well-made American film, failing to use what were seen by many as the most up-to-date and appropriate methods for story construction and film style? Or were they to be seen as specifically British (which very often meant English), working over national themes in a distinctively national style?

A number of observers in the 1910s and early 1920s commented on what they saw as just such a national cinema, especially in the work of Cecil Hepworth's company. They focused on the many tasteful and respectable adaptations of canonic British literature which emerged in these years, and on those films which used a particular picturesque version of the English rural landscape for their setting. Perhaps the high point of this tradition of filmmaking, and the critical discourse which valorized it, was Hepworth's final feature film, *Comin' thro' the Rye*, an elegant and slow-moving literary adaptation, which was first released, significantly, during the British Film Weeks of 1923 and 1924 (Higson 1995).

From the perspective of the late 1920s, by which time the critical landscape had changed dramatically, such films, and the discourse which supported them, seemed far too parasitic upon the other more established and respectable arts, and especially literature and theatre. But this particular conception of the quality British film has never been entirely displaced. Tasteful and reverential adaptations of canonic novels or plays, performed by the cream of British theatre-trained actors, have always been able to curry critical favour, most recently in the form of heritage films such as the Merchant–Ivory version of E. M. Forster's *Howards End* (1993) (Higson 1993, 1996a). There are many who feel that this is what British filmmakers do best, even as there are others who feel this has little to do with what they would define as cinema (or the specifically cinematic).

This tension between different ideas of what constitutes good cinema can already be seen in the 1920s. If Hepworth's films dominated critical thinking about British cinema as a national cinema in the early 1920s, the agenda had changed radically by the late 1920s. In the intervening years, a new intellectual film culture had emerged in Britain, around the Film Society, founded in 1925, and specialist publications such as the periodical *Close Up*, which first appeared in 1927, and Paul Rotha's influential *The Film till Now*, first published in 1930. The critical discourses put into circulation in this period had a major impact over the next three decades on the way in which British cinema was understood and written about by those who preferred not to have their film tastes dictated by the box-office.

The prevailing concern was to find a way of treating cinema as an art form in line with the main tenets of modernist thinking. The most significant films from this point of view were those of the emergent European art cinema, and especially German Expressionism, French Impressionism, and Soviet montage cinema. British cinema was berated for failing to develop along the same lines as these film movements, and for remaining too attached to the pre-modernist sensibility of a Hepworth. Rotha and the *Close-Up* critics could perceive no British film movement with a distinctively modernist national style. The exception that proved the rule was the young Alfred Hitchcock, described in *Close-Up* as 'the one man in this country who can think cinema' (Castle 1930: 189). What was admired in Hitchcock's films was the commitment to visual narration, to metaphor and symbolism, to dynamic lighting and camera angles, and to the meaningfulness of editing, the juxtaposition of one shot with another (Ryall 1986).

By the early 1930s a distinctively British film movement was emerging, a movement that was subsequently to be promoted by its supporters as 'Britain's outstanding contribution to the cinema' (Arts Enquiry 1947: 1). This was the documentary movement, associated above all with the name of John Grierson. Interest in the movement was initially assured among intellectuals because of its commitment to a modernist understanding of cinema as an art form, and especially to montage. But it was the commitment to the realist representation of contemporary Britain and of ordinary British people which secured the reputation of the documentary movement as the foundation of a specifically national cinema (Hood 1983; Lovell and Hillier 1972). The documentarists not only made films, but also wrote extensively about their films (e.g. Rotha 1936; Hardy 1946). Their influence on thinking about British cinema can be seen in the extent to which subsequent histories privileged the documentary movement, as if this was the only development of significance in the British cinema of the 1930s.

> **It was the commitment to the realist representation of contemporary Britain and of ordinary British people which secured the reputation of the documentary movement as the foundation of a specifically national cinema.**

The commitment to realism and to the documentary idea persisted into the 1940s, under the peculiar conditions of wartime filmmaking. By now the centre-ground of critical debate had been won by a prominent group of mainly journalistic film reviewers (Ellis 1996) who were familiar with the achievements of the documentary film movement but who felt that the pure documentary was too austere and needed to be tempered by the more imaginative and populist elements of the narrative feature film. These critics promoted a series of quality British films, from *In which we Serve* (1942) to *This Happy Breed* (1944) and beyond, which, like documentary, dealt with the contemporary lives of ordinary people. They saw in these films the emergence of a distinctively national cinema, in which the nation was represented as a consensual community, with people of different classes, regions, and genders pulling together for the common good (Barr 1977; Higson 1995).

One of the key features of the realist-dominated critical debates of the 1930s and 1940s was an anxiety about popular cinema and what was perceived as a standardized, artistically impoverished, trivial, and escapist mass culture. What was desired was a culturally respectable quality national cinema, which meant in effect a middle-class cinema. The preferred aesthetic was one of social responsibility, restraint, and sincerity, with individual desire subsumed within the communal enterprise. This was in contradistinction to what critics such as Roger Manvell (1944) saw as the irresponsibility of Hollywood's flamboyance, its wish-fulfilling fantasy and escapist individualism. Britain's popular genre filmmaking fared no better. Indeed, it has only been in the last couple of decades that Britain's popular cinema has been taken seriously within critical debate, with previously discredited genres re-evaluated as significant elements of the national cinema.

Take the costume picture, for instance, one of the most popular genres of the 1930s and 1940s. The effort to promote a realist quality national cinema during those years was pulled in two directions when faced with historical drama. On the one hand, such films seemed escapist, since they apparently refused to confront the realities of the present. On the other hand, certain costume pictures, such as Laurence Olivier's Shakespeare adaptations and David Lean's Dickens adaptations of the 1940s, seemed culturally respectable, either because they were adapted from canonic national literature, or because their representations of the past were promoted as authentic—that is, realist—historical re-creations. Either way, the vast majority of often extremely popular period pictures—the Gainsborough costume dramas like *The Wicked Lady* (1945), for instance—were dismissed by the critical consensus as unworthy of serious consideration.

That consensus became increasingly unstable as the

1940s progressed and, between the late 1940s and the mid-1960s, a split began to emerge. On the one hand, there was a continuing commitment to realism. This culminated in the celebration of, first, a series of documentaries made in the mid-1950s, promoted collectively as Free Cinema, and secondly, the 'kitchen sink' dramas made at the turn of the new decade by the same people who had now graduated to feature filmmaking (Hill 1986). From this point of view, films like *Saturday Night and Sunday Morning* (1960) and *This Sporting Life* (1963), about working-class life in provincial England, were seen to have inherited the legacy of the documentary movement of the 1930s and the quality film movement of the 1940s.

On the other hand, there was in this same period, through magazines such as *Sequence* and *Movie*, a renewed critical interest in cinemas outside Britain, from the post-war European art cinemas to Hollywood. What held these interests together was the concern for the idea of the director as author. When critics attached to this auteurist perspective turned their attention to British cinema, they could find almost no signs of the distinctive world-view or the dynamic and consistent style that they associated with the true film author. This was in many ways a return to the critical debates of the late 1920s, with Michael Powell this time the exception that proved the rule. Here was a filmmaker whose career had been virtually destroyed by the realist critics, who were unable to cope with the extravagance and internationalism of his films, and their poetic and often fantastic qualities. But it was precisely these qualities that appealed to *Movie*'s brand of auteurism and that singled out Powell from the rest of British cinema (Christie 1978).

Even so, critical support for Powell is hard to find in the 1960s. By the 1990s the tide had turned completely and, for many commentators, Powell's work between the 1930s and the 1960s, much of it made in collaboration with Emeric Pressburger, is considered among the most significant and interesting in the whole of British cinema history. This critical rehabilitation is a sign of the eclipse of the realist discourse in British film criticism, and the ascendance of auteurism, at least among mainstream film journalists.

As genre cinema has all but disappeared from the production schedules in Britain in the 1980s and 1990s, British cinema has been increasingly promoted in terms of authorship. What the mainstream film journalists have considered significant and distinctive about British cinema in this period has not been a sense of national style, or a coherent movement, or a concern with representing the nation, but the particular styles and world-views of a number of critically successful directors whose allegiance is more to the art-house than to the multiplex mainstream: Nicolas Roeg, Peter Greenaway, Derek Jarman, Stephen Frears, Mike Leigh . . . Even realist filmmakers, like Ken Loach, are now treated as auteurs (see Park 1984).

The other key development in critical discussion of British cinema in the last two decades has been the establishment of film studies as an academic discipline. In such circles, auteurism has played a much weaker, though still significant, role in critical debate about British cinema. That role can be seen in three books written on the edges of the academy in the first half of the 1970s which have since been very influential in academic writing about British cinema (see also Armes 1978). All three emerge from a *Movie*-influenced auteurist perspective, yet all go off in new directions.

Raymond Durgnat's *A Mirror for England* (1970) blends auteurist criticism with a thematic analysis of a whole range of popular British genre films of the late 1940s and 1950s. What is significant about this work is its revisionist concern with both fashionable films and the unfashionable, and the effort to read the films collectively in terms of how they speak to the nation about itself.

Charles Barr's *Ealing Studios* (1977) took a much narrower focus. Like Durgnat, Barr was concerned with how the films of Ealing Studios projected a particular image of the nation. And once again, the consideration of the studio was tinged with an auteurist interest in the work of particular directors, and a developing fascination with the fantastic as much as the realist.

David Pirie's *A Heritage of Horror* (1973) was a study of the British horror film in the post-war period. Like Barr, this involved looking at the work of key studios (notably Hammer) and key directors (notably Terence Fisher) in terms of style and theme. Perhaps the most radical aspect of Pirie's book was the fact that the object of study was one of the popular genres most despised by the adherents of the realist critical discourse which studies such as these were helping to displace.

Over the next two decades, the developments set in train by these three books were followed up with a wealth of writing, much of it emanating from the academy. The greater part of this writing has taken the form

'Poetic' and 'fantastic'—Powell and Pressburger's *A Matter of Life and Death* (1946)

of revisionist historiography, rewriting the history of British cinema from the point of view of new critical perspectives which reject the value judgements of earlier commentators. There have been perhaps three dominant concerns in this historical work: first, a critical reappraisal of the realist tradition; secondly, an attention to films which defy the norms of that tradition; and thirdly, an interest in cinema as institution and in the political economy of the film industry.

A key part of the revisionist enterprise has involved revisiting the films promoted within the realist discourse, examining them in the light of more recent critical debates, particularly in terms of the issues they raise around gender and national identity (e.g. Hill 1983, 1986; Lant 1991; Higson 1995; Dodd and Dodd 1996). At the same time, there has been a concern to foreground the assumptions about realism, about national cinema, and about cultural production which underlie the claims made for these films. The concern thus shifted from whether or not these films were realist to why they seemed realist (and significant) to a particular group of critics. This meant the films and the discourses through which they were valorized were explored in light of their socio-historical conditions of existence. While the conclusions reached often seemed very different from those of Grierson, Manvell, and others, it has been argued that, simply by virtue of attending to the same body of films, those films retain a central place in our understanding of British cinema, at the expense of other, marginalized British film traditions (Cook 1996).

> **A key part of the revisionist enterprise has involved revisiting the films promoted within the realist discourse, examining them in the light of more recent critical debates, particularly in terms of the issues they raise around gender and national identity.**

If one of the concerns of recent academic writing about British cinema has been to reconsider the documentary-realist debate, another has been precisely to bring to critical attention those films which had fallen outside the terms of that debate. This tendency had already been set in motion by Durgnat, Barr, and Pirie,

given their evident interest in the popular and the fantastic. Auteurism has played an important revisionist role here in promoting previously neglected filmmakers as significant artists. Ian Christie's (1985) re-evaluation of the work of Powell and Pressburger is the most prominent example of auteurist writing revising the received wisdoms of British film criticism. Even so, it remains attached to a conception of film as an art which leaves little place for the popular. Nevertheless, it is the sustained attempt to find worth in popular but discredited genre filmmaking, and especially horror, comedy, and the woman's film, which has been one of the defining characteristics of academic writing of the last two decades (e.g. Hutchings 1993; Murphy 1989, 1992; Jordan 1983; Medhurst 1986; Petley 1986; Landy 1991; King 1996).

If we return to the popular costume dramas of the 1930s and 1940s, so harshly dismissed by the realist critics, we can find more recent historians arguing that such films are vital to any consideration of British cinema as a national cinema precisely because of their popularity (Richards 1984; Landy 1991; Harper 1994; Cook 1996). Moreover, it is argued, they should not be seen as escapist: very often they confront contemporary fears, anxieties, desires, and pleasures by displacing those concerns into another time and place. And, as Pam Cook (1996) has shown, they have also played a vital role in enabling audiences, especially female audiences, to construct their identities in relation to ideas of the nation, *inter alia*.

On occasion, it seems the popular is valued simply because it is popular, and there is a refusal to confront the problems and complexities of popular films and film culture. On the whole, however, such work provides a powerful antidote to the masculinism and élitism of other traditions of writing about British cinema.

A third tendency in recent work on British cinema has been the move away from textual analysis and evaluation towards an interest in institutions, state policy, censorship, and related issues. This work has been characterized above all by its attention to archival empirical detail, following in the tradition of Rachael Low's now standard multi-volume *History of the British Film* (1948–85). The tendency can be seen at work in John Barnes's excavations of the very early years of British filmmaking (1976, 1983, 1988, 1992), and in Robert Murphy's revisionist surveys of the 1940s and 1960s (1989, 1992). There have also been thoroughgoing investigations of key aspects of the organization of the cinema industry (e.g. Dickinson and Street 1985;

Macnab 1993) and of the systems of censorship of British films (e.g. Richards 1984; Aldgate 1995).

Informing each of these three tendencies in recent writing about British cinema have been a series of often overlapping critical perspectives, including structuralism and post-structuralism, feminism, and cultural history. Thus much of the recent writing about films as texts, whether inside or outside the realist canon, has resisted the assumption (sometimes apparent in more archive-based work) that meanings can effortlessly be read off film texts. They have employed the insights of structuralist and post-structuralist theory to reveal the narrational and ideological complexities of texts and their potential for multiple readings. Such work, however, frequently turns a blind eye to questions of historical reception (e.g. Landy 1991).

> **If we return to the popular costume dramas of the 1930s and 1940s, so harshly dismissed by the realist critics, we can find more recent historians arguing that such films are vital to any consideration of British cinema as a national cinema precisely because of their popularity.**

The influence of feminist perspectives has encouraged an interest in questions of gender, displacing the focus on class in earlier debates about the documentary-realist tradition. This has opened up to investigation a whole array of highly popular films, addressed primarily to a female audience, which had previously escaped the attention of earlier generations of critics.

The turn to cultural history has been equally influential, situating film within a much broader set of historical coordinates. Thus, there have been studies looking at the ways in which popular genre filmmaking draws on already established indigenous cultural traditions (e.g. Ryall 1986; Higson 1995). Others have explored the relationship between prevailing social, political, and economic forces and the cinema which emerged from them (e.g. Chanan 1980; Richards and Aldgate 1983; Hill 1986; Lant 1991). Yet others have examined the formation of popular taste and its impact on the reception of films by audiences (Harper 1994).

It is clearly no longer possible to talk about British cinema as an unknown cinema. It has always been known in some form or other, even if changing critical perspectives mean that the boundaries are constantly being redrawn. The realist discourse promoted a very narrow understanding of British cinema. More recent debates have made it possible to acknowledge the diversity and richness of British filmmaking, from the actualities and gag films at the turn of the century to the Ivor Novello star vehicles of the 1920s, from early Hitchcock to Sally Potter, from the documentary movement to Hammer horror, from Alexander Korda's costume films of the 1930s to *My Beautiful Laundrette* (1985), *Naked* (1993), and *Trainspotting* (1995), from vulgar comedy to the new black British cinema.

Charles Barr (1986a), has suggested what is most exciting about British cinema is not the realist in itself, but the dynamic relation between the real and the fantastic. None the less, it still seems reductive to define a whole film culture in terms of a binary opposition, however productive that opposition may be. The complexity, fluidity, and heterogeneity of British cinema constantly escapes exhaustive analysis. The realist critics could only define the national cinema in terms of an aesthetic of restraint and a thematic of consensual community by ignoring some of the most popular films of the moment, films which often transgressed those very conventions.

Each of the discourses which has dominated British film criticism has had its own axe to grind, its own favoured films, its own version of the national cinema. In the relativism of the 1980s and 1990s, no single discourse predominates over all others. In collections such as Curran and Porter (1983), Barr (1986b), and Higson (1996b), a sense of the diversity of British cinema emerges. If that in itself sounds like a celebration of a national cinema rich enough to diversify but secure within its own boundaries, it is important to remind ourselves that those boundaries are in fact by no means secure. Some of the most 'English' films of the 1930s were made by Alexander Korda, a Hungarian; some of the most 'English' films of the last decade were made by James Ivory, an American. In both cases, they worked with a truly cosmopolitan team of collaborators. If the realist discourse defined British cinema against Hollywood and in terms of a narrow nationalism, it is equally possible to define British cinema in terms of internationalism.

Another avenue of possibilities has been opened up by writers who have attempted to deconstruct the consensual and predominantly Anglo-Saxon English nationalism of British cinema by exploring the differing constructions of 'nationality' in Scottish, Welsh, and Irish cinema (e.g. McArthur 1982; Dick 1990; Berry 1994; Hill *et al.* 1994) and the cinema of the new black Britons (e.g. Mercer 1988; Malik 1996). Such writing—and the filmmaking it discusses—is very much about redrawing the boundaries of national cinema, revising long-established wisdoms about the 'Britishness' of British cinema.

BIBLIOGRAPHY

Aldgate, Anthony (1995), *Censorship and the Permissive Society: British Cinema and Theatre 1955–1965* (Oxford: Clarendon Press).

Armes, Roy (1978), *A Critical History of British Cinema* (London: Secker & Warburg).

Arts Enquiry (1947), *The Factual Film* (London: PEP and Oxford University Press).

Barnes, John (1976), *The Beginnings of the Cinema in Britain* (London: David & Charles).

—— (1983), *The Rise of the Cinema in Britain* (London: Bishopsgate Press).

—— (1988), *Pioneers of the British Cinema* (London: Bishopsgate Press).

—— (1992), *Filming the Boer War* (London: Bishopsgate Press).

Barr, Charles (1977/1993), *Ealing Studios* (London: Cameron & Tayleur and David & Charles; rev. London: Studio Vista).

—— (1986a), 'Introduction: Amnesia and Schizophrenia', in Barr (1986b).

*—— (1986b), *All our Yesterdays: Ninety Years of British Cinema* (London: British Film Institute).

Berry, David (1994), *Wales and Cinema: The First Hundred Years* (London: British Film Institute and University of Wales Press).

Castle, Hugh (1930), 'Attitude and Interlude', *Close Up*, 7/3: 184–90.

Chanan, Michael (1980/1996), *The Dream that Kicks: The Prehistory and Early Years of Cinema in Britain* (London: Routledge).

Christie, Ian (ed.) (1978), *Powell, Pressburger and Others* (London: British Film Institute).

—— (1985/1994), *Arrows of Desire: The Films of Michael Powell and Emeric Pressburger* (London: Waterstone).

Cook, Pam (1996), *Fashioning the Nation: Costume and Identity in British Cinema* (London: British Film Institute).

*Curran, James, and Vincent Porter (eds.) (1983), *British Cinema History* (London: Weidenfeld & Nicolson).

Dick, Eddie (ed.) (1990), *From Limelight to Satellite: A*

Scottish Film Book (London: Scottish Film Council and British Film Institute).

Dickinson, Margaret, and Sarah Street (1985), *Cinema and State: The Film Industry and the British Government 1927–1984* (London: British Film Institute).

Dodd, Kathryn, and Philip Dodd (1996), 'Engendering the Nation: British Documentary Film 1930–1939', in Higson (1996b).

Durgnat, Raymond (1970), *A Mirror for England: British Movies from Austerity to Affluence* (London: Faber & Faber).

Ellis, John (1996), 'The Quality Film Adventure: British Critics and the Cinema 1942–1948', in Higson (1996b).

Hardy, Forsyth (ed.) (1946/1979), *Grierson on Documentary* (London: Faber & Faber).

Harper, Sue (1994), *Picturing the Past: The Rise and Fall of the British Costume Film* (London: British Film Institute).

Higson, Andrew (1993), 'Re-Presenting the National Past: Nostalgia and Pastiche in the Heritage Film', in Lester Friedman (ed.), *Fires were Started: British Cinema and Thatcherism* (Minneapolis: University of Minnesota Press; London: UCL Press).

*—— (1995), *Waving the Flag: Constructing a National Cinema in Britain* (Oxford: Clarendon Press).

—— (1996a), 'The Heritage Film and British Cinema', in Higson (1996b).

*—— (ed.) (1996b), *Dissolving Views: Key Writings on British Cinema* (London: Cassell).

Hill, John (1983), 'Working Class Realism and Sexual Reaction: Some Theses on the British "New Wave"', in Curran and Porter (1983).

—— (1986), *Sex, Class and Realism: British Cinema 1956–1963* (London: British Film Institute).

—— Martin, McLoone, and Paul Hainsworth (eds.) (1994), *Border Crossing: Film in Ireland, Britain and Europe* (Belfast: Institute of Irish Studies; London: British Film Institute).

Hood, Stuart (1983), 'The Documentary Film Movement', in Curran and Porter (1983).

Hutchings, Peter (1993), *Hammer and Beyond* (Manchester: Manchester University Press).

Jordan, Marion (1983), 'Carry On . . . Follow that Stereotype', in Curran and Porter (1983).

King, Justine (1996), 'Crossing Thresholds: The Contemporary British Woman's Film', in Higson (1996b).

Landy, Marcia (1991), *British Genres: Cinema and Society 1930–1960* (Princeton: Princeton University Press).

Lant, Antonia (1991), *Blackout: Reinventing Women for Wartime British Cinema* (Princeton: Princeton University Press).

Lovell, Alan (1969), 'British Cinema: The Unknown Cinema', stencilled seminar paper (London: British Film Institute Education Department).

—— and **Jim Hillier** (1972), *Studies in Documentary* (London: Secker & Warburg and BFI).

Low, Rachael (1948–85), *A History of the British Film* (London: George Allen & Unwin): *1896–1906* (with Roger Manvell; 1948); *1906–1914* (1949); *1914–1918* (1950); *1918–1929* (1971); *1929–1939* (*Film Making in 1930s Britain*; 1985).

McArthur, Colin (ed.) (1982), *Scotch Reels: Scotland in Cinema and Television* (London: British Film Institute).

MacNab, Geoffrey (1993), *J. Arthur Rank and the British Film Industry* (London: Routledge).

Malik, Sarita (1996), 'Beyond "The Cinema of Duty"? The Pleasures of Hybridity: Black British Film of the 1980s and 1990s', in Higson (1996*b*).

Manvell, Roger (1944/1946), *Film* (London: Penguin).

Medhurst, Andy (1986), 'Music Hall and British Cinema', in Barr (1986*b*).

Mercer, Kobena (ed.) (1988), *Black Film, British Cinema*, ICA Document No. 7 (London: Institute of Contemporary Arts).

Murphy, Robert (1989), *Realism and Tinsel: Cinema and Society in Britain 1939–1948* (London: Routledge).

—— (1992), *Sixties British Cinema* (London: British Film Institute).

Park, James (1984), *Learning to Dream* (London: Faber).

Petley, Julian (1986), 'The Lost Continent', in Barr (1986*b*).

Pirie, David (1973), *A Heritage of Horror: The English Gothic Cinema 1946–1972* (New York: Avon).

Richards, Jeffrey (1984), *The Age of the Dream Palace: Cinema and Society in Britain 1930–1939* (London: Routledge & Kegan Paul).

—— and **Anthony Aldgate** (1983), *Best of British: Cinema and Society 1930–1970* (Oxford: Blackwell).

Rotha, Paul (1930), *The Film till Now* (London: Jonathan Cape).

—— (1936/1952), *Documentary Film* (London: Faber & Faber).

Ryall, Tom (1986), *Alfred Hitchcock and the British Cinema* (London: Croom Helm).

Wollen, Peter (1969), *Signs and Meaning in the Cinema* (London: Secker & Warburg and British Film Institute).

15 Ireland and cinema

Martin McLoone

In his *Irish Filmography*, Kevin Rockett makes the point that, of over 2,000 feature films on an Irish theme produced world-wide since the beginnings of the cinema, rather less than 200 have been made in Ireland itself and most of these only in the last fifteen years or so (Rockett 1996). This stark statistic helps to explain much about the nature of the cinema debate in and about Ireland. On the one hand, despite the relative poverty of indigenous film production until the 1980s, Ireland has enjoyed a considerable presence in the cinemas of other cultures, especially that of the United States and the United Kingdom, and Irish men and women have exerted perhaps a disproportionate influence on the development of cinema, again especially in the United States. The result has been that a lot of literature on the cinema and Ireland has been concerned to excavate the contribution of the Irish to the development of the cinema and to write up a 'lost' history, both of the Irish in cinema and of Ireland in cinema.

On the other hand, this considerable presence has drawn the attention of scholars in both the United States and Ireland to the representation of Irishness contained in these 'outsider' views. Debate in Ireland itself, not surprisingly, has focused on the need not only to develop an indigenous film industry but to develop a film culture that is sensitive to the issues of representation and which is prepared to interrogate the nature of any indigenous cinematic response to these domi-

nant images. In this regard, the key academic work continues to be Kevin Rockett, Luke Gibbons, and John Hill's *Cinema and Ireland* (1987), published originally at a crucial point in the development of both an indigenous film industry and the emergence of a recognizable critical film culture. In retrospect, it can now be seen not only that this study achieved a synthesis and development of much work that had preceded it but that it also mapped out the critical agenda for debates that were to follow.

Rockett's historical analysis of film production in Ireland since the earliest days of the cinema encapsulates a number of key themes that continue to have relevance in Ireland today and are echoed in film cultures across the globe: the difficulty of a small and economically weak country in sustaining a consistent level of film production without state support; the need for film lobbyists to mount a cultural as well as an economic argument for such state support; and finally the need for a national film culture to be aware of the dangers inherent in an overly essentialist response to the dominance of more powerful cultures, like Hollywood.

Indeed, Rockett's historical survey considers the effect on the cinema in Ireland of the narrow and restrictive mores of Catholic nationalism in the period down to the 1960s. Censorship, and a negative or defensive attitude to the cinema in general, created a cultural and ideological impediment to the growth of native filmmaking that was as decisive as the lack of economic support. In later writings, Rockett argues that in the censorious and morally constricting culture that emerged in nationalist Ireland, the images that emanated from Hollywood, and which dominated the cinemas of Catholic Ireland from the 1920s to the 1960s, were positively liberating (Rockett 1991). The polemical thrust of this argument has been picked up by other critics (McLoone 1994) and has considerably muddied the debate over what constitutes a national cinema in Ireland—once again a polemic that is familiar to parallel debates in other cultures.

Rockett's later concerns have focused on what he has called 'the cinema of the diaspora'—precisely that large and influential Irish presence in the cinema of the United States in particular (Rockett and Finn 1995; Rockett 1996). His *Irish Filmography* (1996) represents the most comprehensive listing of the field, but the impulse to track and critically engage with this cinematic heritage has long been a concern with film scholars of Hollywood's ethnic representations. Much of this literature has been concerned merely with establishing the Irish contribution as a matter of historical record—as in Liam O'Leary's (1980) study of Dublin-born Rex Ingram, for example—or tracing the emerging cinematic stereotypes embodied in artists of Irish descent, such as James Cagney, Spencer Tracy, and Maureen O'Hara (Clark and Lynch 1980; Slide 1988; Curran 1989). The most interesting explorations of the Irish influence have often been in the context of auteur studies of eminent filmmakers of Irish descent, and the Irishness of John Ford, a preoccupation with many critics, is paradigmatic here (McBride and Wilmington 1974; Ford 1979; Anderson 1981).

The most sustained work on the Irish influence on American cinema is Lee Lourdeaux (1990) and it is here that the purely historical gives way to a deeper concern with questions of ethnicity (a comparative study of Irish and Italian in this case). His analysis of the Irish and Italian presence in Hollywood emphasizes the essentially dialectic relationship between the global and the local, between the universal and the particular, and draws attention to the fact that Hollywood itself is deeply imbued with the cultural influences of many of those indigenous cultures now struggling to find a cinematic presence in its global shadow. Lourdeaux's approach to the question of ethnicity also demonstrates how the cinematic debate about Ireland and Irishness now exists in a wider cultural studies, as much as in a purely film studies, framework. This is a trend

again anticipated in Rockett *et al.*'s *Cinema and Ireland*, in the section written by Gibbons (1987).

Gibbons approaches the cinematic debates about representation and Ireland through a wide-ranging consideration of pre-cinematic and extra-cinematic cultural discourses (eighteenth- and nineteenth-century European romanticism, the melodramas of Dion Boucicault, landscape painting, travel writing, and the myth of the West in Ireland and America are some of his reference-points). Unlike Rockett, whose rejection of nationalism as a motivating impulse behind an indigenous cinema is clear and unequivocal, Gibbons is more concerned to explore the radical edges of nationalism, and of cultural practice in general, precisely to rediscover the 'unapproved roads' that were blocked and the 'unruly and refractory narratives of vernacular history' that were silenced by the hegemony of Catholic nationalism. While clearly rejecting essentialism and sensitive to the materialist nature of cultural production, Gibbons is, none the less, concerned to establish the 'peculiarities' of the Irish cultural experience and to validate those films, indigenous or international, that he sees as laying bare the nature of these peculiarities. Thus a film as influential and as controversial in its depiction of the Irish as John Ford's *The Quiet Man* (1953) is reread in a positive light, its playfulness and internal self-consciousness revealing the 'ability of certain strains of Irish romanticism to conduct a process of self-interrogation, to raise doubts at key moments about their own veracity, which cuts across any tendency to take romantic images as realistic accounts of Irish life' (Gibbons 1987: 200).

This project is amplified in a series of important and influential pieces gathered together in a later publication (Gibbons 1996) where his focus has shifted more to the 'myth of modernization', which he sees, if anything, as a more paralysing hegemony than the nationalist myths which it has attempted to supplant. For Gibbons, tradition is not necessarily always reactionary and modernity is not always progressive and in his rejection of the grand narrative of modernization, his postmodern, post-colonial arguments echo many of the concerns posed by post-colonial theorists of other cultures.

Gibbons is motivated by a desire to theorize the constituents of a national culture, including a national cinema, and as the production of indigenous filmmaking gathered pace in the early 1990s, stimulated by an enlightened government funding policy (the

Irish culture—complexity and contradictions (*Maeve*, 1981)

emergence of which is traced by Rockett 1994), the question of what the parameters of an 'Irish' national cinema might be has become more acute. For example, McLoone agrees with Gibbons that the stark juxtaposition between the local and the global, or the centre and the periphery, is more complex and more dialectical than it is often assumed (McLoone 1990, 1994). In his analysis of recent indigenous filmmaking, he appropriates from postmodern theory the concept of 'critical regionalism' (Frampton 1985) to explain the thematic and filmic concerns of the emerging Irish 'new wave' (for example, the films of Bob Quinn, Joe Comerford, Cathal Black, Pat Murphy, Margo Harkin, and many of the younger directors of short films who emerged in great numbers after 1987). In his analysis, films like Black's *Our Boys* (1980) and *Pigs* (1984),

Comerford's *Reefer and the Model* (1987), Murphy's *Maeve* (1981) and *Ann Devlin* (1984), and Harkin's *Hush-a-Bye Baby* (1989), are seen to appropriate the forms of dominant narrative cinema and not merely to mimic them. The best of recent Irish cinema, therefore, explores indigenous culture, in all its contradictions, with an outsider's eye, but at the same time subjects this outsider's perspective to the peculiar interrogation of the local culture. It is a dialectical *pas de deux* and it achieves the double effect of avoiding a tendency towards essentialism while offering a critical response to the influences of the outside.

Central to McLoone's project is the relationship between the local and the global—in cinematic terms the relationship between indigenous filmmaking and Hollywood. He is concerned that a national cinema (and national cultural policies) should avoid falling between 'a self-defeating essentialism and a self-abusing domination'. But unlike Gibbons's rejection of the myth of modernization, McLoone argues that it is precisely the grand narrative of modernization, as represented in the increasingly global cinema of Hollywood, which has stimulated the great national cinemas of Europe over the last fifty years. Thus for him, Italian Neo-Realism, the French New Wave, New German Cinema, and even the intermittent flurries from Australia, New Zealand, and a host of other cultures not normally associated with sustained film production, can all be described as forms of critical regionalism. The difference in perspective between Gibbons and McLoone, therefore, might be characterized thus: while the latter offers a definition of national cinema as a critical regionalism, the former might propose a notion of 'critical nationalism'.

The concern, however, to theorize and understand what might constitute a national culture and a national cinema in Ireland is considerably complicated by the contested nature of Irish identity in the first place. The important differences of emphasis in the work of Rockett, Gibbons, and McLoone indicates a much wider debate that exists in culture and politics generally (especially in literary and historical studies) about identity in Ireland. The revisionist, anti-revisionist, and postcolonial theoretical positions now being articulated and challenged have been given added urgency by the increasing modernization of the Irish economy and the gathering pace of Europeanization. However, hanging over these sometimes strident and increasingly acrimonious academic debates is the shadow of Northern Ireland, where contested notions of identity have led to civil strife, violence, and over 3,000 deaths in the last thirty years and which, recently, has witnessed increasing sectarian polarization. It is hardly surprising, therefore, that the representation of Northern Ireland has been a major concern for media academics in Ireland generally (Rolston 1990; Butler 1995; Miller 1994) and that the fall-out from the crisis in Northern Ireland has been explored in film and television studies in particular (McLoone 1991, 1996; Hill et al. 1994).

Again, though, the seminal study is in Rockett et al.'s Cinema and Ireland, in the section written by Hill on the cinema's representation of violence in Ireland (Hill (1987). Like his co-authors Rockett and Gibbons, Hill is concerned to place his study in a historical context. He traces the dominant modes of representation in British cinema back to earlier periods of colonial and imperial imagery and locates a central thrust to the image of the Irish that has endured. Violence, he argues, is denied a political or historical context and is represented as a 'manifestation of the Irish character', a tragic flaw inherent in the Irish themselves. Thus, in Hill's analysis, a 'humanist classic' of British cinema, Carol Reed's Odd Man Out (1947), is revisited and reinterpreted in the light of this long tradition of negative imagery. Its refusal to deal directly with the causes of the violence which it portrays and its emphasis on the tragic romanticism of James Mason's gunman-on-the-run have the effect of reinforcing the dominant British view that violence in Ireland is the fault of the Irish themselves. Interestingly enough, Hill applies his analysis to two films made in Ireland by Irish filmmakers—Neil Jordan's Angel (1981) and Pat O'Connor's Cal (1984)—and identifies the same tendency to ignore the historical or socio-political context of the violence in Northern Ireland, as if the dominant mode of representation has become so internalized that it is reproduced unconsciously, even by the Irish themselves.

The reasons for this, though, are matters more of cinematic form than merely failures of perception by individual filmmakers. These formal matters are pursued in more detail in a later piece by Hill, on the political thriller in general and Ken Loach's Hidden Agenda (1990) in particular (Hill 1991). In raising these issues, Hill revisits the debate on film aesthetics and politics that informed much film theory in the 1960s and 1970s and considers again the problems inherent in trying to employ dominant narrative and realist forms in order to explore complex political realities or promote radical politics. The failure of Hidden Agenda to deal with the politics of Northern Ireland (reducing, as it does, complex issues to little more than a conspiracy theory that stretches the viewer's credulity) is, he argues, a failure of form. Interestingly enough, as a solution, Hill canvasses not a film practice based around the modernist avant-garde, which was the argument of radical film theorists in the 1960s and 1970s, but a form of 'third cinema', where matters of form are approached through an engagement with, rather than a rejection of, dominant forms and exhibit a 'sensitivity to place'. In this, he comes close to McLoone's notion of 'critical regionalism', where questions of form are motivated by the encounter of dominant forms with a local cultural agenda. It might be noted here that many of the indigenous films discussed by all these writers do evince a concern with film aesthetics (perhaps, especially, those of Comerford and Murphy) and that, of the film scholars who have engaged with these films, it is Rockett who has canvassed most clearly for a politically engaged avant-garde, locating in the work of the younger filmmakers, emerging through the short-filmmaking route, a greater formal and political conservatism.

There is one final important point to note about the nature of film scholarship in Ireland. Although the work of the male academics discussed above is deeply informed by feminist criticism, it is perhaps surprising that there has been no concerted feminist intervention itself in Irish film studies. This is all the more surprising given that many of the films produced in Ireland over the years have been made by women and explore the questions of identity through a feminist concern with gender (especially, as in the work of Pat Murphy and Margo Harkin, where the gender issues intersect with the wider politics of Irish nationalism). Both Murphy (in Johnston 1981) and Harkin (1991) have themselves contributed to the film debates in detailed discussions of their filmmaking agenda. And, in the wider cultural ferment in Ireland, women have contributed with growing influence to a whole range of literary, historical, and sociological debates, reflecting the strength of feminist studies generally in Ireland and the importance of gender politics to these wider concerns. However, in strictly film studies terms, there have been relatively few direct feminist interventions.

One of these was an important critique of the gender politics of Neil Jordan's The Crying Game (1992), in which Sarah Edge (1995) has argued that the radical nature of the film's discussion of male gender issues was at the expense of the woman character, and that, consequently, the portrayal of women and nationalism in the film may be seen as positively reactionary. The Crying Game, of course, has engendered a mini academic industry in the United States and has featured as a key text both in queer film theory and in the growing academic field of Irish studies. The final irony, then, of film scholarship in Ireland, and the much larger cultural discourse of which it is a part, is that its concerns with nationality, definitions of Irishness, and identity no longer seem like the archaic lingerings of a pre-modern era, as it has sometimes been characterized. On the contrary, these questions now seem to be at the very cutting edge of contemporary cultural debate.

BIBLIOGRAPHY

Anderson, Lindsay (1981), *About John Ford* (London: Plexus).

Butler, David (1995), *The Trouble with Reporting Northern Ireland: The British State, the Broadcast Media and Non-fictional Representations of the Conflict* (Aldershot: Avebury).

Clark, Dennis, and **William J. Lynch** (1980), 'Hollywood and Hibernia: The Irish in the Movies', in Randall M. Miller (ed.), *The Kaleidoscopic Lens: How Hollywood Views Ethnic Groups* (Englewood Cliffs, NJ: James S. Ozer).

Curran, Joseph M. (1989), *Hibernian Green on the Silver Screen: The Irish and American Movies* (Westport, Conn.: Greenwood Press).

Edge, Sarah (1995), '"Women are Trouble, did you know that, Fergus?" Neil Jordan's *The Crying Game*', *Feminist Review*, 50 (Summer), 173–86.

Ford, Dan (1979), *Pappy: The Life of John Ford* (Englewood Cliffs, NJ: Prentice-Hall).

Frampton, Kenneth (1985), 'Towards a Critical Regionalism: Six Points for an Architecture of Resistance', in Hal Foster (ed.), *Postmodern Culture* (London: Pluto Press).

Gibbons, Luke (1987), 'Romanticism, Realism and Irish Cinema', in Rockett *et al.* (1987).

—— (1996), *Transformations in Irish Culture* (Cork: Cork University Press).

Harkin, Margo (1991), 'Broadcasting in a Divided Community', transcript of a talk given at a symposium at the University of Ulster, in McLoone (1991).

Hill, John (1987), 'Images of Violence', in Rockett *et al.* (1987).

—— (1991), 'Hidden Agenda: Politics and the Thriller', *Circa Arts Magazine*, 57 (May–June), 36–41.

*—— **Martin McLoone,** and **Paul Hainsworth** (eds.) (1994), *Border Crossing: Film in Ireland, Britain and Europe* (Belfast: Institute of Irish Studies; London: British Film Institute).

Johnston, Claire (1981), 'Maeve: Interview with Pat Murphy', *Screen*, 22/4: 54–71.

Lourdeaux, Lee (1990), *Italian and Irish Filmmakers in America: Ford, Capra, Coppola and Scorsese* (Philadelphia: Temple University Press).

McBride, Joseph, and **Michael Wilmington** (1974), *John Ford* (London: Secker & Warburg).

McLoone, Martin (1990), 'Lear's Fool, Goya's Dilemma', *Circa Arts Magazine*, 50 (Mar–Apr.), 54–8.

—— (ed.) (1991), *Culture, Identity and Broadcasting in Ireland: Local Issues, Global Perspectives* (Belfast: Institute of Irish Studies).

*—— (1994), 'National Cinema and Cultural Identity: Ireland and Europe', in Hill *et al.* (1994).

—— (ed.) (1996), *Broadcasting in a Divided Community: Seventy Years of the BBC in Northern Ireland* (Belfast: Institute of Irish Studies).

Miller, David (1994), *Don't Mention the War: Northern Ireland, Propaganda and the Media* (London: Pluto Press).

O'Leary, Liam (1980), *Rex Ingram: Master of the Silent Cinema* (Dublin: Academy Press).

Rockett, Kevin (1987), 'History, Politics and Irish Cinema', in Rockett *et al.* (1987).

—— (1991), 'Aspects of the Los Angelesation of Ireland', *Irish Communications Review*, 1: 20–5.

—— (1994), 'Culture, Industry and Irish Cinema', in Hill *et al.* (1994).

—— (1996), *Irish Filmography* (Dublin: Red Mountain Press).

—— and **Eugene Finn** (1995), *Still Irish: A Century of the Irish in Film* (Dublin: Red Mountain Press).

*—— **Luke Gibbons,** and **John Hill** (1987/1988), *Cinema and Ireland* (Beckenham: Croom Helm; rev. London: Routledge).

Rolston, Bill (ed.) (1990), *The Media and Northern Ireland: Covering the Troubles* (London: Macmillan).

Slide, Anthony (1988), *The Cinema and Ireland* (Jefferson, NC: McFarland).

16 Australian cinema

Elizabeth Jacka

Debates in national cinema

Australian scholars (such as Stern 1995; Creed 1993; Berry 1994; Martin 1993; Jayamanne 1994, 1995; Routt 1992; Brooks 1992; Hodsdon 1992; and Mortimer 1995) have made a significant contribution to the discipline of screen studies and the study of various non-Australian cinemas, most notably those of the United States and various countries in Asia. However, it is undoubtedly in the area of Australian cinema that most work has been done. No other country has such a rich tradition of theorizing national cinema, and it is a pity that the scope and variety of the work is not better known in other places. Of course, this is precisely Australia's dilemma—it is not metropolitan enough to be in the international mainstream of either intellectual or artistic life, and not marginal enough to be exotic. It was the struggle to come to terms with, and find a response to, this intermediate position that produced the original polemic around the need for a national cinema, and the film studies literature that has emerged partly grew up in support of the campaign to institute an Australian film industry and culture.

The growth of a distinctive Australian film studies literature was intimately connected with the re-establishment of the Australian film industry after 1970. Just as government intervention and support was a crucial ingredient in the development of a renewed Australian industry, so it also played a role in fostering an Australian film culture, including the support for critical works which examined the history, politics, and aesthetics of Australian cinema. There has been a fruitful collaboration between writers, both inside and outside the academy, publishers, and government-funded film culture organizations which has led to a large body of work, especially on Australian cinema history.

The first serious critical writing about Australian cinema—the first that had some overt connection with the discipline of film studies that was rapidly emerging in the United Kingdom, Europe, and the United States appeared in the 1970s. However, some of the terms which were to govern writing about Australian film well into the 1980s had been set by a series of influential articles from the 1950s and 1960s. In a 1958 article which has come to be seen as the manifesto for a national film industry, and which is resonantly entitled 'No Daydreams of our Own: The film as National Self-Expression', 'Tom Weir' (actually Tom Fitzgerald, editor of the influential journal *Nation*), wrote:

It is typical of the undeveloped personality of our people that we have practically no indigenous films. Every standard that our impressionable mass audiences imbibe is the standard of an alien culture. Like pre-Chaucerian England, tugged between Italy and France, we are also torn between two dominant cultures, those of America and Britain. No wonder our voices are so thin and so weakly articulated as to be barely audible to visitors when they first step ashore. The daydreams we get from celluloid are not Australian daydreams. Our kingdom is not of this world. (Weir 1985: 144)

Along with the work of other significant writers and campaigners, such as Sylvia Lawson (1965, 1979), this was to set the tone for much of the work on Australian cinema in the 1970s and into the 1980s. It was framed by the idea of a national culture and involved a set of explorations of Australia's complicated colonial and post-colonial relationships with Britain and America, and the influence this had on its film culture.

Indeed, Graeme Turner goes so far as to declare that the revival of the Australian cinema was not only an economic project but that it 'also represented a semi-official project of nation formation' (1994: 202). He argues that, by the end of the 1960s, a developing nationalist mythology in Australia had come to 'recognise film as the most desirable medium for projecting an image of new confidence and maturity seen to mark contemporary Australian culture and society' (Turner 1989: 101). Therefore, both the films of the first few years of the revival and the writing about these films all in some ways engage with this idea of a national project.

This interest in Australian cinema became manifest in the number of histories which had appeared by the beginning of the 1980s. These include the indispensable Pike and Cooper (1981), Shirley and Adams (1983), Tulloch (1981, 1982), Bertrand and Collins (1981), Moran and O'Regan (1989), Moran (1991), and Cunningham (1991), all of which were histories of the pre-1970 period. Histories of the period after 1970 include Dermody and Jacka (1987, 1988a, b), Hinde (1981), and Stratton (1980, 1990). The film historians of the 1980s were almost all part of, or influenced by, the 1970s campaign for government support for a contemporary film industry. This explained their desire to cast the cinema of the past as something to be praised and celebrated; and also motivated their explanations—in terms of the concepts of media or cultural imperialism—of why this cinema had all but disappeared. Such an analysis sees the fragile national culture of countries like Australia as threatened and ultimately conquered by the imperialist invasion from outside, usually from the United States. Some of this early work was undoubtedly flawed conceptually in so far as it did not always avoid posing an essentialist notion of national culture: culture was seen as somehow being

born naturally out of landscape or people and waiting to find expression in words and images, rather than being something syncretic, acquired, and constructed from a complex and politically implicated set of influences. However, much of it was highly sophisticated and, conscious of the traps of essentialism, evolved a nuanced view of Australian culture and film which was able to acknowledge both the local particularities of Australian cinema and its position as the product of a complex set of aesthetic influences and industrial pressures (Lawson 1979; Martin 1988; Tulloch 1982; Cunningham 1991).

> **Some of this work was highly sophisticated and, conscious of the traps of essentialism, evolved a nuanced view of Australian culture and film which was able to acknowledge both the local particularities of Australian cinema and its position as the product of a complex set of aesthetic influences and industrial pressures.**

Contesting the bush legend

Because there has been such a strong interconnection between Australian cinema studies and the process of recognizing and extending Australia's national culture, the methodologies and approaches used in the study of Australian cinema have been broad and eclectic. Australian film scholars have been less concerned with narrowly conceived formal and aesthetic questions about the film texts produced (though this has not been ignored—see e.g. Tulloch 1982; Dermody and Jacka 1988a) than with reading them symptomatically as both signs of, and producers of, a whole culture.

So, many Australian film writers have fruitfully used a combination of cultural studies, literary criticism, visual art theory, and film studies approaches in their highly sophisticated readings of particular films or film movements. During the 1970s critical work tended to be concerned with promoting an Australian cinema which could be an authentic site on which to articulate the unique Australian experience. There was an anxiety that the cinema was derivative or that it was so con-strained by its economic marginality that it could not afford to take thematic or formal risks (see Dermody and Jacka 1987, 1988a). There was also criticism of the limitations of the 'bush legend' as an expression of national identity. During the period leading up to the constitution of Australia as a federated state in 1901, there was a cultural flowering manifested in popular literature, most notably the journal *Bulletin*, which glor-ified the idea of the 'essential' Australia as a land of 'sunlight, wattle, the bush, the future, freedom, mate-ship and egalitarianism' (White 1981: 97). This bush legend, however, was criticized for its obvious mascu-linist and Anglo-Irish bias and remoteness from the experience of contemporary modern urban Australia (see Turner 1986).

As John Tulloch's pioneering account of the Austra-lian cinema of the 1920s shows, the bush legend, and the opposition of city and the bush, was the key struc-turing narrative device of many of the films of that period (Tulloch 1981). This, in turn, may be linked to a long tradition of finding in landscape the source of an 'authentic' Australian identity. This opposition of city and country is not, of course, unique to Australia; it tends to be a constant theme in all cultures where the dynamic but destructive forces of modernity are in contest with an Arcadian vision of traditional ways of life. However, it takes on a particular colour in frontier societies where the rural landscape has a dual charac-ter as either a place of innocence and refuge against the predations of the city or a threatening wilderness inimical to human life.

A number of film scholars have explored the place of landscape in Australian cinema (Turner 1986; Cunning-ham 1991); but it is in the work of Ross Gibson that it is given its fullest treatment. In his films (for example *Camera Natura*, 1986) and scholarly work, Gibson has examined the way that the Australian continent has been imagined by Europeans in writings of exploration and travel and in the cultural artefacts of the colonial period (Gibson 1984). In an essay which has become an often reprinted classic—'The Nature of a Nation: Landscape in Australian Feature Films'—Gib-son uses the perspective developed in this work to look at the rich variety of depictions of the landscape in Australian cinema. Gibson argues that in virtually every plot 'outside city limits', the land is a 'leitmotif and ubiquitous character' (1992: 63). The reason for this, he argues, is that 'non-Aboriginal Australia is a young society, underendowed with myths of "belonging".

The country is still sparsely populated and meagrely historicized. Alienation and the fragility of culture have been the refrains during two hundred years of white Australian images and stories' (64). In another essay, Gibson applies his formidable critical skills to the Mad Max cycle of films, and using a combination of cultural theory, art history, and film studies, sees *Mad Max 2* (1981) and *Mad Max 3* (1985) as both allegories of failure—the continual failure of white explorers to mas-ter the land (thus linking to Gibson's interest in land-scape films)—and, in their baroque mise-en-scène and editing style (a surprising discovery of a parallel between Mad Max and Tintoretto), a representation of a 'world peopled with signs, figures and emblems, where all objects and beings . . . exchange attributes and properties in a perpetual semantic shift', a condi-tion Gibson sees as common to both late Renaissance Europe and (post)modern Australia.

The ongoing engagement with, and contestation of, the bush version of the Australian legend in Australian films often displayed a distaste for the popular idioms with which Australian films worked, especially when they depended on stylistic traits seen to be derived from Hollywood (see Hinde 1981). However, in the early 1980s work began to appear which challenged these initial positions and which celebrated rather than deplored the necessarily syncretic nature of Australian cinema. Two essays in particular—one by Tom O'Re-gan, the other by Meaghan Morris—opened up some new directions for Australian film criticism.

In '*The Man from Snowy River* [1982] and Australian Popular Culture', O'Regan (1985) argued against those who saw that film as simply crude melodrama, an imi-tation western, or an opportunistic attempt to appro-priate an Australian legend, and traced the complex ways in which the film represented a non-metropolitan Australia and how it intersected with the popular cul-tural desires of city-based Australians and their diverse set of imaginings about the 'bush'. Meaghan Morris's (1988) article on *Crocodile Dundee* (1986) also saw beyond local critics' distaste for the movie's apparent rerunning of the 'ocker' stereotype and argued that its 'positive-unoriginality' acted as a cunning export alle-gory, a '*take-over* fantasy of breaking into the circuit of [American] media power', involving both admiration and resistance. She goes on: 'In this admiration, appro-priation as positive-unoriginality figures as a means of resolving the practical problems of a peripheral cinema, while reconciling conflicting desires for power and independence: symbolic nationalist victory is declared, but on internationalist (American) grounds' (Morris 1988: 250).

Cinema and post-coloniality

More recently, as theories of post-coloniality have developed, there has been an increasing interest in conceptualizing Australia as post-colonial. The relations between Aboriginal and non-Aboriginal Australia have naturally been a major focus of this work. In 1992 Aboriginal scholar Marcia Langton was commissioned by the Australian Film Commission to investigate the politics and aesthetics of filmmaking by and about Aboriginal people from an Aboriginal perspective. The book which resulted (Langton 1993) was a landmark, both because it redressed a gap in the film literature in Australia, but also because it was such a fruitful and creative combination of post-structuralist theory, film studies, and Aboriginal perspectives. As critic Stephen Muecke (1994) argues, it signalled 'the collapse of a long-felt antagonistic opposition between Aboriginal essentialism and non-Aboriginal theory'. For Langton, film and television are the main ways in which non-Aboriginal Australians know about Aborigines and thus their knowledge is always a second-order one (Langton 1993: 33). As a result, the way films construct Aboriginality is of the utmost political concern. She analyses well-known 'Aboriginal' films like Charles Chauvel's *Jedda* (1955), drawing out its colonialist constructions of the 'native' and showing its affinities with long-standing Western traditions as exemplified, for example, in the Tarzan legend. She then goes on to examine Aboriginal filmmaker Tracey Moffat's 'deconstruction' of *Jedda* in her 1989 film *Night Cries*, which depicts the white mother and Aboriginal adopted daughter (played incidentally by Marcia Langton) forty years on. Moffat's film is a highly stylized 'experimental' film, in which the original dependency relation between the white homesteaders and their adopted black child is reversed. As Langton suggests, 'the worst nightmare of the adoptive parents is to end life with the black adoptive child as the only family' (1993: 47).

Tracey Moffat's treatment of the 'Jedda text' is also the subject of an influential article by Laleen Jayamanne. Jayamanne—a Sri Lankan Australian who was educated partly in the United States—brings a combination of intellectual influences, including performance theory, film studies, and visual art theory, to

> More recently, as theories of post-coloniality have developed, there has been an increasing interest in conceptualizing Australia as post-colonial. The relations between Aboriginal and non-Aboriginal Australia have naturally been a major focus of this work.

bear on both her own film work (such as *A Song of Ceylon* (1985), a kind of 'reply' to Basil Wright's celebrated 1937 documentary), and to her film criticism. In her essay on *Night Cries*, Jayamanne (1993) offers a 'Sri Lankan reading' of the film, linking its concerns with the general field of post-colonial studies, but also tracing some of what is specific to the colonial and post-colonial situation in Australia, by linking the visual style of the film to Aboriginal painters (such as Albert Namatjira) who had reappropriated the work of European landscape artists. She uses the film to ruminate on the politics of artistic assimilation, appropriation, hybridization, and decolonization that is involved in Aboriginal cultural production and the challenge to Eurocentric artistic practice (Jayamanne 1993: 83).

Colonialism has also been a rich subject for Australian documentary filmmaking, notably in the work of Denis O'Rourke. His controversial 1991 film *The Good Woman of Bangkok* provoked an extended discussion (see Berry et al., forthcoming) which debated the film's treatment of gender, sexuality, and the colonial subject, the ethics of documentary filmmaking, as well as the way in which O'Rourke positions himself as both author and subject of the film. Apart from this debate about *The Good Woman of Bangkok*, there has been surprisingly little work done in documentary theory and criticism for a country which has contributed so much to the documentary form. There has also been a small but robust Australian avant-garde sector which has produced a considerable body of commentary and theory, mainly in the pages of the leading critical avant-garde journal, published since 1971, *Cantrills Film-notes*. Film critic Adrian Martin (1989) has written the best general history of Australia's avant-garde.

As already indicated, while the general field of film studies in Australia was heavily influenced by intellectual debates which originated in Europe and the United States (especially the *Screen* tradition, which was

A 'challenge to Eurocentric artistic practice'—Aboriginal film maker Tracey Moffat's *Night Cries* (1989)

dominant in Australian scholarship and teaching from about 1976 to 1984), the more formalist and psycho-analytic frameworks associated with this tradition have not been dominant in the study of Australian film, because they were not found serviceable in the wider study of the interpenetration of cinema and the wider culture. These frameworks, however, have been more relevant to the theory and practice of feminist film in Australia. Taking a lead from early work done in the United States on feminism and cinema (notably the journal *Women and Film*), the feminist debate was vigorously joined in Australia from about 1974 onwards. The work of the *Screen* theorists, especially Laura Mulvey and Claire Johnston, as interpreted by writers like Lesley Stern was extremely influential on both filmmaking and film criticism (Macallan 1995). As in other Western countries in this period, a large body of films made from a feminist perspective was pro-duced (usually with government support), and their

reception was accompanied by intense debate about the politics of feminist filmmaking, most of which was carried on in the pages of film journals and magazines like *Filmnews*, *Cinema Papers*, and less regular and less long-lived newsletters. The history of Australian feminist filmmaking and theory is well covered in Blonski, Creed, and Freiberg (1987) and Collins (1995) and usefully summarized in Sands (1988).

While a number of Australian film writers have made a considerable contribution to the general field of feminist film studies (e.g. Stern 1982; Creed 1993)—and notwithstanding the fact that there is a rich tradi-tion of Australian women's films—there has been remarkably little written on Australian cinema from within the tradition of feminist film studies (apart from Collins 1995). Much general commentary on Australian films, especially that written by women, has a feminist inflexion or notes the role of gender representations in films from various periods, but there has been virtually no sustained treatment of individual women film-makers, nor detailed critical or formal analysis of film texts using the protocols of feminist film theory. The reasons for this have been suggested above: the primary concerns of the Australian cinema and its commentaries have been questions of national identity and, while gender is clearly an essential aspect of the construction of such an identity, the more general questions seem so far to have blocked the development of a strong feminist intellectual tradition in Australian cinema studies. It is, therefore, interesting to note that in a recent Australian collection on feminism and film (Jayamanne 1995) the only writer to engage with Australian film was the only non-Australian contributor!

Conclusion

Australia has produced a significant body of work on its own national cinema. This work has been made possible because of both the institutionalization of screen studies within academia, which occurred in the late 1970s, as well as a significant level of awareness and support from government funding bodies, where a commitment to film culture was seen as an important ingredient for the production and reception of Australian films. Scholarly work on Australian cinema has also been intimately linked to film practice and to the politics of film funding. Many of the theorists were also filmmakers, but futher than that the fragility of the Australian industry vis-à-vis the massive forces of the international audiovisual industry has lent an urgency and a strategic value to much of the writing—an ongoing connection to the struggle to retain a space for local filmmaking in the face of what is perceived to threaten it.

BIBLIOGRAPHY

Berry, Chris (1994), A Bit on the Side: East–West Topographies of Desire (Sydney: IMPress).

—— Annette Hamilton, and Laleen Jayamanne et al. (1997), The Good Woman of Bangkok: The Debate (Sydney: Power Institute of Fine Arts, University of Sydney).

Bertrand, Ina, and Dianne Collins (1981), Government and Film in Australia (Sydney: Currency Press).

Blonski, Annette, Barbara Creed, and Freda Freiberg (1987), Don't Shoot Darling: Women's Independent Film-making in Australia (Richmond, Victoria: Greenhouse Publications).

Brooks, Jodi (1992), 'Fascination and the Grotesque: Whatever Happened to Baby Jane?', Continuum: The Australian Journal of Media and Culture, 5/2: 225–34.

Collins, Felicity (1995), 'Ties that Bind: The Psyche of Feminist Filmmaking Sydney 1969–89', Ph.D. thesis (Sydney: University of Technology, Sydney).

Creed, Barbara (1993), The Monstrous-Feminine: Film, Feminism, Psychoanalysis (London: Routledge).

Cunningham, Stuart (1991), Featuring Australia: The Cinema of Charles Chauvel (Sydney: Allen & Unwin).

*Dermody, Susan, and Elizabeth Jacka (1987), The Screening of Australia, i: Anatomy of a Film Industry (Sydney: Currency Press).

*—— (1988a), The Screening of Australia, ii: Anatomy of a National Cinema (Sydney: Currency Press).

—— (1988b), The Imaginary Industry: Australian Cinema in the Late Eighties (North Ryde: Australian Film, Television and Radio School).

Gibson, Ross (1984), The Diminishing Paradise: Changing Literary Perceptions of Australia (Sydney: Angus & Robertson).

—— (1992), South of the West: Postcolonialism and the Narrative Construction of Australia (Bloomington: Indiana University Press).

Hinde, John (1981), Other People's Pictures (Sydney: Australian Broadcasting Commission).

Hodsdon, Barrett (1992), 'The Mystique of Mise en Scène Revisited', Continuum: The Australian Journal of Media and Culture, 5/2: 68–86.

Jayamanne, Laleen (1993), '"Love me Tender, Love me True, never Let me Go . . .": A Sri Lankan Reading of Tracey Moffatt's Night Cries—A Rural Tragedy', in Sneja Gunew and Anna Yeatman (eds.), Feminism and the Politics of Difference (Sydney: Allen & Unwin).

—— (1994), 'Postcolonial Gothic: The Narcissistic Wound in Jane Campion's The Piano', Department of Fine Arts, University of Sydney.

—— (ed.) (1995), Kiss me Deadly: Feminism and Cinema for the Moment (Sydney: Power Institute of Fine Arts, University of Sydney).

Langton, Marcia (1993), 'Well, I Heard it on the Radio and I Saw it on the Television . . .' (Sydney: Australian Film Commission).

Lawson, Sylvia (1965/1985), 'Not for the Likes of Us', in Moran and O'Regan (1985).

—— (1979) 'Towards Decolonization: Some Problems and Issues for Film History in Australia', Film Reader 4 (Chicago: Northwestern University).

Macallan, Helen (1995), Travelling in Circles (The Screen Project 1971–1981), Ph.D. thesis, (Sydney: University of Technology).

Martin, A. (1988), 'No Flowers for the Cinephile: The Fates of Cultural Populism 1960–1988', in Paul Foss (ed.), *Islands in the Stream: Myths of Place in Australian Culture* (Sydney: Pluto Press).

—— (1989), 'Indefinite Objects: Independent Film and Video', in Moran and O'Regan (1989).

—— (1993), *Phantasms: The Dreams and Desires at the Heart of our Popular Culture* (Melbourne: McPhee Gribble).

Moran, Albert (1991), *Projecting Australia: Government Film since 1945* (Sydney: Currency Press).

—— and **Tom O'Regan** (eds.) (1985), *An Australian Film Reader* (Sydney: currency Press).

—— —— (eds.) (1989), *The Australian Screen* (Melbourne: Penguin).

Morris, Meaghan (1988), 'Tooth and Claw: Tales of Survival and *Crocodile Dundee*' in *The Pirate's Fiancée: Feminism, Reading, Postmodernism* (London: Verso).

Mortimer, Lorraine (1995), 'The Grim Enchantment of *It's a Wonderful Life*', *Massachusetts Review* 36/4 (Dec.) 656–86.

Muecke, Stephen (1994), 'Narrative and Intervention in Aboriginal Filmmaking and Policy', *Continuum: The Australian Journal of Media and Culture*, 8/2: 248–57.

O'Regan, Tom (1985), '*The Man from Snowy River* and Australian Popular Culture', in Moran and O'Regan (1985).

*—— (1996), *Australian National Cinema* (London: Routledge).

Pike, Andrew, and **Ross Cooper** (1981), *Australian Film 1900–1977* (Melbourne: Oxford University Press and Australian Film Institute).

Routt, William (1992), 'L'Évidence', *Continuum: The Australian Journal of Media and Culture*, 5/2: 40–67.

Sands, Kate (1988), 'Women of the Wave', in Scott Murray (ed.), *Back of Beyond: Discovering Australian Film and Television*, catalogue for exhibition held by the Australian Film Commission and the UCLA Film and Television Archive, Sydney (Sydney: Australian Film Commission).

Shirley, Graham, and **Brian Adams** (1983), *Australian Cinema: The First Eighty Years* (Sydney: Angus & Robertson and Currency Press).

Stern, Lesley (1982), 'The Body as Evidence', *Screen*, 23/5: 39–62.

—— (1995), *The Scorsese Connection* (London: British Film Institute).

Stratton, David (1980), *The Last New Wave: The Australian Film Revival* (Sydney: Angus & Robertson).

—— (1990), *The Avocado Plantation: Boom and Bust in the Australian Film Industry* (Sydney: Pan Macmillan).

Tulloch, John (1981), *Legends on the Screen* (Sydney: Currency Press).

—— (1982), *Australian Cinema: Industry, Narrative, Meaning* (Sydney: Allen & Unwin).

*Turner, Graeme** (1986), *National Fictions: Literature, Film and the Construction of Australian Narrative* (Sydney: Allen & Unwin).

—— (1989), 'Art-Directing History: The Period Film', in Moran and O'Regan (1989).

—— (1994), 'The End of the National Project? Australian Cinema in the 1990s', in Wissal Dissayanake (ed.), *Questions of Nationhood and History in Asian Cinema* (Bloomington: University of Indiana Press).

Weir, Tom (1985), 'No Daydreams of our Own: The Film as National Self-Expression', in Moran and O'Regan (1985).

White, Richard (1981), *Inventing Australia: Images and Identity 1688–1980* (Sydney: George Allen & Unwin).

17

Canadian cinema

Will Straw

The academic study of English Canadian film has followed two broad lines of development since its emergence in the 1960s. Each of these is rooted in a form of cultural nationalism, the predominant impulse in post war English Canadian intellectual culture. One such line of development is that of cultural policy studies, the chronicling of the Canadian state's response to the perceived threat to Canadian national culture represented by the United States. Like Canadian media studies generally, this work is inspired by the political economy of Harold Innis (e.g. 1995), whose theorization of Canada's economic and political dependence, first on Great Britain and, subsequently, on the United States, has been a prominent influence on Canadian scholarship in a variety of fields.

For several decades, the most substantial analyses of Canadian film policy were published in the research appendices which accompanied the reports of government commissions. Such reports still provide the most comprehensive overviews of the Canadian film industry and of state policies directed at this industsy. In the last decade, however, communications scholars have undertaken a more highly theorized and comprehensive analysis of the long-term structural problems blocking the development of a Canadian cinema. Dorland (1991), Pendakur (1990), and Magder (1993) have offered analyses, rooted in the traditions of political economy, of that long process whereby Canadian film exhibition and distribution has remained under US control with disastrous effects on levels of investment in a national film industry.

The significant role played by policy studies within English Canadian film scholarship is evidence of a more general privileging of state action within the cultural sphere in Canada. Those involved in film culture in Canada have long reiterated the claim, first made by public-broadcasting activist Gordon Sparling in the 1930s, that Canadians must choose between 'the State and the United States' (cited in Magder 1993: 13). Popular and scholarly histories of Canadian cinema have typically offered a narrative in which a continuous experience of failure, beginning with the earliest arrival of cinema in Canada, is broken only with the heroic emergence of the National Film Board in 1939. A more recent wave of historical scholarship has challenged such accounts, noting the rich (albeit intermittent and unstable) legacy of attempts to found a national industry dating back to the turn of the century (e.g. Morris 1975).

It is partly in terms of the role played by policy studies that divergences between French-language and English-language film studies in Canada become clear. While English-language work has concentrated on the absence of an indigenous feature film industry, and chronicled the economic and political reasons for this absence, histories of French-language, Québécois cinema have displayed a higher degree of triumphalism. (Not all French-language culture within

Canada, it must be noted, is produced within Quebec; nor is the entirety of Quebec culture produced in the French-language.) While, arguably, the dominant barrier to the development of an English Canadian cinema has been imposed by the US industry, Québécois historians have tended to see the historical weakness of their own cinema as rooted in the long-standing underdevelopment of a distinctive francophone culture within Canada and Quebec. The sense that this underdevelopment was overcome in the 1960s and 1970s, as part of what has come to be known as Quebec's Quiet Revolution, allows histories of French-language cinema in Canada to offer a more heroic tone. In the post-war emergence of a Québécois cinema, we may note two paradoxes.

One is that federal institutions, such as the National Film Board and Canadian Broadcasting Corporation, played crucial (if unintended) roles in fostering a sense of nationalist, even separatist, consciousness in Quebec in the post-war period, in large measure by sponsoring and disseminating images of a population and geographical space undergoing a process of rapid modernization. The second is that, despite an even smaller population base than English Canada, francophone Quebec has produced a popular cinema (alongside its art–auteur cinema), one which, while of variable stability, is embedded in a star system, publicity apparatus, and constellation of collective cultural reference-points lacking in English Canada. Prominent examples of this popular cinema include *Mon Oncle Antoine* (Claude Jutra, 1971) and *Les Noces de papier* ('Paper Wedding', Michel Brault, 1989).

The other line of development in the study of English Canadian cinema has had a more direct impact on the development of Canadian film studies itself as a discipline. This is the attempt to define the specificity of English Canadian culture, an enterprise which flourished amidst the surge of interest in the late 1960s and 1970s in defining a national culture. From a present-day perspective, these attempts bear the mark of an all too obvious essentialism, but in seeking to establish the thematic and formal basis of national cultural traditions, Canadian writers were replicating processes observable in other national cultures before them. Margaret Atwood's *Survival* (1972) was perhaps the most influential of the texts produced as part of this project. Through a detailed study of Canadian fiction, poetry, and drama, she concluded that the thematic unity of Canadian literature (in both its English and French language forms) was based on a persistent

preoccupation with the notion of survival. Writers on the visual arts were very often drawn to the argument that Canadian artistic practice was marked by a preoccupation with landscape, and with the oppressiveness (as much as the sublime beauty) of nature (e.g. McGregor 1985).

In his influential book *Movies and Mythologies*, Peter Harcourt (1977) found a thematic unity for English Canadian cinema in a crisis of character motivation. Looking at the scattered feature film tradition of the 1960s and early 1970s, and at such works as *Paperback Hero* (Peter Pearson, 1973) or *Rowdyman* (Peter Carter, 1971) for example, he noted that the heroes of Canadian films were typically trapped in a real or emotional adolescence. Later, Geoff Pevere (1992: 36) would write of the stubbornly worrisome character of English Canadian films, regarding this as the appropriate response of one national culture to a powerful neighbour whose cultural artefacts include the constant exhortation to be happy. The sense that English Canadian feature films are typically more elliptical, unresolved, and restrained in narrative and stylistic terms is by now a commonplace within discussions of this cinema. Less frequently addressed is the extent to which these attributes are typical of art-house cinematic practices generally, rather than the necessary expression of a national character.

The project of defining a national film tradition found itself increasingly marginalized within the discipline of film studies, as that discipline settled into the departmental structure of Canadian universities in the late 1970s and early 1980s. The first degree programme in film studies in Canada was offered at York University in Toronto in 1969 (Morris 1991: 97). In Canada, as elsewhere in the English-speaking world, the rise of psychoanalytic, formalist, and ideological forms of analysis displaced, for a time, the question of the specificity of national cinematic practices. Indeed, for several years, there were evident tensions between the hermeneutics of suspicion which dominated film theory and the impulse to validate a national tradition which underlay much work on Canadian cinema. Feminist scholars and critics, writing in such magazines as *Cine Action* and *Borderlines*, were virtually alone in undertaking to address Canadian film practice from the perspective of those forms of analysis developed in such non-Canadian journals as *Screen* adnd *Camera Obscura*. More recently, as cultural theory in its Anglo-American variants has come to take up the question of nationhood, this work has served to revitalize Canadian film studies in important ways (e.g. Acland 1994). Indeed, Canadian studies itself, as a broadly interdisciplinary intellectual enterprise, has in recent years been marked by more sustained and vital dialogue with cultural studies.

For two decades teachers of film studies in Canada have met regularly within the Film Studies Association of Canada (FSAC). While FSAC is a bilingual organization (in spirit, if not in practice), French-language scholars in Quebec are more likely to belong to the Association québécoises des études cinématographiques. The sole academic publication devoted exclusively to film studies work in English Canada is the *Canadian Journal of Film Studies*, founded in 1990. (*Cinémas*, a French-language journal published in Montreal, is, characteristically, glossier and receives wider distribution.) Most of the significant debates over Canadian film have transpired in a cultural space in which the academic world and a broader sphere of intellectual culture overlap. Magazines such as *Cinema Canada* (now defunct), *Take One*, *Cine Action*, and *Point of View*, or periodicals of the political and cultural left, such as *Canadian Forum* and *Borderlines*, have done much to establish a critical tradition around English-Canadian cinema. Indeed, the most important controversy over the future of English Canadian cinema, the so-called 'Cinema we Need' debate, began within non-academic magazines and has since became standard assigned reading for courses in Canadian cinema. (It is collected in Featherling 1988.)

This debate was significant, in part, because it departed from the long-standing notion that a Canadian cinematic sensibility found its most natural expression in documentary forms. Typically, all participants concurred that the appropriate Canadian aesthetic was one which offered an alternative to the hegemony of Hollywood forms, but there was significant disagreement over whether the most effective alternative lay in the traditions of materialist experimental film or in new variations of the narrative feature. Bruce Elder, a prominent Canadian filmmaker himself, argued that only an experimental, non-narrative cinema, focused on the 'present' of perception, might successfully challenge the means–end rationality of US narrative cinema. Among those responding, Peter Harcourt (1985) and Piers Handling (1985) insisted on the need for the links to the social world offered by so-called New Narrative films, a cycle represented by such films as *Sonatine* (Micheline Lanctot, 1983) and *Family Viewing* (Atom Egoyan, 1987).

In a variety of ways, this debate echoed similar debates of a decade earlier within film studies and radical film culture internationally, and it was easy to dismiss arguments in favour of a phenomenological, experimental cinema as outmoded. By the mid-to-late 1980s, however, when the debate over 'The Cinema we Need' erupted, there were good reasons to believe that an indigenous tradition of experimental filmmaking, from the work of Michael Snow through that of Brenda Longfellow, Chris Gallagher, and Bruce Elder himself, offered a firmer foundation for a Canadian film culture than the intermittently successful feature, narrative films held up as an alternative. At the same time, as Kass Banning (1992) has noted, the tendency to dismiss documentary filmmaking as an anachronistic legacy of the Grierson period ignored the importance of documentary film in the development of a feminist film practice in Canada. Such films as *Our Marilyn* (Brenda Longfellow, 1988) and *Speak Body* (Kay Armitage, 1979) rework documentary within new, hybrid forms in which the influence of an indigenous experimental tradition is evident.

As might be expected, the most interesting recent work in Canadian film studies is that which challenges long-established orthodoxies. Nelson (1990) set out to undermine the National Film Board's status as the most powerful expression of our national cultural autonomy, noting the Board's role within the Canadian state's broader acquiescence to the security interests of the United States in the post-war period. More recently, Michael Dorland (1996, forthcoming) has suggested that the endless attempt within Canada to found a national feature film industry is in important ways the history of a 'fetish'. Young countries, he suggests, long for a feature film industry to serve as a sign of their national maturity and legitimacy. The principal effect of this longing, Dorland (forthcoming) argues, 'has not been a film industry *per se*, but elements of a film production infrastructure sufficiently established to support the periodic emergence of discursive formations that produce talk about an imaginary or potential industry'.

Arguably, the 'fetish' of a national feature film industry has withered over the last decade, the effect of three interrelated developments. One of these is the emergence of an English Canadian auteur cinema, evident in the works of such directors as Atom Egoyan (e.g. *Family Viewing* 1987; *Speaking Parts*, 1989; *Calendar*, 1994), Patricia Rozema (*I've Heard the Mermaids Singing*, 1987; *White Room*, 1991), Bruce

McDonald (*Road Kill*, 1989; *Highway 61*, 1991), and William D. MacGillivray (*Stations*, 1983; *Life Classes*, 1987). These works have reinvigorated a critical discourse of auteurist interpretation, just as their success has inspired the acknowledgement that an English Canadian cinema may only ever be an art-house cinema with occasional cross-overs to mainstream success. At the same time, the number of Canadian firms producing speciality television programming has expanded, as part of a broader growth in the international markets for television programmes. A national industry which services these markets (particularly in such genres as animated and children's programming, in which Canadian producers have traditionally done well) has taken shape, offering the levels of employment and return on investment which, it was once hoped, would come from the production of feature films. Finally, Canada is home to an elaborate network of independent film and video co-operatives, an infrastructure nourished by the cultural activism of municipal artistic scenes. Much of the important discourse of and about Canadian film is now to be found in independent short films and videos (and in the critical apparatus which surrounds such works), of which *Sally's Beauty Spot* (Helen Lee, 1990) and *Ten Cents a Dance* (Midi Onodera, 1989) offer noteworthy examples. It is here that the debate over cultural identity has moved from the conventional preoccupation with national specificity to embrace the complexities of identity politics and the shifting status of the nation-state (for an overview, see Marchessault 1995).

BIBLIOGRAPHY

Acland, Charles (1994), 'National Dreams, International Encounters: The Formation of Canadian Film Culture in the 1930s', *Canadian Journal of Film Studies*, 3/1: 3–26.

Atwood, Margaret (1972), *Survival: A Thematic Guide to Canadian Literature* (Toronto: Anansi).

Banning, Kass (1992), 'The Canadian Feminist Hybrid Documentary', *CineAction*, 26–7 (Winter), 108–13.

Dorland, Michael (1991), 'The War Machine: American Culture, Canadian Cultural Sovereignty and Film Policy', *Canadian Journal of Film Studies*, 1/2: 35–48.

—— (1996), 'Policy Rhetorics of an Imaginary Cinema: The Discursive Economy of the Emergence of the Australian and Canadian Feature Film', in Albert Moran (ed.), *Film Policy* (London: Routledge).

—— (forthcoming), *The Three Percent Solution: The Discursive Economy of the Emergence of the Canadian Feature Film 1957–1968* (Toronto: University of Toronto Press).

Featherling, Doug (ed.) (1988), *Documents in Canadian Film* (Peterborough: Broadview Press).

Handling, Piers (1985), 'The Cinema we Need?', *Cinema Canada*, nos. 120–1 (July–Aug.), 29–30.

Harcourt, Peter (1977), *Movies and Mythologies: Towards a National Cinema* (Toronto: Canadian Broadcasting Corporation Publications).

—— (1985), 'Politics or Paranoia?', *Cinema Canada*, nos. 120–1 (July–Aug.), 31–2.

Innis, Harold (1995), *Staples, Markets and Cultural Change: Selected Essays* (Montreal: McGill-Queen's University Press).

McGregor, Gaile (1985), *The Wacousta Syndrome: Explorations in the Canadian Landscape* (Toronto: University of Toronto Press).

Magder, Ted (1993), *Canada's Hollywood: The Canadian State and Feature Films* (Toronto: University of Toronto Press).

Marchessault, Janine (ed.) (1995), *Mirror Machine: Video and Identity* (Toronto: YYZ Books and CRCCII).

Morris, Peter (1975), *Embattled Shadows: A History of Canadian Cinema 1895–1939* (Montreal: McGill-Queen's University Press).

—— (1991), 'From Film Club to Academy: The Beginnings of Film Education in Canada', in Réal La Rochelle (ed.), *Québec/Canada: l'enseignement du cinéma et de l'audiovisuel/The Study of Film and Video* (Condé-sur-Noireau: CinémaAction).

Nelson, Joyce (1990), *The Colonized Eye* (Toronto: Between the Lines).

Pendakur, Manjunath (1990), *Canadian Dreams and American Control: The Political Economy of the Canadian Film Industry* (Toronto: Garamond Press).

Pevere, Geoff (1992), 'On the Brink', *CineAction*, 28 (Spring), 34–8.

18

Issues in world cinema

Wimal Dissanayake

Dadasaheb Phalke, who is generally regarded by Indian film historians as the father of Indian cinema, relates an interesting anecdote (1970). His *Raja Harish-chandra*, released on 3 May 1913, is highlighted by scholars as the first Indian feature film. Phalke tells us that he was inspired to make this film after seeing the movie *The Life of Christ* (USA, 1906) in the America–India Picture Palace in Bombay in 1910. As he was watching the film, he was overwhelmed by both a deep religiosity and an awareness of the potentialities of the art of cinematography. As he watched the life of Christ unfold before his eyes, he thought of the gods Krishna and Ramachandra and wondered how long it would be before Indians would be able to see Indian images of their divinities on screen. In fact, it was not long: three years later Phalke made the first Indian feature film based on the celebrated Indian epic the *Ramayana* (see Rajadhyaksha, Chapter 19). However, what this anecdote—and many similar ones by the early filmmakers in Asia, Latin America, and Africa—points to is a series of binaries that underpin the discourse of cinema in those continents: binaries of Westernization and indigenization, tradition and modernity, the local and the global. Any discussion of these cinemas, and the trajectories of their development, must necessarily address these crucial issues.

However, it is important that we do not lump these cinemas together indiscriminately as 'non-Western'. It is, of course, true that, geographically, they are from the non-Western world (with 'Western' here referring to North America and Europe), and that they share many interests and preoccupations. However, as the following chapters clearly demonstrate, while they may display commonalities of interest, each of the countries, because of its specific social formations and historical conjunctures, has its own distinctive trajectories of cinematic development and concerns.

In the same way, we must also avoid treating non-Western cinemas as expressive of some unchanging 'essence'. Instead, we must see them as sites of discursive contestations, or representational spaces, in which changing social and cultural meanings are

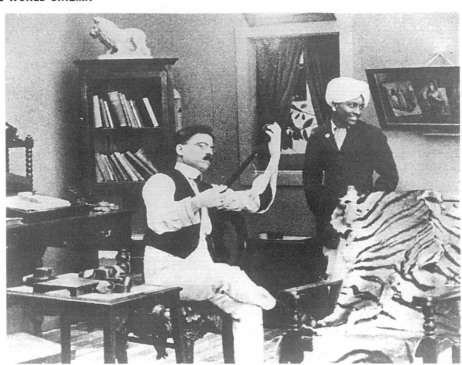

The first Indian feature film,
Raja Harischandra (1913)

generated and fought over. The discursive boundaries of the various societies that constitute the non-Western world are constantly expanding and cannot be accounted for in essentialist terms. Moreover, the filmmakers and film commentators (critics as well as scholars) who are at the leading edge of development of the film cultures of their respective societies have been exposed to, and in many cases trained in, Western countries so that their self-positioning in relation to the contours of their specific cultures is understandably complex and multifaceted (see Burton-Carvajal, Chapter 25).

The concept of Third Cinema, originally formulated by the Argentinian film directors Fernando Solanas and

> **We must also avoid treating non-Western cinemas as expressive of some unchanging 'essence'. Instead, we must see them as sites of discursive contestations, or representational spaces, in which changing social and cultural meanings are generated and fought over.**

Octavio Getino (1973) and later expanded by film scholars such as Teshome H. Gabriel (1982), addresses a number of issues related to non-Western cinemas. Put simply, one can say that First Cinema refers to mainstream Hollywood cinema, and Second Cinema to European 'art' cinema. In distinguishing it from First and Second Cinemas, proponents of Third Cinema see it as the articulation of a new culture and a vehicle of social transformation (see Burton-Carvajal). Paul Willemen (1989), however, suggests how the manifestos laying out the guiding ideas of Third Cinema give the impression that it was developed by Latin Americans for Latin America and that its wider applicability was added as an afterthought. He also argues that there is a danger in the concept of Third Cinema of homogenizing non-Western cinema and not grappling sufficiently with questions of ethnic and gender divisions as well as the vexed relationship between cinema and nationhood. It is this complicated relationship between nationhood and cinema with which we shall begin.

Nationhood and cinema

Nationhood, as with all other forms of identity, revolves around the question of difference, with how the uniqueness of one nation differs from the uniqueness of other comparable nations. Benedict Anderson (1983) suggests that nationhood may be understood as an 'imagined community', and indicates how nationhood is a cultural artefact of a particular kind. It is imagined, because the members of even the smallest nation can never get to know, or even meet, most of their fellow members; yet in the imagination of each the notion of the nation persists. The nation is also imagined as a community because, regardless of the very real inequities and injustices that exist in society, it is always perceived as deep and horizontal comradeship. It is important, however, to note that Anderson employed the term 'imagined' and not 'imaginary'. 'Imaginary' signifies absence, or nothingness, while 'imagined' foregrounds a nice balance between the real and not the real. The critical weakness of Benedict Anderson's formulaton, however, is that it pays scant attention to materialities and underplays the discontinuities of history. It also minimizes the salience of the political character of nationhood and the role which ethnicity and religion have played in the construction of the nation. Any investigation into the ways in which cinema constructs nationhood, therefore, has to consider these thorny issues of ethnic loyalties, religious affinities, and local patriotism. It must also recognize that the nation also contains within itself diverse local narratives of resistance and memory and therefore take into account the full force of these local and dissenting narratives which are embedded in the larger narrative of the nation.

It is evident that cinema is a very powerful cultural practice and institution which both reflects and inflects the discourse of nationhood. As a result, the concept of national cinema is at the base of many discussions of popular culture in Africa, Asia, the Middle East, and Latin America. It is generally analysed at two interrelated levels: the textual and the industrial (although see Crofts, Chapter 1, for a full discussion of the complexities involved in theorizing the concept of 'national cinema'). The textual level involves a focus upon the distinctiveness of a given cinema—whether it be Indonesian or Nigerian, Mexican or Senegalese—in terms of content, style, and indigenous aesthetics. The industrial level involves a focus upon the relationship between cinema and industry, the nature of film production, distribution, and consumption, and the ways in which the ever-present threats from Hollywood are met. However, it should also be noted that the concept of national cinema serves to privilege notions of coherence and unity and to stabilize cultural meanings linked to the perceived uniqueness of a given nation. As I have pointed out (Dissanayake 1994), it is implicated in national myth-making and ideological production and serves to delineate both otherness and legitimate selfhood.

How a nation tells its unifying and legitimizing story about itself to its citizens is crucial in the understanding of nationhood, and after the popularization of cinema as a medium of mass entertainment in Latin America, Asia, the Middle East, and Africa, the role of cinema in this endeavour has come to occupy a significant place (see Rajadhyaksha and Burton-Carvajal, Chapters 19 and 25 below). Benedict Anderson (1983) focused attention on the centrality of print capitalism in giving rise to the idea of the nation and the deep horizontal comradeship it promoted. He observed that newspapers and nationalistic novels were primarily responsible for the creation of a national consciousness. In social circumstances that were antecedent to the establishment of nation-states, newspapers, journals, and fiction served to co-ordinate time and space in a way that enabled the formation of the imagined community that is the nation. In the contemporary world, cinema has assumed the status of a dominant medium of communication, and its role in conjuring up the imagined community among both the literate and illiterate strata of society is both profound and far-reaching. David Harvey (1989) suggests that the way in which cinema works to capture the complex and dynamic relationship between temporality and spatiality is not available to other media, and this becomes a significant issue for non-Western cinemas.

The *topos* of nationhood becomes significant for another reason as well. Cinema in most countries in Africa, the Middle East, Asia, and Latin America is closely linked to the concept and functioning of the nation-state. Questions of economics—production, distribution, and exhibition—and control of content through overt and covert censorship have much to do with this. For most film producers in Latin American, African, and Asian countries that depend on the patronage of local audiences for returns on their investments, the assistance, intervention, and co-ordination of governments become extremely important (in the form of film corporations, training institutes, script boards, censorship panels, national festivals, and the honouring of filmmakers). It is evident, therefore, that the demands of the economics of film industries and the imperatives of the nation-state are interlinked in complex, and at times disconcertingly intrusive, ways.

Speaking in very broad terms, we can divide films made in Asia, Africa, and South America into three main groups: the popular, the artistic, and the experimental (again, see Crofts, Chapter 1, for a further elaboration of these categories). The popular films are commercial by nature and are designed to appeal to the vast mass of moviegoers and to secure the largest profit. The artistic films, while not immune to commercial pressures, are, none the less, driven by 'high art' concerns and tend to be showcased at international film festivals. The experimental films are much smaller in number and much less visible in the filmic landscape; they are committed to the creation of an oppositional cinema characterized by an audacious attempt to interrogate the Establishment and its values. Thus, if we take India as an example, filmmakers such as Raj Kapoor, Manmohan Desai, and Ramesh Sippy represent the popular tradition, directors such as Satyajit Ray and Adoor Gopalakrishnan belong to the 'art' tradition, while some of the work of Kumar Sahani and Mani Kaul may be categorized as experimental (see Rajadhyaksha, Chapter 19). What is of interest in terms of the relationship between the nation-state and cinema is that—again in general terms—while popular cinema generally upholds notions of a unified nation, the artistic cinema tends to offer critiques of the nation-state (and its associated economic, social, political, and cultural discourses and institutions) and the experimental cinema characteristically calls into question the hegemonic project of the nation-state and the privileged vocabularies of national narration. Thus, in a large country like India with its numerous languages and religions, films produced in regional languages like Bengali or Malayalam tend to valorize, directly or obliquely, the regional at the expense of the national, thereby revealing certain fissures and fault lines in the national discourse. The artistic and experimental filmmakers seek to draw attention to the ambiguous unities, silenced voices, emergent and oppositional discourses, that occupy the national space, and thereby instigate a de-totalizing project.

For filmmakers in Asia, Africa, and Latin America, the cinematic representation of minorities presents a challenging problem, and this issue is inseparable from the dictates of the nation-state. The putatively homogeneous nature of the nation-state and its legitimizing meta-narratives begin to come under scrutiny as film-makers attempt to articulate the experiences and life-worlds of the minorities, whether they be ethnic, religious, linguistic, or caste, who inhabit the national space. Films that thematize the hardships of minorities create a representational space from where the hegemonic discourse of the state can be usefully subverted, and the idea of social and cultural difference emphasized. Indeed, one can see a wholly understandable tension between the idea of the unitary nation and cultural difference in many works of cinema produced in Asian, Latin American, and African countries. This tension is discernible in some of the works of internationally celebrated film directors like Nagisa Oshima of Japan, as well as in the creations of less well-known filmmakers such as Ji Qingchun (China), Park (Korea), and Euthana Mukdasnit (Thailand).

> **Artistic and experimental filmmakers seek to draw attention to the ambiguous unities, silenced voices, emergent and oppositional discourses, that occupy the national space, and thereby instigate a de-totalizing project.**

Film commentators in Latin America and Africa also display such propensities to rethink issues and repose questions. For example, if we take Mexican cinema, we find that in the past the concept of *mexicanidad* (Mexicanness) was privileged in intellectual and aesthetic discussions, and was perceived as a leading *topos* guiding Mexican cinema. Distinguished writers, such as the Nobel laureate Octavio Paz, underlined its significance, and both filmmakers and film critics positively valorized it. However, modern commentators of Mexican cinema now highlight how *mexicanidad*, as it was formulated, was élitist, sexist, and class-bound, and privileged the *criollo* over the *mestizo* and the Indians. Through the interrogation of such concepts as 'Japaneseness' and 'Mexicanness' associated with filmic discourse, scholars are emphasizing the need for the reacquisition of subaltern agency and the repossessing of history. The discursive spaces that they are opening up can have profound consequences in examining afresh the cinemas of the non-West.

The public sphere

This discussion of the interconnections between cinema and nationhood leads to the importance of cinema in the public sphere. From the very beginning, cinemas in South America, Africa, and Asia were involved in the public sphere, addressing important questions related to tradition, Westernization, democracy, the caste system, and cultural identity. The pioneering work of the German social philosopher Jurgen Habermas (1991) has resulted in the widespread interest in the concept of the public sphere which has helped to foreground issues of democratization, public participation, and oppositionality. Others such as Oskar Negt and Alexander Kluge (1993) have built upon Habermas's work and discussed the ability of cinema to provide a site for the contestation of meaning in an increasingly technologically saturated public sphere, where democratic self-realization and community participation have become much more problematic. The question of the public sphere is particularly important in the case of the nations of Asia, Africa, and Latin America. In many of these countries, cinema has always been perceived as playing a social role and continues to be a significant form of mass communication, even in the face of the censorship which many countries—be it Indonesia or the Philippines or Nigeria—impose.

Many examples of the mutual animation of cinema and the public sphere may be provided. In the 1930s Indian filmmakers addressed the issue of untouchability, which continues to be extremely sensitive. In 1946 Akira Kurosawa made *No Regrets for Youth*, which had a profound impact on Japanese society, raising the whole issue of the democratization of society and leaving an indelible mark on later filmmakers such as Oshima, Kei Kumai, and Kazuo Kuroki. Oshima, in his earlier films, made cinema a vital part of the public sphere by raising issues related to the plight of Korean minorities in Japan, capital punishment, and sexuality. The Indian film director Ritwik Ghatak, in his works, sought to focus on important issues related to the Indian public sphere such as the partitioning of India, the plight of the poor, the predicament of the artists, and the nature of mechanization. Many of the most interesting films made in Argentina after 1983, when the country returned to constitutional democracy, textualize the nature, significance, and urgency of re-democratization and the sweeping-aside of fascistic tendencies. African filmmakers like Idrissa Ouedraogo

have sought to make cinema a vital adjunct of the public sphere by raising questions concerning tradition, cultural identity, stereotypes, and misleading Western representations of African society.

However, it is in China where this relationship between cinema and the public sphere can be seen in its most vivid form. The work of the post-1980 group of filmmakers, generally referred to as the Fifth Generation of filmmakers, stirred up a great deal of interest both inside and ouside China (see Reynaud, Part 3, Chapter 20). Many of these films deal with the Cultural Revolution and seek to textualize directly or indirectly the phenomenon of the Cultural Revolution and its effects on the rural population, in particular, through an innovative filmmaking approach characterized by minimal narration, striking camera movements, a stress on spatiality, and disruptive montage. Films such as Chen Kaige's *Yellow Earth* (1984), *King of the Children* (1985), *The Big Parade* (1986), and *Farewell, my Concubine* (1993), Zhang Yimou's *Red Sorghum* (1988) and *To Live* (1994), Tian Zhuangzhuang's *The Horse Thief* (1986) and *The Blue Kite* (1991), to mention but a few titles, all bear testimony to a desire to make cinema an indispensable facet of the public sphere.

Intertextuality

As indicated at the start of this chapter, cinema was an imported art form that quickly became indigenized in the non-Western world. In a similar manner, European–American theories of cinema are impinging ever more strongly on the thought and sensibility of both filmmakers and film critics in Asian, African, and Latin American countries. The impact of European–American film scholarship on the non-Western world raises some fundamental issues related to comparative film study.

Is it possible to broaden the European–American referents that guide Western film theories so as to accommodate the cinematic experiences of the non-Western world? Do those African, Asian, Middle Eastern, and Latin American intellectuals and film scholars who are vigorously antipathetic to these Western theories subscribe to a merely spurious notion of cultural authenticity and purity? What is the nature of the theoretical space from which Asian, Latin American, and African film scholars and theorists speak? Writing in the context of literature, African-born Harvard professor

Kwame Anthony Appiah (1992) argues against both the pseudo-universalism of Eurocentric theorizations which pose as universal and a 'nativism' which nostalgically appeals to an apparently 'pure' and 'authentic' indigeneous culture. As Appiah points out, while 'nativism' may challenge Western norms, the way in which the contest is framed remains unchanged. 'The Western emperor has ordered the natives to exchange their robes for trousers: their act of defiance is to insist on tailoring them from homespun material. Given their arguments, plainly, the cultural nationalists do not go far enough; they are blind to the fact that their nativist demands inhabit a Western architecture' (1992: 60). These remarks also have a relevance for film theory.

It is clear that Eurocentric paradigms cannot take on the mantle of universal templates or they will hamper a deeper understanding and appreciation of cinemas in the non-Western world (see Ukadike, Chapter 24). During the last fifteen years or so, following a retheorization of such issues as the nature of cinematic representation, the role of ideology in cultural production, and the importance of female subjectivity in cinema, the genre of melodrama, for example, has been critically rehabilitated in Western film studies. However, melodramas produced in Latin America, Africa, and Asia—and the majority of films made in these regions have been melodramas—cannot be judged in terms of Western conceptualizations of melodrama. Melodrama functions differently in different cultural contexts and the melodramatic traditions evolved in these countries, especially in the theatre, have acquired highly distinctive characteristics. For example, in India, film melodramas bear the cultural inscriptions of folk theatre as well as the Parsee theatre of the nineteenth century. Other analytical tools developed by Western film scholars—such as those relating to point of view, the gaze, and textual subjectivity—may also be seen to have limited application. Paul Willemen (1994), for example, has perceptively demonstrated, in relation to the work of the Israeli filmmaker Amos Gitai, how in his cinema it is most decidedly not through point-of-view shots that we are mobilized, but through the differences between one point of view and another even within the one shot. The role of the aesthetic inter-texts and cultural contexts, in this respect, are crucial to the understanding of the various non-Western cinemas.

Film is not an isolated art form; it inhabits a common expressive culture fed by tradition, cultural memory, and indigenous modes of symbolic representation.

> **It is clear that Eurocentric paradigms cannot take on the mantle of universal templates or they will hamper a deeper understanding and appreciation of cinemas in the non-Western world.**

Therefore, films and other arts are mutually implicated in the production of meaning and pleasure, and this deserves to be examined more closely. In most African, Latin American, and Asian countries cinema, from the very beginning, has had a symbiotic relationship with the theatre, and continues to do so. Similarly with painting. The complex ways in which traditional arts inspire modern filmmaking would reward further exploration and are vitally connected to what Paul Willemen refers to as the 'orchestration of meaning' in cinema.

Let us, for example, consider the filmmaker Yasujiro Ozu. In his films, stillness and emptiness play a crucial role in the production of meaning. On the surface, if seen through Western eyes, nothing happens. But at a deeper level of emotional and cultural apprehension, much is going on in those stillnesses and emptinesses. This is, of course, connected with traditional Japanese aesthetics. For example, in Japanese manuals of painting it is remarked that emptiness does not occur until the first ink mark is inscribed on the paper, thereby calling attention to the vital interplay between emptiness and inscriptions as co-producers of meaning. In the same way, African filmmakers have made a conscious attempt to draw on the traditional African arts in filmmaking, especially the art of oral storytelling, and the use of dreams, fantasies, narrative detours, and parallelisms in the films of Ousmane Sembene, Haile Gerima, Souleymane Cissé, and Idrissa Ouedraogo demonstrate this link (see Ukadike, Chapter 24).

The interconnections between cinema and painting in most Asian countries is a fascinating one. Japanese, Chinese, and Korean filmmakers in the past have tapped the rich resources of painting in framing their shots, creating mise-en-scène, and organizing their visual material, and they continue to do so. For example, in the visual style of films such as Chen Kaige's *Yellow Earth*, one can see the impact of Taoism and traditional Chinese paintings of nature. The towering presence of hills and mountains and the diminutive human beings etched against them, the use of a limited range of colours, natural lighting, and the nonperspectival deployment of space, bear testimony to this fact. Similarly, in the work of Ritwik Ghatak, one perceives an attempt to use creatively and innovatively traditional Indian iconography associated with painting in order to communicate a cinematic experience that is anchored in the past but reaching out to the present.

However, we also need to bear in mind that this is not only a question of aesthetics; there is also an ideological and political aspect to it. For example, in *Yellow Earth*, the extreme long shots, the absence of depth, and the empty spaces that fill the frame can be read as a critique of the Cultural Revolution and its excesses. The supposedly apolitical visuals inscribed in the massive presence of nature therefore make a political statement. Going beyond this reading, as Rey Chow (1995) points out, we need to examine the film in terms of its material makings and rethink the cognitive value of emptiness and blankness. As she rightly observes, in order to make sense of 'space' the viewer would have to 'view' space from a position whose locality would 'see' non-signifying blankness in relation to the representational presence itself. Hence, in order to grasp the complexities of the enunciative positions and spectatorships that characterize non-Western cinemas, texts—and their inter-texts—must be analysed in terms of ideology and politics as well as artistic apprehension.

Any meaningful discussion of the cinemas of the non-Western world would compel us to confront issues of economics, politics, aesthetics, institutions, technology, and cultural discourse in general. What is the nature of the national film industry? What role do governments play, both positive and negative? How are the cinema industries located at the local and the global? How are they dealing with the hegemony of Hollywood? How do filmmakers seek to construct alternative histories and cultural identities? These, and similar issues that merit closer anlaysis, will be dealt with at length in the specific case-studies that follow. What I have sought to do in this introductory chapter is to raise some salient issues related to the cinemas of the non-Western world. As Paul Willemen (1989) observes, what the outstanding filmmakers from Asia, Africa, and Latin America have done is to start from a recognition of the multilayeredness of their own cultural-historical formations, with each layer being shaped by intricate linkages between local as well as international forces. As a consequence, these filmmakers suggest a way of inhabiting one's culture which is neither myopically nationalist nor evasively cosmopolitan. This is the ideal that stands before the filmmakers of the non-Western world.

> **What the outstanding filmmakers from Asia, Africa, and Latin America have done is to start from a recognition of the multilayeredness of their own cultural-historical formations, with each layer being shaped by intricate linkages between local as well as international forces.**

BIBLIOGRAPHY

Anderson, Benedict (1983), *Imagined Communities: Reflections on the Origin and Spread of Nationalism* (London: Verso).

Appiah, Kwame Anthony (1992), *In my Father's House: Africa in the Philosophy of Culture* (Oxford: Oxford University Press).

Chow, Rey (1995), *Primitive Passions: Visibility, Ethnography, and Contemporary Chinese Cinema* (New York: Columbia University Press).

Davis, Darrell William (1996), *Picturing Japaneseness: Monumental Style, National Identity, Japanese Films* (New York: Columbia University Press).

Dissanayake, Wimal (ed.) (1994), *Colonialism and Nationalism in Asian Cinema* (Bloomington: Indiana University Press).

Gabriel, Teshome K. (1982), *Third Cinema in the Third World* (Ann Arbor, Mi.: UMI Research Press).

Habermas, Jurgen (1991), *The Structural Transformation of the Public Sphere: An Inquiry into a Category of Bourgeois Society*, trans. Thomas Burger and Frederick Lawrence (Cambridge, Mass.: MIT Press).

Harvey, David (1989), *The Condition of Postmodernity: An Enquiry into the Origins of Cultural Change* (Oxford: Blackwell).

Negt, Oskar, and **Alexander Kluge** (1993), *Public Sphere and Experience: Towards an Analysis of the Bourgeois and Proletarian Public Sphere* (Minneapolis: University of Minnesota Press).

Phalke: Commemoration Souvenir (1970), (Bombay: Phalke Centenary Celebrations Committee).

Rajadhyaksha, Ashish (1985), 'The Phalke Era: Conflict of Traditional Forms and Modern Techology', *Journal of Arts and Ideas*, nos. 14–15.

Solanas, Fernando E., and Octavio Getino (1973), *Cine: cultura y descolonizacion* (Buenos Aires: Siglo XXI Argentino Editores).

*Willemen, Paul (ed.) (1989), *Questions of Third Cinema* (London: British Film Institute).

—— (1994), *Looks and Frictions: Essays in Cultural Studies and Film Theory* (Bloomington: Indiana University Press).

19   Indian cinema

Ashish Rajadhyaksha

As with the history of modern India itself, the history of the Indian cinema has until recently been written mainly with nationalist intention. India became an independent 'sovereign democratic republic' in 1947, with the transfer of power from the British into the hands of a nationalist ruling élite. In the process, the independent nation-state was heir to a century-old history of engagment with modernity, social reform, and democracy that culminated in something like a seventy-year freedom struggle from colonization. It has been the business of India's most important historians to write, from this vantage-point of political independence, what Gyanendra Pandey calls the 'biography of the nation-state', and from its ensuing contention that

the [Indian political] 'centre' remains the recognised vantage point for a meaningful reconstruction of 'Indian' history, and the 'official' archive . . . the primary source for its construction. By attributing a 'natural' quality to a particular unity, such as 'India', and adopting its 'official' archive as the primary source for historical knowledge . . . the history of India since the early 19th century has tended to become

the biography of the emerging nation-state. It has also become the history in which the story of Partition, and the accompanying Hindu–Muslim and Muslim–Sikh riots . . . is written up as a secondary story . . . one that, for all its consequences miraculously left the course of Indian history unaltered [as] 'India' started firmly . . . and naturally on its secular, democratic, non-violent course. (Pandey 1991)

Part of the history of modern India has been the enormously influential presence of what is now famous as the 'world's largest film industry'. This was one of the legacies of the colonial state that Independence bestowed upon free India and, as with nationalist political history, India's film history has been largely written up from the standpoint of state policy on Indian cinema after 1947, with its efforts to install a respectable 'realist cinema'. A concern with respectability and, occasionally, political usefulness is also evident in critical-theoretical efforts to make sense of Indian cinema in the era of high nationalism.

In recent years, however, there has emerged a body of new writing that is as influenced by what we could call 'post-nationalist' historiography, notably that pioneered by the famed Subaltern Studies collective (see Guha 1982–9), as by new theory in the West, such as cultural studies and post-colonial theory. In the following survey, I shall first briefly outline Indian cinema's own history, asking readers to bear in mind that the periodizations I use are still mainly orthodox ones, the cinematic equivalents of the 'biography of the nation-state'. They are used mainly because newer ones are still not sufficiently common as to be useful for such a brief survey. Then I shall outline an influential critical tradition that I have identified as largely 'nationalist', including important film journalism; and in the final section, I shall provide a brief summary of recent theoretical writing on Indian film.

Indian cinema: a brief history

Virtually all conventional history of Indian cinema begins with the man considered its pioneer: Dhundiraj Govind Phalke (also known as Dadasaheb Phalke). Born in Nasik in 1870, Phalke had had a colourful history an an artist, photographer, and printer before he launched his film career with the mythological *Raja Harishchandra* in 1914 (see Rajadhyaksha 1987). This was the first Indian fiction film we know of, but it was hardly India's first movie. Since 1896 India had had a thriving nascent film industry mainly on the periphery of a vast and well-entrenched theatre industry, including in particular the Parsee theatre and commercial theatrical troupes in its main presidency cities of Bombay, Calcutta (see Mukherjee 1980), and Madras, as well as many other cities (e.g. Lucknow and Lahore).

> **Part of the history of modern India has been the enormously influential presence of what is now famous as the 'world's largest film industry'. This was one of the legacies of the colonial state that Independence bestowed upon free India and, as with nationalist political history, India's film history has been largely written up from the standpoint of state policy on Indian cinema after 1947, with its efforts to install a respectable 'realist cinema'.**

India also had a nearly century-old history of popular visual art, extending into what has come to be called 'Company School' painting (Indian art made for British clients and Indian bureaucracy and aristocracy, named after the East India Company) and further developing at the turn of the century, into bazaar paintings, notably in Calcutta, and art for a growing publishing industry (e.g. woodcut print-making) (see Archer 1953, 1962; Archer 1977). This practice, constituting among other things India's first encounter with Western oil-painting and naturalism—exemplified by the painter Raja Ravi Varma, who started as a portraitist, went on to paint Indian mythological scenes in naturalist style, and finally became a mass producer of religious oleographs and lithographs (see Kapur 1989)—also extended into still photography, which then formed a key bridge into cinema itself.

A great deal of recent writing has investigated the cultural practices of the pre-cinema traditions of popular art, as industry, and politically in its gradual assimilation of nationalist identity, for example Guha-Thakurta's landmark book *The Making of New 'Indian' Art* (1992). This now well-charted territory has not, however, been duplicated by significant research into early Indian cinema before Phalke, although biographical material on other contemporaries, notably Hiralal Sen in Calcutta (who started by filming plays; see Mukherjee 1966) and Nataraja Mudaliar in Madras, is available. Phalke's own undoubtedly influential cinema has, however, been enhanced by two further factors: first, his accompaniment of that cinema with an early effort towards theory, especially Swadeshi (or national-indigenism), which allowed him to claim a political character to his staple genre of the Hindu mythological. The survival of the genre well into recent times (and the new lease of life that television has recently given it) partly explains Phalke's key presence in all nationalist Indian film histories ever since, especially those written up by the film industry itself or on its behalf by 'official' historians. There has, however, been a major recent revival of interest in the silent film, mainly as a result of a restoration project at the National Film Archive of India and the showcasing of surviving silents in the Pordenone Film Festival (see Chabria 1994).

The more concrete historiography of Indian cinema, however, emerges only from the 1920s with the founding of major studios—notably the Kohinoor and Ranjit in Bombay, the New Theatres in Calcutta, the Maharashtra Film Company (Kolhapur), and its famous off-shoot, Prabhat, which moved to Poona. These studios, and their famed sound versions—which coalesced mainly into the 'dominant' three: New Theatres, Prabhat, and Bombay Talkies—introduced professional distribution systems, as well as star manufacture, establishing a substantial base for the Indian cinema before the Second World War (by which time audiences for local products already far exceeded those for imported films).

Conventional film histories of this period usually focus on the three studios mentioned above, and its famous film directors—V. Shantaram (Prabhat), the German Franz Osten and his producer Himansu Rai (Bombay Talkies), and the whole stable of directors at New Theatres, notably P. C. Barua and Nitin and Debaki Bose—for having introduced many of the tenets of modernism, 'art' cinema, and respectable nationalism. It is less noticed that even at this time the considerably larger bulk of production already came out of independent production outfits based in Bombay, Calcutta, and Madras, which often reduced the major studios into hirers of studio space. As with Phalke, here too the survival of studio productions from the 'big three' has further reinforced claims regarding the admittedly major cultural influence of these houses.

The Second World War was crucial for perhaps exactly the opposite reason of its impact in the West. The war economy, it has been extensively documented, actually stimulated independently financed industry, and after the war the big studios were overwhelmed by independent financier-producers entering the film industry with mainly short-term benefits in mind.

Three main trends in Indian cinema are evident after the war. First, there is the founding of something like a national, or nation-wide, audience for the Hindi cinema, which benefited from the Partition of India as the former movie industries of Lahore and Karachi, in what became Pakistan, migrated to Bombay. Secondly there is an extension of the 'all-India' aesthetic—of fantasies that often came to be called 'masala' films—into other languages, notably Tamil, Teluga, Bengali, and Marathi, and new production bases in Hyderabad, Bangalore, and Coimbatore, for example. Thirdly, a major political influence came with the founding of the Indian state itself, and the adoption of official measures to discipline the film industry into adhering to new cultural and ideological priorities. This latter initiative led to the government itself entering

film production, and to the establishment of an art cinema movement that produced India's best-known filmmaker, Satyajit Ray.

To a great extent the ideological tensions that characterize these three developments decide the priorities of much nationalist film writing and have been analysed notably by Ravi Vasudevan (1993). This period, when several 'all-time hits' by filmmakers like Guru Dutt, Raj Kapoor, Mehboob, and V. Shantaram were made, has also been written up as the 'golden age' of the Indian cinema and in numerous books and essays on the work of Satyajit Ray (notably Das Gupta 1980, 1981).

In the late 1960s direct state action realized some of the recommendations of the 1951 Film Enquiry Committee to 'provide, afford or procure finance or other facilities for the production of films of good standard', by designating new priorities for the Film Finance Corporation (FFC), which helped to launch the famed New Indian Cinema movement. Launched in part by Mrinal Sen's *Bhuvan Shome* (1969) and Mani Kaul's highly experimental *Uski Roti* (1969), the FFC produced both self-consciously avant-garde film—especially the work of Kaul and Kumar Shahani (see Shahani 1986)—as well as what came, with the work especially of Shyam Benegal, to define further an aesthetic of 'state realism'. Emphasizing what is usually interpreted as a romantic realism with a major investment in regional roots (i.e. as against the Hindi cinema's 'rootless' pan-nationalism), the New Cinema helped establish local industries, notably in Kerala, Assam, and Orissa, which were all relatively marginal until the 1970s.

However, this was also the time when the mainstream Hindi cinema transformed itself yet again, in the light of political developments that culminated in the National Emergency declared by Indira Gandhi in 1975, a transformation usually equated with the star who was to dominate Hindi cinema until the present, Amitabh Bachchan. Associated in the 1970s with a vigilante 'angry young man' stereotype, which often appropriated rhetorically the political movements of the peasantry and working classes that had led to the Emergency, the Bachchan phenomenon in many ways encapsulates this turbulent period in Indian history, which only transformed itself in the late 1980s with economic liberalization, the arrival of satellite television, and the founding of Doordarshan, the massive Indian state television infrastructure.

Nationalist film theory: a brief history

In 1948, a year after Independence, Satyajit Ray wrote his influential essay 'What is Wrong with Indian Films?' to launch a now well-entrenched attack on the Indian cinema for its inability to comprehend what is basic to film, namely temporality and movement. 'In India, it would seem that the fundamental concept of a coherent dramatic pattern existing in time was generally misunderstood . . . often by a queer process of reasoning, movement was equated with action and action with melodrama'.

Ray's own cinema, which has conventionally been seen as the point at which Indian cinema's initiatives towards realism, and the mastering of the storytelling idiom, were finally realized, has also provided the post-Independence focus for debates about divisions between realism versus modernism, high art versus low, and, after the avant-garde practice of some New Indian Cinema filmmakers, modernism versus avant-garde (usually mapped onto the two very different legacies of Ray himself as against his equally influential, but less well-known, contemporary Ritwik Ghatak; for Ghatak, see Rajadhyaksha 1982, 1987; Ghatak 1987). One of the key figures embodying the Ray aesthetic is the writer Chidananda Das Gupta, his long-time colleague, with whom Ray launched the seminal Calcutta Film Society in 1947. Das Gupta's important collection of essays, published mainly in film society periodicals like the Indian Film Review and Indian Film Culture—a crucial forum for educating people into modernist filmmaking and film seeing practices—includes the classic 'The Cultural Basis of Indian Cinema' (1968). In that article Das Gupta argued for the 'all-India film', a genre of the nationalist mass entertainer that played the political function of culturally integrating the country and in that sense performed by default a role that Ray also, with greater self-consciousness, was attempting in his practice. Another key writer from this period, addressing a range of issues from the viewpoint of this modernist divide, was Kobita Sarkar (1975, 1982).

As the question of art cinema merged into that of the specific reformist role of the Indian state in the area of film, there emerged a substantial body of both historical writing (see notably Barnouw and Krishnaswamy (1963), the best-known book on Indian cinema until recently) and writings on film policy, the nature of state funding, questions of censorship, and the role of the reviewer in popular journals. Key roles were played by mass circulation periodicals like Filmfare (a fortnightly owned by the Times of India) and Screen (a film weekly owned by the Indian Express group); and by B. K. Karanjia, a film journalist who at different times in his career edited both journals, and was responsible, as chairman of the FFC in the late 1960s for many of the aesthetic decisions and choices made by that organization regarding the New Indian Cinema.

> Ray's own cinema, which has conventionally been seen as the point at which Indian cinema's initiatives towards realism, and the mastering of the storytelling idiom, were finally realized, has also provided the post-Independence focus for debates about divisions between realism versus modernism, high art versus low, and, after the avant-garde practice of some New Indian Cinema filmmakers, modernism versus avant-garde.

This body of nationalist film writing also addressed the 'pre-Ray' era through an often evolutionist notion of history which saw filmmakers like Barua, Bimal Roy, and those associated with the left-wing Indian Peoples' Theatre Association as the precursors of what reached fruition with Independence. Much of this earlier 'author' cinema, produced by the major studios, has also been seen in terms of bringing literary respectability to cinema, notably at the New Theatres. This also constitutes a major feature of early critical writing in films of this time (see Jha 1990). Alongside this critical writing are two other influences: the film reviewers and journalists who took upon themselves the responsibility of 'educating' viewers into realism (e.g. Kalki, in Tamil, and the critic with the pseudonym Cynic in Malayalam), and the government reports addressing state intervention (the Film Enquiry Committee Report, 1951), censorship (the Khosla Report on Film Censorship, 1969), and the role of the FFC (Committee on Public Undertakings Report on the Film Finance Corporation, 1976).

Much recent theory on this period has addressed the role of melodrama, rather than realism in its orthodox sense, as having played a pivotal role in the cinematic 'writing of the biography of the nation-state' (see Chakravarty 1993). Both Ravi Vasudevan (1993) and Madhava Prasad (1994) examine melodrama as a system of cohering narratives addressing post-Independence urbanization in particular.

Recent film theory: a brief history

A politically well-researched area in India is the 1970s, when the earlier nationalist definition of the state underwent a series of crises: the emergence of the extreme left Naxalite movement, working-class agitations culminating in the Nav Nirman movements in Bihar and Gujarat and the declaration of an internal Emergency by Indira Gandhi in 1975 (see Frankel 1978).

The later New Indian Cinema in this period also yielded a specifically avant-garde practice in the films, teachings, and writings of Kumar Shahani. A student of Ritwik Ghatak, Shahani's cinema and his body of writing constitutes, alongside the political developments of that decade, the first major shift in the 'national modernist' writing of Indian film history (Shahani 1986). Shahani's work parallels a range of practices in Indian visual art, music, and theatre that systematically sought both formal and ideological alternatives to realism, often reworking pre-colonial practices with the awareness of a historical internationalist avant-garde. The key theories of this time are mainly encapsulated in an influential journal, the *Journal of Arts and Ideas*, founded in the late 1980s. The journal demonstrates at least three phases through which Indian cultural and film theory have gone since the Emergency. The immediate and specifically political crises following the Emergency led to numerous inquiries into an aesthetic that might resurrect the still-valuable nationalist imperative, but on lines other than those which had prevailed in 'official' histories and which were incarnated in official cultural institutions. Geeta Kapur's writings covering this period (Kapur 1990, 1991, 1993) are key markers of this shift towards investigating the history of a specifically Indian, and generally non-Western, modernism. Other important writings from this time, criticizing state formations, include M. S. S. Pandian's landmark book (1992) on the movie megastar and Chief Minister M. G. Ramachandran and his despotic rule even as he became an almost unreachable icon in Tamil Nadu.

The second phase constituted the formal entry of

> Shahani's work parallels a range of practices in Indian visual art, music, and theatre that systematically sought both formal and ideological alternatives to realism, often reworking pre-colonial practices with the awareness of a historical internationalist avant-garde.

post-colonial theory, and with this the reinvestigation of the history of Indian nationalism itself as one that specifically opened up the 'biography of the nation-state'. *Arts and Ideas'* special issue *Careers of Modernity*, edited by Tejaswini Niranjana, goes alongside Niranjana, P. Sudhir, and Vivek Dhareshwar's seminal anthology *Interrogating Modernity* (1993), to form the definitive material on this area. This by-now-substantial body of work has been mainly influenced by the new terrain of analysing nationalist historiography opened up by the Subaltern Studies historians, and notably Partha Chatterjee (1986, 1994). Chatterjee's work is premissed on the Gramscian concept of the passive revolution, in which the state first exists and then constructs the pre-conditions of its existence, which include the terms of normative and designative interpellation of its 'citizen subjects'.

The third, and perhaps most recent, dimension opened up specifically in the realm of film studies in India follows the founding of the first postgraduate department of film studies at Jadavpur University, Calcutta. Apart from Prasad's own thesis (1994) and Vasudevan's writings, recent developments in film studies include the now-famous '*Roja* debate', around Mani Rathnam's film, following Niranjana's (1994) essay in the *Economic and Political Weekly*. In late 1995 conferences in film studies in Simla (at the Indian Institute of Advanced Studies), Poona (at the National Film Archive of India), and on cultural studies (organized by the Centre for Studies in Social Sciences) indicate a growing academic acceptance of film studies in orthodox literature, history, and social science departments.

BIBLIOGRAPHY

Archer, Mildred (1977), *Indian Popular Paintings in the India Office Library* (London: HMSO).

Archer, W. G. (1953), *Bazaar Paintings of Calcutta* (London: Victoria and Albert Museum).

—— (1962), *Kalighat Drawings* (Bombay: Marg Publications).

*__Barnouw, Eric__, and **S. Krishnaswamy** (1963/1980), *Indian Film* (New York: Columbia University Press; rev. edn. (incl. New Indian Cinema) Oxford: Oxford University Press).

Chabria, Suresh, and **Paolo Cherchi Usai** (eds.) (1994), *Light of Asia* (National Film Archive of India and Le Giornate del Cinema Muto).

*__Chakravarty, Sumita S.__ (1993), *National Identity in Indian Popular Cinema 1947–1987* (Austin: University of Texas Press).

Chatterjee, Partha (1986), *Nationalist Thought and the Colonial World: A Derivative Discourse* (New Delhi: Oxford University Press).

—— (1994), *The Nation and its Fragments: Colonial and Postcolonial Histories* (New Delhi: Oxford University Press).

Das Gupta, Chidananda (1980), *The Cinema of Satyajit Ray* (New Delhi: Vikas).

—— (1968/1981a), 'The Cultural Basis of the Indian Cinema', in *Talking about Films* (New Delhi: Orient Longman).

—— (ed.) (1981b), *Satyajit Ray* (New Delhi: Directorate of Film Festivals).

Film Enquiry Committee (1951) (Chairman, S. K. Patil), *Report of the Film Enquiry Committee* (New Delhi: Government of India Press).

Frankel, Francine (1978), *India's Political Economy 1947–1977: The Gradual Revolution* (Princeton: Princeton University Press).

Ghatak, Ritwik (1987), *Cinema and I* (Calcutta: Ritwik Memorial Trust and Rupa).

Guha, Ranajit (ed.), *Subaltern Studies*, 1 (1982), 2 (1983), 3 (1984), 4 (1985), 5 (1987), 6 (1989) (New Delhi: Oxford University Press).

Guha-Thakurta, Tapati (1992), *The Making of a New 'Indian' Art: Artists, Aesthetics and Nationalism in Bengal c.1850–1920* (Cambridge: Cambridge University Press).

Gutman, Judith Mara (1982), *Through Indian Eyes: Nineteenth and Early Twentieth Century Still Photography in India* (New York: Oxford University Press and International Centre of Photography).

Jha, Bagishwar (ed.) (1990), *B. N. Sircar* (Calcutta: NFAI and Seagull Books).

Kapur, Geeta (1989), 'Ravi Varma: Representational Dilemmas of a Nineteenth Century Indian Painter', *Journal of Arts and Ideas*, 17–18 (June).

—— (1990), 'Contemporary Cultural Practice: Some Polemical Categories', *Social Scientist*, 18/3 (Mar.).

—— (1991), 'The Place of the Modern in Contemporary Cultural Practice', *Economic and Political Weekly*, 26/49 (7 Dec.).

—— (1993), 'When was Modernism in Indian/Third World Art?', *South Atlantic Quarterly*, 92/3 (Summer).

Mukherjee, Prabhat (1966), *Hiralal Sen: India's First Filmmaker* (Calcutta: Cine Central).

Mukherjee, Sushil Kumar (1980), *The Story of the Calcutta Theatres 1753–1980* (Calcutta: K. P. Bagchi).

Niranjana, Tejaswini (1994), 'Integrating whose Nation? Tourists and Terrorists in *Roja*', *Economic and Political Weekly* 24/3 (15 Jan.).

—— **P. Sudhir,** and **Vivek Dhareshwar** (1993), *Interrogating Modernity: Culture and Colonialism in India* (Calcutta: Seagull Books).

Pandey, Gyanendra (1991), 'In Defence of the Fragment: Writing about Hindu–Muslim Riots in India Today', *Economic and Political Weekly*, 26/11–12 (Annual).

Pandian, M. S. S. (1992), *The Image Trap: M. G. Ramachandran in Film and Politics* (New Delhi: Sage).

Prasad, Madhava (1994, forthcoming), *The State and Culture: Hindi Cinema in the Passive Revolution*, Ph.D. thesis, University of Pittsburgh (New Delhi: Oxford University Press).

Rajadhyaksha, Ashish (1982), *Ritwik Ghatak: A Return to the Epic* (Bombay: Screen Unit).

—— (1987), 'The Phalke Era: Conflict of Traditional Form and Modern Technology', *Journal of Arts and Ideas*, 14–15 (July–Dec.).

—— and **Amrit Gangar** (1987), *Ghatak: Arguments/Stories* (Bombay: Screen Unit).

*—— and **Paul Willemen** (1994–5), *Encyclopaedia of Indian Cinema* (London and New Delhi: British Film Institute and Oxford University Press).

Ray, Satyajit (1948/1976), 'What is Wrong with Indian Films?', in *Our Films, Their Films* (New Delhi: Orient Longman).

Sarkar, Kobita (1975), *Indian Cinema Today* (New Delhi: Sterling).

—— (1982), *You Can't Please All: Film Censorship, the Inside Story* (Bombay: IBH).

Shahani, Kumar (1986), 'Dossier on Kumar Shahani', *Framework*, 30–1.

Vasudevan, Ravi (1993), 'Shifting Codes, Dissolving Identities: The Hindi Social Film of the 1950s as Popular Culture', *Journal of Arts and Ideas*, 23–4.

Popular Hindi cinema

Rosie Thomas from Rosie Thomas, 'Indian Cinema: Pleasures and Popularity', *Screen*, 26/3–4 (May–Aug. 1985), 116–31.

Discussion of Indian popular cinema as 'other'cinema is immediately problematic. There is no disputing that, within the context of First World culture and society, this cinema has always been marginalized, if not ignored completely. It has been defined primarily through its 'otherness' or 'difference' from First World cinema, and consumption of it in the West, whether by Asians or non-Asians, is something of an assertion: one has chosen to view an 'alternative' type of cinema. However, this is a cinema which, in the Indian context, is an overridingly dominant, mainstream form, and is itself opposed by an 'Other': the 'new', 'parallel', 'art' (or often simply 'other') cinema which ranges from the work of Satyajit Ray, Shyam Benegal, and various regional filmmakers, to Mani Kaul's 'avant-garde' or Anand Patwardhan's 'agitational' political practice. In these terms Indian popular cinema is neither alternative nor a minority form. Moreover, in a global context, by virtue of its sheer volume of output, the Indian entertainment cinema still dominates world film production, and its films are distributed throughout large areas of the Third World, where they are frequently consumed more avidly than both Hollywood and indigenous 'alternative' or political cinemas. Such preference suggests that these films are seen to be offering something

positively different from Hollywood, and, in fact, largely because it has always had its own vast distribution markets, Indian cinema has, throughout its long history, evolved as a form which has resisted the cultural imperialism of Hollywood. This is not, of course, to say that it has been 'uninfluenced' by Hollywood: the form has undergone continual change and there has been both inspiration and assimilation from Hollywood and elsewhere, but thematically and structurally, Indian cinema has remained remarkably distinctive.

Bombay filmmakers repeatedly stress that they are aiming to make films which differ in both format and content from Western films, that there is a definite skill to making films for the Indian audience, that this audience has specific needs and expectations, and that to compare Hindi films to those of the West, or of the Indian 'art' cinema is irrelevant.

Compared with the conventions of much Western cinema, Hindi films appear to have patently preposterous narratives, overblown dialogue (frequently evaluated by filmmakers on whether or not it is 'clapworthy'), exaggeratedly stylized acting, and to show disregard for psychological

Making a popular Hindi film—Dev Anand on location in *Lootmaar* (1980)

Popular Hindi cinema continued

characterization, history, geography, and even, sometimes, camera placement rules. (Camera placement rules can be disregarded, particularly in action (fight) scenes, which seem to be allowed something of the non-continuity conventions of song sequences.)

Tolerance of overt fantasy has always been high in Hindi cinema, with little need to anchor the material in what Western conventions might recognize as a discourse of 'realism', and slippage between registers does not have to be marked or rationalized. The most obvious example is the song sequences, which are much less commonly 'justified' within the story (for example, introduced as stage performances by the fictional characters) than in Hollywood musicals. Hindi film songs are usually tightly integrated, through words and mood, within the *flow* of the film—and misguided attempts to doctor Hindi films for Western audiences by cutting out the songs are always fatal. However, the song sequences (often also dream sequences) do permit excesses of fantasy which are more problematic elsewhere in the film, for they specifically allow that continuities of time and place be disregarded, that heroines may change saris between shots and the scenery skip continents between verses, whenever the interests or spectacle or mood require it.

However, this is not to say that 'anything goes': there is a firm sense of 'acceptable realism and logic', beyond which material is rejected as 'unbelievable'. In fact, the criteria of verisimilitude in Hindi cinema appear to refer primarily to a film's skill in manipulating the rules of the film's moral universe, and one is more likely to hear accusations of

'unbelievability' if the codes of, for example, ideal kinship behaviour are ineptly transgressed (i.e. a son kills his mother; or a father knowingly and callously causes his son to suffer), than if the hero is a superman who single-handedly knocks out a dozen burly henchmen and then bursts into song.

It would appear that the spectator-subject of Hindi cinema is positioned rather differently from that of much Western cinema. In fact, even on the most overt level, Indian cinema audience behaviour is distinctive: involvement in the films is intense, and audiences clap, sing, recite familiar dialogue with the actors, throw coins at the screen (in appreciation of spectacle), 'tut-tut' at emotionally moving scenes, cry openly and laugh and jeer knowingly. Moreover, it is expected that audiences will see a film they like several times, and so-called 'repeat value' is deliberately built into a production by the filmmakers, who believe that the keys to this are primarily the stars, music, spectacle, emotion, and dialogue—this last having a greater significance than in Western cinema.

What seems to emerge in Hindi cinema is an emphasis on emotion and spectacle rather than tight narrative, on *how* things will happen rather than *what* will happen next, on a succession of modes rather than linear denouement, on familiarity and repeated viewings rather than 'originality' and novelty, on a moral disordering to be (temporarily) resolved rather than an enigma to be solved. The spectator is addressed and moved through the films primarily via affect, although this is structured and contained by narratives whose power and insistence derives from their very familiarity, coupled with the fact that they are deeply rooted (in the psyche and in traditional mythology).

20

Chinese cinema

Bérénice Reynaud

The rise of critical interest in Chinese cinema

Geopolitical events of the last thirty years have drastically affected Western scholarship on Chinese cinema—including even the transcription of proper names into the Latin alphabet. In the early 1980s the old Wade–Giles system was eventually replaced by the internationally standardized Pinyin developed in the People's Republic of China (PRC). Mao Tse-tung (Mao Tsé-toung in French) became Mao Zedong, and the filmmaker Tsai Chu-sheng (Tsai Tchou-cheng in French) is now spelled Cai Chusheng. Some major texts, such as Jay Leyda's *Dianying* (1972) and Régis Bergeron's first volume (1977), pre-date the adoption of Pinyin, which makes cross-referencing difficult. And, since Western habits contrast with the Chinese custom of placing the family name *before* the given name, some historians prefer to print the family name in capital letters. However, perhaps the major problem confronting scholars working on Chinese cinema is access to films. Deng Xiaoping's open-door policy of the late 1970s has facilitated cultural exchanges, but Chinese cinema largely remains an uncharted sea, even if a few islands have now come into view.

The highly successful screening of Chen Kaige's *Huang tudi* ('The Yellow Earth', 1984) at the 1985 Hong Kong Film Festival (McDougall 1991: 55–114) prompted a new interest in Chinese cinema. While ignored and criticized in the PRC, the film launched the concept of the 'Fifth Generation' at an international level. Specifically, the 'Fifth Generation' denotes filmmakers such as Zhang Yimou, Tian Zhuangzhuang, and Huang Jianxin, who, like Chen Kaige, had entered the Beijing Film Academy in 1978, the year it reopened after the Cultural Revolution. The first Fifth Generation film therefore is actually not *The Yellow Earth*, but Zhang Junzhao's *Yige he bage* ('One and Eight', 1984).

The term 'Fifth Generation' echoes the various 'new wave' movements taking place in the early 1980s in Hong Kong and Taiwan (Browne *et al.* 1994). It is often assumed that the term 'generation' is used to designate the distinct role that each decade's filmmakers have played in the political and aesthetic construction of a national cinema in China. Tony Rayns, however, states that Fifth Generation directors were simply 'the fifth class to graduate from the school's Directing Department' (Rayns, 1991: 104) while, for Chris Berry, the term highlights the stylistic breakthrough between Fifth Generation films and those which preceded them (Berry 1991: 116).

Since 1985 scholarship in the West has focused on a few films and a few directors: in particular, the detailed essays of Esther C. M. Yau (1991) on Chen Kaige's *Yellow Earth* and Wang Yuejin (1991) on Zhang Yimou's *Hong gaoliang* ('Red Sorghum', 1987) as well as Rey Chow (1995) on Chen Kaige's *Yellow Earth* and *Haizi*

Chen Kaige's *King of the Children* (1984) prompted a new interest in Chinese cinema

Wang ('King of the Children', 1987), which all employ the various strategies of textual analysis (psychoanalysis, structuralism, feminist and cultural theory). The work of other filmmakers, both within and without the Fifth Generation, has been much less explored. There are, however, some exceptions: most notably Berry's research on the viewing subject of Chinese cinema, as it is constructed in films from the 1960s and 1980s (Berry 1991a; 1994), Ma Ning's (1994) and Nick Browne's (1994: 40–56) work on Xie Jin's melodramas, and Paul G. Pickowicz's (1994) study of Huang Jianxin's 'post-socialist' films.

Recent scholarship on Fifth Generation films and melodramas of the 1980s has often focused on the construction of sexual difference and the representation of women. Yet, the 'placement' of femininity and masculinity within the Chinese tradition (especially Confucianism) does not coincide with the Western construction of gender, which problematizes the application of cross-cultural analyses. While Esther C. M. Yau makes a brilliant case for the use of Western analysis of a non-Western text (Yau 1991), prompting a debate taken up in particular by Rey Chow (1995), issues of gender are often combined with explorations of other forms of difference in Chinese culture: such as those of insider–outsider and moral–immoral (Ma Ning 1994), yin–yang and class differences (Wang 1991), or ethnic differences (Yau 1994).

The great emphasis of recent scholarship and criticism on Chen and Zhang, often in the form of comparisons between the style of the two directors (Chow 1995: 160–3), has, however, marginalized the contributions of Fifth Generation women filmmakers (Hu Mei, Peng Xiaolian, Li Shaohong, Ning Ying). Two notable exceptions are Berry's text 'Chinese "Women's Cinema"' (1988) and E. Ann Kaplan's feminist analysis of Hu Mei's *Nü'er lou* ('Army Nurse', 1986) (Kaplan 1991*b*).

While Browne's and Berry's essays contextualize Fifth Generation work within the history of Chinese cinema, most texts on recent films consist purely of synchronic analyses. Pickowicz (1993: 295) sees the 'new research on Chinese cinema' as too 'narrowly focused' as a result of the 'absence of a large scholarly literature that covers all the decades of the twentieth century', while Clark (1987: 1) was prompted to write his book by the lack of a 'full-length scholarly study of film in China after 1949'. Apart from Clark's book, the three major contributions to the history of Chinese cinema are those of Leyda (1972), Bergeron (1977, 1983–4), and a French collection that covers Chinese cinema from 1922 to 1984 from a variety of point of views (historical, aesthetic, cultural, theoretical) and includes very comprehensive data on 141 films and 54 filmmakers (Quiquemelle and Passek 1985). Unfortunately these books were completed too early to include the Fifth Generation (although Clark briefly mentions *The Yellow Earth*). The texts dealing with post-1985 Chinese cinema (Berry 1991; Browne 1994; Chow 1995) are collections of essays written at different times without claim to exhaustiveness or a unified point of view.

How Chinese is it?

The interest raised in the West by the Fifth Generation has reopened an old question: is Chinese cinema merely derivative of Western forms, or has it made an original use of the medium? The Chinese detractors of *The Yellow Earth* found its success abroad 'suspect' (McDougall 1991: 102): if foreigners liked the film, it was argued, it was because it presented a 'bad' image of China. Since 1949 foreignness and cosmopolitanism have been associated with an implicit betrayal of Maoist ideology. For Rey Chow (1995: 37–8), the question of the image projected to Western audiences implies the fetishization and commodification of China in a post-colonial circulation of filmic signifiers. Yet, while comparing this presentation of China to the West accomplished by Fifth Generation filmmakers like Chen and Zhang to the state of mind of colonized subjects trying to 'engage with the colonizer's own terms' (38), Chow also finds them guilty of a 'form of

primitive passion that is sinocentrism' (51) and generating the nativist belief that foreign audiences 'cannot understand China . . . the ultimate essence beyond representation' (49–50). The dual nature of Chinese cinema underlines this contradiction: produced by and for Chinese, it also belongs to an international film history through which China and the West have constructed exotic spectacles for each other.

> **The dual nature of Chinese cinema underlines this contradiction: produced by and for Chinese, it also belongs to an international film history through which China and the West have constructed exotic spectacles for each other.**

The 1995 centenary prompted renewed inquiries about the introduction of cinema into China, especially among Hong Kong scholars (Law and Teo 1995); a matter which had previously been investigated by Leyda's (1972) generous and enthusiastic curiosity. However, while the genesis of the filmic images in China's early cinema raises a number of theoretical and epistemological issues, it has mostly been presented by historians as a collection of facts. China discovered cinema when in a state of semi-colonial domination, having had a series of unequal treaties imposed upon it by the Western powers following the two Opium Wars (1840–2 and 1856–60). The first screening of 'electric shadows' took place in Shanghai in 1896, but historians disagree about the system of projection: a Lumière camera (Leyda 1972: 1; Clark 1987: 6, 1988: 176) or Edison's Vitascope (Law and Teo 1995: 33–6). After 1898 Edison cameramen, the American Mutoscope and Biograph company, Pathé Frères, and the French banker Albert Kahn all made documentaries about China. The first images shot by Chinese (1905–8) were scenes from famous Peking operas (Leyda 1972: 10). In 1913 the first two Chinese narrative features were directed in Hong Kong by Li Minwei (*Zhuang Zi Shi Qi*, 'Zhuang Zi Tests His Wife'), who had formed the Sino-American Company in partnership with an American businessman, Benjamin Brodsky (Law and Teo 1995: 28), and in Shanghai by Zhang Schichuan (*Nan fu nan qi*, 'An Unfortunate Couple'), an employee of the American-owned Asian Motion Pictures Company. In 1922 both men set up their own studios, and these ranked among the most influential film companies in Hong Kong and Shanghai (He 1985). A combination of Western and local entrepreneurship, Chinese cinema was therefore produced as a hybrid form: in China 'the association of film art with foreignness is overwhelming' (Clark 1988: 176).

The majority of films shown on Chinese screens were imported (mostly from Hollywood), yet in the 1920s and 1930s film companies mushroomed in Shanghai, and a star system developed quickly (He 1985). Ruan Lingyu, 'the Chinese Garbo', who appeared in such classics as Sun Yu's *Xiao wanyi* ('Small Toys', 1933) and Cai Chusheng's *Xin nüxing* ('New Women', 1935) before committing suicide at 25, has retained an enduring fascination among film lovers, historians, and intellectuals (Shu 1985). Analysing *Small Toys*, Pickowicz (1993: 305–8) argues that China's struggle with modernity at the beginning of the twentieth century was largely experienced as a crisis in family values. The cinematic representation of women was already a central question for left-wing filmmakers in the 1930s. As Ma Ning notes, 'because the woman's position is lowest in traditional Chinese society, she has become a metonymic figure for other disadvantaged social groups' (Ma 1994: 22). As a result, before and after 1949, woman was constantly used to signify the necessity of social change, and this may help to explain the recurrence of melodrama in Chinese cinema. Bergeron (1977), who admires the genre in post-revolutionary fictions, dismisses the films of the Republican era for 'their lack of class consciousness'. Other historians and analysts (Leyda, Rayns, Tadao Sato, Li Cheuk-to) emphasize the formal experimentation and political subtlety of pre-revolutionary cinema, and for most historians the 1930s and the post-war years represent two 'golden ages' of pre-revolutionary Chinese cinema (Lau 1985).

Whether they criticize it (Bergeron 1977) or merely report it, historians agree on the paramount influence of Hollywood on Chinese cinema of the 1920s and 1930s. Classic films, such as Shen Xiling's *Shizi jietou* ('Crossroads', 1937) achieved an original combination of forms borrowed from Hollywood and a commentary on China's social reality. Since the Shanghai studios continued to produce silent films until 1935–6, their point of reference, however, was, as Rayns aptly observes, 'the visual expressiveness' and formal experimentation of American *silent* cinema (Rayns 1995: 105). With the advent of the talkies, Hollywood's influence continued to be felt, but cinema also devel-

oped close ties with literature and theatre, a feature that has remained a major characteristic of Chinese cinema until the present day and which has given an emphasis to the screenplay over the mise-en-scène (Clark 1987: 20, 94–5).

In its 'most escapist period' of the 1910s and 1920s (Leyda 1972: 64), cinema, often drawing its inspiration from the popular 'Mandarin Duck and Butterfly' literature, was divorced from the intellectuals. Politicized by the 1931 Japanese invasion, leftist artists and intellectuals subsequently infiltrated the major studios, and some formed underground communist cells, such as the one headed by the screenwriter Xia Yan. A key figure in Chinese cinema, Xia was the first to adapt to the screen a May Fourth literary work, Mao Dun's *Chun can* ('Spring Silkworms', 1933). Started on 4 May 1919 as a protest and mass demonstration regrouping students and intellectuals against the Chinese government's compromising policies towards the Western powers and Japan, the May Fourth movement criticized the stifling effects of Chinese tradition and Confucianism and promoted a democratic, modernized 'new China', that would be patriotic and self-sufficient yet open to foreign ideas. Consequently, May Fourth intellectuals advocated various forms of literary experimentation. While its importance in Chinese intellectual life is a known fact in Chinese studies, Pickowicz (1993) questions the nature of its influence on cinema, as he examines the leftist melodramas of the 1930s and the 1980s. Arguing that May Fourth fiction lost its relevance as protest literature when adapted to the screen after 1949, he does not discuss the films it directly inspired: so the attacks they underwent remain the domain of the historian.

Politics and censorship

In 1949 nine Chinese out of ten had never seen a film; in 1952, 600 million admissions were recorded, and this number continued to grow (2.05 billion admissions in 1957, 25.5 billion in 1982). Party leaders set out to shape cinema, with a Leninist enthusiasm, into a national mass culture for the benefit of the new heroes of the Revolution: soldiers, workers, and peasants. As Mao Zedong implied in his 1942 talks at the Yan'an Conference on Literature and Art (Mao 1980), this meant a break with the May Fourth tradition represented by the urban-educated and Westernized Shanghai filmmakers. The new cultural cadres had been formed after 1936 in Yan'an, where the Communist People's Liberation Army was based. Clark (1987) reads the history of post-1949 cinema as a constant struggle between the Yan'an and Shanghai traditions, with the Party favouring the former. This also reflects a defiance against the foreign origin of the medium, and a drive towards the sinification of cinema.

The Communist Party set out to establish 'a national system for the production, censorship, distribution and projection of films' (Clark 1987: 34) and limit the number of American movies available to Chinese spectators (while simultaneously exposing them to Soviet cinema). After the completion of a few landmark films such as Wang Bin and Shui Ha's *Baimao nü* ('The White-Haired Girl', 1950), political pressure caused production to drop. Sun Yu's *Wu Xun zhuan* ('The Life of Wu Xun', 1950) has been often written about as an example of the early interference of politics into filmmaking in the PRC (Leyda 1972: 197–8; Bergeron 1983–4: i. 72–84; Clark 1987: 38, 45–54). While the film depicted the protagonist as a generous educator, Maoist attacks denounced him as an opportunist, reformist, and feudal exploiter. The campaign against the film helped speed the nationalization of the Shanghai studios, completed in 1953.

After 1956 the Soviet-inspired commitment to socialist realism was replaced by a demand for the combination of 'revolutionary realism and revolutionary romanticism'. This encouraged filmmakers to seek inspiration in the Chinese past—in particular May Fourth fiction and a modified operatic tradition. In the following decades Chinese cinema developed unevenly. It was expanding, experimenting, and gaining audiences when creativity was encouraged by the Party—such as the 1956–7 'Hundred Flowers' period (during which the slogan 'let a hundred flowers blossom and a hundred schools of thought contend' encouraged people, but especially artists and intellectuals to make suggestions to the Communist Party and even criticize its line), the political relaxation of the early 1960s, and the 'new period' initiated by Deng Xiaoping in 1979; conversely, there were times of heightened censorship during which films were banned, filmmakers persecuted, and production drastically curtailed, such as the 1957 'Anti-Rightist' campaign (during which the people who had taken the freedom of the 'Hundred Flowers' too literally were severely punished) and the Cultural Revolution (1966–78). Following the liberalization of the late 1970s, victims of both campaigns appeared in melodramas of the 1980s (Ma

1994: 15–39, 40–56; Pickowicz 1993: 295–326) and later in a (banned) Fifth Generation film, Tian Zhuangzhuang's *Lan Fengzheng* ('The Blue Kite', 1993).

One of the first targets of the Cultural Revolution was the screenwriter Xia Yan (head of the Film Bureau since 1951). In addition to *Spring Silkworms*, he had, since 1949, written the screen adaptation of two May Fourth stories, Lu Xun's *Zhufu* ('The New Year's Sacrifice', 1956) and Mao Dun's *Linjia puzi* ('The Lin Family Shop', 1959), and endorsed the adaptation of another one, Rou Shi's *Zaochun eryue* ('Early Spring in February', 1963); these films were denounced by the Red Guards, and Xia Yan spent ten years in jail. Despite the key roles many had played in building their national cinema, both before and after 1949 at least thirty filmmakers (including the President of the Filmmakers' Association, Cai Chusheng) died as a result of this persecution. Many more lost their jobs, were tortured, imprisoned, or exiled. Film production dropped dramatically (and later completely halted in 1967–9) and was not restored to its 1965 level until 1978 (Khang 1985: 143; Clark 1987: 187–8).

Because the names of Xia Yan and Cai Chusheng are still unfamiliar in the West, it remains difficult to evaluate the tragedy involved in their imprisonment or death. Leyda completed his book at the onset of the Cultural Revolution, too soon to fully understand and describe it; Bergeron's communist sympathies distract him from an accurate assessment of the damages of Maoist censorship; Clark provides a detailed, well-documented account of the Cultural Revolution years, but his book deals only with the post-1949 era, and its object is therefore *not* to write Chinese film history as a continuum since 1896.

Historians, theoreticians, and critics have therefore inherited a conceptualization of cinema history as a series of political ruptures whose origin is extra-cinematographic. Accordingly, the fetishization of the Fifth Generation, which cultural critics such as Chow denounce, may be seen to result from such a fragmented approach to Chinese film history. Moreover, apart from Rayns's journalistic pieces in *Sight and Sound*, there is no serious essay on the emergence of the 'Sixth Generation' (Zhang Yuan, Wang Xioashuai, He Yi). Zhang Yuan's *Mama* ('Mama', 1990), 'the first Chinese independent film since 1949' according to Rayns, was produced illegally outside the state-run studios. Sixth Generation films are often banned, and depend on international circuits for exposure and/or funding, which raises the old question of how Chinese they are. Articulating a post-Tiananmen Square dilemma, the Sixth Generation is part of a nascent counter-cultural milieu centred in Beijing, which also includes underground rock musicians (such as Cui Jian), visual artists and, significantly, independent videomakers (Wu Wenguang, the 'Structure, Wave, Youth, Cinema Experimental Group') (Reynaud 1996: 253–8).

The Western gaze

If the history of Chinese cinema before and after the Fifth Generation remains a war waged by anonymous soldiers, the name of one filmmaker emerges: Xie Jin. His importance is stressed by Browne (1994), Berry and Clark (1991: 198), Pickowicz (1993: 313), and Ma Ning (1994: 15). He directed melodramas and revolutionary operas before combining both genres in *Wutai jiemei* ('Stage Sisters', 1965), considered his masterpiece but criticized during the Cultural Revolution. He directed a number of successful 'tear-jerkers' in the 1980s, the most famous being *Furongzhen* ('Hibiscus Town', 1987). The first half of his career is a successful example of combining revolutionary realism with revolutionary romanticism, while his work during the 1980s has been used to test and expand Western theories about melodrama. His work reflects the ruptures used to write the history of Chineses cinema—the Communist takeover, the Cultural Revolution, the aesthetic break of the Fifth Generation (whose members define themselves *against* him)—as well as articulating the tensions between Chinese tradition and Western influence and realism and melodrama.

In his case, melodrama and realism are in a dialectical relationship with one another and pose the question of cross-cultural interpretation. For Catherine Yi-Yu Cho Woo, Bazin-inspired filmic realism 'seems incompatible with traditional Chinese art' (Woo 1991: 21), and Browne cautions that applying 'the category of melodrama' to Chinese cinema 'entails a shift of cultural perspective' (1994: 40). Melodrama's schematic, theatrical opposition between good and evil, it is argued, are 'incommensurable' with the aesthetic and ethical categories at work in Chinese society—either in classical painting and poetry, Confucianism, or the post-1949 ideological order. The question Chinese film studies will have to face in the next few years, therefore, is how to contain Western theoretical imperialism while simultaneously avoiding the fetishization of the specificity of Chinese culture—the turning

of it into an exotic Other knowable only through the critical analyses of native insiders. The concept of realism, when combined with that of authenticity, has often been used to construct or perpetuate an exotic image of China and/or Chinese cinema: it is well known, for example, that the most popular films in the West are those that present Chinese rural landscapes rather than urban scenes. On the other hand, if Western scholars are to eschew 'nativist' criticism, the way forward is to base their theoretical arguments on an ever-increasing knowledge of Chinese culture, film, and political history.

BIBLIOGRAPHY

Bergeron, Régis (1977), *Le Cinéma chinois*, i: *1905–1949* (Lausanne: Alfred Eibel).

—— (1983–4), *Le Cinéma chinois 1949–1983*, 3 vols. (Paris: L'Harmattan).

Berry, Chris (1982), 'Stereotypes and Ambiguities: An Examination of the Feature Films of the Chinese Cultural Revolution', *Journal of Asian Culture*, 6: 37–72.

—— (1988), 'Chinese "Women's Cinema"', *Camera Obscura*, 18: 4–41.

—— (1991a), 'Sexual Difference and the Viewing Subject in *Li Shuanghuang* and *The In-Laws*', in Berry (1991c).

—— (1991b), 'Market Forces: China's 'Fifth Generation' Faces the Bottom Line', in Berry (1991c).

*—— (ed.) (1991c), *Perspectives on Chinese Cinema* (London: British Film Institute).

—— (1994), 'Neither One Thing nor Another: Toward a Study of the Viewing Subject in Chinese Cinema in the 1980s', in Browne et al. (1994).

—— and **Paul Clark** (1991), 'Appendix 1: Major Directors', in Berry (1991c).

Browne, Nick (1994), 'Society and Subjectivity: On the Political Economy of Chinese Melodrama', in Browne et al. (1994).

*—— **Paul G. Pickowicz, Vivian Sobchack,** and **Esther Yau** (eds.) (1994), *New Chinese Cinemas: Forms, Identities, Politics* (Cambridge: Cambridge University Press).

Chow, Rey (1995), *Primitive Passions: Visuality, Sexuality, Ethnography, and Contemporary Chinese Cinema* (New York: Columbia University Press).

*Clark, Paul** (1987), *Chinese Cinema: Culture and Politics since 1949* (Cambridge: Cambridge University Press).

—— (1988), 'The Sinification of Cinema: The Foreignness of Film in China', in Wimal Dissanayake (ed.), *Cinema and Cultural Identity: Reflections on Films from Japan, India, and China* (Lanham, Md.: University Press of America).

Dissanayake, Wimal (ed.) (1988), *Cinema and Cultural*

Identity: Reflections of Films from Japan, India, and China (Lanham, Md.: University Press of America).

He Xiujun (1985), 'Histoire de la compagnie shanghaienne *Mingxing* et son fondateur Zhang Shickuan', in Quiquemelle and Passek 1985.

Kaplan, E. Ann (1991a), 'Melodrama/Subjectivity/Ideology: The Relevance of Western Melodrama Theories to Recent Chinese Cinema', *East–West Film Journal*, 5/1 (Jan.), 6–27.

—— (1991b), 'Problematising Cross-Cultural Analysis: The Care of Women in the Recent Chinese Cinema', in Berry (1991c).

Khang Budong (1985), 'Convalescence', in Quiquemelle and Passek (1985).

Kwok and **Marie-Claire Quiquemelle** (1986), 'Chinese Cinema and Realism', in John D. H. Downing (ed.), *Film and Politics in the Third World* (Brooklyn: Automedia).

Lau Shing Hon (1985), 'Deux Ages d'or du cinéma chinois: Les années trente et l'après-guerre', in Quiquemelle and Passek (1985).

Law, Kar, and **Stephen Teo** (eds.) (1995), *Early Images of Hong Kong and China: the Nineteenth Hong Kong International Film Festival* (Hong Kong: Urban Council).

Leyda, Jay (1972), *Dianying: An Account of Films and the Film Audience in China* (Cambridge: MIT Press).

McDougall, Bonnie S. (1991), *The Yellow Earth: A Film by Chen Kaige*, with complete trans. of the filmscript (Hong Kong: Chinese University Press).

Ma Ning (1994), 'Spatiality and Subjectivity in Xie Jin's Film Melodrama of the New Period', in Browne *et al.* (1994).

Mao Zedong (1980), *Mao Zedong's 'Talks at the Yan'an Conference on Literature and Art:' A Translation of the 1943 Text with Commentary*, ed. and trans. Bonnie S. McDougall (Ann Arbor: Center for Chinese Studies, University of Michigan).

Pickowicz, Paul G. (1993), 'Melodramatic Representation and the "May Fourth" Tradition of Chinese Cinema', in Ellen Widem and David Der-Wei Wang (eds.), *From May Fourth to June Fourth: Fiction and Film in Twentieth-Century China* (Cambridge: Harvard University Press).

—— (1994), 'Huang Jianxin and the Notion of Post-Socialism', in Browne *et al.* (1994).

Quiquemelle, Marie-Claire, and **Jean-Loup Passek** (eds.) (1985), *Le cinéma chinois* (Paris: Centre national d'art et de culture Georges Pompidou).

Rayns, Tony (ed.) (1985), *More Electric Shadows: Chinese Cinema 1922–1984* (London: British Film Institute).

—— (1991), 'Breakthrough and Setbacks: The Origins of the New Chinese Cinema', in Berry (1991c).

—— (1995), 'Missing Links: Chinese Cinema in Shanghai and Hong Kong from the 1930s to the 1940s', in Law and Teo (1995).

—— and **Scott Meek** (eds.) (1980), *Electric Shadows: Forty-Five Years of Chinese Cinema* (London: British Film Institute).

Reynaud, Bérénice (1994), 'Gong Li and the Glamour of the Chinese Stars', in Pam Cook and Philip Dodd (eds.), *Women and Film: A Sight and Sound Reader* (London: Scarlet Press).

—— (1996), 'New Visions/New Chinas—Video: Art, Documentation and the Chinese Modernity in Question', in Michael Renov and Erika Suderburg (eds.), *Resolutions: Essays on Contemporary Video Practices* (Minneapolis: Minnesota University Press).

Semsel, George S. (ed.) (1987), *Chinese Film: The State of Art in the People's Republic* (New York: Praeger).

—— **Hong Xia,** and **Jianping Hou** (eds.) (1990), *Chinese Film Theory: A Guide to the New Era* (New York: Praeger).

—— **Xihe Chen,** and **Hong Xia** (eds.) (1993), *Film in Contemporary China: Cultural Debates 1979–1989* (Westport, Conn.: Praeger).

Shu Kei (1985), 'La Légende de Ruan Lingyu', in Quiquemelle and Passek (1985).

Yau, Esther C. M. (1989), 'Cultural and Economic Dislocation: Filmic Phantasies of Chinese Women in the 1980s', *Wide Angle*, 11/2: 6–21.

—— (1989/1994), 'Is China the End of Hermeneutics? or, Political and Cultural Usage of Non-Han Women in Mainland Chinese Films', *Discourse*, 11/2: 115–38; repr. in Diane Carson, Linda Dittmar, and Janice R. Welsch (eds.), *Multiple Voices in Feminist Film Criticism* (Minneapolis: University of Minnesota Press).

—— (1991), '*Yellow Earth*: Western Analysis and a Non-Western Text', in Berry (1991c).

Wang Yuejin (1989), 'The Cinematic Other and the Cultural Self? De-Centering the Cultural Identity on Cinema', *Wide Angle*, 11/2: 32–9.

—— (1991), '*Red Sorghum*: Mixing Memory and Desire', in Berry (1991c).

Woo, Catherine Yi-Yu Cho (1991), 'The Chinese Montage: From Poetry and Painting to the Silver Screen', in Berry (1991c).

21

Hong Kong cinema

(a) Discovery and pre-discovery   STEPHEN TEO

The discovery of Hong Kong cinema in the West essentially began in the 1970s with the importation of kung fu action pot-boilers. Traditionally, the Hong Kong film industry drew its audiences from Taiwan and key Southeast Asian countries like Malaysia and Singapore. But the films of Bruce Lee and director King Hu made non-Chinese audiences in non-traditional markets like Europe and America sit up and take notice for the first time.

This somewhat facile 'discovery' of Hong Kong cinema was supplemented by the rise of the Hong Kong New Wave in 1979. New Wave films such as Ann Hui's *The Secret* (1979) and *The Boat People* (1983), Tsui Hark's *The Butterfly Murders* (1979) and *Dangerous Encounter—1st Kind* (1980), and Allen Fong's *Father and Son* (1981) made Western audiences realize that Hong Kong cinema was more than kung fu and martial arts.

However, it is really the action genres that gained a cult following for Hong Kong cinema, spawning a certain misconception that the strength of the cinema is founded on only one genre, and that its history started in the early 1970s, when Bruce Lee became popular. We can therefore divide the whole history of Hong Kong cinema into two distinct phases: a 'Discovery History' and a 'Pre-Discovery History'.

> **It is really the action genres that gained a cult following for Hong Kong cinema, spawning a certain misconception that the strength of the cinema is founded on only one genre, and that its history started in the early 1970s, when Bruce Lee became popular.**

The 'Discovery History' is relatively well known since it covers the contemporary development of Hong Kong cinema and may, in fact, be subdivided into a 'Post-Discovery' phase that takes into account the subsequent progress of the Hong Kong New Wave into a 'second wave' in the 1990s. This post-discovery phase covers mature and sophisticated works (such as Stanley Kwan's *Rouge*, 1989 and *Actress*, 1993, Wong Kar-wai's *Days of Being Wild*, 1991, *Chungking Express*, 1994, and *Ashes of Time*, 1994) that are more recognizably art-house-type movies and acknowledged as such by critics in the West.

While it is too much of a generalization to refer to the whole period of the development of Hong Kong cinema from its beginnings up to 1970 as a 'Pre-Discovery History', the fact remains that a large chunk of the history of Hong Kong cinema before the kung fu wave hit Western shores is largely undiscovered and unappreciated. However, Hong Kong critics and scholars have, for the last twenty years, emphasized its importance in a continuing series of thematic studies (published in book-length catalogues) organized by the Hong Kong International Film Festival (see Leung, Chapter 21).

The early history

The first production of a fictional film occurred in 1909. *Stealing the Roast Duck* was produced by the Asia Film Company, founded by an American businessman, Benjamin Brodsky, who went on to produce films in Shanghai. The key figure to emerge during this pioneering period was Li Minwei, who founded the Sino-American Film Company (Huamei) with Brodsky, and produced *Zhuang Zi Tests his Wife* (1913), in which Li himself appeared in drag, playing the wife. Li was also a major figure in the founding of two other important companies, China Sun (Minxin) in 1922 and United Photoplay Services (Lianhua) in 1930, that would dominate the fledgling film industries of Hong Kong and Shanghai, the centres of filmmaking in the Chinese-speaking world. In the 1930s, with the arrival of sound, Hong Kong's film industry found a niche as the production centre of Cantonese-dialect movies. Shanghai's Tianyi Company, which produced the first Cantonese-dialect movie *Platinum Dragon* in 1933, relocated to Hong Kong in 1934 to take advantage of the resources there and its distribution markets. It was followed by the establishment of the Grandview Company (Daguan) in 1935, which began to make patriotic films that exploited the Chinese antipathy towards the Japanese, who had embarked on a militarist policy and were slowly eating up Chinese territory.

When full-scale war got under way in 1937, Hong Kong was turned into a production base for 'national defence films'—war films lauding the war effort and exhorting the Chinese populace to rise up against the Japanese. These films, such as Situ Huimin's *March of the Guerrillas* (1938) and Cai Chusheng's *Devils' Paradise* (1939), were made by Shanghai filmmakers who had fled the occupation and voluntarily exiled themselves in the colony, thus initiating the first migratory movement of Shanghai filmmakers into Hong Kong. When Hong Kong itself was occupied by the Japanese in December 1941, the film industry came to a complete stop.

Post-war renaissance

The Hong Kong cinema as we know it today owes its existence to post-war developments. The years between 1946 and 1949 were crucial in laying the foundations for Hong Kong to replace Shanghai as the 'Hollywood of the East'. Once again, Hong Kong was the receiving centre of filmmaking talent fleeing Shanghai. The exodus occurred in two waves. First, immediately after the war, actors and directors who had elected to stay on in Shanghai under Japanese occupation were accused of collaborating with the enemy. These filmmakers, including veteran directors Zhu Shilin, Yue Feng, Bu Wancang, Ma-Xu Weibang, Li Pingqian, and producer Zhang Shankun, took off for Hong Kong.

The Great China Film Company was established in 1946 by mainland interests, and many exiled filmmakers found employment with the company. Great China was virtually the only company making movies in the colony during the immediate post-war years. Its output was mainly Mandarin movies scheduled for release in Shanghai and other major cities in the mainland. China was the main market, but when that market effectively vanished with the communist victory in 1949, the Hong Kong film industry began to rely on overseas Chinese communities in South-east Asia, Taiwan, and other countries around the world for its bread and butter.

The second influx of Shanghai talent into Hong Kong took place in 1947 and 1948 as the civil war raged on the mainland. This time many of the directors were communists or sympathizers fleeing white terror campaigns launched by the Kuomintang government. When the Great China company closed down in 1948, the gap was filled by Yonghua, founded by Li Zuyong, another mainland entrepreneur, and the charismatic producer Zhang Shankun. Yonghua rapidly became the most prestigious company in Hong Kong producing Mandarin movies, beginning with the spectacular epics *Soul of China*, directed by Bu Wancang, and *Sorrows of the Forbidden City*, directed by Zhu Shilin (both released in 1948).

While social conscience dramas such as Li's *A Strange Woman* and *The Awful Truth* (both 1950) and Zhu Shilin's *The Flower Girl* (an adaptation of Maupassant's *Boule de suif*) and *Spoiling the Wedding Day* (both 1951) proved popular in the early 1950s, popular genres such as the comedies and musicals produced by the Motion Picture and General Investment Company (MP and GI) were more successful in the second half of the decade. In 1957 the Shaws, a remarkable family of film entrepreneurs and producers from Shanghai, established a new studio named Shaw Brothers. Its logo, a close copy of the Warner Bros. logo, became one of the dominant symbols of Hong Kong cinema in the next decade.

Like Yonghua before it, the studio built its success on costume pictures such as Li Hanxiang's *The Enchanting Shadow* (1960), *The Love Eterne* (1963), and *The Empress Wu* (1963). In the late 1960s a spate of martial arts sword-fighting movies, mostly directed by Zhang Che (*The One-Armed Swordsman*, 1967, *The Assassin*, 1967, *The Golden Swallow*, 1968), consolidated the Shaws' supremacy in the market. The sword-fighting movies also signalled the rise of the kung fu genre that would dominate the 1970s. Shaw Brothers had tried to sign Bruce Lee to a contract, but Lee made a better deal with a new studio, Golden Harvest, established in 1970 and run by a new-generation studio mogul, Raymond Chow. Chow was the ex-production chief at Shaw Brothers. His departure from Shaws dealt a blow to the studio, and it never fully recovered from the loss and the competition Chow presented with Golden Harvest.

The Cantonese cinema

The 1950s was also the golden age of Cantonese cinema. The film that first won the attention of critics was *Tears of the Pearl River* (1950), made by a left-wing company whose founders included the mainland director Cai Chusheng. The left-wing movement in Cantonese cinema initiated a campaign to inject more social substance and progressive thinking into Cantonese movies. A filmmaking co-operative was formed, which made a multi-episodic film *Kaleidoscope* (1950), with each episode directed by a leading director. However, it was the establishment of the

Union Film Company (Chung-luen) in 1952 that launched Cantonese cinema into a period of creative growth during the next two decades. Some of the greatest classics of Cantonese cinema were made by Union: *In the Face of Demolition* (Lee Sun-fung, 1953), *Father and Son* (Ng Wui, 1954), *Cold Nights* (Lee Sun-fung, 1955), *Parents' Hearts* (Chun Kim, 1955).

Cantonese movies, however, were primarily a popular mass medium, with comedies, opera films martial arts action movies, and melodramas making up the standard genres. About sixteen pictures were released each month, and stars and directors would make several films back to back. Quantity overwhelmed quality and Cantonese movies never got over the image of being a 'fast-food' cinema: cheap, mass-produced, easily consumed and discarded. Cantonese production continued its quantitative push into the 1960s, but in 1965 the market reached saturation-point, sparking off an economic crisis and fall in production which presaged the decline of Cantonese cinema that would come to pass at the end of the decade. Despite the releases of some memorable Cantonese pictures during the 1960s—Lee Sun-fung's father-and-son melodrama *The Orphan* (1960, starring a teenage Bruce Lee) and Lee's reverential costume picture *So Siu-siu* (1962); Chan Lit-bun's gothic martial arts masterpiece *Green-Eyed Demoness* (1967); Chor Yuen's comic parodies *The Black Rose* (1965) and *Young, Unmarried and Pregnant* (1967); and Lung Kong's vivid portrait of a middle-class teenager's fall from social grace, *Teddy Girls* (1969)—Cantonese film production had come to an end by 1973. This decline of the Cantonese cinema has been attributed to various factors, such as the perception that it was outdated, technically inferior, and lacking quality, and thus unable to compete with the more sophisticated Mandarin cinema. However, perhaps a more important factor was the rise of local Cantonese-dialect broadcast television in 1967, which siphoned off audience support from Cantonese movies and allowed Mandarin movies to enjoy predominance (see Leung, Chapter 21).

The Cantonese dialect was to make a come-back in Hong Kong cinema in 1973, when Chor Yuen's *The*

> **Cantonese movies never got over the image of being a 'fast-food' cinema: cheap, mass-produced, easily consumed and discarded.**

House of 72 Tenants featured the dialect, spoken by a cast of familiar actors from television and became one of the biggest box-office successes of that year. It was the television comedian Michael Hui who did much to re-establish Cantonese as the lingua franca of Hong Kong screens when he switched to a cinema career with the films *Games Gamblers Play* (1975), *The Last Message* (1975), and *The Private Eyes* (1976).

The cultural significance of Cantonese cinema has been substantial. Cantonese opera film in the 1950s is unimaginable without the distinctive use of Cantonese lyrics, while Cantonese comedies relied upon Cantonese colloquial humour and slang. Cantonese melodrama in the 1950s introduced realism and explored family values against the background of an industrializing and urbanizing society. Cantonese martial arts movies from the 1950s to the 1960s popularized the serial adventure and standardized kung fu as the predominant martial art of Hong Kong movies. Cantonese action movies in the 1960s also contained a fine sense of parody that would lay the foundations of the postmodern humour of later films.

Indeed, the achievements of Cantonese cinema have been recognized by New Wave directors who have evoked old Cantonese movies in their films: Tsui Hark, going back to the tradition of Cantonese martial arts serials in *Once upon a Time in China* (1991); Allen Fong, quoting from Cantonese melodramas which deal with the father-and-son relationship in his 1981 movie *Father and Son*; John Woo, remaking a Cantonese action-movie-with-a-social-conscience with his *A Better Tomorrow* (1986). What these few examples also highlight is the role of the Cantonese cinema in awakening the new-found identity of the younger generation of directors known as the New Wave.

Generational change

The Hong Kong New Wave was prefigured as far back as 1969 in *The Arch*, a seminal work about the impact of feudalism on a widow in ancient China filmed by a woman director, Tang Shuxuan. With her next film, *China Behind* (1974), Tang condemned the Cultural Revolution before it was fashionable to do so. Experimental New Wave styles embellished standard genres like the martial arts, in Chor Yuen's *The Magic Blade* (1976), and the crime thriller, in Leong Po-chih and Josephine Siao's *Jumping Ash* (1976). These works,

plus those of the comedian Michael Hui, signalled generational change in Hong Kong cinema. The generation that was born after the war and grew up in the 1950s and 1960s now stood at the forefront of the industry. Many of the new filmmakers had studied in film schools abroad. Upon their return to Hong Kong they had gone into television and made drama series, short films, documentaries. Television, which had earlier robbed Cantonese cinema of its audience, now became a training-ground of new talent for the cinema. These talents included Ann Hui, Yim Ho, Tsui Hark, Allen Fong, Alex Cheung, Patrick Tam, all of whom made their film debuts in the years 1979–80.

The New Wave ushered Hong Kong cinema into the modern age, winning international recognition for the industry and a cult following for some of its directors. However, the Hong Kong cinema has always remained true to the tenets of commercialism and popular cinema even in the films made by New Wave directors. The kung fu films of Jackie Chan are perhaps the most representative of commercial Hong Kong cinema at its best.

In the mid-1980s directors began to tackle the question of 1997 (the year of China's take-over of Hong Kong as a Special Administrative Region) in a series of allegorical dramas: Yim Ho's *Homecoming* (1984), Leong Po-chih's *Hong Kong 1941* (1984), and Ann Hui's *Love in a Fallen City* (1984). As the 1980s ended Hong Kong cinema had gained a new sophistication and even more international attention through the films of Stanley Kwan (*Rouge*) and John Woo (*The Killer*, 1989).

In the 1990s Hong Kong cinema entered a period of uncertainty. The 'postmodern' comedies of Stephen Chiau and outlandish martial arts movies (utilizing a gender-bending motif such as the 1992 release *Swordsman II*) secured cult followings. International interest was maintained through the stylish movies of Wong Kar-wai (*Days of being Wild*, *Ashes of Time*), Clara Law (*Autumn Moon*, 1993), and Stanley Kwan (*Actress*). However, since 1993 the film industry has experienced a period of sluggish box-office returns, escalating costs, and shrinking markets (with only 29 million tickets sold in 1994 compared with 44.8 million tickets sold in 1989). As a result, the China market is destined to become especially important for the future Hong Kong film industry given the hand-over of Hong Kong in 1997.

(b) China and 1997   N. K. LEUNG

In 1997 Hong Kong ceased to be a British colony and became a Special Administrative Region of the People's Republic of China. This political watershed has overshadowed almost all aspects of life in Hong Kong, including its cinema. Indeed, how the relations between Hong Kong and China have been represented in films has been one of the more ostensible themes in the study of Hong Kong cinema since the 1980s. However, it is also possible to look at the way Hong Kong cinema has handled its relationship with China over a longer period, and this will shed light on aspects of the history of film studies of Hong Kong.

Three historical periods may be identified, starting with the most recent. From the 1980s onwards the Hong Kong cinema has been in what might be described as its 'Post-1997 Consciousness' period, a period when the Hong Kong cinema finally caught up with this issue of paramount political importance and began to express, not always overtly, its sentiments on the matter. The period between the late 1960s and the late 1970s represents a kind of 'Mirror Stage' (to borrow a Lacanian phrase) of the Hong Kong cinema, when it only cared to see its own body as its source of pleasure and was oblivious to the ever-present law as symbolized by China. According to this periodization, the whole period of the Hong Kong cinema up to 1966 could be described as its gestation period, during which time it battled with the problems of language, genre, and subjectivity, and, in doing so, indicated the extent to which Hong Kong cinema has seen Hong Kong as the legitimate master of its own fate.

The year 1966, as we know, was the year of the Great Cultural Revolution in China, the reverberations of which would result in a large-scale riot in Hong Kong in 1967 and which indirectly contributed to the student revolt in much of Europe and across America in 1968. Before the revolution, films both in Cantonese (the Chinese dialect spoken in Hong Kong and China's southern province Guangdong) and in Mandarin (China's national 'dialect', commonly spoken by people from the north) were being made. The coexistence of the two languages also reflected the fact that the Hong Kong film industry had been perodically augmented by filmmakers emigrating down south from China, not

only throughout the 1930s and 1940s, but also in the years immediately after China officially established its communist government in 1949. The gradual development of and indigenous film culture in Hong Kong, therefore, was always paralleled by an influx of external, if not alien, cultural elements, resulting in various kinds of tension between the two languages, different literary and cinematic genres, and, most importantly, a Hong Kong and Chinese subjectivity.

Film studies in Hong Kong from the 1940s to the 1960s reflected this state of affairs. Critical studies were mainly concerned with the Hong Kong cinema in its two language versions: either the Cantonese cinema or the Mandarin cinema with, occasionally, some comparisons between the two. Within each language domain, the focus was mainly on genre study (of social realism, melodrama, musicals, and so on) and historical periodization (such as the 'golden' period of the Cantonese or Mandarin cinema and the years before or after the Second World War). The aesthetics employed were derived from literature rather than from film, and the practice of film criticism, with the exception of erratic film publications such as the short-lived *Film Forum* (which appeared from 1947 to 1948), was chiefly in the form of newspaper reviews. Not surprisingly, it was the leftist newspapers in Hong Kong (those that followed the revolutionary politics of mainland China) that carried some of the better-quality film reviews. But, these reviews tended to display traces of early Soviet radical aesthetics (putting politics above all else) and became redundant when the Hong Kong cinema entered its next stage.

The logic of using the year 1966 as a demarcation date seems self-evident. The Great Cultural Revolution of China signified, on a world scale, a peak of social radicalism. However, when Hong Kong recovered from the shocking riots in 1967 and looked forward to a new direction in 1968, its cinema underwent a change. Suddenly, the Cantonese cinema in Hong Kong was proclaimed dead. For the next few years, films were mainly produced in Mandarin. It was as though the people of Hong Kong had lost their voice or the desire to speak in their own language. While other aspects of life in Hong Kong were to embark on an all-out capitalist take-off, its cinema was left to speak in a tone

(Mandarin) which, in the absence of Cantonese, signified an alien Other that was China.

Although the historical approach in film studies would put 1968 or 1969 as the year in which the Cantonese cinema ended, it has found it difficult to offer an explanation for this. However, viewed from the perspective of the Hong Kong–China power relationship, it can be seen that the Hong Kong cinema lost its desire to speak because it sought to forget the 1967 trauma, which was viewed as a Chinese imposition of its fanatical radicalism on an indifferent Hong Kong. The Hong Kong cinema could therefore only speak with its own vioice when it re-emerged as a confident self, as it did in 1972, when the Cantonese cinema came back with a vengeance with director Chu Yuan's box-office hit *The House of 72 Tenants*. In the decade which followed, the Hong Kong cinema pursued a path of pure pleasure and sensuality, leaving politics out of the scene as much as it could, relecting a Hong Kong which seemingly only knew the pursuit of wealth and materialism.

> **Although the historical approach in film studies would put 1968 or 1969 as the year in which the Cantonese cinema ended, it has found it difficult to offer an explanation for this.**

As far as tracing the evolution of film studies in Hong Kong is concerned, other things began to happen in the late 1960s as well. A group of young film critics began to gather around a weekly magazine called the *Chinese Student Weekly*, aimed primarily at college and high-school students, and attempted to write film reviews from a more unorthodox perspective. Helped by the screening of international art films (made available by the budding film club activities at the time) and inspired by new critical approaches in film studies from overseas, particularly the auteurism of Andrew Sarris and the new stream of film writings from England (such as *Movie* and the *Cinema One* series), these film critics sought to bring a fresh and more vigorous approach to the analysis of both Chinese and international films. Although they did not formulate any original theoretical models, the influence they exerted on the film culture of Hong Kong was undeniably huge. Some of them went on to become film directors, such as Patrick Tam (*The Sword*, 1980) and

Shu Kei (*Days without the Sun*, 1989) while some have continued to write to this day, such as Law Kar and Sek Kei, who has now become Hong Kong's most popular film reviewer and critic. There were also other film personalities who initially were either associated with the activities around the group and the weekly publication, such as director John Woo (now working in Hollywood), or grew up under the group's influence, such as director Ann Hui (*The Secret*, 1979; *The Story of Wu Viet*, 1981; *Woman at 40*, 1995). In its own way, the *Chinese Student Weekly* was like the *Cahiers du cinéma* in miniature for the Hong Kong cinema, and marked a turning-point in the evolution of its film studies.

> **In its own way, the *Chinese Student Weekly* was like the *Cahiers du cinéma* in miniature for the Hong Kong cinema, and marked a turning-point in the evolution of its film studies.**

The development of this new film culture, in the context of a commercially buoyant cinema in Hong Kong, provided the setting for the birth of the Hong Kong International Film Festival in 1977. In its second year, the festival started publishing an annual book to go along with its Hong Kong Cinema Retrospective section, which was organized around a different theme each year. This project has not only been breathtaking in its scope of coverage, but has also provided an effective guide to the history of film studies in Hong Kong over the past two decades. Moreover, the key essays of this yearly volume appear in both Chinese and English and thus represent the most useful means for English-speaking readers to find out about the Hong Kong cinema.

While the work done in this area has been impressive, it is also clear from this project that film studies in Hong Kong has not delivered as much as might have been expected. The approaches adopted have largely been the conventional ones of historical periodization and genre study, as some of the early thematic titles indicate: *Cantonese Cinema 1950–1959* for 1978, *Cantonese Cinema 1960–1969* for 1982, *A Study of Hong Kong Martial Arts Film* for 1980, and so on. The project was at its most stimulating when it dealt with *Changes in Hong Kong Society through Cinema* in

A 'sophisticated . . . art-house type movie'?
Chungking Express (1995)

1988 and *The China Factor in Hong Kong Cinema* in 1990, just as the Hong Kong cinema was entering its 'Post-1997 Consciousness' period, described above. Since the 1990s the Hong Kong cinema has shown signs of losing direction, and the themes selected by this project have looked fatigued as well, as *Mandarin Films and Popular Songs from the 1940s to 1960s* for 1993 and *The Restless Breed: Cantonese Stars of the Sixties* for 1996 would indicate. On the whole, a critical project that is grounded in a more in-depth synthesis of Chinese and Western aesthetics, and which faces up to the politics of the Greater China region in an open manner, has yet to be accomplished. Just as the hand-over of Hong Kong in 1997 raises important questions about the future of the Hong Kong film industry (will China open up new audiences for an ailing industry or will Hong Kong filmmakers need to move to China to cultivate a new political and cinematic space), so the future of Hong Kong film studies is likely to depend upon the way these questions are answered.

22

Taiwanese New Cinema

Kuan-Hsing Chen

My central task in this short chapter is to question the very notion of the Taiwan New Cinema (hereafter TNC). I shall argue that the TNC was born out of, and participated in facilitating the nativist movement (by which I mean not only the 'self-rediscovery' movement in the specific case of Taiwan, but a general historical reaction to the end of colonial domination in the colony). However, it has ultimately been taken over by the new nation-building and state-making project and become part of the mechanism of transnational corporations (TNCs of a different kind, known as Hollywood). Indeed, one of the future trends of 'world cinema' will be a move into what I shall term a 'global nativism', a nativism predicated upon the commodification of the implicit dialectic between nationalism and transnationalism.

Throughout this chapter the term 'TNC' refers generally to a range of cinematic practices from the early 1980s to the present. As a sign that gathers together a whole set of activities (including production, film criticism, promotion, consumption), 'TNC' was initially coined by critics and later accepted by a wider population. According to such critics, 'TNC' strictly refers to the alternative cinematic movement, which began with *In our Time* (1982), co-directed by four then younger-generation directors, and ended with *All for Tomorrow* (1986; a military school recruitment advertising clip) co-directed with Chen Kuo-fu by the foremost director of TNC, Hou Hsiao-Hsien. According to this definition,

what has come after that can be termed 'post-TNC'. On the other hand, critics have also recognized that there has been continuity between the 'new' (of the Taiwan New Cinema) and the 'post', and that while the 'new' has lost its original commitment to 'alternative' cinematic practices, the 'post' has none the less inherited its concerns with the cinematic representation of Taiwan's local histories. The question them becomes: how does one position and understand this obsession with 'histories'?

Unlike most Third World countries which mobilized nativism in the movement towards independence and global decolonization after the Second World War, Taiwan's 'self-rediscovery' was blocked by the kuo-mingtang government (the nationalist party, or KMT). Although it can be argued that the tradition of an 'oppositional' nativist movement began at the end of Japanese occupation, especially immediately after the 28 February 1947 massacre, and was culturally crystallized in the 'homeland' literary movement (*hsiang-t'u wen-hsue yun-dong*) of the 1970s, the drive towards nativism could not develop fully under this authoritarian, semi-colonial regime. The full-blown nativization movement (*ben-tu-hua yun-dong*) did not come about until the late 1970s and early 1980s, when the late President Chiang Ching-kuo, the son of Chiang Kai-shek, began, in recognition of 'no hope of recovering the mainland' (*fan-kung wu-wang*), to nativize (or more accurately, to ethnicize) his political regime, as a strategy for maintaining government legitimacy. (The term to 'ethnicize' is used here deliberately, because, from the point of view of the most deprived population—the aboriginals—the Han people are, and have been, the colonizer, no matter whether they came before or after 1945, when the Japanese handed the regime back to the Han Chinese. In the decade-long nativist-nationalist movement, aboriginals have been excluded and marginalized. They contest the imposed categories classifying 'ethnic' differences as Taiwanese (Tai-wan-jen) or Mainlander (Wai-shen-jen, or people coming from outside the province) between 1945 and the late 1980s, and as 'four main ethnic groups' which include the dominant Min-nan-jen, Hakka (Ker-jia-jen), Wai-shen-jen, and the aborigines, since the late 1980s. For the aboriginals, it is not so much an ethnic as a racial difference between aboriginal and the Han Chinese.)

When the political spaces were opened up and the export-oriented national economy was fully incorporated into the structure of global capital to become an often exaggerated member of the 'four tigers' or NICs (Korea, Hong Kong, Singapore, Taiwan), TNC, along with other forms of cultural practices (literature, music, dancing, painting, academic production, religion, and so on), seized the chance to look back on (or, more accurately, to begin a desperate search for) the historical formation of the 'lost self' from the imaginary location of this geopolitical space—Taiwan rather than China. In this sense, the invention of histories where a new identity could be constructed and struggled over, and which had been suppressed in history textbooks, found a new arena in cinematic writing.

However, this wider social mood and ideological structure of feeling cannot alone explain the birth of TNC: the inner logic of the film industry and the cinematic apparatus have also to be understood. From the mid-1970s onwards Taiwan's film industry lost its battle with Hong Kong, which had gradually become the little Hollywood throughout the region (Lii, forthcoming). The formation of a TNC movement was thus in part an attempt to revive the local film industry. As critic Tung Wa explained in 1986, 'TNC was born in the chaotic situations of demand–supply dysfunction in the local market and defeat in the external market' (1986: 31). Furthermore, with the so-called 'Taiwan Miracle', a consumer society was to take shape in the late 1970s which had diversified and shifted the landscape of cultural tastes in the market. Hence, a new generation of moviegoers demanded something directly connected to their own experiences, a need

to which the older generation of directors had failed to respond. In short, the formation of TNC was historically overdetermined by economic and political forces.

What was new about the TNC since the 1980s in relation to previous cinematic production was essentially this reclamation of the 'real' home space from which to construct the popular memory of people's lives on the island, especially in the post-war era. Moreover, the call for an alternative 'national cinema' by critics was self-consciously placed against Hollywood's 'global expansion' (Tung 1986: 34). As Wu Chi-yen (1993: 7) summarizes it, the newness of the TNC expressed itself on two levels: in the use of historical 'materials . . . from the local and the exploration and creation of new cinematic languages (mise-en-scène, cutting, narrative structure)', in other words the use of the long take, non-linear narrative, and critical social realism. However, whether TNC possesses its own language in the history of world cinema remains a open-ended. Critic Cheng Chund-shing points out that, if there is one, it is a 'parrot' language, imitating and assembling various outside elements. Therefore, the crucial point about TNC is not so much the originality of its aesthetic forms as its strategic ideological function within the wider cultural history of Taiwan and, more precisely, its historical turn on the discovery and construction of the 'Taiwanese self'.

> **The crucial point about TNC is not so much the originality of its aesthetic forms as its strategic ideological function within the wider cultural history of Taiwan and, more precisely, its historical turn on the discovery and construction of the 'Taiwanese self'.**

There is a general consensus among critics that TNC was born in 1982, when the low-budget film *In our Time*, co-directed by newcomers Edward Yang, Tao Te-chen, Ko I-cheng, and Chang Yi and produced by the state-owned Central Motion Picture Company (CMPC), was released. The success of *In our Time* provided the incentive for the CMPC to produce a second film, *The Sandwich Man* (1983), based on three short stories by Huang Tsuen-ming from the homeland literary movement and co-directed by Hou Hsiao-

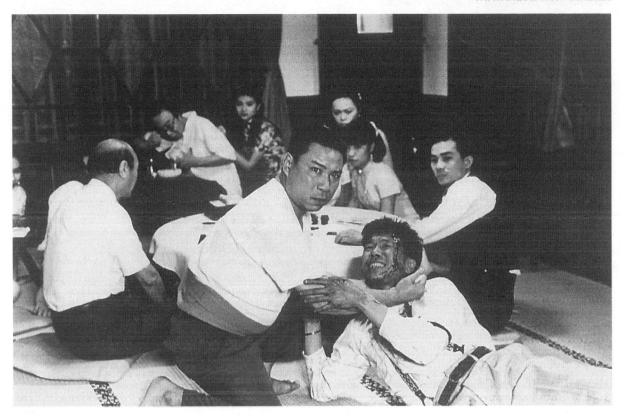

The controversial *City of Sadness* (1989) explores the taboos of ethnic conflict and state violence

hsien, Zeng Zhuang-xiang, and Wang Jen. This borrowing from nativist literature constituted a defining feature of the TNC which was in evidence throughout the 1980s. What can be termed as *Bildungsroman* narrative—expressed in *Ah-Fei* ('Rape Seed', 1983), *The Boys from Fengkuei* (1983), *Growing Up* (1983), *Summer at Grandpa's* (1984), *Dust in the Wind* (1986), *Taipei Story* (1985), *A Time to Live and a Time to Die* (1985), *Banana Paradise* (1989), and *A Brighter Summer Day* (1991)—not only retraced their youth in the memory of the post-war generation, but also charted the trajectories of changing environments, political and economic. In this sense, the TNC's obsession with history signals the end of an era and the beginning of a new one: the move from an agricultural to an industrial society, from poor rural life to the urban centres, from political identification with China to that with Taiwan.

Perhaps because the ethnic background of the directors, as well as those who were in control of the film industry, was largely ethnically Mainlander (Wai-

shen-jen), historical memory did not stretch back to the era of Japanese occupation or earlier, until the appearance of recent films such as *Hills of no Return* (Wang Tong, 1992), *The Puppetmaster* (Hou Hsiao-hsien, 1993), and *A Borrowed Life* (Wu Nien-chen, 1995). With the explosion of identity politics in various forms of social movements (women, labour, aboriginals, older soldiers, lesbians and gays, and youth) from the late 1980s onward, there emerged a set of movies that concerned themselves with the politics of identity such as the critically important *Banana Paradise*, *Two Painters* (1990), *Rebels of the Neon God* (1992), *Dust of Angels* (1992), *The Wedding Banquet* (1993), and *Vive l'amore* (1995). However, unlike Hong Kong cinema, TNC has been predominantly male; indeed, it is difficult to claim the existence of any women's film in TNC.

In retrospect, two rounds of heated debate may be seen to have taken place in the history of TNC: the first surrounding *All for Tomorrow* and the second surrounding *A City of Sadness* (1989). In 1988 the key players of the TNC, including directors Hou Hsiao-hsien and Chen Kuo-fu and scriptwriters Hsiao Yeh and Wu Nien-chen, jointly produced *All for Tomorrow*, an MTV-style promotion film for military school recruitment funded by the Ministry of Defence. This association between TNC and militarism came as a shock to critics, who lamented that what had begun as an alternative cultural movement had been co-opted into the Establishment and announced the death of the TNC (see the articles collected and documented in Mi-chou and Liang 1991: 33–79). Perhaps, the 'death' of TNC as a conscientious intellectual project was inevitable: TNC never operated outside 'the system' (of production, distribution, and consumption) and the Party–state-owned CMPC was its production base. In effect, the launching of the TNC could be read as a generational struggle over power, apparent in the 1987 'Manifesto on Taiwan's Cinema', drafted and signed by this new generation. Once the resources fell into the hands of this new generation, and they learned how to survive within commercial industry, the radicalness of the initial project was inevitably diluted.

By far the most politically controversial debate on history centred around *A City of Sadness*, directed by Hou. Departing from the *Bildungsroman* mode typical of TNC, *A City of Sadness* attempted to deal with the taboos of ethnic conflict and state violence. The film reinvoked the violent 'white horror' (*bai-se kung-bu*) experiences of the 1940s, especially the massacre of 28 February 1947, when some 30,000 people were killed. More than any other film, *A City of Sadness* provoked response from large sections of society. As Mi-chou and Liang (1991, p. xii) put it, the film triggered off a 'sudden explosion' of debate that forced critics to face neglected social and historical problems. Through this emotionally charged film event, the debate confronted a wide range of issues such as historical narration (who has the power to write history, in what directions, and to what ends), the ideological role of cinema, and the system of popular film criticism. It can be argued that TNC's contribution has been precisely its ability to cut into the social fabric in interpellating cultural identities of different constituencies, sparking off the hitherto suppressed collective flow of desire, and offering itself as a sounding-board against which to articulate affective responses.

Ironically, the seemingly taboo film *A City of Sadness* also marked the TNC's entrance into the international circuit. In 1987 martial law had been lifted, but the habit of self-censorship was not broken overnight and, as the 'packager' of the film Tsan Hung-chih

explained, he decided upon a strategy of 'promote expansively overseas, play low key back home' (quoted in Mi-chou 1991: 109), a policy which helped the film to win the Golden Lion award at the 1989 Cannes Film Festival. The success of this strategy also made the producers aware that there was a potential market overseas for its exotic aliennesss. This new discovery (by the local and international industry) marked a shift in the character of TNC, as well as in its financing: *A Brighter Summer Day*, for example, was produced with Japanese investment.

In its concern to join the United Nations (in order to gain bargaining-chips with the Chinese state), the Taiwanese government recognized the value of TNC as registering the name of Taiwan in the American mind. In 1992 the Government Information Office, in charge of international propaganda and local censorship, signed a contract with Warner Bros. to distribute TNC. To facilitate the process further, the diasporic director Lee Ang, who had been living in New York for over a decade, was contracted to make films such as *Pushing Hands* (1991) and later *The Wedding Banquet*, both of which were funded by the Central Studio. It is no accident that the setting for both films was New York, thus permitting the 'transnationalization' of TNC and 'Ang Lee', who has almost achieved the status of national hero since the release of *Sense and Sensibility* (1996). For the state, what matters is not so much the ideological content of the film, but whether it will disseminate the name of Taiwan (and ensure that the world-wide audience is able to distinguish 'Taiwan' from 'Thailand').

In 1993 the crew of *The Wedding Banquet* was warmly received by President Lee Teng-hui, while the movie's homosexual question was of course comple-

While national cinema is partly under threat from the rise of the international co-production, there is also an awareness on the part of Hollywood of the importance of the local. This might be characterized as a form of 'global nativism', in which exotic images of natives and national local histories and signs are employed as selling-points in the world cinema.

tely ignored. From then on, the production of TNC was no longer simply locally oriented (the supposed nativist mode of production), but was also geared to the foreign market, and *The Wedding Banquet* became the first TNC circulated in US theatres. So while national cinema is partly under threat from the rise of the international co-production, there is also an awareness on the part of Hollywood of the importance of the local. This might be characterized as a form of 'global nativism', in which exotic images of natives and national local histories and signs are employed as selling-points in the world cinema. Whether nation-states are in decline, the transnational corporations (the other TNCs) are taking over the world is, of course, a matter for debate. But there is no sign that nationalism is disappearing; quite the contrary, transnationalism and nationalism seem to be bonded together. In this respect, TNC may be seen to be becoming a TNC.

BIBLIOGRAPHY

Chen, Robert R. S. (1993), *The Historical and Cultural Experiences of the Taiwan New Cinema* (Taipei: Wuan-Hsiong).

Lii Ding-tzann (forthcoming), 'A Colonized Empire: Reflections on the Expansion of Hong Kong Film Industry in Asian Countries', in Kuan-Hsing Chen (ed.), *The Trajectories of Cultural Studies: The Decolonization Effects* (London: Routledge).

Mi-chou (1991), 'The Foggy Discourses surrounding *A City of Sadness*: On the Problems of Film Criticism', in Mi-chou and Liang Hsing-hua (1991).

—— and **Liang Hsing-hua** (eds.) (1991), *The Death of New Cinema: from 'All for Tomorrow' to 'City of Sadness'*, War Machine 3 (Taipei: Tonsan Books).

—— (eds.) (1994), *After/Outside the New Cinema*, War Machine, 13 (Taipei: Tonsan Books).

Nandy, Ashis (1982), *Intimate Enemy: The Loss and Rediscovery of the Self under Colonialism* (India: Oxford University Press).

Tung, Wa (1986), 'Language Law and Color Pen: Notes on the 1985 Taiwan New Cinema', *Film Appreciation Journal*, 22: 29–36.

Wang Fei-ling (1994), *An Unfinished Film Dream: In Memory of Wang Fei-Ling*, ed. Chien Cheng et al. (Taipei: Klim).

Wu, Chi-yen (1993), *Underdeveloped Memories*, War Machine, 8 (Taipei: Tonsan Books).

Wuo, Young-yie (1993), 'Hong Kong, Pig King, Nation: Mainlander's National Identity in "Home Coming" Films', *Chung Wai Literary Monthly*, 22/1: 32–44.

23

Japanese cinema

Freda Freiberg

In the second half of the Showa imperial era, from the 1950s until the end of the 1980s, the art cinema of Japan exerted a particular fascination over film critics and film scholars in the West. This fascination was maintained through a number of shifts in critical orientations, shifts both in film studies and in attitudes to Japan. This phenomenon, the Western critic's seduction, my own included, is truly worthy of deconstruction, as suggested by Yoshimoto (1993).

Initially, there was the thrill of the first encounter with a strange culture, and one which displayed a highly developed aesthetic consciousness. The exotic settings, costumes, rituals, and performance styles of Akira Kurosawa and Kenji Mizoguchi's *jidai geki* (period films), exhibited at Venice and then other international film festivals in the early 1950s, doubtless appealed to our orientalist fantasies of a mysterious exotic Japan, totally other from the world we knew. (In retrospect, we may recognize a self-orientalizing tactic on the part of the Japanese film industry, in its attempt to break into foreign markets and achieve critical attention overseas, not unlike the successful strategy deployed by Fifth Generation Chinese filmmakers, such as Chen Kaige and Zhang Yimou, in recent times (see Reynaud, Part 3, Chapter 20). For, just as Chinese viewers find the feudal China of Chinese cinema far removed from their experience, and knowledge of Chinese history, so too did Japanese critics question the veracity of Kurosawa and Mizoguchi's feudal Japan and deplore the neglect

of films that addressed contemporary Japanese social problems.)

But the masterly film direction—the exquisitely orchestrated long takes and deliciously fluid dissolves of late Mizoguchi, and the dazzling display of dynamic editing techniques by Kurosawa—were also totally seductive. Perhaps this rediscovery of an aesthetic Japan, of Japan as the locus of supreme style, fitted a post-war political agenda to reinstate Japan in the Western alliance against Eastern communism, offsetting the image of a brutal and primitive Japan cultivated by the Allies during the Second World War (Dower 1986). These films also included snatches of 'democratic' and 'pacifist' rhetoric, calculated to make Western audiences believe that the American occupation had succeeded in taming and reforming its former enemy. It was now the Soviet Union and China which were awarded the traits of oriental despotism.

However, the discovery of the Japanese cinema also coincided with the rise of auteurism in film studies, so that the idea of Japanese cinema came to be conflated with the work of a few directors, those who were accorded the status of 'auteurs', true authors. Initially the canon was confined to Mizoguchi and Kurosawa; soon, however, a third name was introduced, that of Yasujiro Ozu, who finally eclipsed the other two both in terms of the number of publications devoted to analysis of his work and in terms of his centrality to theoretical debates about the Japanese cinema. The fact that these three masters emerged from three different company studios (Mizoguchi from Nikkatsu, Ozu from Shochiku, and Kurosawa from Toho) that specialized in three different genres (the melodrama, the home drama (*shomin-geki*), and the period film (*jidai-geki*)) was overlooked; for industrial contexts and genre conventions were deemed barriers to true artistic expression: the true artist transcended them.

> **The discovery of the Japanese cinema also coincided with the rise of auteurism in film studies, so that the idea of Japanese cinema came to be conflated with the work of a few directors, those who were accorded the status of 'auteurs'.**

If the French critics around *Cahiers du cinéma*, many of whom later became leaders of the French New Wave cinema, acclaimed Mizoguchi for his transcendental style, judging him a superior artist to Kurosawa (the filmmaker who had long reigned unrivalled in the United States and the British Commonwealth), it was Paul Schrader (1972) in America (another film critic who was to become a writer-director) who located transcendental style in the films of Ozu, alongside those of the Dane Theodor Dreyer and Frenchman Robert Bresson. Prefiguring David Bordwell's (1985) 'parametric' stylists, Schrader's 'transcendental' stylists share a common approach to filmmaking, rather than a common culture. For Schrader, they document, with extreme precision, banal, everyday rituals; introduce disparities and disjunctions which disturb the equilibrium; and finally transcend rather than resolve the disturbances through aesthetic strategies that are imbued with spiritual, religious, and philosophical meaning. In Ozu's case, the transcendence is achieved through his use of 'codas', a montage of still-life shots that partake of the spirit of Zen.

Schrader relates Ozu's spiritual aesthetic to a Zen aesthetic which permeates the Japanese arts in general and is evident in haiku, the tea ceremony, ink painting, Noh drama, and the martial arts. This aesthetic is marked by a creative use of silences and voids (*mu*), and a predominant mood of *mono no aware*

(literally, the pathos of things) based on a sorrowing awareness of the transience and mutability of all living things (*mujo*). Schrader has not been alone in identifying this aesthetic at work in the Japanese cinema. Although she does not specifically identify it with Zen, Japanese American academic Keiko McDonald (1983) finds several major Japanese films of the 1950s—Kon Ichikawa's *Biruma no tategoto* ('The Harp of Burma', 1956), Mizoguchi's *Ugetsu monogatari* ('Tales of Ugetsu', 1953), Kurosawa's *Kumonosu-jo* ('Throne of Blood', 1957), Keisuke Kinoshita's *Nijushi no hitomi* ('Twenty-Four Eyes', 1954) and Ozu's *Tokyo monogatari* ('Tokyo Story', 1953)—imbued with the philosophy of *mujo*, which she describes as a traditional philosophical concept or traditional Japanese attitude to life.

McDonald sees her role as a native informant who can explicate Japanese cinema to the Western viewer not versed in Japanese culture, and, in this respect, she follows Richie rather than Schrader. Donald Richie, who has lived for many years in Japan, and has familiarized himself with Japanese theatre, art and culture, cinema and society, has performed the role of mediator between Japanese cinema and the West, helping to make it accessible to the uninitiated. In both his collaborative work with J. L. Anderson (1959), and his own books, he has functioned as an interpreter of a largely unknown territory—assuming the seductive role of pioneer and explorer. Because there are very few film scholars in the West who can speak and understand Japanese, and who have more than a cursory knowledge of Japanese culture and society, art, and history these few are easily seduced into performing the role of experts with specialist knowledge of Japan and the Japanese, of educators who can open doors to an understanding of Japanese cinema and Japanese culture. Unlike the current situation in Chinese cinema scholarship, there have been few Japanese who write in English, French, or German, or work in the Western academy, who could contest their readings; little Japanese-language material has been translated into English; and the fact that Japan has been an imperial power itself, rather than a direct victim of European imperialism, seemed to exonerate such Western forays into Japanese culture from the charge of cultural imperialism.

In fact, an American tradition of using the Japanese cinema as a mirror of, or door into, Japan and the Japanese has its origins in wartime Washington. Researchers there studied Japanese films, documen-

Tokyo Story (1953)—Ozu's 'narrational playfulness'

tary and fiction, in an effort to understand the Japanese national character, so as to better ensure defeat of the Japanese military forces and a smooth transition to the post-war American occupation. Richie came to Japan with the occupation and remained there to write, among other things, a book on Japanese cinema, sub-titled 'Film Style and National Character', for the Japan Travel Bureau in 1961, a work which was revised, expanded, and updated for Doubleday in New York a decade later. Apart from working as film critic for the *Japan Times* and writing book-length studies of the life and films of Kurosawa and Ozu, Richie was also very generous with his time, knowledge, and contacts towards the next generation of Western researchers on Japanese film, who started arriving in Japan in the 1970s. Their debt to Richie is evident, not merely in

their formal acknowledgements of his assistance, and their deference to his opinions, but also in their emula-tion of his methodology. Both Audie Bock (1978) and Joan Mellen (1976) survey a wide historical field, cover a broad range of directors, mix biographical informa-tion with summary accounts of the films, give some attention to film style, but generally concentrate on thematic readings of the work of the surveyed direc-tors. In her introduction, Mellen echoes Richie's description of Japanese cinema as 'the most perfect reflection of a people' (Richie 1961/1971, p. xix): it is, she suggests, 'a mirror into the hearts of a people' (Mellen 1976, p. xxvii). If reflection theory has fallen out of favour, even more questionable, in the light of deconstruction and post-colonial theory, is her state-ment that '[t]hrough the Japanese film, we, as well as the Japanese, are able to penetrate this society and its history' (Mellen 1976, p. xxvi).

On the other hand, Mellen does offer a new slant in her sustained feminist critique of Ozu and Kurosawa. Unfortunately, her readings of films, unlike Bock's, suffer from the categorical imperative, and a failure to perceive ambiguities and ambivalences. Swept up in the rhetorical mode of a universalist Western feminist film criticism, she is very quick to label a text or a director either feminist or misogynist, pacifist or militarist, feudal or democratic, when these labels may not be appropriate or accurate, given the historical and industrial constraints of the conditions of Japanese film production and reception. On the other hand, the paucity of politically committed criticism in Western writing on Japanese film makes her work seductive: here is a woman daring to criticize some of the acknowledged great masters of the cinema, while praising some others for their commitment to social change and resistance to dominant values. Empowered by feminist ideology, she may be unaware of her privilege as a Western woman, but she confidently cuts through the cant of mysticism and aestheticism that surrounds the reception of Japanese film and directly addresses social issues.

Since Mellen, one of the few Western researchers to investigate the relevance of social issues to Japanese cinema has been David Desser, another American scholar. In his *Eros Plus Massacre* (1988), he undertakes an explication of the New Wave Japanese Cinema of the 1960s in the light of contemporary Japanese social and political issues and debates, supplying the historical context of production and reception, and attributing political motivations to the filmmakers. His stated intention was to balance the neo-formalist bias of contemporary theoretical debates about the Japanese cinema by putting film content and social context back into the picture.

Until the late 1970s the field of Japanese film studies was dominated by film critics and historical researchers, some from inside and others from outside the Japanese studies area. In the late 1970s a crucial shift occurred: film theorists from outside the Japanese studies area entered the terrain. Three major publications were significant in this shift: first, a special issue of *Screen* magazine in 1976, devoted to an analysis of Ozu film texts; secondly, the publication of Noël Burch's *To the Distant Observer* in 1979; and thirdly, the publication of David Bordwell's book on Ozu in 1988.

These projects coincided with the arrival, and rapid expansion, of cinema studies in the Western academy that seemed to demand a greater theoretical, quasi-scientific rigour than had been hitherto practised in film study; detailed close analysis of the construction of film texts (made possible by new technology); and systematic investigations of the relations between cinema and psychoanalysis, sociology, history, linguistics, and aesthetics. Radical intellectuals around *Screen* in London drew upon the exciting work of French structuralist and post-structuralist theorists, as well as Russian Formalists, in their search for a total theory of the cinema and for strategies of film analysis. Theorizations and analyses of mainstream Hollywood cinema led to investigations of alternative cinemas (the Soviet silent cinema; Godard; German Expressionism; primitive cinema; the avant-garde) and here the Japanese cinema was seized upon as another alternative. In the *Screen* issue on Ozu, Branigan (1976) and Thompson and Bordwell (1976) presented the Ozu text as a modernist text. With evidence gleaned from close textual analysis, they argued that, in Ozu's film practice, unlike the Hollywood system, space was prioritized over narrative. They did not argue that Ozu represented the Japanese cinema: it was the author Ozu who posed the difference. But Noël Burch went further and argued that the Japanese cinema as a whole provides a formidable example of a totally other system from the 'institutional mode of representation' (the dominant style of international filmmaking) in prioritizing presentation over representation, decentred composition over centred composition, surface over depth . . .

In his grand master-theory, Burch employed the language of Marxist historiography and French post-structuralism interlarded with bold (and questionable) assertions about the uniqueness of Japanese society, culture, and art, due to national isolation, unoriginality, and uniformity. He traced a history of Japanese cinema, based on its imitation, adaptation, and ultimate transgression of Western codes of filmmaking, illustrating it with close formal analyses of the editing techniques, shot composition, and camera deployments in isolated sequences from a large number of films. He concluded that the classical (pre-American occupation) Japanese cinema displayed a preference for the long shot over the medium shot and close-up; editing codes that draw attention to themselves (showy, excessive editing or exceptionally long takes); non-anthropocentric composition; and other departures from standard Hollywood practice.

Although he included in his argument an extended range of film directors active in the 1930s (Teinosuke Kinugasa, Hiroshi Shimizu, Sadao Yamanaka, Mikio Naruse, Tamizo Ishida, Tomotaka Tasaka, *et al.*, as well as the Big Three), he was prone to ignore or dismiss as un-Japanese or (implicitly) as non-art industrial practice that did not fit his argument. He was just not interested in the popular generic cinema that is not formally aberrant (in relation to dominant codes of Western realism), and that is not art cinema.

Fascination for a profoundly other aesthetic tradition, one not based on Cartesian perspectivalism, links Schrader, Burch, and recent art historians, such as Norman Bryson (1988). However, where this other tradition is other than the Euro-American, its links with other Asian aesthetic traditions (Chinese and Indian) are unexplored. With the rise of the Chinese art cinema, some of the arguments posed about its aesthetic antecedents (Ehrlich and Desser 1994, part 1) give a strong sense of *déjà-vu*. The explication of a Chinese artistic tradition—one with multiple perspectives rather than a fixed one, flat composition rather than composition in depth, even lighting rather than chiaroscuro, and one that allots an active role to emptiness—suggests that the supposedly exceptional 'aesthetic tradition' of Japan was derived from China and not uniquely Japanese. Beyond that, Willemen (1995) has argued for the persistence of a feudal mode of visuality alongside other modes of visuality in the modern cinema generally. In support of his argument, one may note that flat composition, character typology and frontality, and even lighting are attributes of European feudal art, as well as of Ozu's cinema.

Bordwell takes issue with Burch over his notion of a pure Japanese tradition, arguing that Ozu developed a unique set of 'intrinsic norms' (unique in the Japanese cinema as well as the West), which draw on Taisho era popular cultural forms heavily influenced by modern Western culture. In his later work, Bordwell (1988, chs. 2 and 3) explored the historical and industrial, as well as the cultural, context of Ozu's filmmaking career. However, he continues to assert his belief that Ozu's formal strategies make his work exciting and interesting, while dismissing his thematic material as reiterations of trite cultural clichés. In other short papers on Mizoguchi (Bordwell 1983) and the pre-war Japanese cinema (Bordwell 1992: 328–46), Bordwell continues to concentrate on the departures of Japanese directors from Hollywood and European filmmaking norms, identifying a different treatment of deep space in the case of

(pre-war) Mizoguchi, and a stylistic preference for the decorative or ornamental flourish in the case of the Japanese cinema generally.

> **Bordwell continues to concentrate on the departures of Japanese directors from Hollywood and European filmmaking norms, identifying a different treatment of deep space in the case of (pre-war) Mizoguchi, and a stylistic preference for the decorative or ornamental flourish in the case of the Japanese cinema generally.**

Even though celebrating Ozu's narrational playfulness, and identifying it as rooted in a love of fun and games, rather than a ponderous aesthetic rigour, Bordwell himself pursues his subject with such exhaustive rigour, with such a welter of (formal) analytic detail, and with such polemical insistence that he kills the charm and fun. Characteristically, too, he refuses to pursue the symptoms of anything beneath the surface. In contrast, French critic Sylvie Pierre (1992) responds to the Ozu films with a sense of wonder and in a spirit of exploration, pursuing various lines of approach. *Inter alia*, she suggests that one could read the lack of serious attention to sex and politics, and prankish humour, and the low-angle shooting style in Ozu's cinema as symptoms of arrested development; his obsession with perceptual games and quasi-electric charging of the living texture of the passing moment as a displacement of eroticism. Pierre's tentative deployment of psychoanalytic terminology is uncommon in criticism of Japanese film. The only case of a sustained application of (Western feminist) psychoanalytic theory to Japanese film that I am aware of is Robert Cohen's (1992) analysis of Mizoguchi's film *Saikaku Ichidai Onna* ('The Life of Oharu', 1952).

Both Thompson and Bordwell's (1976) and Branigan's (1976) rigorous analyses of the clearly perceptible surface structures of the Ozu text, and Burch's (1979) ambitious argument about the essential difference of the Japanese cinema in general, rely on Barthes's proposition that 'the Japanese text' is pure surface, with no depth—a proposition they have applied literally and metaphorically. Their syntactic, anti-semantic approach has been very seductive to film scholars unfamiliar with Japanese language, culture, history, and politics, because it seems to make these knowledges redundant: since there is no depth to this cinema, there is no need to pursue the matter further. Until now, despite extensive criticism of their approach in book reviews and academic journalism (see esp. Lehman 1987), there have been no substantially developed counter-theories. Two reasons could be proposed for this failure to pursue the matter: the decline of interest in the Japanese cinema, and its replacement, in the later 1980s and 1990s, by the Chinese cinema(s); and the dearth of scholars equally qualified in Japanese studies and film theory.

However, the question of Nagisa Oshima intervened. Stephen Heath 1976, 1977) found his work of paramount interest to questions and debates about subjectivity, politics, and aesthetics, which preoccupied Marxist and Lacanian British film scholars around *Screen* magazine. Oshima, rather than Ozu, offered a breakthrough for the political avant-garde in the West. The translation of Tadao Sato's work (1982), along with Desser's (1988) book on the Japanese New Wave, enabled us to position this work in a Japanese political context. Oshima's agenda shared with the international New Left movement an attack on the doctrinaire Old Left, and a stress on personal and sexual liberation, but also had specifically local targets: the victim mentality and sentimentality of Japanese leftist filmmaking; Japan's legacy of imperialism, militarism, racism, and sexism; the oppression of Koreans by the Japanese state.

One could say that the Big Three (Ozu, Kurosawa, and Mizoguchi) had become the Big Four (the former three plus Oshima), in the West's understanding of Japanese cinema. The industry's reliance on staple genres was acknowledged but usually dismissed with disdain (Anderson and Richie 1959/1982: 315–22; Burch 1979: 151–3). Some spasmodic attention has been given to the yakuza movie (Schrader 1974; Keiko McDonald, in Nolletti and Desser 1992; Mellen 1976: 121–33) and to the samurai film (David Desser, in Nolletti and Desser 145–64), but generally one could say that we are still awaiting the substantial kinds of analysis of the Japanese popular genres that have been undertaken in regard to the popular Hollywood genres. The same could be said of the star system in the Japanese cinema. Since the classical Japanese film industry was, like Hollywood, based on genre specialization (and diversification) and the star system, these absences would seem to be serious gaps.

In their absence, two racy texts on archetypes of Japanese popular culture, written by two knowledgeable non-academics, Buruma (1984) and Barrett (1989), are useful antidotes to the academic preoccupation with art cinema. Both entertaining and informative, these texts trace the continuities and shifts in the dominant archetypes as manifested in a variety of popular media (comic strips, popular literature, theatre, radio, film, oral storytelling), bringing out the rich intertextual texture of Japanese popular culture. More scholarly historical research on pre-war Japanese popular culture has been undertaken by Miriam Silverberg (1993), who gives welcome attention to the mobility of gender and cultural identifications in pre-war Japan, thus breaking down the sharp split between 'them' and 'us' (women and men, Japanese and non-Japanese).

The dominance of Japanese commerce and capital in the international arena in the 1980s produced renewed speculations about Japan's relation to modernity and postmodernity, both within and outside Japan. Film scholars had long been debating whether Ozu, Mizoguchi, or Kurosawa were traditional or modern (terms often conflated with the essentially Japanese and the Westernized, or with the conservative and the progressive). But now, in the light of postcolonial theory, the terms have become problematic. Scott Nygren (1989) has suggested a considerable amount of cross-cultural confusion in their application, in both East and West: in both cases, conservative, traditional norms have been read as 'modern' or 'modernist' in the other context. Yoshimoto (1991) sees the terminology of modernity and postmodernity as unavoidably tainted by imperialism: the non-West by definition cannot be modern. The vaunted postmodernity of Japan, which has supposedly surpassed that of the West, masks the survival of feudal and politically despotic social and cultural forms, and allows them to be rationalized and naturalized as authentic and desirable national differences. Yoshimoto (1993) decries the emphasis of recent scholarship on the problems of cross-cultural analysis, and advocates a return to politically engaged and informed criticism.

CRITICAL APPROACHES TO WORLD CINEMA

BIBLIOGRAPHY

*Anderson, Joseph A., and Donald Richie (1959/1982), *The Japanese Film: Art and Industry* (rev. Princeton: Princeton University Press).

Barrett, Gregory (1989), *Archetypes in Japanese Film: The Socio-political and Religious Significance of the Principal Heroes and Heroines* (Selinsgrove: Susquehanna University Press).

Bock, Audie (1978), *Japanese Film Directors* (Tokyo: Kodansha).

Bordwell, David (1983), 'Mizoguchi and the Evolution of Film Language', in Stephen Heath and Patricia Mellencamp (eds.), *Cinema and Language* (Los Angeles: American Film Institute).

—— (1985), *Narration in the Fiction Film* (London: Methuen).

—— (1988), *Ozu and the Poetics of Cinema* (London: British Film Institute; Princeton University Press).

—— (1992), 'A Cinema of Flourishes: Japanese Decorative Classicism of the Prewar Era', in Nolletti and Desser (1992).

Branigan, Edward (1976), 'The Space of *Equinox Flower*', *Screen*, 17/2 (Summer), 74–105.

Bryson, Norman (1988), 'The Gaze in the Expanded Field', in Hal Foster (ed.), *Vision and Visionality* (Seattle: Bay Press).

*Burch, Noël (1979), *To the Distant Observer: Form and Meaning in the Japanese Cinema* (London: Scolar Press).

—— (1983), 'Approaching Japanese Film', in Stephen Heath and Patricia Mellencamp (eds.), *Cinema and Language* (Los Angeles: American Film Institute).

Buruma, Ian (1984), *A Japanese Mirror: Heroes and Villains of Japanese Culture* (London: Jonathan Cape).

Cohen, Robert (1992), 'Why does Oharu Faint? Mizoguchi's *The Life of Oharu* and Patriarchal Discourse', in Nolletti and Desser (1992).

Desser, David (1988), *Eros plus Massacre: An Introduction to the Japanese New Wave Cinema* (Bloomington: Indiana University Press).

Dower, John (1986), *War without Mercy: Race and Power in the Pacific War* (New York: Pantheon Books).

Ehrlich, Linda C., and David Desser (eds.) (1994), *Cinematic Landscapes: Observations on the Visual Arts and Cinema of China and Japan* (Austin: University of Texas Press).

Freiberg, Freda (1992), 'Genre and Gender in World War II Japanese Feature Films', *Historical Journal of Film, Radio and Television*, 12/3: 245–52.

Heath, Stephen (1981), 'Narrative Space', *Screen*, 17/3 (Autumn), 68–112; repr. in *Questions of Cinema* (Bloomington: Indiana University Press).

—— (1977/1981), 'The Question Oshima', *Wide Angle* 2/1: 48–57; repr. rev. in *Questions of Cinema* (Bloomington: Indiana University Press).

Lehman, Peter (1987), 'The Mysterious Orient, the Crystal Clear Orient, the Non-existent Orient: Dilemmas of Western Scholars of Japanese Film', *Journal of Film and Video*, 39 (Winter), 5–15.

McDonald, Keiko (1983), *Cinema East: A Critical Study of Major Japanese Films* (London: Associated University Presses).

Mellen, Joan (1976), *The Waves at Genji's Door: Japan through its Cinema* (New York: Pantheon Books).

Nolletti, Arthur, and David Desser (eds.) (1992), *Reframing Japanese Cinema: Authorship, Genre, History* (Bloomington: Indiana University Press).

Nygren, Scott (1989), 'Reconsidering Modernism: Japanese Film and the Postmodern Context', *Wide Angle*, 11/3 (July), 6–15.

Pierre, Sylvie (1992), 'Le Monde d'Ozu' ou, L'Empire de la décence', *Trafic*, 4 (Autumn), 68–87.

Richie, Donald (1961/1971), *Japanese Cinema: Film Style and National Character* (rev. expanded New York: Doubleday).

Sato, Tadao (1982), *Currents in Japanese Cinema*, trans. Gregory Barrett (Tokyo: Kodansha International).

Schrader, Paul (1972/1988), *Transcendental Style in Film: Ozu, Bresson, Dreyer* (Berkeley: University of California Press; repr. New York: Da Capo Press).

—— (1974), 'Yakuza-Eiga, a Primer', *Film Comment*, 10/1 (Jan.–Feb.), 8–17.

Silverberg, Miriam (1993), 'Remembering Pearl Harbour, Forgetting Charlie Chaplin and the Case of the Disappearing Western Woman: A Picture Story', *Positions*, 1/11: 24–76.

Thompson, Kristin, and David Bordwell (1976), 'Space and Narrative in The Films of Ozu', *Screen*, 17/2 (Summer), 41–73.

Willemen, Paul (1995), 'Regimes of Subjectivity and Looking', *UTS Review* 1/2 (Oct.), 101–29.

Yoshimoto, Mitsuhiro (1991), 'Melodrama, Postmodernism, and the Japanese Cinema', *East–West Film Journal*, 5/1 (Jan.), 28–55.

—— (1993) 'The Difficulty of being Radical: The Discipline of Film Studies and the Postcolonial World Order', in Masao Miyoshi and H. D. Harootunian (eds.), *Japan in the World* (Durham, NC: Duke University Press).

24

African cinema

N. Frank Ukadike

In recent times scholarly inquiries into African cinema have proliferated. These have involved multidisciplinary perspectives and have resulted in a diversity of both African and non-African perspectives. The major concerns of this academic writing have been the relationship of African cinematic discourse to the 'dominant' modes of representation and the theoretical contexts and frameworks necessary for their understanding. However, the term 'dominant' has also become problematic in so far as it privileges the hierarchical standing of Hollywood and other Western cinemas, in relation to which all other cinemas, including Africa's, are considered to be either different, alternative, or oppositional. This categorization has also posed other important questions such as: Can there be an autonomous African cinema? What makes African cinema different from Hollywood and other Western cinemas? Can African cinema's uniqueness be understood from the perspectives of other cinemas outside the dominant traditions? In order to begin to answer these questions, it is necessary to examine not only the history of African film production but also the critical and theoretical perspectives employed to account for this history and the difference of African film.

Problems of production

African filmmaking is a very recent phenomenon that has, after independence, developed differently in the anglophone, francophone, and lusophone regions. The shifting conditions and changes which have taken place during the colonial and post-independence periods demonstrate that the cinemas were born under unique circumstances not common to other national cinemas. In short, the varied character of African films today reflects a convulated historical pattern of development. An account of their histories must, therefore, identify factors which have led to their growth or retardation, focusing specifically on socio-political, cultural, and economic issues as well as the state practices which have impacted upon the production of films. In terms of creativity, narrative refinement, and quantity of films produced in the continent, it is now possible to speak of genuine growth, but this success is threatened by a number of economic and political factors. As Kenneth Harrow (1996) has argued, 'it is hard to imagine any other aspect of culture so controlled by neo-colonial forces as in African film'—a control as retrogressive in many ways as the outmoded myths which permeate the interpretation of African history and culture.

Indeed, much 'African' film production is scarcely African at all and results from foreign exploitation of African resources, cheap labour, and production facilities in Zimbabwe and Kenya (which are made available to the highest bidder). This situation helps to explain the unfortunate case in Zimbabwe, where films such as *Neria* (Jit, 1993), *Consequences* (1987), and *More*

Time (1992) are marketed as African films when the producers and distributors are foreign. A number of blockbuster foreign films have also been produced in Africa. These include *Out of Africa* (USA, 1985), shot in Kenya, *Gorillas in the Mist* (USA, 1988), shot in Rwanda, *Mr Johnson* (GB, 1990), shot in Nigeria, and most recently, *The Ghost and the Darkness* (USA, 1996), shot in the South African animal reserves. Although shot in Africa, however, these foreign films none the less deny Africans any point of view. In the same way it is difficult to explain the legitimacy of *Cry Freedom* (1987) and *Sarafina* (USA, 1993) being paraded as black South African films, given the time at which they were made.

In order to understand the various factors which have limited the growth of African film, it is therefore necessary to examine Africa's relationship with other producing nations and assess the impact of 'hegemonic foreign' (Cham 1995) tendencies on the situation in Africa today. Hollywood virtually monopolizes sub-Saharan African theatres, along with foreign distributors and exhibitors of Hong Kong, kung fu, and Indian musical melodramas, with the result that very few African films get seen. This problem is exacerbated by the proliferation of satellite television transmitted live across the continent. South Africa is the home base of MNET, the satellite television network that beams foreign cable networks to most African countries. Because it does not give prominence to African films, it has become the worst perpetrator of cultural colonialism inside Africa.

> **Hollywood virtually monopolizes sub-Saharan African theatres, along with foreign distributors and exhibitors of Hong Kong, kung fu, and Indian musical melodramas, with the result that very few African films get seen.**

In the 1990s this situation of African film worsened, and filmmakers appealed, to no avail, for government intervention as the only way to compel foreign theatre-owners to promote indigenous African films. This has, however, forced the promotion of video production in anglophone Ghana and Nigeria, in particular. What has been the impact of this video boom on the film industries of Ghana and Nigeria? Are we witnessing the demise of celluloid film production in Africa? Is African film history being rewritten with the video revolution? Most middle-class workers in Nigeria and Ghana, for example, have never seen African films (as opposed to the new video films, as they are popularly called) but can mention numerous American films that even US citizens have never seen or heard of. With the advent of video, however, Ghana has been able to cultivate an indigenous film and video culture. So far it is the only country in Africa I know where Hollywood has lost out to African video films.

The United States and Europe have designed strategies to protect their film industries and Africa needs to do the same, especially with regard to economic viability. How can African film practice be encouraged to reach the industrial level? In what ways can effective control of free flow of foreign films and satellite television be channelled to work for the transformation of African film practices? This worked in Europe in the 1920s (and is still working for the United States). Is it applicable to Africa, as we approach the twenty-first century? Burkina Faso has set precedents which should inspire other African countries. A country of about 6.5 million people with meagre economic resources, it organizes, every other year, the world's largest film festival, the Pan-African Festival of Film and Television of Ouagadougou (FESPACO), which it uses to showcase African films. Burkina Faso has also sponsored inter-state co-productions, an initiative which has helped to produce some award-winning films, and runs a film archive in Ouagadougou, which provides an invaluable facility for research on African cinema.

What, then, is African cinema? or toward an African world cinema?

The first question has been addressed in several studies (Diawara 1992; Ukadike 1994; Tomaselli 1993; Pfaff 1986) and in the writings of Teshome H. Gabriel (1982), Clyde Taylor (1985), Mark A. Reid (1985), Mbye B. Cham (1982) and so on. It is interesting that Africa is no longer regarded as the filmic cul-de-sac it was once thought. Over the years African cinema has undergone a radical transformation by widening its scope and offering an expanded definition of the continent's cinemas as work which expresses the diversity and plurality of the cultures of the producing nations. Indeed, the term 'African cinema' may be seen as outdated, now used only for convenience. For it is important to make it clear that the cinema in Tunisia may not have anything in common with the cinema in Cameroon. Each nation's cinema is a loose assortment of films by individual filmmakers of various backgrounds and with different agendas. Their ostensible goals may be the same with regard to the representation of continental issues, but stylistic trends do not mirror the unity that we find in the filmmakers' declamations. Still, some broad trends link all the generations of filmmakers.

As independence paved the way for the acquisition of cinematic know-how and filmmaking infrastructure, it is understandable how, in the pioneering period of the 1960s–1970s, it became the concern of African film practitioners to link the emerging cinema with politics and education and to stress African histories and culture which Euro-American cinemas often caricature. The African cinema of this period is didactic and unabashedly political and denunciative. For example, Ousmane Sembene, widely regarded as the father of African cinema, proclaimed that 'the cinema is the night school of my people'. For him, the film theatre could provide the forum for education unavailable under colonialism.

This also implied the adoption of particular filmmaking strategies. Simply put, the effect of Sembene's ideology can be seen in the narrative style employed in his film *Borom Sarret* (Senegal, 1963), a twenty-minute short which, arguably, initiated the model African film in which the synthesis of fiction and documentary, meticulous attention to detail, and oral narrative technique coalesce into an indigenous aesthetic. This approach suggests new ways of seeing and interpreting African history through cinematic images, and highlights the dichotomy between African cinema and Euro-American cinema, in this case between a social cinema and a commercial cinema orientated towards profit.

As the leading pioneer, Sembene exerted enormous influence on other African filmmakers. However, his

Borom Sarret **(Senegal, 1963), is a twenty-minute short which, arguably, initiated the model African film in which the synthesis of fiction and documentary, meticulous attention to detail, and oral narrative technique coalesce into an indigenous aesthetic.**

narrative style has been neither prescriptive nor binding on other pioneer African filmmakers such as Med Hondo, Souleymane Cissé, Haile Gerima, Safi Faye, and Sarah Maldoror. Although these pioneers differ in their narrative approaches to African issues, they are unanimous in eschewing the dominant notion of a cinema geared towards entertainment. These African filmmakers initiated interrogative narrative patterns by appropriating and subverting 'dominant' conventions, blending them with their own cultural codes (oral narrative art) to create a novel aesthetic formula. Dubbed 'the aesthetics of decolonization', it is this aesthetic, and its difference from Western notions of art, that some critics have argued has invested the language of cinema with new meaning and encouraged new methods of critical orientation.

Although African filmmakers invoke oral tradition as a primary influence, they have appropriated it and applied it in various ways to create paradigms for addressing the broad range of social, political, cultural, and historical issues of Africa. Even among critics of African film practice, oral tradition as a creative matrix has generated controversies and disagreements regarding its application to African films (Akudinobi 1995). Although their styles are diametrically opposed to each other, this use of oral tradition and African film language can be identified and analysed in the films of Ousmane Sembene and Med Hondo. While Sembene's narrative is more linear than Hondo's and imbued with straightforward didacticism (as in *Borrom Sarret*, *Mandabi*, 'The Money Order', 1968, *Xala*, 1974, and *Camp de Thiaroye*, 1987), Hondo's films (*Soleil O*, 1969, and *West Indies*, 1979) are, as Pfaff (1986) suggests, syncopated and eruptive in tone, and reminiscent of the stylistically disruptive tone of black French liberationist literature. The two filmmakers not only share a number of Western influences (such as Italian Neo-Realism, Hollywood, Latin American documentary, and Soviet montage) but are indebted to indigenous oral storytelling techniques as well. Thus, while Western critics have tended to read Hondo's style as avante-garde and Godardian, Africanist discourse has emphasized its links with oral tradition (see Pfaff 1986; Ukadike 1994).

Specific applications of the oral storytelling art abound in African films. In Désiré Écaré's exuberant film *Faces of Women* (Côte d'Ivoire, 1988), music, song, and dance intersperse the narrative. Unlike Western films, where music is used to contradict or complement the visual information, song and dance in *Faces* are narrative components working together to

Senegalese filmmaking—*Xala* (1974)

advance the film's structure and to create continuity between images or what they signify. Moussa Kemoko Diakite's *Naitou* (Guinea, 1982) employs no dialogue—only music and dance—to show how the cultural power of art can be used to tell the tale of a young orphan girl in a polygamous home, who has been badly mistreated by the stepmother who killed her real mother. In *Angano . . . Angano . . . Tales from Madagascar* (Madagascar and France, 1989), Marie-Clemence and Cesar Paes use oral storytelling techniques to demystify dominant documentary film practice. In this film, storytelling is foregrounded as art, and oral tradition becomes the principal actor which renders vivid an eyewitness account of the myths and belief systems of the Malagasy culture. They include tales about the origins of life, rice cultivation, and the

ritual practice of the exhumation of the dead. The images captured are presented without trivializing or folklorizing the ritual as in conventional ethnographic films. Close-ups are judiciously employed, but not the type of psychologizing close-ups used in Jean Rouch's psychodrama *Les Maîtres fous* (1953).

For some critics the quest of Africanizing film language has and is being achieved in the films themselves and has initiated a set of critical assumptions that include a counter-discourse against the 'dominant' aesthetic. If this suggests modification and revision of cinematic discourse and the cinematic canon, what theoretical and critical methodology is applicable? Can the pan-Africanist model intermingle with the European–American model to initiate a new inquiry into the means of signification? Both cinemas require

> **Is the time ripe now for an African film historiography to address the works of exiled filmmakers and situate them within the global concept of African world cinema?**

different critical or theoretical methodologies, or a blend of methodologies, for formulating discourses on their evolution.

South Africa offers another dimension to African film history and the discourse of African cinema. The cinema in South Africa which was once referred to as the cinema of apartheid is now simply known as South African cinema since the country has been admitted to the Organization of African Unity following the demise of apartheid. South Africa is a multiracial society that is unlike many other countries in Africa. Film production in this Southern hemisphere is dominated by South African whites. In the 1995 Pan-African Film and Television Festival of Ouagadougou, the question of who is a South African filmmaker or whether white South African filmmakers fit into this category arose. Although the delegation was predominantly black, it was a white South African 'queer' film that sparked a mass exodus from the theatre where the film was shown. It suggests that homosexuality has not begun to be publicly addressed in Africa as it has been in other societies, or, to put it in another way, African audiences outside South Africa may not yet be prepared for such a cultural shock.

Notable filmmakers who live outside the continent such as Med Hondo, Ngangura Nweze, Jean-Marie Teno, Safi Faye, and Haile Gerima identify their works as African. But how does African historiography position John Akomfrah, a Ghanaian-born filmmaker, or Nigeria's Ngozi Onwurah, whose works are identified with black British film practice? Also, there have been important films set in Africa that deal with African issues in serious terms which have been categorized as African films, even though their makers are diasporan blacks. A few of these filmmakers are Sarah Maldoror (*Sambizanga*, Angola and Congo, 1972), Raoul Peck (*Lumumba*, France and Germany, 1992), and Marie-Clemence Blanc-Paes (the producer of *Angango . . . Angango*). Is the time ripe now for an African film historiography to address the works of exiled filmmakers and situate them within the global concept of African world cinema?

Critical and theoretical concepts

Another perspective from which to view African cinema concerns the critical theories used in their appraisal and appreciation. Until recently, writings on African cinema were dominated by the French. With few exceptions, the approach was Eurocentric and more journalistic than academic. But with the coming of a new breed of critics, such as Françoise Pfaff, Teshome Gabriel, Mbye B. Cham, Mark A. Reid, Clyde Taylor, Keyan Tomaselli, myself and others, critical theories and academic assessment of African cinematic practices have taken new and innovative paths. These new critics have begun to blend what are perceived as dominant theories and criticisms into pan-Africanist discourses which provide new interpretations of the configurations and significations of this new aesthetic. The strategy recalls the Latin American film practices of the 1960s, when filmmakers were not only able to use film as a weapon of liberation but also generated the critical theory that was relevant to the cultural, political, and historical transformations that led to the consideration of alternative (read: indigenous) aesthetics (see Burton-Carvajal, Chapter 25).

> **African critics have tended to differ from their Western counterparts, and have argued that it is not adequate to formulate African film discourse only within the critical and theoretical frameworks of European–American contexts.**

In the late 1990s, as the field of African film studies expanded, a plethora of African film theory and criticism began to emerge. This has been beneficial to African cinema, but has also initiated debates regarding the adequacy of critical methodologies. There are two schools of thought—the one advocating the adequacy of Western critical canons, and the other arguing for a reassessment of the canon so that African cinematic discourse should not be merely appended to dominant cinematic discourse. Thus, African critics have tended to differ from their Western counterparts, and have argued that it is not adequate to formulate

African film discourse only within the critical and theoretical frameworks of European–American contexts.

Keyan Tomaselli (1993), for example, has raised concerns regarding imported theories 'grounded in deconstruction and post-Freudian Lacanian psychoanalysis'. He argues that it may be inappropriate to apply such theories, which were developed to explain Westernized subjectivities, for interpeting cultural images of Africa. Thus, Sheila Petty's (1995) analysis of Djibril Mambety's *Hyenas* (Senegal, 1992) shows how Western feminist film theory may not be appropriate in the African film discourse. Similarly, the limitations of psychoanalytically informed feminist readings of African film may also be seen in the case of Sembene's *Xala* (Senegal, 1974), where the cultural meaning of the pestle for pounding food has been interpreted as a phallic symbol and misread to fit Western feminist discourse. In *Xala*, the pestle is used as a metaphor to reinforce the impact of the collusion of African and Western cultures, which contributes to the tearing-apart of El Hadj's life. This is an important cultural motif in the film, for, irrespective of wealth or how well placed in society a person may be, African customs demand that one must respect one's mother-in-law. El Hadj contravenes this simple rule by denying the obligation to take off his Western suit, sit on the wooden chair provided for him, and pound the grain in the mortar. One can therefore understand why an African reader would be amused to see the pestle equated with phallocentrism.

In order to advance the understanding of African film, it is necessary to reformulate film theory and criticism in order to do justice to the specificity of African cinemas and the particular socio-political and cultural situations in which they occur. This does not mean, as Harrow contends, that this would entail that only 'African perspectives are appropriate in the consideration and theorizing of African film' (Harrow 1996). This approach can be seen in the special issue of the journal *Iris* on African cinema, entitled *New Discourses of African Cinema* (Ukadike 1995): the content of this volume is rich and the ways in which contributors have engaged the issues is diverse. The theoretical models employed in the studies represent critical interventions whose orientations range from Western critical paradigms and anthropological reading of film images to pan-Africanist readings of the significance of images. The essays, for example, display a concern to criticize the concepts of tradition and modernity as applied to African films (and surrounding discourses) such as Henri Duparc's *Bal poussière* (Côte d'Ivoire, 1988)

and Jean-Pierre Bekolo's *Quartier Mozart* (Cameroon, 1992). The theory and criticism of the documentary film is also seen to be expanded by such African documentaries as *Afrique je te plumerai* ('Africa, I Will Fleece You', Cameroon, 1992) and *Allah Tantou* ('God's Will', Guinea, 1991). The transposition of an alien story (a play by the Swiss writer Friedrich Dürrenmatt) into an African setting in Djibril Mambety's *Hyenas* is seen to explore the socio-political contradictions of contemporary Africa through an exploratory and hybrid style which compels viewers to re-examine their ways of seeing and reacting to African issues.

The introduction to this special issue also suggests the direction African cinematic discourse should take. It calls for an informed critical dialogue that does not need to be an African-centred discourse, as this would 'imply new forms of hegemony', and 'a retrenchment to the tyranny of a [new] canon'. The articles published therefore, eschew 'monolithic dialogue' even if they do 'signify a monolithic tendency—a tendency which argues for the broadening of investigations' (Ukadike 1995: 4), but not at the expense of the cultural, political, historical, and economic determinants of African film initiatives. The history and discussion of African cinema and of world film should go along this route. Inclusion, not exclusion, is the buzz-word for proliferation of ideas.

BIBLIOGRAPHY

Akudinobi, Jude (1995), 'Tradition/Modernity and the Discourse of African Cinema', *Iris: A Journal of Theory on Image and Sound*, N. Frank Ukadike, ed., 18: 25–37.

Bakari, Imruh, and Mbye Cham (eds.) (1996), *African Experiences of Cinema* (London: British Film Institute).

Cham, Mbye B. (1982), 'Ousmane Sembene and the Aesthetics of African Oral Traditions', *Africana Journal*, 13/1 and 4: 24–40.

—— (1995), 'Filming the African Experience', in Gaston Kaboré (ed.), *Africa and the Centenary of Cinema* (Paris: Présence africaine).

*Diawara, Manthia (1992), *African Cinema: Politics and Culture* (Bloomington: Indiana University Press).

Gabriel, Teshome (1982), *Third Cinema in the Third World: The Aesthetics of Liberation* (Ann Arbor: University of Michigan Research Press).

Harrow, Kenneth (1993), *Critical Arts*, 7/1–2, Special Issue: *African Cinema*.

—— (1996), *Research in African Literatures*, 27/3: 173–7.

*Martin, Michael T. (ed.) (1995), *Cinemas of the Black Diaspora: Diversity, Dependence and Oppositionality* (Detroit: Wayne State University Press).

Petty, Sheila (1995), 'Whose Nation is it Anyhow? The Politics of Reading African Cinema in the West' in Gaston Kaboré (ed.), *Africa and the Centenary of Cinema* (Paris: Présence africaine).

Pfaff, Françoise (1986), 'Films of Med Hondo: An African Filmmaker in Paris', *Jump Cut*, 31: 44–6.

Reid, Mark A.(1985), 'Dialogic Modes of Representing Africa's Womanist Film', *African American Review*, 25/2: 375–88.

Taylor, Clyde (1985), 'FESPACO '85 was a Dream Come True', *Black Film Review*, 1/4: 6–9.

Tomaselli, Keyan (1993), African Cinema: Theoretical Perspectives on Some Unresolved Questions', *Critical Arts: A Journal for Cultural Studies*, 7/1–2: 1–10.

*Ukadike, N. Frank (1994), *Black African Cinema* (Berkeley, University of California Press).

—— (ed.) (1995), *Iris: A Journal of Theory on Image and Sound*, 18, Special Issue: *New Discourses of African Cinema*.

Hyenas

Richard Porton from Richard Porton, 'Mambety's *Hyenas*: Between Anti-Colonialism and the Critique of Modernity', *Iris*, 18 (Spring 1995), 95–103.

Hyenas (Senegal 1992) revolves around a wealthy old woman's return to the village where, years before, whe was 'seduced and abandoned' by a man who now seems completely benign. Yet despite the film's apparent embrace of grim determinism, Djbril Diop Mambety strips Friedrich Dürrenmatt's parable of its quasi-theological veneer. The desolate town of Colobane encapsulates many of the contradictions of Senegalese society as both revolutionary hopes and traditional bonds of solidarity erode. With its faded bourgeoisie and rapacious petty bourgeoisie, Colobane serves as a microcosm reflecting Africa's current economic crisis.

Linguère Ramatou, the film's vengeful elderly woman, agitates Colobane's populace to the point of frenzy by promising a future of untold wealth. 'Ramatou is coming back to us . . . richer than the World Bank . . . only the lady can save us' is the townspeople's hopeful exhortation. The local politicians and clergy, immobolized by despair, view Ramatou's largess as the only possible solution to the never-ending cycle of poverty and exploitation. Dramaan Drameh, the amiable shopkeeper who never fails to sip calvados with his eager customers, awaits the eminent *grande dame* with more anticipation than any of the other inhabitants. Ramatou's beneficence eventually turns sour, of course, and the cataclysmic series of events that inevitably bedevil Calobane seem designed to frustrate critics and audiences who might be tempted to indulge themselves with moralistic interpretations.

The film's allegorical structure is directly mediated by the suffering imposed on African countries by 'structural adjustment', the World Bank's attempt to control the internal policies of debtor nations by coercing them to increase exports and seriously curtail social spending, thus insuring misery for the the poor. Given these constricting material realities, a misguided moralist might, for example, see the film merely as an indictment of consumerism, a tract that apparently blames the victims of structural adjustment for their yearnings to enjoy some paltry material pleasures. In the final analysis, however, the film seems more like an intermittently comic dirge than a sermon.

Despite Mambety's occasional rhetorical flourishes—the juxtaposition of a Sony sign and shots of African starvation is one of the flashier examples—the film is far removed from earlier examples of African social realism, whether exemplified by the novels and films of Ousmane Sembene or Safi Faye's synthesis of documentary and autobiography.

Hyenas's overlapping ironies and tragicomic tone shares a kinship with an earlier Mambety film, *Touki-Bouki* (1973). In that film, rather ethnocentrically stereotyped as an African *Breathless* by some critics, the rebellious protagonists hope to escape to France, but their nihilistic exaltation of violence dooms them. The lure of Parisian glamour proves a hollow fantasy, but the film does not promote an artificial recuperation of pre-colonial tradition. Similarly, *Hyenas* presents a bleak sketch of contemporary acquisitiveness, without endorsing, however hesitantly, a return to some sort of Edenic, pre-colonial bliss. In discussing various African films including *Touki-Bouki*, Roy Armes and Lizbeth Malkmus claim, in a vein of dubious essentialism, that the pre-eminent directors 'structure their films around a series of external oppositions (e.g. past/present, tradition/modernity)'. Yet the interest of Mambety's films seems to lie in their concerted attempts to explode this kind of binarism, posing these alternatives not as choices but as self-consuming artefacts.

The gruesome carnivalesque crescendo of *Hyenas* turns out to be a case in point. As the villagers satisfy their cravings for shoes from Burkina Faso and sparkling refrigerators, Ramatou imports an actual carnival to Colobane, with a dazzling Ferris wheel as the fair's centrepiece. If these diversions are meant to pacify the townspeople while Dramaan is made a scapegoat, Ramatou's plan succeeds all too well. Despite his genial manner, we are resigned to accept Dramaan as the man responsible for the millionairess's former life of privation and forced prostitution, yet Ramatou herself does not embody moral probity of any sort. Dramaan's plaintive outburst—'Madam, we hold fast to the principles of our civilization'—evokes more the pain of a self-inflicted wound than the shrillness of a rallying-cry. Unlike the unambiguously affirmative heroines of *Sambizanga (Angola, 1972)* and Med Hondo's *Sarraounia* (Mauritania, 1986), Ramatou is not an icon of empowerment. She can only offer the mere negative freedom of ruthless demystification.

In the final analysis, therefore, Mambety's thematic tapestry is geared more towards narrative polyphony than a series of sterile oppositions; as in all complex parables, the interpretive work is left to the audience. The film suggests several disparate, if complementary, points of departure: a materialist gloss, as well as a contextualization within African cinema's elaboration of the oral tradition.

In his recent comprehensive survey of African oral literature, Isidore Okpewho demonstrates how contemporary writers

Hyenas continued

....

such as Ousmane Sembene and Wole Soyinka transform and subvert traditional trickster narratives for the purpose of radical social critique. In works such as *The Road, and Kongi's Harvest, traditional solidarity with victims is transformed into barbed attacks on entrenched power. Hyenas*'s relationship to the critical legacy of oral tradition is somewhat different. Mambety's tragicomic stance contains the seeds of social critique, but is not prescriptive or programmatic in the tradition of Soyinka or Sembene. Mambety's approach is abrasively parodic. With a skilful deployment of what Mikhail Bakhtin termed 'double-voiced discourse', *Hyenas* expertly reframes motifs from both the oral tradition and more earnest, hopeful African films. The film could not be characterized as cynical, but this example of good-humoured despair is a far cry from the insurrectionary cinema of years past.

In addition, the film deviates from the simple observational style of recent Africn films such as *Yaaba* (Burkina Faso, 1987). Unlike that film's unobtrusive lyrical realism, Mambety's film employs a form of rhetoric that unashamedly calls attention to itself. Autonomous shots of hyenas herald the villagers' joyous anticipation of wealth, and stark overhead shots punctuate Dramaan's interrogation by the town's clergy. The rhetorical overlay cannot be viewed as heavy-handed, however, since it is impossible to distil a monolithic credo from the ornate, self-conscious editing style.

Hyenas's carefully modulated syncretism helps to modify—perhaps even undermine—some of the strictures laid down in studiously nationalist works such as *Toward the Decolonization of African Literature*. The Nigerian literary critics who collaborated on this lively polemic provide a derisive account of the condescension endemic to most accounts of African literature, and the 'severance' of contemporary African fiction and poetry from the roots of oral tradition. The authors reserve their choicest epithets for Wole Soyinka; the playwright and novelist who would

eventually win the Nobel Prize is condemned for his capitulation to 'Euro-modernism'. Conversely, other authors are seen as more exemplary representatives of anti-colonialist zeal, and more genuine progenitors of a new African tradition. Ousmane Sembene, for example, is praised as a 'people's *griot'*.

If European modernism and indigenous African modes were irreconcilable polarities, Mambety's cinematic parable would prove unsettling indeed. Mambety is certainly not ashamed to proclaim that 'it is a joy for me to pay tribute to Friedrich Dürrenmatt'. Yet this homage to a modernist European playwright is as politically acute as Sembene's most didactic novels and films and, in paradoxical ways, as attuned to important currents in African tradition as the stories of Amos Tutuola. It could be plausibly asserted that *Hyenas* incorporates a 'double consciousness' that is almost endemic to many African co-productions of recent vintage. While W. E. B. Du Bois's use of the term 'double consciousness' described African Americans' anguished oscillation between black identity and American selfhood, filmmakers like Mambety must delicately balance African identity with a modernist legacy that influenced an earlier generation of African intellectuals, most notably the founders of *Présence africaine* (a journal founded in Paris in 1956).

Several sequences in *Hyenas* can be viewed as sardonic (and subtly parodic) interludes which chronicle the contradictions stemming from Africa's ambivalent embrace of both modernity and literary and cinematic modernism. The fact that *Hyenas* can reject a Manichean traditionalism, while poking fun at the fatuities of modernist Europhiles (despite the fact that the film itself is an example of an idiosyncratic modernism) reveals an unusually sophisticated sensibility. Mambety's film is more a slyly subversive appropriation of Western modernism than a concession to its homogenizing lingua franca. Like the West Indian cricketers celebrated by C. L. R. James in *Beyond a Boundary*, Mambety transforms a petrified Western aesthetic into a vibrantly critical practice.

25

South American cinema

Julianne Burton-Carvajal

Introduction

The bibliography on Latin American cinema has grown exponentially from the 1940s to the present, with the most explosive increase taking place over the past decade. Between 1960 and 1972 the British film journal *Sight and Sound* published only two articles on Latin American film. The 1970s saw some 150 articles (excluding film and book reviews) on related topics published in English, and the 1980s doubled that number. Of the roughly 100 books written on Argentine cinema, to take one example, more than 25 per cent date from the 1990s.

The multiple and sometimes overlapping motives for expanding the bibliography on film in Latin America are not always scholarly. Promotion, commemoration, and the will to register personal testimony have been prevalent alongside more academic impulses. Emphases also differ according to the national-cultural, institutional, and historical contexts of the writers. A survey of the international panorama of books and monographs indicates, perhaps predictably, that commemoration, documentation, and the recuperation of submerged histories dominate the early phases of Latin American publishing (1940s to 1960), promotion and critical assessment the 1970s, scholarly investigation, and historiography the 1980s and 1990s. Critical discourses currently emerging from cultural studies,

queer theory, post-colonial, and post-national (e.g. border, exile, globalization) studies are also leading to a re-examination of consecrated texts and reconceptualizations of the critical object. This chapter, therefore, begins with a consideration of the problems involved in defining and conceptualizing South American cinema followed by an overview of South American filmmaking practices and the issues to which they give rise. These include the relationship between the film medium and processes of social change; the modes most appropriate for the representation of 'national' realities; questions of modes of production and consumption; and the role of the filmmaker in societies characterized by severe inequalities.

Mass, popular, and élite culture

Understanding the historical role and cultural impact of cinema in South or Latin or, more accurately, Indo-Ibero-Afro-America, presupposes a recognition that the film medium has intervened in this multi-ethnic, multilingual, multinational (and increasingly transnational) hemisphere, not simply as a manifestation of mass or popular or high culture but—in varying degrees and at different times—as all three of these. As the first mass art form, film was introduced in most nations and proto-nations of the region within a few years of its 'invention' in 1895, and in the intervening century the creation of—or the impulse to create—a national cinema has been viewed as one of the obligatory indices of both modernity and nationhood.

> **As the first mass art form, film was introduced in most nations and proto-nations of the region within a few years of its 'invention' in 1895, and in the intervening century the creation of—or the impulse to create—a national cinema has been viewed as one of the obligatory indices of both modernity and nationhood.**

No national cinema tradition sustained the goal of replicating Hollywood's studio-based, industrial model of film production, but in the three that came closest to this persistent if impractical aspiration—Mexico, Argentina, and Brazil, in descending order of magnitude—the film medium became the most important register of popular culture, in part through its ability selectively to hegemonize social types, costumes, customs, landscapes, and eventually speech patterns and musical traditions into composites that came to symbolize both the national and the popular. These composites took on a life of their own in the sphere of reception, eliciting reproduction in popular song, speech, dress, social habits, and self-conception. In the case of Mexican cinema more than any other, unrivalled dissemination throughout the Spanish-speaking world and Brazil helps explain why the cultural imaginary invoked was widely embraced as an expression of a shared supranational imaginary. Finally, television's successful conquest of the mass audience has helped make cinema an increasingly élite form of expression. The international success of recent films from Mexico or Brazil, Chile or Bolivia, for example, occurs in a radically altered context, since these films now circulate as part of an international art cinema that is relatively indifferent to national specificity and targets privileged rather than popular audiences.

In no country has the cinema been more central to the deliberate construction of a new, homogenizing national consciousness than in Mexico, especially during the 1930s, when the coming of sound coincided with the consolidation phase of the post-revolutionary regime. Yet Aurelio de los Reyes (1983), historian of the silent period of Mexican film production, argues that the nationalist impulse is inherent in the entire trajectory of Mexican filmmaking, marking the uses to which the fledgling medium was put in the waning years of the dictatorship of Porfirio Díaz (whose overthrow in 1910 inaugurated the Mexican Revolution). It also marks the zeal that prevailed during the subsequent decade, under Venustiano Carranza, to export on film 'the richness, beauty, civilized and useful aspects' (de los Reyes 1983: 228) of national culture to a world already woefully misled by Hollywood's distorted representations of Mexico and Mexicans.

Subsequent to the Second World War in nearly every instance of socio-political transformation towards a more inclusive conceptualization of the nation—the initiation of the Castro regime in Cuba in 1959, peasant and student mobilizations in Brazil prior to the 1964 military coup, student and worker mobilization in Mexico City prior to the Tlatelolco massacre of 1968, the Popular Unity period in Chile (1970–3) and the decade preceding it, the Sandinista regime in Nicaragua (1979–90), the Salvadorean civil war and processes of redemocratizaton in the Southern Cone nations during the 1980s, Bolivia's ethno-democratic resurgence in the mid-1990s—film has been a weapon of choice in the (re)definition of the national project and the enlistment of previously excluded or under-represented national constituencies. Two of these historical conjunctures in particular, Cuban cinema of the 1960s and 1970s and post-dictatorship Argentine cinema of the 1980s, offer exemplary instances of film as the register through which a revised national project can be both formulated and promulgated. The new social movements of the 1980s and 1990s—women's, indigenous, and environmental movements, for example—are also associated with this audiovisual imperative, though their medium of choice is most often video because of its lower costs, greater flexibility, and ease of use.

However, the failure to achieve infranational integration has also been one of the primary symptoms of the incompleteness of the process of nation-building throughout continental Latin America, where people continue to self-identify primarily on the basis of their province or region. The existence of sporadic regional filmmaking traditions should therefore be no less surprising than the attempts to subsume them into a single national tradition often centred in and subordinated to the capital. Sometimes these regional cinematic traditions are associated with individuals; in other instances, a regional production centre has focused the efforts of numerous individuals across one or more generation (e.g. Guadalajara in Mexico and Medellín and Cali in Colombia). Therefore, many Latin American nations demonstrate both 'metropolitan' and 'peripheral' traditions not only in the evolution of commercial filmmaking initiatives but also in oppositional ones.

Nation and anti-nation: the new Latin American cinema movement, artist-intellectuals, and the notion of the popular

The recent focusing of international critical attention on questions of how cinema implicates and expresses the national has made it obvious that all cinemas, even that perennially dominant construct known as Hollywood, are national cinemas. Some, however, have been more transparently—that is, hegemonically—'national' than others. In dependent countries, questions of film and nation-(hood) are incomparably fraught because 'a sense of national powerlessness generates a sisyphean struggle to conquer an elusive "authenticity" (that must be) constructed anew with every generation' (Stam *et al.* 1995: 395). Haunted by spectres of dependency and cultural colonialism, national cinemas throughout the post-colonial world have been habitually evaluated in terms of their service to national 'consolidation' and 'integration' and later 'development' and 'national liberation'. Both individual and generational creative expression have been subordinated to the larger project of vindicating a national image and/or consolidating a national cinema. In Latin America from the late 1960s to the 1980s a 'continental project', unifiying in its diversity and tied to the larger project of continental revolution, was superimposed upon the mandate to (re)assert the nation in cinematic terms.

Predictably, the nation that film culture has been (self-)mandated to (re)assert has varied according to particular national–historical–political conjunctures. *Utopia Unarmed*, Jorge Castañeda's (1993) analysis of the Latin American left before and after the Cold War, dissects the perennial commitment to nationalism on the part of the many strands of the left alliance.

According to Castañeda, in terms of its power to mobilize and elicit the ultimate sacrifices from Latin American populations, nationalism has no rival in Latin America except for the region's (now waning) devotion to the Catholic Church. The characteristically populist strain that flourished in Latin American nationalisms from the 1930s to the 1950s and occasionally beyond, a strain that reflected 'the unfulfilled Latin American dream of a painless modernity' (1993: 43), conferred upon the artist-intellectual sector the role of representational agent of the national citizenry, and mediator between the latter and the state as well as the extranational realm. During this period the Latin American nation was understood as being made up of two incompatible populations: the *comprador* élites, a foreign-identified 'anti-nation'; and the people, (re)defined as the true nation. The latter category consisted of the excluded or marginalized masses—socially, economically, racially, ethnically, and often culturally 'other'. Regarded as voiceless and socially invisible, they were perceived to require the intervention of self-appointed mediators to give them voice and visibility. For three decades this shared 'social imaginary' was constitutive of the supraregional and pan-nationalism that the New Latin American Cinema movement both catalysed and reflected.

For roughly the same thirty-year period—from the takeover of Havana by the Fidelistas on 1 January 1959 to the electoral defeat of the Nicaraguan Sandinistas in February 1990—the idea of armed revolution occupied centre-stage in the left's pageant of history while the interpretive filter was provided by dependency theory. The first autochthonous theoretical discourse to emerge from the hemisphere, dependency theory, as characterized by Castañeda, posited the colonial status of the hemisphere, the dysfunctional nature of capitalism in the region due to the impotence and/or treacherousness of the local business classes, the dearth of democratic channels, and the non-viability of any form of non-socialist development (Castañeda 1993: 71). The revolution was to be anti-imperialist, anti-capitalist, and hemispheric; hence it needed hemispherically viable cultural expressions. Film, foremost among these because its massive reception did not require literacy, needed to be dissociated from its origins, both imperialist and capitalist, by emphasizing anti-industrial, artisanal modes of production; original, autochthonous (as opposed to derivative and dependent) modes of expression; and participatory, activating modes of reception.

Motivated by social concern rather than economic ambition, seeking to make films about, for, and with 'the people', filmmakers were artist-intellectuals with an impulse to activism. Socially, and often politically as well, they were part of an alternative élite, almost invariably upper middle class. Though earnest and consequential, their efforts to realign their class affiliation were seldom unproblematic. Bolivian filmmaker Jorge Sanjinés, for example, gives an account of how he and his Grupo Ukamau learned almost too late, that hierarchically individualistic cultural perspectives anchored in inherited class and ethnic privilege, however 'natural' they may seem to those who subscribe to them, are incompatible with any aspiration to a genuinely popular, indigenous-centred cinema. High in the remote Andes, prepared to begin filming *Yawar Mallku* ('Blood of the Condor', 1969), Sanjinés and his La Paz-based crew were mystified by initial resistance from the local community that quickly evolved into open hostility. Faced with the prospect of complete failure, the filmmakers offered to submit to the judgement of the community through the time-honoured *jawaico* ritual, the casting and reading of the coca leaves, and finally secured their support.

Fernando Birri, in a manifesto from the early 1960s, called for a national, realist, and popular cinema, according to which filmmakers should not only re-examine biases inherent to their social and educational level, but also develop effective modes of expression capable of connecting to actual audiences and reception practices. A double challenge is inherent in the dual sense of the word 'popular': of the people and acclaimed by them. The career trajectories of Brazilian Nelson Pereira dos Santos, revered 'father' of Cinema Novo, and the comparatively unsung Venezuelan auteur Román Chalbaud, are exemplary in this regard.

Pereira dos Santos's career has spanned almost five decades and produced seventeen features to date. The quest for resonance with ordinary Brazilians from all walks of life, if occasionally detoured, has never been abandoned. Following the itineraries of several young peanut-vendors, *Rio 40 grams* ('Rio 100 Degrees', 1956) traces the socioeconomic panorama of Brazil's (then) capital city. His second, *Rio zona norte* ('Rio Northern Zone', 1957), enlists melodrama and popular music into new regimes of social sensitivity as it retrospectively pieces together the story of a brilliant Afro-Brazilian samba composer from Rio's most marginal sector who dies without ever getting his due. Commissioned by the British Film Institute and Chan-nel 4 telelvision to make a feature commemorating the hundredth anniversary of the film medium, Pereira dos Santos brought forth a tribute to and meditation on the popular appeal of the 'old' cinema. His *Cinema das lagrimas* ('Cinema of Tears', 1995) charts a thinly plotted pilgrimage, shared by an ageing director and a young but tragically afflicted critic, through the ecstatic excesses of dozens of Mexican melodramas and one climactic Argentine tear-jerker.

Intriguingly, one of the most successful examples of this impulse to produce a cinema that is both genuinely popular in the dual sense and also socially meaningful occurs outside the radius of the New Latin American Cinema. Venezuelan cinema began sporadically in the 1950s and only emerged as a national-cultural movement in the mid-1970s after reiterated demands for state support finally bore fruit. Of Venezuela's several dozen active feature filmmakers, Román Chalbaud is widely recognized locally as the country's foremost cinematic auteur.

Chalbaud was a pioneer first in theatre and then in television. From the late 1950s his career has alternated between these and film. From his début film, *Caín adolescente* ('Teenage Cain', 1959) to his sixteenth, *Cuchillos de fuego* ('Knives of Fire', 1990), Chalbaud's films have won a large following in Venezuela, helping to create a significant audience for national cinema where none existed before. Almost invariably set and shot in marginal areas of contemporary Caracas, Chalbaud's films enlist a panoply of popular types, invoke recognizably idiosyncratic modes of speech and ritualized belief systems, and employ an affectionate and humorous yet also ironic and mildly allegorical *costumbrismo*. Despite his characteristic social concern, Chalbaud neither embraced nor was embraced by the New Latin American Cinema movement, perhaps in large part because, unlike that cadre, his commitment to the expressive potential and popular appeal of melodrama has never wavered.

Exile, diaspora, international co-productions, and migrations of creative talent

Simple models of 'national' cinema in Latin America are complicated by transatlantic and trans-hemispheric migrations of talent, international co-productions, exile, and diasporic film production (including the rise of 'Latino' cinemas in North America). In most Latin American nations, the first practitioners of the new mode of expression were not nationals but foreigners. Incipient film production in Brazil, Argentina, Mexico, Colombia, and elsewhere enlisted numerous Europeans, primarily Italian, French, and Spanish. In the late 1940s and early 1950s Vera Cruz, São Paulo's infamous attempt to establish a Brazilian MGM, imported its technical talent from Italy and the United States in the late 1940s and early 1950s. The prevalence of co-production strategies in the 1980s and 1990s calls the very concept of national cinema into question. The aspiration to an autonomous national filmmaking tradition is complicated, therefore, not only by the founding presence of Europeans and North Americans, but also by the often sustained nature of this 'foreign' contribution. As Ann Marie Stock (1996) suggests, the concepts of 'migrancy' and border crossings counter the perceived fixedness of critical emphases on national and regional paradigms as well as the associated, and anachronistic, constructs of authenticity and inauthenticity.

> **Simple models of 'national' cinema in Latin America are complicated by transatlantic and trans-hemispheric migrations of talent, international co-productions, exile, and diasporic film production (including the rise of 'Latino' cinemas in North America).**

The results of Irene Castillo de Rodríguez's (1995) research into the Spanish contribution to the visual media in Colombia may not be atypical. Colombia's first feature film, *María* (1920), and its first talking feature, *Flores del Valle* ('Flowers of the Valley', 1940) were both directed by the Spaniard Máximo Calvo. Colombia's first film society was founded in Bogotá in 1949 by the Catalonian Luis Vicens. The country's first socially committed film movement was initiated by José María Arzuaga, a Spaniard who is credited with drawing attention to the incipient problematics of urbanization in *Raíces de piedra* ('Roots of Stone', 1961) and *Pasado meridiano* ('Post-Meridian', 1963). Sergio Cabrera, the most prominent director of the present generation (*Técnicas de duelo*, 'Details of a Duel', 1988; *La estra-*

tegia del caracol, 'The Snail's Strategem', 1993), is a first-generation Colombian of Spanish parentage.

Examples of migrations of talent *within* Ibero-America are rife if infrequently cited, and go back to the 1930s (e.g. Cuban director and producer Ramón Peón's contribution to Mexican cinema in the 1930s or Argentinian director Carlos Hugo Christensen's involvement in both Brazilian and Venezuelan filmmaking from the 1950s onwards). Dolores Del Rio and Carmen Miranda, on the other hand, are the foremost examples of Latin American actresses successfully transplanted from their respective national contexts to Hollywood, where they were (re)cast as ubiquitous pan-ethnic signifiers. Dolores Del Rio had the unique distinction of two consecutive careers. After twenty years in Hollywood she returned to Mexico, on the verge of 40, to undertake a second star trajectory as an emblem of 'authentic' Mexico during the most gilded years of Mexican cinema's 'golden age', beginning in 1943 with *Flor silvestre* and *María Candelaria*.

Co-productions are often perceived as a recent phenomenon, when in fact interhemispheric co-productions were key to maintaining the international reach of the 'old' Mexican cinema during the late 1940s and 1950s. Countless New Latin American Cinema projects depended on more or less formalized international co-production arrangements, from series sponsored by Radio-televisione italiana (RAI) in the 1970s and Televisión española (TVE) in the 1980s to personal interventions like French film-essayist Chris Marker's on behalf of Patricio Guzmán's *Grupo tercer año*. Marker provided film stock for what turned out to be the three-part documentary epic *La batalla de Chile* ('The Battle of Chile', 1975–9), which nevertheless would not have seen the light of day without extensive post-production support from the Cuban national film institute, Instituo cubano del arte y industria cinematográficos (ICAIC). Before the collapse of the Soviet Union and related internal economic pressures curtailed ICAIC's activities, a significant percentage of New Latin American Cinema output was the beneficiary of co-production with Cuba, acknowledged or unacknowledged.

The assumption that co-productions inevitably undermine and even erase national differences has been persuasively challenged by Laura Podalsky's (1994) study of pre-revolutionary Cuban filmmaking from the 1930s to the 1950s. Contrasting national productions with Cuban–Mexican and Cuban–Spanish collaborations, she demonstrates how cross-national co-productions function to mark national differences

The 'formally audacious' epic documentary *Hour of the Furnaces* (1968), a film counterpart to Solanas and Getino's manifesto *Towards a Third Cinema*

rather than occlude them. Podalsky also illustrates how intraregional, cross-national influences can be as explanatory as neo-colonial impositions.

Latin American filmmakers who have developed portions of their careers in involuntary exile include Argentines Fernando Solanas, Gerardo Vallejo, and (Spanish-born) Octavio Getino, collaborators on the epic documentary trilogy *La hora de los hornos* ('The Hour of the Furnaces', 1968) and the theorization of 'third cinema'. After the restitution of democratic rule, all subsequently returned to Argentina, where they remain active on the national film scene. Other leading Argentines whose careers were interrupted by political exile include Fernando Birri, Lautaro Murúa, Leonardo Favio, and countless other leading artists and performers.

Brazil's *enfant terrible* of the Cinema Novo, director and polemicist Glauber Rocha, sought to establish a base in numerous Latin American and European countries in the late 1960s, when the military government's repressive measures were at their height. After filming *Der leone have sept cabezas* ('The Lion has Seven Heads') and *Cabezas cortadas* ('Severed Heads', both 1970) in North Africa and Spain, the *apertura* (opening-up) of the military regime enabled him to return to Brazil and make several additional films including his last, *A idade da terra* ('The Age of Earth', 1980). The Bolivian director Jorge Sanjinés was doing post-production in Italy when a 1971 military coup made his return to his native country imprudent. He dedicated the next several years to tracing an itinerary through the Andes, making collaborative features with the Quechua and Aymara populations of Peru, Ecuador, and Colombia until conditions permitted his return to Bolivia in 1979.

The Chilean case is the most notable example of how a national cinema transcends its own borders in response to historical–political conjunctures, becoming diasporic. The foundations of Chilean film culture prior to Salvador Allende's socialist coalition regime (1970–3) were disjunctive: an ill-fated attempt at government-sponsored commercial production in Santiago under Chile Films (1938–49); a later decade of oppositional activity catalysed by Dutch documentarist Joris Ivens's 1962 visit to Valparaiso and climaxing with the 1973 *coup d'état*. Massive exodus over the subsequent decade resulted in 176 Chilean exile productions made in France, Italy, Spain, Holland, Belgium, Great Britain, Germany, Switzerland, the Soviet Union, Sweden, Finland, Romania, Canada, Cuba, Nicaragua, Mexico, Venezuela, Colombia, and the United States. If exile disperses, *desexilio* (the process of returning home and reintegrating into a national culture that has not remained frozen in time) coalesces. As Zuzana Pick has argued, both processes 'expand conceptual and aesthetic boundaries' and 'contribute to a decentering of views on identity, nationality and difference' (1993: 158).

The inverse instance, one of influx rather than scattering, is demonstrated by Mexico in the 1930s, Cuba in the early 1960s, and Nicaragua in the early 1980s. Newly inaugurated revolutionary regimes in each of these countries placed film among their foremost cultural priorities and struggled to recruit and/or accommodate an influx of international talent and assistance. Though he was never permitted to edit his footage, Sergei Eisenstein's US-financed effort to film *Que viva Mexico!* (1932), an epic of Mexican culture across regions and centuries, was pivotal to both the director's career trajectory and the country's subsequent film aesthetics. A year earlier Fred Zinneman and Paul Strand from the United States had collaborated with Mexican peers on *Redes* ('The Wave', 1931), a documentary-style feature denouncing exploitation in a Vera Cruz fishing community. The following decade, novelist John Steinbeck and director John Ford both engaged in major collaborations with the Mexican director Emilio Fernández. In the Cuban case, Italian Neo-Realist screenwriter Cesare Zavattini and cinematographer Otello Martelli, Mexican producer Manuel Barbachano Ponce, Dutch documentarist Joris Ivens, Soviet director Mikhail Kalatozov and his virtuoso cinematographer Sergei Urusevsky, French New Wave director Agnès Varda and cinéma vérité documentarist Chris Marker, as well as emerging filmmakers Ugo Ulive from Uruguay and Alejandro Saderman from Argentina, all participated in a kind of 'solidarity co-production' with uneven success. Nicaragua's INCINE (the national film insititute during the Sandinista government) has facilitated international co-productions and numerous independent productions by Cubans, Mexicans, Puerto Ricans, Bolivians, Chileans, North Americans, and others.

Finally, both long-standing territorial appropriations and ongoing population displacements have contributed to the production of independent Chicano and Latino cinemas across the United States (e.g. the films of Luis Valdez and Gregorio Nava) and, to a lesser extent, Canada. Zuzana Pick's characterization of the New Latin American Cinema movement as a 'continental project' might also be applied to such cinemas in a resignifying move calculated to underline the successful pan-ethnic, transnational breeching of borders characteristic of this body of audiovisual expression which, as product of and response to the increasing arbitrariness and ineffectiveness of geopolitical bor-

ders, is also, though not unproblematically, 'unified in its diversity'. The concept of transculturation is also helpful in this regard.

The notion of transculturation

The concept of transculturation, first articulated in 1940 by Cuban anthropologist and ethnographer Fernando Ortiz in his study *Contrapunteo cubano del tabaco y azúcar* (1940) and subsequently adapted by Uruguayan literary critic Angel Rama in his 1982 work *Transculturación narrativa en América Latina*, can be usefully applied to the long-standing debate about national cultural autonomy and the denial, dismissal, or disparagement of 'foreign' components. Ortiz proposed the term 'transculturation' as an alternative to the term 'acculturation'. He emphasized that the process of transition from one culture to another entails complex and almost inevitably reciprocal 'transmutations of culture' (1947/1995: 98) in a triple process of new cultural acquisition (acculturation), the uprooting of previous cultural characteristics (deculturation), and the creation of new cultural phenomena (neoculturation) (102–3). Ortiz's 'modest proposal' for a modification in terminology, itself an example of transculturation, is an early and still-generative instance of local theory originating in the periphery.

Rama, writing four decades later, argued that the concept of transculturation 'visibly translated a Latin American perspectivism' (1982: 33) in its explicit recognition, on the one hand, that Cuban culture in particular and Latin American culture in general are the products of permanent, ongoing transcultural dynamics and in its implicit recognition, on the other, of the dynamism and creative agency involved in achieving characteristically original re-elaborations of 'cultural norms, behaviors, beliefs and objects' (34). Rama identified a dual dynamic of transculturation around the potentially overlapping impact of an *external* and an *internal* metropolis. The 'mother country' under a colonial regime and the dominant country in a neo-colonial situation are both external metropolises which relegate the nation as a whole to peripheral status. Within each Latin American nation, however, Rama recognized how the capital often exerts an analogous impact as overly dominant centre *vis-à-vis* the doubly peripheralized 'provinces' (34).

Applying this notion of Latin American cultural production as 'transculturative' to the evolution of cinema in Latin America offers a way of breaking out of national versus foreign, autonomous versus imposed, authentic versus inauthentic dichotomies and their impossible either/or mandate. It suggests how visitor and visited are mutually transformed by their encounter and how exile both reinforces and reinflects national identity. This view of cultural, and film, expression as the transformed and transforming product of ongoing—and to some extent selective and self-renovating—processes of transculturation also appropriately relativizes the perceived novelty of the nowadays much-touted globalization process, which, despite the current intensification of its pace and impact, must be seen as historically rooted in processes that pre-date even the European conquest of the New World.

> **Applying this notion of Latin American cultural production as 'transculturative' to the evolution of cinema in Latin America offers a way of breaking out of national versus foreign, autonomous versus imposed, authentic versus inauthentic dichotomies and their impossible either/or mandate.**

Film historiography and production: industries and artisans

Historiographical debates and dilemmas have been central to the formation of the discourses—political–ideological, critical, theoretical, methodological—that circulate in and around the cinematic traditions and practices of the Ibero-American region. These dilemmas have been exacerbated by the fact of dependency in that these histories are always written against other, dominant histories and inflected by political partisanship and ideological inclinations.

Four phases of Ibero-American film history may be identified: the silent period, the consolidation of national cinemas after the introduction of sound, the development of counter-cinemas—most strongly manifest in the 1960s and 1970s but continuing into the 1980s and beyond—and the uneven realignment of commercial and committed cinemas in the face of television and video that characterizes the 1980s and 1990s. Within these later periods two 'moments' stand out. The years 1968–9 saw the release of an inordinate number of landmark political films, all of which challenged both their socio-political context and the film medium itself in radical ways: *Yawar Mallku*, *Terra em transe* ('Land in Anguish', Brazil, Glauber Rocha), *El Chacal de Nahueltoro* ('The Jackal of Nahueltoro', Chile, Miguel Littín), *Memorias del subdesarrollo* ('Memories of Underdevelopment', Cuba, Tomás Gutiérrez Alea), *Lucía* (Cuba, Humberto Solás), and *La hora de los hornos*. A decade and a half later, the years 1984–5 can also be retrospectively seen as a watershed in terms of works that broke new thematic ground and signalled new formal directions. These included three from Argentina: María Luisa Bemberg's *Camila*, Fernando Solanas's *Tangos: el exilio de Gardel* ('Tangos: The Exile of Gardel'), and Luis Puenzós *La historia oficial* ('The Official Version'); three from Brazil: Nelson Pereira dos Santos's *Memorias do carcere* ('Prison Memoirs'), Tizuka Yamasaki's *Patriamada* ('Beloved Country'), Eduardo Coutinho's *Cabra marcado pra morer: vinte anos depois* ('Man Marked to Die: Twenty Years Later'); as well as Jorge Ali Triana's *Tiempo de morir* ('Time to Die', Colombia), Paul Leduc's *Frida: naturaleza viva* (Mexico), and Fina Torres's *Oriana* (Venezuela).

Like other historical subdivisions, these are, of course, heuristic conveniences and remain subject to modification. Of the four, the two intermediate periods—commercially focused cinemas of national consolidation, and subnational–supranational oppositional movements—have been the object of more sustained and systematic historical and critical inquiry than either the silent era or the contemporary 'post-national' moment (Newman 1993).

Each (post-)national tradition also elicits individualized periodization as well. In 1982 Randal Johnson and Robert Stam divided Brazilian Cinema Nôvo into a preparatory phase (1954–60); an initial phase lasting until the military coup (1960–4); a third phase (1964–8), when the 'coup-within-the-coup' severely restricted expressive freedom; and a final tropicalist–allegorical phase (1968–72), after which, they argued, Cinema Nôvo as a movement fragmented into the multiple practices of Brazilian cinema. Paulo Antonio Paranaguá (1993) divided Mexican film history into seven periods. Ana Lopez (1996) identified three generations of exiled Cuban filmmakers. As heuristic conveniences, these and all other historical subdivisions remain subject to future modification.

Throughout these histories, Latin American cinema practices have oscillated between industrial aspirations and artisanal necessities. A significant number of recently rediscovered female film pioneers from the 1920s to the 1940s—Brazil's Carmen Santos and Gilda de Abreu, Mexico's Mimi Derba, Adela Sequeyro, and Matilde Landeta—were involved in attempts to found production companies. Like those of most their male counterparts, their efforts turned out to be ephemeral, their mode of production more artisanal than industrial. Even a country as tiny as Uruguay aspired (futilely) to a national film industry as early as the late 1930s. Chile, which saw its high point of film production in 1925 with fifteen features, made a concerted attempt in the 1940s under Chile Films to produce films for a domestic and export audience, importing talent from elsewhere in the hemisphere. Venezuela's Bolívar Films, founded in 1940, employed a similar trans-hemispheric strategy in the production of eight features between 1949 and the mid-1950s. In the 1960s the appropriateness of the industrial model began to be questioned at the same time that critics began to emphasize the personal stamp of individualized directional expression over formulaic genre pictures with a characteristic studio stamp.

Mexico's major studies were founded over three decades: Chapultepec (later Nacional productora) in 1922, Clasa in 1935, Azteca in 1937, Churubusco in 1944, Tepeyac in 1946, San Angel Inn in 1949. If the fifty features produced in 1938 marked the attainment of industrial stature, the drop to twenty-nine two years later signalled the precariousness of an enterprise that would persistently oscillate between boom and crisis. Major Mexican studios began to be broken up in the 1980s with sell-outs to foreign production companies and reconversion to other uses.

Neither Brazil nor Argentina, Mexico's only potential competitors in the hemisphere, saw sustained studio-based production on the Mexican scale, though at its short-lived high point in 1942, when fifty-six features were produced, Argentina employed 4,000 technicians in thirty studios. Filmmaking, along with other forms of cultural expression, was later chronically curtailed by censorship; despite the notable resurgence of national film production with the return to democratic government in 1983, the massive closing of theatres and decline in audiences has meant that even the most long-lived of the Argentine studios, Argentina Sono Films and Aries, have now disappeared or been reoriented towards distribution or the production of *telenovelas* (televised soap operas).

In Brazil, Rio de Janeiro's Atlântida studios saw their heyday in the 1940s and 1950s with the production of hundreds of carnival-linked *chanchadas*, an autochthonous parodic genre, usually musical, that was as adored by audiences as it was reviled by critics. The last and most spectacular attempt at industrialization on the Hollywood model took place in Brazil in the late 1940s. On the strength of his association with the French avant-garde and British documentary movements, Brazilian-born Alberto Cavalcanti was invited to take the helm of the state-of-the-art Vera Cruz film studio, an ambitious post-Second World War 'import subsitution' venture by São Paulo's powerful Matarazzo investment group. The financial failure of this controversial initiative, which produced eighteen features between 1949 and 1954, generated much rancour and recrimination. According to Maria Rita Galvão, a specialist in the history of São Paulo-based film production, 'Vera Cruz was historically the most complete realization Brazil has known of the film industry myth . . . It implanted a mode of production that, despite its total inappropriateness to the conditions of the national film market, tended to impose itself as a standard to be followed' (Johnson and Stam 1982/1995: 271).

Politicizing *la politique des auteurs*

Reacting against formulaic studio production, a generation formed by the film societies and film study circles that proliferated in many Latin American cities after the Second World War attempted to carve out a space for personalized expression in independent productions. The phenomenon was first registered in Argentina with the generation of the 1960s. Because few of these young Turks succeeded in finding production support for subsequent features in a deteriorating political climate, this generation failed to coalesce into a movement. Its legacy endures in films like Lautaro Murúa's *Alias Gardelito*, David José Kohon's *Tres veces Ana* ('Three Times Ana'), both from 1961, and Rodolfo Kuhn's *Pajarito Gómez* and Leonardo Favio's *Crónica de un niño solo* ('Chronicle of a Boy Alone'), both released in 1965.

Similar conditions existed in Brazil in the late 1950s and early 1960s, but there sporadic and geographically distant attempts to produce another kind of

A 'landmark of political filmmaking'—*Blood of the Condor* (1969), a film that 'touched a national nerve'

cinema did successfully coalesce into the paradigmatic new cinema movement, Cinema Nôvo, characterized by new modes and philosophies of production and a new aesthetics. Various models, selectively appropriated—such as Italian Neo-Realism, the French New Wave, and assorted trends in international documentary—were conjugated into a self-consciously contestatory national imaginary: whether urban or rural, Brazil was best seen from below. The industrial model was now abandoned by choice rather than default.

Invoking the antithesis of the industrial model, Glauber Rocha turned a phrase attributed to Jean-Luc Godard, 'a camera in your hand and an idea in your head,' into a slogan. Endorsing the prevalent trend towards nationalization of the country's natural resources, and echoing the nationalist-developmentalist rhetoric of the period, Rocha (1963) argued that 'Brazilian art forms had to nationalize their modes of expression'. Rocha's invocation of an aesthetics of hunger, and of the violence that hunger engenders (1965b), was translated into signification practices based on scarcity, as anticipated in films like Linduarte Noronha's documentary *Aruanda* (1959) and quintessentially embodied in others like Nelson Pereira dos Santos's feature *Vidas secas* ('Barren Lives', 1963). Yet for all its creative energy, contentious cohesion, and international recognition, Cinema Nôvo, which inspired oppositional film movements throughout Latin America, never succeeded in sustaining the popular response its advocates and practitioners sought because the transformations it cultivated remained incomplete.

Transforming modes of production and consumption

Oppositional Latin American cinema took as its point of departure not only the introduction of new content or the transformation of cinematic forms, but the transformation of the conditions of film production and viewing. Where dominant cinema prioritized exchange value (profit), oppositional filmmakers emphasized use values (social benefits). Where industrializing modes of production turned filmmakers into virtual 'piece-workers' or managers, alternative procedures sought reintegrative participation at all levels of the creative process. Where dominant practices required large amounts of capital and a complex infrastructure with expensive equipment, studio sets, professional actors, polished screenplays, fixed shooting-schedules, and a large crew, oppositional filmmakers opted for simplified, artisanal modes of production using location shooting, non-professional actors or a mix of professionals and non-professionals, improvised scripts, and a less technologically mediated style of filming. These efforts were financed by a variety of means: personal loans, local co-operatives, international co-productions, partial state subsidy, and, in Cuba and Nicaragua, complete state subsidy.

Where the structures and conventions of traditional filmmaking required passive, socially fragmented audiences who did their viewing in the ritualized space of the conventional movie theatre, oppositional filmmakers sought to transform diffusion and reception practices in order to encourage broader audience participation, response, and feedback. Distribution strategies included bringing films to often remote targeted audiences through self-distribution, organized mobile cinema projects, and sustained parallel circuits utilizing community spaces. Reception strategies included organized discussions and debates, the enlistment of indigenous narrators to reprise film content, and stylistic modifications in the films themselves in order to catalyse audience intervention. Cuba's popular prime-time television programme *24 × segune* ('Twenty-Four Frames a Second'), hosted by filmmaker and humorist Enrique Colina, exemplified the commitment to a broadly disseminated, demystificatory film literacy. These transformations in modes of production and consumption reached their apogee in Argentina during the late 1960s and early 1970s with the semi-clandestine production and completely clandestine exhibition of the formally audacious epic documentary *La hora de los hornos* and the Cine de la base group's ambitious clandestine feature *Los traidores* ('The Traitors', Raymundo Gleyzer, 1973).

Practical theories: third and other imperfect cinemas

Through manifestos, founding documents, film festival proclamations, occasional essays, and eventual books, a series of practical theories began to circulate centred on naming oppositional filmmaking practices. First among these was Argentina's Fernando Solanas and Octavio Getino's Third (or guerrilla) Cinema as an alternative to 'First' (industrial) and 'Second' (auteurist) Cinema (1969a). The following year, Cuban Julio García Espinosa called for a rejection of technically perfect cinema modelled on Hollywood in favour of a deliberately imperfect, process-oriented cinema that exposes

and questions genre conventions even as it utilizes them to forge a pleasurable link with audiences. Bolivian Jorge Sanjinés's concept of *une cine junto al pueblo* (a cinema close to the people, 1979), a cinema close to the people, shuns individual close-ups and strives to re-create historical events in long takes with the collaboration of the historical actors, using a dramaturgy compatible with indigenous narrato-logical traditions. Of these, Third Cinema was the concept that enjoyed the widest circulation beyond Latin America, having been promoted, for example, by Zuzana Pick in Canada, Guy Hennebelle in France, Teshome Gabriel in the United States, and Paul Willemen in Great Britain, while within Latin America (the equally imprecise) concept of imperfect cinema generated the most resounding echo.

> **The theoretical propositions contained in all these manifestos derive from the concrete practice of attempting to make specific films under specific historical conditions. This is the source of both their strengths and their weaknesses: because these praxis-based theories were eminently conjunctural, bound by history and geography, they proved resistant to transplantation.**

Solanas and Getino's 'Towards a Third Cinema' was the most widely circulated of a set of theoretical statements formulated by the pair between 1969 and 1971, though not published until 1973. In 1979, from his Peruvian exile, Octavio Getino published a reappraisal of Third Cinema 'ten years later' (Getino 1982). Stressing the particular national-historical circumstances and concrete cinematic practice that generated the theoretical reflections, as well as the ambivalent social location of its authors as middle-class intellectuals, Getino regretted the group's rhetorical stridency and their animosity towards other militant film groups working in Argentina at the same time, and expressed scepticism regarding the reported diffusion of the Third Cinema concept in Europe, Africa, and North America. The theoretical propositions contained in all these manifestos derive from the concrete practice of attempting to make specific films under specific historical conditions. This is the source of both their strengths and their weaknesses: because these praxis-based theories were eminently conjunctural, bound by history and geography, they proved resistant to transplantation.

With the proliferation of film practices apparent since the 1980s, the advent of new generations less oriented to ideology, the end of filmmaking conceived as collective crusade, and the recogntiion that marginal and mainstream, dominant and oppositional film cultures are inextricably interrelated, the impetus to manifestos has declined. In a kind of counter-manifesto delivered at the 1989 Havana festival, Mexican director Paul Leduc called for a 'cinema of the salamanders' as the only viable successor to the two-principal models of world filmmaking, Hollywood and European (auteur) cinema, both of which have now gone the way of the dinosaurs. This 'salamander cinema' would be characterized by organized collective action on the one hand and the embracing of the new technologies on the other.

Genre, gender, history, documentary, realism, and the rest

Comedy, epic, and melodrama are the three major generic categories of Latin American fictional filmmaking, with the disposition to melodrama powerful enough to subtend the other two. Particular subgenres, often hybridized, began to characterize the major national cinemas of Latin America with the coming of sound and the incorporation of incipiently national musical traditions whose primary outlet for massive diffusion until that time had been radio. These autochthonous subgenres include Argentine tango melodramas, Brazilian *chanchadas* with carnival-inspired plots and celebration of samba, and Mexican cabaret melodramas (*cabareteras*) with their imported Caribbean dance rhythms and signature boleros. The most popular Latin American film of all time—*Allá en el Rancho Grande* ('Over at the Big Ranch', Mexico, Fernando de Fuentes, 1936, remade 1948) inaugurated a national genre, the *comedia ranchera*, a regionally idiosyncratic version of the American western. Epics inspired by history and folk-heroes—the Mexican revolutionary, the Brazilian *cangaçeiro* (backlands rebel), the Argentine gaucho—configured characteristic

national subgenres equally indebted to the Hollywood western.

Another characteristic Latin American subgenre, the street chronicle depicting the lives of indigent children, has its most famous exponent in Luis Bruñuel's *Los olvidados* ('The Young and the Damned', Mexico, 1950). A Venezuelan prototype, *Juan de la calle* ('Juan of the Streets'), directed by Rafael Rivero, appeared nearly a decade earlier, in 1941. Two pioneering Mexican women directors worked in this subgenre in its incipient stages: Adela Sequeyro in *Diablillos del arrabal* ('Little Slum Devils', 1938) and Matilde Landeta in her award-winning screenplay 'Tribunal de menores' ('Juvenile Court'), written in the late 1940s and filmed as *El camino de la vida* under the direction of Alfonso Corona Blake in 1956.

With the rise in the 1960s of alternative filmmaking practices centred around auteurism and more artisanal modes of production, the importance of genre tended to diminish as melodramatic forms were rejected on the grounds of their alleged imperial contamination and escapist (apolitical, ahistorical) orientation. While some new cinema products reworked national generic traditions (Glauber Rocha's *Deus e o diabo na terra do sol*, 'Black God, White Devil', 1963, and *Antonio das Mortes*, 1969, invoked the *cangaçeiro* genre, for example), most directors chose to work 'outside' genre by enlisting history as a documentary presence both stylistically and narratologically.

History and melodrama are two pillars of Latin America cinema that most practitioners and promoters of New Latin American Cinema believed to be at odds with one another and throughout the 1960s and 1970s most of these filmmakers shunned melodrama in order to privilege the historical. Much of the stylistic innovation characteristic of this period was a product of filmmakers' aggressive undermining of conventional dichotomies between documentary and fictional modes of representation, favouring the former in order to insert history into the imaginary construct that is cinema.

This is the case, for example, with three of the best-known Cuban films. Tomás Cutiérrez Alea's *Memorias del subdesarrollo* is a fictional collage composed of fragments in every conceivable documentary register. Sara Gómez's *De cierta manera* ('One Way or Another', 1974, 1979) disrupts its cross-class, interracial love story with pseudo-sociological discourses and reconstructed biographies of social actors. Humberto Solás's *Lucía* puts the experience of women from three key periods at the centre of the epic of Cuban history, using stylistic and subgeneric markers to 'document' the dominant modes of perception characteristic of each era.

Deliberately counter- and anti-epic modes of (re)writing history in cinema are exemplified by Jorge Sanjinés's *El coraje del pueblo* ('The Courage of the People', 1971), Leon Hirszman's *São Bernardo* (Brazil, 1972), Paul Leduc's *Frida: Naturaleza viva* (Mexico, 1984), María Luisa Bemberg's *Miss Mary* (Argentina, 1986) and *Yo, la peor de todas* ('I, the Worst Woman of All', 1990). Significantly, feminine experience lies at the narrative core of each of these films and seems inseparable from the stylistic choices that contribute to their appeal. A gendered reckoning with history, and a reconceptualization of history capable of reckoning with gender, reinvigorated cinematic expression in Latin America from the 1970s not only in the films directed by women that began to appear for the first time in significant numbers, but also in the approaches of their male counterparts. (Cuban director Humberto Solás and Brazilian director Leon Hirszman were among the pioneers of gender-sensitive representation with *Lucía* and *São Bernardo*).

During the 1980s the break-up of the Soviet Union and proliferation of neo-liberal economic policies coincided in Latin America with political redemocratization processes and the disintegration of the utopian vision of revolutionary socialism. A return to the melodramatic mode on the part of Latin American filmmakers (many of them women) coincided with a critical-theoretical reassessment of melodrama, particularly among Euro-American scholars. In films like *Camila* (María Luisa Bemberg, 1984) and *The Official Story* (Luis Puenzó, 1985), both products of post-dictatorship Argentina, melodrama and history are no longer at odds. Political (in)justice is the secular substitute for the absent sacred which, in Peter Brooks's (1991) theorization, is the generative impetus of melodrama. The Brazilian film *Patriamada* (Tizuka Yamasaki, 1984) also recuperates melodrama in order to exceed and subjectivize the documentary-based representations that were the dominant markers of Brazil's analogous moment of political transition.

A suspicion of illusionism characterized the era of heroic militancy. Alfredo Guevara, head of Cuba's ICAIC, described the goal of the Cuban film project as 'demystification of cinema for the entire population', the deliberate dismantling of 'all the mechanisms of cinematic hypnosis' (in Rosen 1972: 53). The empha-

sis on asserting the presence of history through the multiple modalities of documentary has been one of the many ways that realist discourses have dominated the Latin American feature film scene. Documentary realism, social realism, critical realism are multiple ways of naming this insistence on reality as made up of external, observable phenomena. The diversifying of the filmmaking ranks that began in the 1970s with the incorporation of female talent on a significant scale and the widespread questioning of political ideologies during the following decade have led to a heightened valuation of subjectivity, fantasy, and emotion, to what B. Ruby Rich has described as a shift from exteriority to interiority (1993: 12).

Magical realism, so prone to hackneyed appropriation, is hardly a credible counterweight to the predominant realist bias. The narrative and stylistic exuberance and rich allegorical layering of Brazilian Tropicalismo, a form of allegorized expressionism generated during the darkest period of the dictatorship in films like Glauber Rocha's *Terra en transe* and Joaquim Pedro de Andrade's *Macunaíma* (1969), is a more viable example of an efficacious counter-modality, as is the oneric subversiveness of Ana Carolina Teixeira Soares's *Das tripas coração* ('Bending over Backwards', 1980). In *Julio comienza en julio* ('Julio Begins in July', Chile, 1978), the first and only feature film released under the seventeen-year Pinochet dictatorship, offers another deconstructive variation. Simultaneously enlisting and undermining realism, director Silvio Caiozzi created cognitive dissonance by combining sepia photography, enlisting and exceeding realism in stylistic terms, and an early twentieth-century mise-en-scène with a hypermodern shooting and editing style.

It must be stressed that documentarists also questioned received wisdom regarding mechanisms of perception, cognition, and socio-political transformation early and often, beginning with the parodic statistics of the opening voice-over of Fernando Birri's foundational social documentary *Tire dié* ('Toss me a Dime', 1958, 1960). In *Hombres de Mal Tiempo* ('Men of Mal Tiempo', Cuba, 1968) Argentine Alejandro Saderman used solarization, negative reversal, slow motion, and other experimental techniques to externalize the subjective 'fiesta of memory' evoked by the reunion of five centenarian veterans of Cuba's war for independence. Numerous documentaries of the Chilean diaspora also use highly subjectivized modes, such as *Por debajo de la mesa* ('Under the Table', Luis Osvaldo García and

Tony Venturi, Canada, 1983), which uses the visual metaphor of a hearing-aid to evoke one illegal immigrant's sense of non-personhood through assumed deafness.

Old and new media in the era of globalization

Examining audiovisual production in terms of the parameters and practices of critical discourse since the transition from dictatorship to democracy in Chile, Gastón Lillo has identified a series of *nudos tensionales* (tensional knots) characteristic of the discourse of the contemporary period: concepts of history, the subject, and identity (national, social, sexual), notions of the people, the national, and the popular (and the national-popular), and the opposition between tradition and modernity (Lillo 1995: 32). As this century dominated by cinema draws to a close, questions regarding the fate of national cinemas in a post-national era and the film medium's prospects for survival in an electronic, globalizing age comes to the fore.

Since its inception, and particularly since the Second World War, the film medium in Latin America has been central to the definition of national and pan-regional identity, to its redefinition in times of crisis, and to the enlistment of generalized support for the national (or transnational) project. As the key components of a mass visual culture, film and television structured the imaginary of modernizing developmentalism and socialized citizens of traditional societies by showing them how to act 'modern' as they migrated to the swelling cities. The mass media (radio, film, and television) were agents and promoters of technological innovation: by socializing consumers into consuming what was expected of them, they helped unify patterns of consumption and behaviour. Today national projects, if they exist at all, must compete with the post-national and transnational realities to which the electronic media, thanks to neo-liberal economics and other globalizing forces, are currently socializing their citizenry.

As film production and consumption have declined by as much as 90 per cent in the principal countries (due to rising production costs, lack of infrastructural reinvestment, massive theatre closings, and changing patterns of cultural consumption), cultural access in the private domestic sphere (via television, video, cable, laser, satellite) has increased proportionately. Collective use of public space and basic forms of sociability and civility have declined as a result, while national identities are being reconfigured transnationally because—despite the increasingly global reach of regional television networks like Brazil's TV Globo and Mexico's Televisa—the forms of culture being consumed derive increasingly from a single extra-national source, the United States. US products dominate Latin American home video and cable markets, where space for national and hemispheric products has been minuscule or non-existent.

Geo-economic realignments since the late 1980s have transformed modes of cinematic consumption to a degree unimaginable only a decade earlier. Ever more costly to produce, a film now has to recover its investment in several media markets, since the theatrical return is no longer sufficient. This is more difficult to achieve in dependent countries given market saturation by US products and limited access to the new technologies.

Reversing the 1970s trend to increased state participation in audiovisual cultural production, the current trend to privatization and transnationalization of film, television, video, and other techno-cultures aggravates communicational dependency. The vacuum created by the dearth of national policies regarding cultural production and new technologies risks allowing the default privatization and mercantilization of everything from scientific research and artistic innovation to the symbolic construction of national history. The increasing de-territorialization of the audiovisual media is minimally counterbalanced by reterritorialization: regional radio and television stations, musical micro-markets, grass-roots video movements, specialized cable broadcasters, the perhaps quixotic efforts of two prominent *cinematecas* at opposite ends of the hemisphere (Caracas and Montevideo) to operate a major commercial theatre dedicated exclusively to screening films from Latin America.

> **Today national projects, if they exist at all, must compete with the post-national and transnational realities to which the electronic media, thanks to neo-liberal economics and other globalizing forces, are currently socializing their citizenry.**

In countries throughout Latin America, filmmakers have united for decades to lobby for national film legislation, meaning that in numerous Latin American countries this is the only cultural sphere with a precedent in policy formation. The European Union's practice of consolidating film, television, and video under the unifying designation 'audiovisual space' correlates with both the increasing technological and aesthetic integration of the three media and their practical integration in the public's habits of consumption. Film's fate is globally tied to television, video, and satellite, and in order to survive and prosper, filmmakers must cast in their lot with their counterparts working in television, video, computer imaging, and other new technologies, guiding the evolution of state policy in the realm of culture and communications and encouraging co-production with television.

What are the implications of the hybridizations that transnationality and globalization produce? How will ethnic, regional, national, and hemispheric identities reconstitute themselves in response to contemporary processes of transcultural hybridization, and what will be the role of the film medium in that process? In '¿Habrá cine latinoamericano en el año 2000?' ('Will there be Latin American Cinema in the Year 2000?') Néstor García Canclini proposes a concept of identity that is 'not simply sociospatial but sociocommunicational' in its simultaneous articulation of local, national, and post-national referents. He sees multi-media and multicontextuality as the two key notions for redefining the social role of film and other communications systems: film will only survive as part of a complex of visual media; constructs of identity will and must evolve as part of an ongoing 'co-production' process (1993: 33).

As the century draws to a close and the silver screen is everywhere upstaged by the computer screen, there is a marked over-production of filmmakers in Latin America. Where no film schools existed until the late 1950s, over thirty have been founded during the past three decades. On the other hand, Latin America boasts 300 million potential image consumers. The voracious expansion of televisual markets and broadcast slots promises to keep the cinema of the past in circulation as well as offering contemporary production a potential outlet that has barely begun to be tapped.

Peruvian novelist and erstwhile politician Mario Vargas Llosa once declared bitterly that the real revolution in Latin America would be the end of revolution. Movies and revolutions have been characteristic if not essential spectacles in the hemisphere since the turn of the century. If the Mexican Revolution, the first such popular uprising, inaugurated the century with a prolonged conflict that produced a vast cinevisual archive, the outbreak of the Zapatista rebellion as the century draws to its close poses both a fitting symmetry and a radical difference. The Cuban Revolution in the 1960s, the Chilean struggle for electoral socialism in the 1970s, the reinauguration of democracy in Brazil and Argentina in the 1980s all privileged cinema, as did the Central American revolutionary movements of the past two decades. As recently as the 1980s Salvador's Sistema Radio Venceremos Film and Television Collective prioritized radio, film, and video as the key communications media. In their cinematic production, they utilized an eclectic synthesis of media (16mm, Super-8, video, black and white interspersed with colour), creating a characteristic 'look' that was both the result of accommodation to practical limitations and an original expressive synthesis. In marked contrast, a decade later the Zapatistas of remote Chiapas went directly to the Internet. Immediacy, portability, minimal cost, and massive global dissemination made this option irresistible. 'Reverting' to the primacy of the written word, and opting to let others gather and disseminate moving images of their movement in whatever formats they choose, the Zapatistas look simultaneously backward and forward in time from their uniquely pre-/postmodern vantage-point.

As the next century unfolds, creators of Latin American audiovisual media could do worse than follow the example of the media-savvy Zapatistas in their selective recombination of traditional and hypermodern elements. The world-wide trend towards ever greater concentration of media technologies and information systems and their subordination to exclusively market forces coexists with its antithesis: the increasing democratization inherent in those same new technologies, along with their actual and potential adaptability to heterogeneous non-commercial uses.

BIBLIOGRAPHY

*Barnard, Timothy,** and **Peter Rist** (eds.) (1996), *South American Cinema: A Critical Filmography 1915–1994* (New York: Garland).

Birri, Fernando, interviewed by Julianne Burton, 'The Roots of Documentary Realism', in Burton (1986).

Brooks, Peter (1991), 'The Melodramatic Imagination', in Marcia Landy (ed.), *Imitations of Life: A Reader in Film* *and Television Melodrama* (Detroit: Wayne State University Press).

*Burton, Julianne (1986), *Cinema and Social Change in Latin America: Conversations with Filmmakers* (Austin: University of Texas Press).

—— (1990), *The Social Documentary in Latin America* (Pittsburgh: University of Pennsylvania Press).

Castañada, Jorge (1993), *Utopia Unarmed: The Latin American Left after the Cold War* (New York: Knopf).

Castillo de Rodríguez, Irene (1995), 'Cien años de presencia de Espaã en el cine colombiano', *Españo en Colombia. Revista de la Embajada de España*, 3 (May), 52–3.

Chanan, Michael (1985), *The Cuban Image* (London: British Film Institute).

Colina, Enrique, and **Daniel Díaz** (1971), 'Ideología del melodrama en el viejo cine latinoamericano', *Cine cubano*, 73–5: 14–26.

de los Reyes, Aurelio (1983), *Cine y sociedad en México 1896–1930,* i: *Vivir de sueños 1896–1920* (Mexico City: Universidad nacional autónoma).

Galvão, Maria Rita (1995), 'Vera Cruz: A Brazilian Hollywood', in Johnson and Stam (1982/1995).

García Canclini, Néstor (1993/1997), '¿Habrá cine latinoamericano en el año 2000?', *Jornada Semanal*, 193 (17 Feb.), 27–33; trans. as 'Will there be a Latin American Cinema in the Year 2000?', in Ann Marie Stock (ed.), *Framing Latin American Cinema: Contemporary Critical Directions* (Minneapolis: University of Minnesota Press).

García Espinosa, Julio (1970/1983), 'Por un cine imperfecto', trans. as 'Towards an Imperfect Cinema'; Julianne Burton in Michael Chanan (ed.), *Twenty-Five Years of the New Latin American Cinema* (London: British Film Institute and Channel 4).

—— (1985), 'Meditations on Imperfect Cinema . . . Fifteen Years Later', *Screen*, 26/3–4: 93–5.

—— (1995), 'Por un cine imperfecto: Veinte años después', in *La doble moral del cine* (Bogotá: Editorial Voluntad).

Getino, Octavio (1982), *A diez años del 'Hacia un tercer cine'* (Mexico: Filmoteca UNAM).

Johnson, Randal (1991), 'The Rise and Fall of Brazilian Cinema 1960–1990', *Iris*, 13 (Summer), Special Issue: *Latin American Cinema*, ed. Kathleen Newman, 97–124; repr. Johnson and Stam (1982/1995).

*—— and **Robert Stam** (eds.) (1982/1995), *Brazilian Cinema* (New Brunswick, NJ: Associated University Presses; expanded edn. New York: Columbia University Press).

*King, John (1990), *Magical Reels: A History of Cinema in Latin America* (London: Verso).

Leduc, Paul (1989), 'Dinosaurs and Lizards', in Pat Aufderheide (ed.), *Latin American Visions* (Philadelphia: International House).

Lillo, Gastón (1995), 'El cine y el contexto político-cultural en el Chile de la posdictadura', *Revista canadiense de estudios hispánicos*, 10/1, Special Issue: *Mundos contemporáneos en el cine español e hispanoamericano*, ed. Robert Young, 31–42.

Lopez, Ana M. (1996), 'Memorias of a Home: Mapping the Revolution (and the Making of Exiles?).' *Revista canadiense de estudios hispánicos*, 10/1, Special Issue: *Mundos contemporáneos en el cine español e hispanoamericano*, ed. Robert Young, 5–17.

Newman, Kathleen (1993), 'National Cinema after Globalization: Fernando Solanas's *Sur* and the Exiled Nation', in John King, Ana Lopez, and Manuel Alvarado (eds), *Mediating Two Worlds: Cinematic Encounters in the Americas* (London: British Film Institute).

Noriega, Chon, and **Ana Lopez** (eds.) (1996), *The Ethnic Eye. Latino Media Arts* (Minneapolis: University of Minnesota Press).

—— and **Steven Ricci** (eds.) (1994), *The Mexican Cinema Project* (Los Angeles: UCLA Film and Television Archive).

O'Grady, Gerald (ed.) (1994), *Nelson Pereira dos Santos: Cinema Novo's 'Spirit of Light'* (New York: Film Society of Lincoln Center and Harvard University).

Ortiz, Fernando (1940/1995), 'On the Social Phenomenon of Transculturation and its Importance in Cuba', in *Contrapunteo urbano del tabaco y azúcar*, trans. Harriet de Onís as *Cuban Counterpoint: Tobacco and Sugar* (New York: Random House and Vintage).

Paranaguá, Paulo Antonio (1988), 'News from Havana: A Restructuring of the Cuban Cinema', *Framework*, 35: 80–103.

*Pick, Zuzana (1993), *The New Latin American Cinema: A Continental Project* (Austin: University of Texas Press).

Podalsky, Laura (1994), 'Negotiating Differences: National Cinemas and Co-Productions in Prerevolutionary Cuba', *Velvet Light Trap*, 34 (Fall), 59–70.

Rama, Angel (1982), *Transculturación narrativa en América Latina* (Mexico City: Siglo XXI).

Ramirez Berg, Charles (1992), *Cinema of Solitude: A Critical Study of Mexican Film 1967–1983* (Austin: University of Texas Press).

Rich, B. Ruby (1991), 'An/Other View of the New Latin American Cinema', *Iris*, 13 (Summer), Special Issue: *Latin American Cinema*, ed. Kathleen Newman, 5–28.

Rocha, Glauber (1963/1965a), *Revisão crítica do cinema brasileiro* (Rio de Janeiro: Editora civilização brasileira); trans. into Spanish as *Revisión crítica del cine brasileiro* (Havana: Ediciones ICAIC).

—— (1965b/1995), 'Estética da fome', trans. Randal Johnson and Burnes Hollyman in Johnson and Stam (1995).

Rosen, Marjorie (1972), 'The Cuban Film Fiasco', *Saturday Review*, 17 June.

Sanjinés, Jorge (1977/1986), 'Cine revolucinario: La experiencia boliviana', trans. as 'Revolutionary Cinema: The Bolivian Experience', in Burton (1986).

Sanjinés, Jorge (1979), *Teoría y práctica de un cine junto al pueblo* (Mexico City: Siglo XXI).

Shohat, Ella, and Robert Stam (1994), *Unthinking Eurocentrism: Multiculturalism and the Media* (London: Routledge).

Solanas, Fernando, and Octavio Getino (1969a/1973a), 'Hacia un Tercer Cine', trans. as 'Towards a Third Cinema', in Solanas and Getino, *Cine, cultura y descolonización* (Buenos Aires: Siglo XXI).

—— —— (1969b), 'La cultura nacional, el cine y *La hora de los hornos*', *Cine cubano*, 56–7 (Mar.).

—— —— (1973b), 'Cine militante: una categoría interna del Tercer Cine', in Solanas and Getino, *Cine, cultura y descolonización* (Buenos Aires: Siglo XXI).

Stam, Robert, João Luiz Viera, and Ismail Xavier (1995), 'The Shape of Brazilian Cinema in the Post-Modern Age', in Johnson and Stam (1982).

Stock, Ann Marie (1996), 'Migrancy and the Latin American Cinemascape: Towards a Post-National Critical Praxis', *Revista canadiense de estudios hispánicos*, 10/1 Special Issue: *Mundos contemporáneos en el cine español e hispanoamericano*, ed. Robert Young, 19–30.

Valjalo, David, and Zuzana M. Pick (eds.) (1984), *Literatura chilena*, 8, Special Issue: *10 añnos de cine chileno 1973–1983*.

Vega, Alicia (1979), *Re-vision del cine chileno* (Santiago: Editorial Aconcagua).

26

Film and changing technologies

Laura Kipnis

The problem in writing this chapter is that by the time you read it, everything will have changed radically, once again. Electronic and digital technologies are having seismic, unsettling effects on the film industry, and film production practices are being transformed and retransformed on practically a monthly basis. Computers are increasingly affecting every stage of production. Traditional filmic processes are disappearing, replaced by new forms of digital image manipulation. Everyone connected with film is waging a valiant struggle to keep up with rapidly changing technologies, trying to make sense of the present, while simultaneously hazarding calculated guesses about the future. Professional organs like *American Cinematographer*, which always viewed encroaching electronic technologies (such as video) with barely contained suspicion, are now suffused with free-floating anxiety, their articles permeated with loss and pathos about film's potentially diminished stature in the digital age. One can hardly help but notice the emotional and at times overwrought language brought to bear on the topic within the world of film production.

The anxiety is not confined to the industry either. At a film studies conference in Chicago in 1996, academic panellists fretted about 'the death of the camera', and 'the end of film'. Academics involved in teaching new technologies routinely speculate about the 'end of narrative', given the various forms of non-linear temporality and interactivity that new digital technologies have made possible. And how is our curriculum supposed to reflect the end of narrative, when we can't even figure out what production technologies to invest in, given that every time you look up, another one is being phased out? And these changes aren't entirely welcome ones. To the great detriment of independent filmmakers, Super-8 film is now virtually extinct (although still making special guest appearances in fieatures like Oliver Stone's *Natural Born Killers* (1994) to signal 'experimentation'), killed off quickly by the introduction of affordable and easy-to-use VHS camcorders *circa* 1985. (On the subject of technological change and uncertainty, let's not even get into the panoply of video formats that have come and gone over the last two decades, and how many carcasses of dead or dying production technologies litter our equipment rooms.)

Even the future of 16mm seems precarious, with support services—labs, sound services, projector-manufacturing—rapidly crumbling. Once Betacam camcorders hit the scene in 1982, news-gathering changed immediately to video, as did industrial and corporate film, as well as much documentary production aimed for broadcast. Eastman Kodak, the world's largest film manufacturer, has been struggling schizophrenically to keep up with these technological changes, shifting corporate strategies virtually from week to week—first moving into videotape, then shoring up film production and fighting to ensure that film would remain the favoured origination medium in image-based mass entertainment, now jumping feet first into digital imaging. Kodak has laid off at least 17,000 employees in the United States and over 30,000 workers abroad since the mid-1980s, in corporate belt-tightening occasioned by a series of bad forecasts about new technologies and heavy world-wide losses. Kodak's Rochester workforce has been downsized—to use the current euphemism—by 40 per cent in the same period. Rochester, NY, had long been something of a company town treated by Kodak like a favourite nephew; more recently the company has vastly retreated from this century-long civic commitment. These changes in technology don't affect filmmakers alone or happen in a social vacuum: they have had sweeping repercussions everywhere, from international markets to local issues like health care for Kodak's retirees—even down to the specifics of the number of hospital charity beds available for the poor in Rochester.

In short, the language of crisis, loss, and uncertainty is endemic to anything connected to film these days. It may be that these are the linguistics of any period of rapid technological transformation, and that at the birth of radio, or of film itself, or the introduction of film sound, or the invention of television and early computers, similar anxieties reigned. Or it may be that digital technology will transform all things, including film, beyond recognition and that what we are hearing now are merely small rumblings compared to the thunder of stampeding elephants coming over the horizon.

At the same time as technological changes in film-related industries are having sweeping material effects in terms of jobs and markets, transformations in image-making procedures brought about by digital technologies are spawning complex theoretical questions about the ontological status of the filmic image itself. Can a photograph be considered *evidence* of anything in the digital age, and if not, what does this mean—aesthetically, socially, or juridically? It has now become routine, via the magic of digital manipulation, to see long-dead cult actors like Humphrey Bogart or Jimmy Cagney 'interacting' with live actors in commercials; or to witness 'character replacement'—for *In the Line of Fire* (1993), footage of George and Barbara Bush disembarking from Air Force One was digitally scanned, and actors playing the First Couple were composited into the image. The truth-status of any given image is anyone's guess. Or if there is no 'original' but only endless perfect digital clones, does this have implications for how value and meaning are assigned or experienced? How photographic technologies work and how they make images available to audiences—questions of reception—open onto an array of impossibly large questions about referentiality and indexicality, onto questions about mimesis and realism. Issues of photographic reproducton, as Walter Benjamin has so famously pointed out, are inseparable from even larger issues of modernity, capital, and their respective ideologies. And *will* the new modes of interactivity make linear narrative obsolete? This is certainly a question with ramifications far beyond film studies, as narrative seems to be one of those basic categories of human conceptualization.

Or, taking the long view, are interactivity, non-linearity, and the 'digital revolution' a bit over-hyped, and are we falling into a romantic and narrow technological determinism if we envision that new technologies alone will alter something so indelible as narrative, or vastly change something so much a facet of contemporary culture as film? And is all of this really so new? After all, the mute button on your television remote control is an interactive technology. Non-linear narrative has been a staple of modernist experimentation for most of this century (or since the invention of the unconscious, if you consider dreams a media form). And are computer-generated images so completely different from the use of models, mattes, optical effects, rear projection, and a host of other ways of inventing and manipulating images that have long been staples of cinematic technology? In other words, did the photographic or filmic image ever have any particular relation to truth or evidence to begin with? And does it really matter whether those dinosaurs are miniatures or computer-generated, optically printed or shot against blue screen or digitally composited? *Should* the mode of production of the image change the kinds of theoretical question we ask about it? So, for example, if a filmic image no longer originates in a 'pro-filmic event', but is generated by a computer, does that necessitate revisions in theories about realism and reception? If a character in a film isn't portrayed by an actor acting, but is the result of manipulating scanned images of numerous faces or bodies, for instance, do new theories about identification need to be devised?

But as technological changes are provoking or reprovoking such epistemological uncertainties, let us remember that these revolutionary new technologies are *social* technologies, meaning that their revolutionary potential is limited to the uses that surrounding social institutions and economic forces allow to be made of them. The captains of industry have a lot invested, in all senses of the word, in hooking us on ideologies of continual technological obsolescence and change: if, as in one proposed scenario for the future, movie theatres stop projecting film and convert to screening high-definition television (HDTV) signals beamed in by satellite, some lucky captain of industry and his stockholders stand to make a megafortune on the deal. Or, will HDTV—the latest much-hyped thing—eventually go the way of 3-D film, into the trash-heap of technological also-rans with all those cute little cardboard 3-D glasses? And do consumers really *care* about television images with better resolution, or do they care to the tune of the several thousand dollars they'll have to spend to convert to the new system, *if* it ever gets off the ground, which still seems doubtful? Do you? It is estimated that consumers will be forced to spend $75 billion to upgrade old television sets once the conversion to HDTV is complete.

But before you whip out your credit card, keep in mind that much of the fascination with newness and innovation, our beliefs in progress and the necessity of change, have ideological implications and serve specific interests, namely those of capitalism's ongoing necessity for new markets and fresh innovations to keep itself viable. And despite the hype about interactivity and revolution, the centres of cultural influence and power are not likely to change one bit, and neither is the direction of the flow of cultural products, or the move towards global domination of cultural markets by big capital. Rather, digital reproduction will most likely simply aid the penetration of new markets by multinational media conglomerates, creating new delivery systems for not-very-new and hardly-very-different images and information.

So if film studies has been somewhat slow to come to terms with a changing apparatus, or to theorize the shifts in film language and grammar that technological change seems to have so rapidly brought about, the reasons are understandable. As I have tried to indicate, these are impossibly large questions, and unfortunately this article too cannot even begin to attempt to answer them: predicting the future, or revamping film theory, or performing large-scale social analysis, or even offering detailed comparative historical case-studies in previous technological changes are all beyond my scope. Instead, let us call this chapter both a case-study in technological innovation (and particularly in the anxiety of technological innovation), *and* an experiment in how to write about technological innovation from within the midst of the maelstrom, where things are both nebulous and hopping about drastically from one moment to the next, like Silicon Valley techno-nerds on No-Doz and caffeine highballs.

Film and video

But another reason for the hesitation around technological change is that film studies is, to a large extent, premised on an understanding of film as a discrete technology. The same understanding permeates the industry's discourse about itself. I would like to suggest that, historically, film has constructed an identity for itself that was maintained by erecting a somewhat fictive separation between itself and neighbouring electronic technologies, and that changes in technology are making this separation increasingly problematic.

One of the ways that film studies has been able to achieve credibility as an academic discipline in the humanities is precisely to distinguish itself from television, to claim (and produce) a more elevated and more high-minded status for itself, that is to distinguish film as art—or 'Film Art' (the title of a well-known introductory film textbook)—from the noisy lower orders of video and television. Perhaps this imperative even factors into which film theories achieve success as paradigms for the field, and which fade away: the emphasis on film as a discrete technology and on cinematic specificity seems to be maintained within the dominant traditions of contemporary film theory, such as apparatus theory (Rosen 1986).

What will be the fate of dominant film studies paradigms in the face of technological shifts that attenuate the distinctions between the film and electronic technologies? It now makes less sense than ever to speak of 'film' as though it were a discrete technology. But, in fact, if you examine the recent history of film technology, it appears that, despite the conventional academic separation of film and television studies, in *practice* film and video have been quite interdependent and increasingly proximate for at least the last twenty years, that is, ever since the introduction of the Rank-Cintel Flying Spot Scanner in 1972. What the Rank-Cintel did was obviate the difference in frame rates between film (24 frames per second) and video (30 frames per second) in film-to-video transfers. You don't really care how—the important point is that this opened the possibility of reinventing the entire method of film post-production and distribution in North America, because now origination medium wouldn't necessarily determine the finishing medium. In other words, something could be shot on film, and edited and finished on videotape, and released on either film *or* video.

The advent of digital non-linear editing (the Avid is the best-known example) has pretty much finished off film editing: even films that are theatrically released on film are almost universally edited electronically (either on tape, or on a non-linear system) before being reconformed on film. And of course film-to-video transfers opened up the possibility of the home rental market, which has had a major transforming effect on all aspects of film financing, production, and viewership, not to mention transforming film studies and education, given the new access and availability of film. The unfortunate casualty has been the 16mm film print business, pretty much dead and buried.

Other major intersections of the two technologies are video assist on film cameras, in which a video tap on the film camera allows the image (or a black-and-white version of it) to be viewed on a television monitor on the film set, instead of waiting for the film to be processed, printed, and returned from the lab the next

day. This, as you can imagine, has had a decisive effect on the directorial process, and on film sets. Francis Ford Coppola now directs from an electronically rigged trailer off the set, where he can view the unfolding scene on television monitors, rather than, as was once the practice, from on the set, and in proximity to the actors.

The ever-greater commingling of film and video seems to provoke a certain state of alarm, and indeed acrimony, on the part of the film profession, or so you would infer from the language used to describe the experience. 'Video technology is encroaching on traditional film production techniques from several directions . . . advances in video assist and addressing the dreams—and nightmares—of many directors of photography' (Brandt 1991: 93). Or 'A lot of film shooters and editors come to video with a queasy feeling, a sense that they're about to surrender control of their work.' Film folk get the 'flutters' when they approach video, according to this author, who begs his reader not to conclude that he has been seduced by the 'mindless and endless proliferation of video technology' (Roland 1992: 53–4). So while there is no argument that computer-based random access editing—which is to video editing what word-processing is to typing on a typewriter—is incredibly convenient *and* allows editors increased flexibility and creativity, it is still an experience fraught with risk. According to *American Cinematographer*, 'It's only natural for an experienced professional to feel some trepidation towards new technology, especially in a historically hands-on task like film editing. One [film] editor who recently tried our system for the first time was very, very nervous,' recalls the vice-president of a company manufacturing digital editing systems; 'He actually got a piece of film and attached it to his desk, so he'd still be able to touch film' (Pizzelo 1994: 22). Or, 'Rostock, like most film editors, initially resisted the idea of editing film on tape . . . She still has fond memories of film cutting, however. "There's this whole cosmic thing about wanting to touch the film, which I still miss, and you can't mark tape with a grease pencil"' (Comer 1992: 26–7). Anecdotes of this sort are quite typical of the curiously *emotional* tone of much of the writing about new technologies from within the film profession—as is the somewhat talismanic and weirdly occult status accorded to film in these accounts. And I can personally testify that one quite often *does* hear filmmakers, when discussing the inferiority of video editing to film editing, invoking this loss of 'touching film' as if editing film were a conduit to something deeply personal, even religious, to which punching buttons on a video edit controller can't compete. (For those unfamiliar with the video-editing process, touching tape is *verboten* and you don't physically splice the tape; rather, an electromagnetic signal is transferred from one piece of tape to another, or, in the case of digital editing, onto computer hard drives before being laid off to tape.)

The film-to-tape transfer—also known as the telecine process—and the site of greatest full-body contact between film and electronic technology, becomes, perhaps predictably, a scene of particular fretting and distinction-making. One reason, of course, is that film and video still do have different aspect ratios, one of the problems HDTV is meant to solve. Film has a wider frame than video, and when transferred to video, only the centre of the film frame makes it to your living-room. To compensate, especially on the widest-screen film formats, video engineers often add camera movements the director never intended (this is known as 'pan and scan'), by panning to the edges of the film frame itself during the transfer process, thus enabling viewers at least to see any crucial action instead of lopping it off. This is a less than happy solution, but so is 'letter-boxing', in which widescreen films are shown full width, but squeezed down to microscopic size, with bands of black at the top and bottom of the video frame. Most directors, knowing their films are eventually destined for television, simply do not employ the edges of the frame for significant story information, in a routine compliance of aesthetics with commerce—another defeat of film's breadth by video's narrow frame.

It is these resonances and connotations that need to be pointed out, rather than focusing on the obvious material differences between film and video. The more interesting question is one of assigned differences: how does value come to be attached to what are mere distinctions, and how has film's discourse about itself relied on hierarchizing such distinctions into relations of value and merit? Like the penchant for touching film, when you start looking closely at these things, they can start to seem rather odd.

In reading over the last ten years of *American Cinematographer* on the subject of film's relation to electronic technologies, one can't help but notice that the vocabulary brought to bear on the subject—which often relies on metaphors involving the lack of a 'shared language' and corresponding concerns about 'relationships', 'communication problems', and 'incompatibility'—seems oddly reminiscent of the vocabularies associated with other hotbed issues involving cultural confrontations with 'others' like race or immigration, in which language differences also become a way of articulating boundary anxieties. And language issues are also typically a mechanism through which the 'other' is imbricated into a structure in which dissimilarity is redefined as inferiority, and in which cultural differences are rearticulated as hierarchized oppositions. So the fact that, from within film discourse, video didn't speak the right language is significant in its fall from value. It is not simply a *different* technology, it is figured as a social inferior. My point here is not that the film–video opposition has crashing social significance on the order of race or immigration issues, or that we should bring humanistic empathy to bear on video's plight, but that discourses about social technologies can be seen to follow certain conventions of the social and linguistic contexts they inhabit. And I am suggesting that these discursive conventions *have* had significance in both the film profession and film studies, and that current shifts in technologies—in which video and electronic technologies are permeating film far more than ever before (and perhaps eventually displacing it)—are making this more apparent.

Typically, an article in the March 1993 *American Cinematographer* on 'Telecine: The Tools and how to Use Them' (Harrell 1993) focused less on material differences like the 'pan and scan' problem than on the cultural differences—the shared-language problem. Film people just don't know how to talk to telecine operators. The kind of 'close relationship' that exists between a film's director of photography and the film's colourist, that is, between two film professionals from the same world 'is very much a personal relationship'. But, conversely, 'telecine color correction and movie color timing are two different worlds'. The shared 'terminology that has been honed and developed for nearly a hundred years [in film] hasn't yet been fully developed'. And, in that what makes film an *art* is the photographic intent of the film, or what director of photography Conrad Hall calls 'the artistic use of color, grain, sharpness, darkness and motion', the fear is that, left to the mercy of the telecine colourist, this art will be lost. So, 'It is up to the telecine operator to make film *art* work for video *technology*' (my emphasis).

So the language difficulties become a way of erecting an art–technology opposition, and that opposition is one of the most frequent ways that film figures its distinction from, and hierarchizes its relation to, video. I think this is worth a closer look. The typical form this distinction takes is that film is human, sensuous, and creative, while video is dominated by machines, engineers, and technocrats. (Thus the control panels of the telecine colourist are described in the *American Cinematographer* article as looking like 'the cockpit of a 747'.)

To those outside the field, film's aversion to video, or its relegation of video to the sphere of technology, might be seen as merely an instance of what Freud referred to as the narcissism of small differences. Many people can't even tell the difference between something shot on film and something shot on video, particularly on broadcast television, which reduces the appearance of the difference anyway, by squashing the number of lines of resolution (a measurement of the quality of picture information) down to television's bandwidth. (If you are one of those who can't tell them apart, think about news, soap operas, live sports: that's video. Hour-long dramas, movies of the week: that's film. See the difference?) The difference between the look of the two is diminishing with the advent of digital video cameras, which feature controls that allow you to shape the look of the picture to make it resemble film, adding grain, flicker, and diffusion.

But video does look different from film. It is not only its lower resolution: video can't reproduce the same contrast ratio from lights to darks, meaning that it has less range, and gives less detail at either end of the light–dark spectrum. A consequence is that there are certain technical rules about how light your video whites can be and how dark your video blacks can be, and how vast a difference between the two there can be, particularly in broadcast situations. So video is routinely bad-mouthed in film discourses for allowing less latitude to the cinematographer, and thus less creative freedom, and less 'art'. And the fact that television engineers do get the final say about what may or may not be broadcast leads to no end of carping by cinematographers that video is a medium overruled by control-room engineers and soulless technocrats, not artists, because if your blacks are below 7.5 and your whites above 100 on a horrible contraption called a waveform monitor, you may have won an Oscar for cinematography, but your masterpiece won't go on the air.

So when filmmakers approach video, it has usually been with great trepidation about losing their souls in a devil's pact with technology. The arm's-length distan-

cing is evident in the jacket copy from a widely used 1985 (that is, pre-digital) American Society of Cinematographers handbook whose project was exactly to forge some heretofore unknown *rapprochement* between film and video via what would have previously been thought an oxymoronic title: *Electronic Cinematography: Achieving Photographic Control over the Video Image*. The jacket reassures the nervous cinematographer:

Here's a book that *uniquely* demystifies video and reveals its creative potential. The authors, who have worked in both film and video, approach electronic cinematography from the point of view of the *cinematographer*, rather than that of the engineer . . . If you are interested in combining the refinements of motion picture film techniques and aesthetics with the technology of video, you will find a wealth of applications . . .

The book requires 'no previous electronics experience', the reader is assured. Once again, film is the realm of aesthetics, video is technology.

But let's get real. Shooting film can *hardly* be considered less technocratic than shooting video, and is actually far *more* technically difficult, requiring precise measurement of light, detailed knowledge of arcane things like sensitometry, and a somewhat overstructured relation to numbers: between film stocks (7287, 5298), film speeds (250, 500 . . .), frame rates, f-stops, lenses, filters, the Kelvin scale (a measurement of colour temperature), footcandles (a measurement of light intensity), and wattage (the power drawn by lights). These hardly seem less 'technological' or more sensuously personal than anything you would encounter on a video shoot.

Perhaps the art–technology distinction starts to seem a little more iffy. Now a hard-core film buff will probably intervene at this point to insist that we talk about the quality of the image, and the 'artfulness' possible with film that simply can't be achieved with video. And video often does look different from film, but that is also largely the result of the uses to which it is put. Video does do a technically less precise job of directly reproducing reality with the same degree of detail and verisimilitude, even though it tends to have a 'harder edge' and a more 'real' look. But this look of 'realness' is, to a great degree, a product of video's historic association with electronic news-gathering, or ENG: it is a convention, not an essence. When videographers want to make video look more like film, they will actually try to fuzz that hard edge somehow: by using diffusion or filtration. Film may tend to look more beautiful, but this is also, to a great degree, a matter of conventions: it is generally lit differently (low-key or arty, as opposed to high-key and functional), and for different purposes.

But the issue is the way in which material distinctions and differences between film and video become expressed as relations of value, and the issue of value is never far away from any discussion of film–video distinctions. One reason may be that, as one filmmaker philosopher put it, 'In shooting on film you're shooting on precious metal, that is, silver. With video technologies, you're shooting on silicon, which is essentially dirt.' It may not be exactly the silver–dirt distinction that lends film its aura of preciousness, but the fact that this makes film costs subject to fluctuations in the silver market. Film *does* cost more to shoot and process. Consequently, video is often shot in situations where money needs to be saved, for example lower-status genres like sitcoms or soap operas, or to advertise lower-status consumer commodities like used cars or down-market furniture, or in live (and thus usually more passing and disposable) programming like news or sports. So it may be that video has come to be associated with cheapness, with the momentary, the real, the quotidian. So it starts to *look* cheap, while film, by contrast, comes away with higher-class status. It starts to look richer, and this, I'd suggest, is a *sub rosa* aspect of the romance about film. And, of course, you only see video on television, for free, in your home, whereas the optimal film-viewing experience is after you have travelled somewhere and paid for your seat. So, in short, the film–video distinction has come to have certain class connotations that are piled on top of the other oppositions already in play: art–technology, silver–dirt, higher genres–lower genres, and cinema–television (even though 75 to 85 per cent of what is broadcast on prime time US television is shot on film).

Film, video, and digital culture

This brings us back to the present, and to the vast changes sweeping the world of production. How exactly do they affect and trouble the status of film? Well, a new generation of digital video cameras has recently been introduced by Sony that is said to rival 35mm film in terms of image quality. New advances in digital cinematography software allow camerapersons to simulate different film stocks on video, by selectively adding graininess or other film characteristics, to boost particular highlights, alter colours, change the overall tonal scale or contrast ratio—all previously activities proprietary to the 'art' of cinematography. The first all-digital live-action filmless movie was shown at last year's Sundance Film Festival, about which *American Cinematographer* wrote, 'The Berlin Wall between film and video may or may not be tumbling down. But if the recent all-digital production of *Mail Bonding* is any indication, there may be some serious cracks in the separation between these two media' (Kaufman 1995: 50). It is interesting to note, though, that three years earlier the magazine's editor had announced breathlessly, 'Cinematography now stands at the crossroads of film, video and computer technologies' (Heuring 1992: 25). The film world still seems unsure, regarding electronic technology, whether the Cold War rages still or *détente* has been achieved: should we pull up the drawbridge or welcome the invaders with cake and punch? Even though video technology has been in bed with film for at least twenty years, the profession, with a certain symptomatic disavowal ('yes I know, but . . .'), seems to keep greeting it anew.

Anxiety and disavowal are typical responses to unwelcome change, but what might also make film particularly prone to a current sense of instability is that, as I have suggested, it had never completely habituated itself to the presence of electronic technologies to begin with, and the technological changes currently under way seriously muck up the distinctions that have traditionally structured film's own discourse about itself. If digital technologies will allow video to rival 35mm film in terms of image quality, positioning electronic technologies to share in 'film art', perhaps it starts to become more apparent that the deeply held conviction that film is art, not technology, is something of a smokescreen for another material issue: that film is, of course, really, a vast business. It is economics, not art, that drives the development of these new technologies and their applications, just as it is economics that has driven the film industry from its inception. It seems fairly clear that one way film has played out its art–commerce ambivalence is by assigning all forms of such crudeness to the realm of video, while clinging to the notion of itself as somehow purer, an 'art form'. Even film academics, who might seem less likely to buy into the art thing in any wholesale way, can regularly be heard disparaging and distancing themselves from television studies. The Society for Cinema Studies,

Digital imaging and box-office success—*Jurassic Park* (1993)

the leading film studies professional organization, has only recently contemplated changing its name to allow some allusion to television.

It may be that film *is* on its last legs. Speculation is currently running high that economic forces will inevitably lead to electronic distribution of theatrical features, and to the demise of projected film. That is because it is ultimately cheaper to distribute electronic images and sound via satellite, fibre optics lines, or another carrier than it is to mass-produce film prints and physically deliver them to theatres. And instant

home distribution of first releases by satellite (with pay-per-view by credit card) is even more financially advantageous because producers could recoup on their investments almost immediately. If 60 per cent of revenues are now generated by video distribution a year after a theatrical release, financiers are carrying those debts until the features hit the home viewer. Why wait so long? The most dire scenario for film is that there won't be sufficient economic incentive for film manufacturers to compete, and that there will even ultimately be a transition away from film as an origination medium, as digital cameras achieve greater and greater sophistication.

Whether or not this is the future is anyone's guess. As I said, a general sense of impeding loss permeates much of these discussions. What seems to provoke ambivalence about so much of this technological change is the sense that something 'human' is being lost, or shunted aside. There is a definite loss of older crafts and craft knowledge: film editing is virtually dead, as are special effects crafts like mould-making, casting, modelling, drawing, not to mention optical compositing and effects. Matte painting is on its way out, replaced by computer workstations. One response has been a defiant quasi-Luddite return to older technologies: Tim Burton's *The Nightmare before Christmas* (1993) had a cast entirely composed of puppets, bringing stop-motion photography back from the edge of extinction because many older technologies like stop-motion, according to Ray Harryhousen—one of the big names in traditional special effects—lend a certain strangeness to fantasy films which is lost if you make a film too realistic: 'You lose that dream quality.' Other special effects old-timers compare the cleanliness of computer workstations to 'accounting procedures' (Magrid 1994: 26–8). Perhaps there *is* the loss of something ineffably human in these new technologies. The two big hits of summer 1996, *Independence Day* (which had the largest opening grosses of any film in history) and *Twister*, are both noted for replacing 'star power' with massive computer-generated special effects. New computer software, such as the infamous 'morphing' technique of *Terminator 2* (1991), become the stars of the big new blockbusters, which now tend increasingly to be written around new special effects rather than special effects being used organically to help tell a compelling story.

There has also been much post-*Jurassic Park* (1993) speculation that computer technologies will ultimately replace actors, sets, and locations with digital simulacra; that 'If an actor's too fat to do movie number four, his head can be grafted onto somebody else's body or recreated digitally'. Whether or not this is the wave of the future, *Jurassic Park* did, in fact, feature a computer-generated actor portraying a human: for the final seconds of the shot in which the T-rex devours the attorney Gennaro head first, a computer re-creation of the actor was used (Magrid 1994: 30). Certainly cutting costs by eliminating actors is always an incentive. In *Forrest Gump* (1994) an anti-war protest scene involved a crowd of 200,000; all but 1,000 of them were digital replicants. Spiralling mega-salaries are the largest factor in out-of-control film costs, and film executives are starting to notice that big stars don't necessarily generate big profits.

Forrest Gump was, of course, the breakthrough movie that digitally put words in former presidents' mouths by 'repixillating' their lips, leading to much commentary and concern about the propagandistic or manipulative potential made available by digital technologies, in which every pixel in a frame can be endlessly manipulated and transformed. Says special effects artist Ken Ralston, '*Forrest Gump*'s shots of Hanks interacting with historical figures definitely pushes the outer edges of effects work, dabbling with what were supposed to be photographic documentations of history. When seeing is no longer believing, the concept of photography as proof of anything seems on the verge of extinction. Here's the technology to do really dangerous work.'

Political and cultural theorists have been writing about the loss of a sense of history for some time now. So does a society get the technology it deserves, or technologies that make its own dominant ideologies more visible, more livable? As *American Cinematographer* wrote with some excitement regarding the then revolutionary morphing techniques in *Terminator 2* (you can now buy a similar programme for your home computer for under $100), 'The big news was that the audience accepted an incredible illusion as reality, and they loved it.' Well, it hardly seems like news, following on the heels of Reagan–Thatcherism, that audiences will accept incredible illusions as reality, or that the relationship between technologies and social ideologies has a certain quality of identity.

The task is then, as usual, for independent image-makers to work to utilize these new technologies to create images and contents that *aren't* simply business as usual. Technology needs to be demystified, as do silly manufactured oppositions between this or that technology on the basis of false notions of 'value'. Instead, technology can be utilized to contest the forces of social amnesia, rather than reproducing the industry's incessant bottom-line drive towards newer, bigger, shinier tech. What does it matter if independents produce more 'artistic' but equally tunnel-visioned technological reveries, that is, succumb to experimentation as an end in itself? Too many young film- and videomakers have got caught up in mastering each successive new technology, each new computer-imaging program, and end up producing pretty, technically competent wallpaper. Many of the most talented students seem to be producing the most vapid work, spending endless hours manipulating pixels into submission without stepping back to wonder what for.

Instead, now that it's possible to alter landscapes digitally, perhaps we can think about using these 'revolutionary' technologies as tools to alter social landscapes in more permanent and even more unsettling ways, rather than being seduced into quiescence by the lure of the new.

BIBLIOGRAPHY

Benjamin, Walter (1936/1969), 'The Work of Art in the Age of Mechanical Reproduction', trans. Harry Zohn in *Illuminations* (New York: Schocken Books).

Bordwell, David, and Kristin Thompson (1990), *Film Art: An Introduction* (New York: McGraw-Hill).

Brandt, James B. (1991), 'Video Assist: Past, Present and Future', *American Cinematographer*, 72/6 (June), 93–8.

Comer, Brooke (1992), 'Incident at Oglala: Advancing the Art of Editing', *American Cinematographer*, 73/4 (Apr.), 26–32.

Film Art: An Introduction (1990) (New York: McGraw-Hill).

Harrell, Alfred D. (1993), 'Telecine: The Tools and how to Use Them', *American Cinematographer*, 74/3: 61–6.

*Hayward, Philip, and Tana Wollen, (eds.) (1993), *Future Visions: New Technologies of the Screen* (London: British Film Institute).

Heuring, David (1992), 'When "Post" Becomes the Main Event', *American Cinematographer*, 73/9 (Sept.), 22–3.

Kaufman, Debra (1995), 'Mail Bonding: Foray into Digital Filmmaking', *American Cinematographer*, 76/4 (Apr.) 50–4.

Lister, Martin (ed.) (1995), *The Photographic Image in Digital Culture* (London: Routledge).

Magrid, Ron (1994), 'Exploring the Future of Special Effects', *American Cinematographer*, 75/2 (Feb.), 52–6.

Millennium Film Journal (1995), Special Issue: *Interactivities*, 28 (Spring).

Petro, Patrice (ed.) (1995), *Fugitive Images: From Photography to Video* (Bloomington: Indiana University Press).

Pizzelo, Chris (1994), 'Forecasting the Digital Future', *American Cinematographer*, 73/9 (Mar.), 25–30.

Roland, Fritz (1992), 'Making Peace with Technology', *American Cinematographer*, 73/9 (Sept.), 53–7.

Rosen, Phillip (ed.) (1986), *Narrative, Apparatus, Ideology* (New York: Columbia University Press).

Williams, Raymond (1975), *Television: Technology and Cultural Form* (New York: Schocken Books).

27

Film and television

John Hill

Despite the centenary of cinema in 1995, it has been common in recent years to talk of the decline of cinema, and even its 'death'. A number of factors have underpinned this kind of thinking: the decline in cinema attendances world-wide and a declining variety in film production, the loss of a certain kind of cinematic experience involved with cinemagoing, and a corresponding dimunition of the cultural importance of film. There is certainly a degree of validity in these claims. Although there has been an upturn in a number of countries in recent years as a result of the opening of multiplexes, the global trend in cinemagoing has been downwards. At the same time, there has been a crisis in film production in a number of countries and a growing domination of the world market, outside Asia, by the output of Hollywood. Cinemagoing is no longer the central leisure activity it once was, even for those who attend the cinema, while the composition of the cinema audience has also changed, no longer consisting of the 'mass' of the population, but only a particular—mainly youthful—segment of it.

However, if we take into account the significance of television and video, this situation looks somewhat different. For while cinemagoing has been in decline, the actual watching of films has not, and is probably greater than ever before. This can be seen in the way in which the economics of film, television, and video have become increasingly entwined. Towards the end of the 1960s and the beginning of the 1970s the Hollywood

majors were faced with economic crisis; by the end of the 1980s, however, they were once again restored to financial health. The key factor in this turn-around lay in the ability of the studios to adapt to, and take advantage of, the new video and pay-TV markets, the revenues from which soon outstripped those from theatrical release. Whereas returns from theatrical release (both domestic and foreign) accounted for nearly 76 per cent of studio revenues in 1980, these were only responsible for 32 per cent of revenues in 1990. In contrast, revenues from pay-TV rose over the same period from 4.8 to 9 per cent, while, most dramatically, revenues from video increased from 1 to over 45 per cent (Screen Finance 1993: 8). Thus, while cinema admissions over the same period fell in the United States as well as globally, this clearly does not indicate that films were watched less—only that they were increasingly viewed on the small screen (Screen Digest 1993: 204–5).

This means that, 100 years on from the first public film screening in 1895, films—whether broadcast or on video—are now more likely to be watched at home on television than in the cinema. But does this matter, and what are the implications of this for an understanding of the current situation of cinema? In order to answer these questions, it may be helpful to examine some of the arguments which have surrounded the development of the increasingly close relationship between film and television and the ways in which this has been perceived as both a loss and a gain.

Economics

As the above suggests, the drive towards a convergence of film and television has been economic. For although film and television have often been seen as clearly distinct (and even as enemies of each other), the relationship between the two has been complex and varied. As William Lafferty has argued, 'contrary to conventional wisdom, the economic relationship between film and television has a lengthy history' (1988: 273). He traces this relationship back to the 1930s, when Hollywood invested in television and radio broadcasting stations and networks as a means of controlling the development of a potential competitor, and also explored the potential of theatre television (see also Gomery 1984). These strategies, however, failed to bear fruit because of the opposition of the Federal Communications Commission, which was already concerned about monopoly tendencies in the film industry. Consequently, it is the 1950s which Lafferty identifies as the period in which a 'symbiotic relation between the film and television industries' was properly sealed (1988: 281). It was at this time that the studios fully opened up their film libraries to television broadcasters and began direct production of programmes specifically for televison, leading to the emergence of the 'made-for-TV movie' in the early 1960s.

In doing so, Peter Kramer argues, the Hollywood majors were involved in a 'dual strategy' (1996: 38). On the one hand, the majors adapted the processes of the old studio system to regular production for the television audience; on the other hand, they sought to 'differentiate' the cinema film from television through investment in special 'blockbuster' movies (characterized by the use of new technological developments, special effects, and spectacle) that would continue to attract audiences into the cinemas. Despite the growing dependence of the big-budget 'event' movie on small-screen media for the generation of revenues, Kramer argues that this is not as contradictory as it might at first seem. For it is precisely 'the lure of the big picture'—the 'grandeur and mystique of cinema'—which he argues provides a major part of a film's appeal for the television and video audience (12).

This 'dual strategy' may also be linked to changing modes of movie consumption. For the majority of people, the actual activity of cinemagoing has become much less regular and more of a 'special' activity than in the heyday of Hollywood's studio system. The social character of the audience has also changed, with the bulk of the moviegoing audience belonging to the 15–24 age-group. In contrast, films on television and video are watched by an older and more socially diverse audience for whom the activity of film viewing is often regular and habitual. Thus, in the case of US telefilms, Laurence Jarvik and Nancy Strickland argue that, despite their low critical status, they often attract audiences well in excess of theatrical releases and that 'the enormous viewership for movies-of-the-week and miniseries parallels the huge regular moviegoing family audience of Hollywood's Golden Age' (1988: 42). However, while much more time is now spent watching films of all kinds on television than in the cinema, questions also remain. As Sylvia Harvey suggests, it is important to consider the significance of the time spent watching films not just in terms of 'quantity' but also in terms of 'quality' (1996: 241). A number of different issues arise in this respect.

Technology

In the first instance, the viewing of film on television or video inevitably involves a drop in technical quality. This has various aspects and includes a certain loss of quality in sound, colour range, and resolution (from 3,500 to 4,000 lines of resolution to 525 lines of resolution in the United States and 625 in Europe). There is also the vexed question of aspect ratio. Whereas the aspect ratio of television is normally 1.33:1, films—since the advent of widescreen processes in the 1950s—have characteristically been shot in much more rectangular ratios (such as 1.85 or 2.35:1). In order to accommodate films to a television format, 'panning and scanning' techniques (ironically developed by the film industry itself) have been adopted, which lead not only to a loss of much of the original image but also to a degree of 'remaking' of films as well. As a result, and despite the appeal of the 'big picture', filmmakers have increasingly had to acknowledge that television is a film's ultimate destination and stick to 'safe-action' areas when filming. Frank Thompson (1990), for example, indicates the differences between John Boorman's *Point Blank* (1967) and Miloš Forman's *Amadeus* (1984) when seen on television. The latter, he argues, was evidently filmed with television in mind, whereas the former was not. As a result, *Amadeus* still 'works' on television; *Point Blank*, by contrast, looks 'jumbled' and 'sloppy' (1990: 41). However, with the growing acceptability to audiences of 'letter-boxing' (whereby films are shown in their proper aspect ratio), some of the problems associated with panning and scanning are beginning to be overcome.

It is also the case, as Dan Fleming (1996) has argued, that there has been nothing inevitable about television's inability to deal with the widescreen image. The technology has existed for some time to provide widescreen television, with high-definition images and good-quality stereo sound, which, if not necessarily matching the quality of the projected film image, is at least capable of approximating it much more closely. That this has not so far been made widely available has more to do with its economic feasibility than any 'essential' difference between the film and television media. This is also true of what are often taken to be other fundamental differences between film and television. Thus, while film involves the watching of a large screen image in a darkened public space whereas television involves the viewing of a small screen image in a private domestic space, this again is largely a historical contingency, resulting from the economic imperatives of the film and television industries, rather than any inevitable difference. As Kramer (1996) indicates, in its early phase of development, film was initially conceived (by pioneers such as Thomas Edison) as a domestic technology, just as television was in turn conceived, and tested (in the form of theatre television), as a public one.

In the same way, television has often been regarded as basically a 'live' medium which is better suited to relaying the 'live' event than transmitting pre-recorded entertainment, such as film (see Barr 1996). However, while television may have exploited this 'live' quality to great effect in relation to news, sport, and important public events, it does not follow that television is 'essentially' a 'live' medium or that it is this 'live' quality which should shape the direction of drama on television. Robert Vianello, for example, argues in relation to US television in the 1950s that 'The question of "live" versus film formats' was not simply a technological or aesthetic matter but an economic one (1984: 210). 'Live' programming, he argues, gained dominance in the early years of US television not only because it was cheaper to produce than filmed programming, but because it was used to justify the power of the television networks and enforce the dependency of local television stations. By the late 1950s, however, when the conditions that had made 'live' programming an advantageous strategy for the networks began to change, production shifted decisively towards the telefilm. In this respect, the legacy of 'live' drama on television has been read in different ways: as something particular to television which the shift to recorded forms has lost, or as an inhibition upon the aesthetic potential of television which the development of a closer relationship with cinema then overcame (McLoone 1996).

Aesthetics

However, if the influence of film forms on television drama may be seen to have encouraged the demise of 'live' television drama, this influence has not always been seen as leading to drama which is then regarded as properly 'cinematic'. This again has been partly a matter of economics. Made-for-TV films or theatrical films made with television money have often been made more quickly and cheaply than those made by Hollywood and often lack the production values associated with the 'big picture'. However, as McLoone argues, there is also a tendency in this kind of discussion to draw a 'false contrast' between film and television: between the extremes of 'television at its least "adventurous" (aesthetically) and cinema in its big picture, "event" mode' (1996: 81). In this respect, it is often the big Hollywood 'event' movie which is used to define 'cinema' even though the bulk of Hollywood's output during the studio era consisted of much more routine, modestly budgeted productions that lacked the special effects or expensive displays that are now associated with the 'event' movie.

As a result, many US television films can be seen to belong to a tradition of low-budget Hollywood film-making, and succeed as cinema despite their television origins. Steven Spielberg's *Duel* (1971) is one of the most celebrated examples of this, but, more recently, John Dahl's *Red Rock West* (1993) and *The Last Seduction* (1994), which were given successful theatrical releases *after* they had been made for, and shown on, cable television, vividly illustrate how television beginnings do not necessarily vitiate against the production of 'proper' cinema (Lyons 1994). Similar examples may also be found in Europe, where television broadcasters have been involved in extensive support of film production. Despite complaints, especially in Britain, that the films which television finances have lacked the cinematic values associated with 'real cinema', it is difficult to identify any shared television influence or 'TV aesthetic' informing such films, especially when it has included work as diverse as that of Federico Fellini, Roberto Rossellini, Ermanno Olmi, and the Taviani brothers in Italy, Rainer Werner Fassbinder, Werner Herzog, and Wim Wenders in Germany, Pedro Almodóvar in Spain, and Peter Greenaway, Derek Jarman, Stephen Frears, Mike Leigh, and Ken Loach in Britain.

However, if it is difficult to isolate clear-cut aesthetic differences between film and television, this is not to say that the way in which film and television have become intertwined has not had aesthetic consequences. Lafferty, for example, argues that although television inherited from film a set of narrative and stylistic conventions, the pressures of time and cost upon television production led to the adoption of new techniques by television which then fed back into film production. He cites, for example, the use of 'non-classical' techniques such as rack-focus, overlapping sound, and, particularly, the zoom which were adopted by television in the interests of speed and cost but subsequently became commonplace in filmmaking practice. Indeed, by the 1970s, Lafferty argues, there had been 'a virtual melding of film and television techniques' (1988: 299). With the advent of video, critics have also argued for more wide-ranging forms of interaction. Timothy Corrigan, for example, argues that the 'distracted' conditions of television and video viewing has encouraged new types of cinematic narration. He indicates how the 'classical' model of film narration has begun to give way to forms of narration in which time is 'wasted' and in which narrative incident and visual display exceed motivational logic (1991: 166). Corrigan, in this respect, identifies some of the features of what has become identified as 'postclassical' cinema in which plots have become looser and more episodic, identification with characters less intense, and the relations between narrative and spectacle less tight-knit than in films of the 'classical' period. In doing so, he is also attributing special significance to the changed viewing conditions of films in so far as such features are connected to the less concentrated manner in which films are likely to be watched on television and video.

Spectatorship

To some extent, it is this interest in spectatorship that has informed some of the more recent writing of film and television. Sylvia Harvey, for example, has sought to differentiate film from television in terms of 'the quality of the viewing experience' and its 'social and public character' (1996: 250). The quality of the viewing experience, she argues, is related not only to the size and density of the film image, but also to the concentrated attention span which it receives in the cinema. Drawing on Bazin's work on the ontology of the photographic image, she calls for a 'recognition of the special, even "sacred" character of the film image', which, she argues, 'derives not from divine authority but from human response' (250). Something of a similar line is taken also by Anne Friedberg, who argues that, with the advent of the video movie, 'the "aura" of the original moment of cinema exhibition also disappears' (1993: 139). There is, however, a slightly paradoxical twist to this argument. For Walter Benjamin (1936), it was precisely the 'mechanical reproducibility' of the mass media, as exemplified by film, which destroyed the 'aura' of traditional art and its attachment to notions of the 'original'. In the age of television and video, however, it is now the film-viewing experience that is seen to possess 'auratic' qualities and provide precisely the experience of the 'original' which, it is argued, the television or video viewing of films now lacks.

In such arguments, it is the concentration and involvement that characterizes watching film in a cinema rather than on television or video which is given emphasis. Television spectatorship, in this respect, is seen to be fundamentally different from cinema spectatorship. Raymond Williams (1974), for example, has defined the key experience of television as one of 'flow', while John Ellis (1982) lays stress on television's dependence on 'segmentalisation'. For both authors, it is the experience of 'watching television' that is considered more important than the watching of individual programmes and, for Ellis, this also involves a particular relationship with the viewer. Thus, unlike the concentrated gaze at the screen expected by cinema, television only invites the 'glance' (163).

It is this 'glance aesthetics' that Corrigan (1991: 31) sees as governing the contemporary viewing of films, while Friedberg (1993: 139–43) discusses the 'spectatorial flânerie' and active relationship to texts permitted by television and video technologies. In both cases, this new form of spectatorship is also linked to changing forms of (postmodern) subjectivity. For Corrigan, the new forms of film reception involve the disappearance of 'a clear and stable viewer' (1991: 2), while, for Friedberg, the new media produce 'a shifting, mobile, fluid subjectivity' (1993: 143). However, although it is clear that television and video have allowed a greater control (and interactivity) over the viewing of films, there is also a tendency in such writing to make overly general claims and draw too strong a contrast between 'old' and 'new' forms of viewing. Thus, the watching of films in cinemas is not, and has not been, as concentrated—just as the viewing of film on television and video is not necessarily as inattentive—as the oppositions drawn between film and television viewing sometimes suggest. The conditions characterizing the viewing of films have varied according to historical and geographical circumstances and, indeed, John Belton suggests how contemporary movie-'going' has echoes of both the peep-show and the nickelodeon era (1994: 342). Moreover, the assumption that the conditions generally taken to be characteristic of cinema spectatorship (large screen, darkness, relative immobility) necessarily 'fix' subjectivity in some straightforward way (as in apparatus theory) is clearly inadequate for an understanding of the complex ways in which audiences have actually responded to films socially and historically. In the same way, it is not possible simply to 'read off' forms of subjectivity from the technologies of television and video. Subjectivity in this respect is 'produced' not by the media, but by a whole set of social and cultural determinants, which may, nevertheless, include film, television, and video.

Cultural identity

This emphasis upon subjectivity also overlaps with concerns regarding the role of film in the shaping of social and cultural identities. As we have seen, one contrast between film and television has been to see television as encouraging a more 'privatized' form of film consumption. However, once again, the opposition is not necessarily clear-cut. As Harvey notes, while cinema may offer a shared experience in a social space, it can also be one which is 'intensely private' (1996: 241). And, while watching film on television may be regarded as private, it can also be a shared experience. This is not simply because television viewing often involves a group of some kind (be it family members or friends), but because watching a film as it is broadcast can involve a sense of collective belonging as well. From this point of view, the simultaneous viewing of a

film by a large audience draws together spectators in a shared experience similar to those provided by other forms of television such as public occasions or episodes of a soap opera.

This also complicates models of television viewing as a relatively undifferentiated 'flow'. While the emphasis upon 'flow' may have drawn attention to important aspects of television viewing, it has also underestimated the role of the independent programme and how it is distinguished from, and often watched separately from, the overall flow of television (Waller 1988; McLoone 1996). Films on television can be important in this regard precisely because television can make use of a film as an 'event' which breaks up the televisual flow and offers a 'special' experience separated out from the rest of television. In doing so, film can also participate in the 'public sphere' of which television is now a central part. Thus, Jarvick and Strickland defend US TV movies in terms of their 'social function', arguing that, in addition to the provision of entertainment, they constitute 'the town hall of public debate on important historical, social and political issues' (1988: 42).

This is an argument which also has relevance to the relations between film and television outside the United States, and especially in Europe. For European television has been much less driven by commercial imperatives than its US counterpart, and the co-operation between film and television which has occurred within European countries has characteristically been linked to public-service values. Thus, while in the United States it has been the networks and the commercial pay-TV channels, such as Home Box Office (HBO) and Showtime, that have financed films, in Europe it has been public-service stations (such as ZDF in Germany, RAI in Italy, Channel 4 in Britain, RTVE in Spain, and RTP in Portugal) that have been of crucial importance in sustaining European film production. In the case of France, the government's legal requirement that broadcasters support French film production has ensured that France is the Continent's largest film-producing country.

The importance of television's support for film production in Europe may be explained by the growing economic might of Hollywood and the problems national cinemas have faced in trying to maintain levels of production. From this point of view, an alliance between film and television has provided not only the most economically prudent form of cinema for European countries, but also the one most likely to offer a culturally distinctive alternative to Hollywood

My Beautiful Laundrette (1985)—a fusion of 'art cinema' and public-service television

norms, by drawing on television's public-service traditions and speaking to their own cultures in ways that Hollywood films, aimed at a global market, cannot. Thus, in the case of films supported by Britain's Channel 4—such as *My Beautiful Laundrette* (1985), *Letter to Brezhnev* (1985), *Riff-Raff* (1990), *The Crying Game* (1992), and *Naked* (1993)—there has been something of a fusion between the formal interests of 'art cinema' and the socio-political concerns of public service television (Hill 1996). The issue in respect of Europe, therefore, is not so much whether it is desirable that television should support film, but whether it will continue to possess the means to do so. This question has become especially pertinent in the 1990s, given the increasingly commercial climate of broadcasting across Europe, which has made support for film, because of its cost, increasingly difficult, as the examples of RAI in Italy and RTVE in Spain have demonstrated.

Conclusion

It is now clear that the future of film is inextricably linked with that of television and video. In this sense, it is an irreversible development, and there is little point in lamenting the 'decline' of cinema in its traditional form. However, this chapter has also suggested that it is misleading to 'essentialize' the differences between the two mediums or homogenize the characteristics of each. It has also pointed out that the relationship between film and television is historically and geographically variable, and, although crucially important, the US experience is but one model of the way in which film and television have reached an alliance. And while there may be certain losses involved in the new relationship between film and television (such as technical quality or type of viewing experience), there have also been corresponding gains (such as the increased accessibility of films and the emergence of more 'active' viewing forms). In this respect, cinema is not so much in 'decline' as entering a new historical era.

BIBLIOGRAPHY

Anderson, Christopher (1994), *Hollywood TV: The Studio System in the Fifties* (Austin: University of Texas Press).

Balio, Tino (ed.) (1990), *Hollywood in the Age of Television* (Boston: Unwin Hyman).

Barr, Charles (1996), '"They Think it's all Over": The Dramatic Legacy of Live Television', in Hill and McLoone (1996).

Belton, John (1994), *American Cinema/American Culture* (New York: McGraw-Hill).

Benjamin, Walter (1936/1973), 'The Work of Art in the Age of Mechanical Reproduction', in *Illuminations*, ed. Hannah Arendt and trans. Harry Zohn (London: Collins).

Corrigan, Timothy (1991), *A Cinema without Walls: Movies and Culture after Vietnam* (London: Routledge).

Ellis, John (1982), *Visible Fictions Cinema: Television: Video* (London: Routledge).

Fleming, Dan (1996), 'Dial "M" for Movies: New Technologies, New Relations', in Hill and McLoone (1996).

Friedberg, Anne (1993), *Window Shopping: Cinema and the Postmodern* (Berkeley: University of California Press).

Gomery, Douglas (1984), 'Failed Opportunities: The Integration of the U.S. Motion Picture and Television Industries', *Quarterly Review of Film Studies*, 9/3 (Summer), 219–28.

****Harvey, Sylvia** (1996), 'What is Cinema? The Sensuous, the Abstract and the Political', in Christopher Williams (ed.), *Cinema: The Beginnings and the Future* (London: University of Westminster Press).

Hill, John (1996), 'British Television and Film: The Making of a Relationship', in Hill and McLoone (eds.), *Big Picture, Small Screen*.

——— and **Martin McLoone (eds.) (1996), *Big Picture, Small Screen: The Relations between Film and Television* (Luton: John Libbey Media and University of Luton Press).

Hilmes, Michèle (1990), *Hollywood and Broadcasting: From Radio to Cable* (Urbana: University of Illinois Press).

Jarvik, Laurence, and **Nancy Strickland** (1988), 'TV Movies: Better than the Real Thing', *American Film* (Dec.), 41–3, 56.

Kramer, Peter (1996), 'The Lure of the Big Picture: Film, Television and Hollywood', in Hill and McLoone (1996).

****Lafferty, William** (1988), 'Film and Television', in Gary R. Edgerton (ed.), *Film and the Arts in Symbiosis: A Resource Guide* (New York: Greenwood Press).

Lyons, Donald (1994), 'Genre and Caste in Cableland', *Film Comment*, 30/5 (Sept–Oct.), 2–7.

McLoone, Martin (1996), 'Boxed In? The Aesthetics of Film and Television', in Hill and McLoone (1996).

Screen Digest (1993), 'World Cinema: Falling Screens and Failing Audiences' (Sept.), 201–8.

Screen Finance (1993), 'Studio Film Revenues Set to Grow by 6.9 per cent in 1993' (5 May), 8–13.

Thompson, Frank (1990), 'The Big Squeeze', *American Film* (Feb.), 40–3.

Vianello, Robert (1984), 'The Rise of the Telefilm and the Networks' Hegemony over the Motion Picture Industry', *Quarterly Review of Film Studies*, 9/3 (Summer), 204–18.

Waller, Gregory A. (1988), 'Flow, Genre and the Television Text', *Journal of Popular Film and Television*, 16/1 (Spring), 6-11.

Williams, Raymond (1974), *Television: Technology and Cultural Form* (London: Fontana).

List of Picture and Reading Sources

PICTURES

Unless otherwise stated all photographic material was reproduced courtesy of the Kobal collection. Whilst every effort has been made to identify copyright holders that has not been possible in a few cases. We apologize for any apparent negligence and any omissions brought to our attention will be remedied in any future editions. 3.1 1969 Embra Line 3.2 Les Grand Films Classiques 3.5 British Post Office 3.6 1990 J & M Entertainment Ltd/Miramax Film Corp. 3.7 Courtesy of the British Film Institute 3.8 Svenskfilmindustri 1957 3.9 Courtesy of Ian Christie 3.10 1945 Excelsa Films 3.11 Contemporary Films 1975 3.12 Artificial Eye 1981 3.13 Courtesy of Paradise Films 3.15 Courtesy of the British Film Institute 3.16 The Rank Organization 1946 3.17 Courtesy of the British Film Institute 3.18 Courtesy of the British Film Institute 3.19 Courtesy of the British Film Institute 3.20 Navketan International Films Ltd from collection of Hyphen Films Ltd 3.21 Guangxi Film Studio/Artificial Eye 1984 3.22 Artificial Eye/Courtesy of the Movie Store 3.23 Courtesy of the British Film Institute/ERA International Ltd 3.25 Contemporary Films 1974 3.26 Courtesy of the British Film Institute 3.27 Ukamau Limitada 3.28 Universal Studios and Amblin

READINGS

Rosie Thomas: 'Popular Hindi Cinema', from Rosie Thomas, 'Indian Cinema: Pleasures and Popularity', reprinted with permission from *Screen* 26(3–4), 1985. Richard Porton: 'Hyenas' from Richard Porton, 'Mambety's *Hyenas*: Between Anti-Colonialism and the Critique of Modernity' *Iris*, 18, 1995 © Richard Porton.

Index of Selected Films and Names